D1231446

The Retirement Researcher's Guide Series

SAFETY-FIRST RETIREMENT PLANNING

An Integrated Approach for a Worry-Free Retirement

Wade D. Pfau
PhD, CFA, RICP

Copyright © 2019 by Wade Donald Pfau. All rights reserved.
Published by Retirement Researcher Media, Vienna, Virginia.

No part of this publication may be reproduced, stored in a retrieval system, or transmitted in any form or by any means, electronic, mechanical, photocopying, recording, scanning, or otherwise, except as permitted under Section 107 or 108 of the 1976 United States Copyright Act, without the prior written permission of the publisher. Requests to the publisher for permission should be addressed to wade@retirementresearcher.com.

Limit of Liability/Disclaimer of Warranty: While the publisher and author have used their best efforts in preparing this book, they make no representations or warranties with respect to the accuracy or completeness of the contents of this book and specifically disclaim any implied warranties of merchantability or fitness for a particular purpose. No warranty may be created or extended by sales representatives or written sales materials. The advice and strategies contained herein may not be suitable for your situation. You should consult with a professional where appropriate. Neither the publisher nor the author shall be liable for any loss of profit or any other commercial damages, including but not limited to special, incidental, consequential, or other damages.

Library of Congress Cataloging-in-Publication Data:
Pfau, Wade D., 1977–
    Safety-First Retirement Planning: An Integrated Approach for a Worry-Free
    Retirement / Wade D. Pfau.
        pages cm
    Includes index.
ISBN [978-1-945640-06-3] (paperback) - ISBN [978-1-945640-07-0] (e-book)

Library of Congress Control Number: 2019912666
Retirement Researcher, Vienna, VIRGINIA

1. Retirement Planning. 2. Financial, Personal. I. Title.

Cover Design: Trevor Alexander & Mineral Interactive
Graphics and Layout: Watermark Design Office
Printed in the United States of America

To those hard workers seeking to someday
enjoy their retirement.

TABLE OF CONTENTS

PREFACE

The challenge in building an effective retirement income plan is to use available income tools and tactics in a strategic manner to meet the financial goals of retirement while also managing the risks confronting those goals. The financial goals of retirement include sustainably meeting a lifestyle spending goal for as long as one lives, providing a legacy for the family or community, and maintaining liquidity to cover unexpected expenses and contingencies in retirement.

Meanwhile, the three major categories of risk for a retirement income plan include longevity, market volatility, and spending shocks. Longevity risk is the possibility of living longer than planned, which could mean not having resources to maintain the retiree's standard of living. Market volatility is the risk that poor market returns are realized, leading to a reduced portfolio value and a reduced ability to maintain the retirement standard of living. Taking distributions from investments in retirement further amplifies market risk by increasing the importance of the ordering of investment returns. This is called sequence-of-returns risk. Finally, spending shocks are the risk that expensive bills materialize, such as for long-term care or health care, which require large expenditures that deplete assets and reduce the ability to maintain lifestyle at later ages.

Retirement income planning is the field of financial planning which addresses this challenge. It is still a relative newcomer within financial services, and it continues to experience growing pains and disagreements about the best way to help retirees succeed. In reviewing existing approaches, I have identified two very distinct schools of thought for managing the finances of retirement.

First, probability-based advocates generally support using an aggressive investment portfolio with a large allocation to stocks to meet retirement goals. My earlier book *How Much Can I Spend in Retirement? A Guide to Investment-Based Retirement Strategies* provides an extensive investigation of probability-based approaches. With these investment solutions, a higher lifestyle may be supported if one is willing to spend and invest aggressively in the hope of subsequently earning higher market returns. Should decent market returns materialize, investment solutions can be sustained indefinitely while also helping to support legacy and liquidity. Probability-based advocates are generally comfortable with the expectation that decent returns will materialize such that these approaches will *probably* work just fine.

However, an investments-only mind-set is not the optimal way to build a retirement income plan. There are pitfalls in retirement that we are less familiar with during the accumulation years. Traditional wealth management is not equipped to handle longevity and sequence risk in a fulfilling way. Retirees must self-manage longevity and market risk, which means more assets are required to cover spending goals over an assumed long time horizon combined with the possibility that poor market returns chip away at the portfolio. Nonetheless, longevity protection is not guaranteed with investments and assets may not be available to support a long life or legacy. For retirees who are worried about outliving their assets and not successfully meeting their lifetime financial goals, probability-based strategies can become excessively conservative and stressful.

This book is primarily about the other school of thought: the safety-first approach to retirement income. Safety-first advocates support a more bifurcated approach to building retirement income plans that integrates investments with insurance, providing lifetime income protections. Probability-based advocates generally view annuities and life insurance as unnecessary in retirement. They see the stock market as a straightforward way to obtain superior retirement outcomes. Safety-first advocates disagree.

Risk pooling with insurance provides an alternative means for potentially earmarking fewer assets to cover lifetime spending goals, effectively reducing the potential overall cost of retirement. With risk pooling, one does not need to plan for the very expensive case of an extremely long life combined with poor market returns. Instead, the retiree pays an insurance premium that will provide a benefit to support spending if those risks materialize and retirement becomes more expensive. An unprotected investment portfolio may otherwise deplete. Insurance companies can pool sequence and longevity risks across a large base of retirees, allowing for retirement spending that is greater than the sustainable withdrawal rate from investments for someone self-managing these risks. When bonds are replaced with insurance-based risk pooling assets, retirees can improve the odds of meeting their spending goals while also supporting more legacy at the end of life, especially in the event of a longer-than-average retirement.

Lifetime income through insurance, whether that be annuities or life insurance, can help to manage market volatility and investment risks, to protect from longevity risk, to more efficiently earmark assets to cover retirement spending, to reduce the fear and worry that many have about outliving their assets in retirement, and to simplify the financial plan.

We walk through this thought process and logic in steps, investigating three basic ways to fund a retirement spending goal: with a bond ladder, with a diversified investment portfolio, and with annuities and life insurance. We consider the potential role for different types of annuities including simple income annuities and their various flavors, variable annuities, and fixed index annuities. When we properly consider the range of risks introduced after retirement, I conclude that the integrated strategies preferred by safety-first advocates, which combine investments and insurance, support more efficient retirement outcomes that better support spending and legacy.

I welcome your feedback and questions. You can reach me at:
wade@retirementresearcher.com.

As a final note, I have avoided including footnotes to make the book more readable and give it a less academic feel. Each chapter ends with a Further Reading list that includes the bibliographic information for resources mentioned.

Wade Pfau
King of Prussia, PA

ACKNOWLEDGEMENTS

Writing a book is a major endeavor, and I have been helped along the way by countless individuals. First and foremost, I would like to thank my colleagues at Retirement Researcher and McLean Asset Management for providing the vision and resources to make this book possible. I'm grateful for the leadership and willingness of Alex Murguia and Dean Umemoto to build a firm that can turn my research on retirement income planning into practical solutions for real-world retirees. I would also like to thank Trevor Alexander, Briana Corbin, Rob Cordeau, Bob French, Paula Friedman, Christian Litscher, Morgan Menzies, Kyle Meyer, and Jessica Wunder.

I am also deeply indebted to Don and Lynne Komai and the Watermark Design Office for their assistance in developing the layout and design for this book.

A special thanks to David Meyers, Jen Dunbar, Steven Hoagland, and other members of the Retirement Researcher Basecamp, as well, for helping to develop the book title.

Furthermore, I am grateful to the American College of Financial Services for their leadership and focus on retirement income planning, particularly David Blanchett, Michael Finke, David Littell, George Nichols, Kirk Okumura, and Steve Parrish.

When it comes to retirement income planning, I also wish to thank countless other practitioners and researchers who have helped me along the way. A partial list must include Bill Bengen, Bill Bernstein, Jason Branning, Jason Brown, J. Brent Burns, Ian Cahill, Bill Cason, Curtis Cloke, Jeremy Cooper, Dirk Cotton, Wade Dokken, Harold Evensky, Francois Gadenne, Jonathan Guyton, David Jacobs, Dean Harder, Rick Hayes, Jamie Hopkins, Robert Huebscher, Stephen Huxley, Michael Kitces, David Lau, Manish Malhotra, Ed McGill, Moshe Milevsky, Aaron Minney, Dan Moisand, Brent Mondoskin, Emilio Pardo, Kerry Pechter, Robert Powell, John M. Prizer, Jr., Art Prunier, Dick Purcell, Jason and Art Sanger, Bill Sharpe, Jeff Smith, Larry Swedroe, Joe Tomlinson, Bob Veres, Steve Vernon, and Mark Wutt.

I also wish to thank my family for their support and the sacrifices made to help me get this book written.

Finally, I wish to thank everyone who has read and participated at RetirementResearcher.com since 2010.

CHAPTER 1

Overview of Retirement Income Planning

Strong disagreements exist about how to position a retiree's assets to best meet retirement goals. Two fundamentally different philosophies for retirement income planning—which I call *probability-based* and *safety-first*—diverge on the critical issue of where a retirement plan is best served: in the risk/reward trade-offs of a diversified and aggressive investment portfolio, or in the contractual protections of insurance products.

On the one side are investments-centric approaches of the probability-based philosophy that rely on the risk premium from the stock market. This is the idea that stocks will outperform bonds over sufficiently long periods, and this investment outperformance will provide retirees with the opportunity to fund a higher lifestyle. Those favoring investments (the probability-based approach) rely on the notion that while the stock market is volatile, it will eventually provide favorable returns for most retirees and will outperform bonds. The upside potential from an investment portfolio is viewed as so significant that insurance products are not needed. Investment approaches are probability-based in the sense that they will *probably* work. My book *How Much Can I Spend in Retirement? A Guide to Investment-Based Retirement Strategies* provided a detailed analysis for these probability-based investment approaches for retirement.

An alternative school of thought for retirement income is the safety-first approach. It is my focus in this book. Safety-first advocates are generally more willing to accept a role for insurance as a source of income protection to help manage various retirement risks. For investments-only strategies, retirement risks are generally managed by spending less in retirement, as longevity risk is managed by assuming a long life, and market risk is managed by assuming poor market returns. But insurance companies pool these market and longevity risks across a large base of retirees—much like a traditional defined-benefit pension—allowing for retirement spending that is more closely aligned with average, long-term, fixed-income returns and average longevity. This could support a higher lifestyle than what is feasible for someone self-managing these risks by assuming low returns and a longer time horizon.

Safety-first advocates recognize that risk pooling can be a more effective way to manage retirement risk because it allows retirees to spend as though they will experience average outcomes; those with average lengths of life and average market returns will have paid an insurance premium that is transferred to those who experience a more costly combination of a longer retirement and poor market returns. This can allow everyone in the risk pool to spend more than they may otherwise feel comfortable spending without this protection in place, or to otherwise earmark a smaller asset base to fund their lifestyle in retirement.

The income protections provide a license to spend assets because the retiree knows that subsidies (or insurance benefits) will be received from the risk pool if risks manifest that otherwise threaten the sustainability of an unprotected investment portfolio. Income protections manage longevity risk and calibrate the planning horizon to something much closer to life expectancy. Those who fall short of life expectancy subsidize the income payments for those who outlive it. Those subsidies are known as *mortality credits*. While receipt of those subsidies clearly benefits the long-lived, arguably both groups can benefit by enjoying higher spending while alive because they have pooled the longevity risk. Their spending can be based on averages, and they do not have to self-manage the risk by planning for an overly long retirement.

Income protections through insurance can also provide peace of mind for retirement lifestyle that leads to a less stressful and more enjoyable retirement experience. Overly conservative retirees become so concerned with running out of money that they spend significantly less than they could. A dependable monthly check from an annuity can provide the explicit permission to spend and enjoy retirement and can simplify life for those with reduced cognitive skills or for surviving spouses who may be less experienced with financial matters.

As for legacy, a death benefit can be created with life insurance to provide a specific legacy amount. Additionally, an annuity supporting lifetime income dedicates assets specifically toward the provision of income, allowing other assets to be earmarked specifically for growth. This can allow for a larger legacy, especially when the retiree enjoys a long life and more of his or her income is supported through the annuity's mortality credits.

With investment solutions, a more comfortable lifestyle may be maintained for those willing to invest aggressively in the hope of subsequently earning higher market returns to support a higher income rate. Should decent market returns materialize and sufficiently outpace inflation, investment solutions can be sustained indefinitely. Upside growth could also support a larger legacy and provide liquidity for unexpected expenses.

However, the dual impact of market and longevity risk leaves an investment portfolio vulnerable to the possibility of being unable to support the desired lifestyle over the full retirement period. These are risks a retiree cannot offset easily or cheaply in an investment portfolio. Investment approaches seek to reduce market and longevity risk by having the retiree spend conservatively. Retirees spend less to avoid depleting their portfolio through a bad sequence of market returns in early retirement and because they must be prepared to live well beyond their life expectancy. The implication is clear: should the market perform reasonably well in retirement, the retiree will significantly underspend relative to their potential and leave an unintentionally large legacy.

At the same time, longevity protection (the risk of outliving savings) is not guaranteed with investments, and assets may not be available to support a long life or legacy. A *reverse legacy* could result if the portfolio is so depleted that the retiree must rely on others (often adult children) for support. This is particularly important in light of the ongoing improvements in mortality. Today's retirees will live longer and have to support longer retirements than their predecessors. For healthy individuals in their sixties, we are approaching the point where forty years must replace thirty years as a conservative planning horizon.

Retirees experience reduced risk capacity as they enter retirement. Their reduced flexibility to earn income leaves them more vulnerable to forced lifestyle reductions resulting from the whims of the market. A probability-based strategy could backfire.

For preretirement wealth accumulation, there has been less focus on appreciating the joint impact that longevity risk and market risk could play on a financial plan after retirement. Investment managers have tended to view risk pooling as unnecessary because the stock market can be expected to perform well over time. However, once distributions begin, any downward volatility in the early years of retirement can disproportionately hurt the sustainability of a retirement spending plan. With longevity risk, retirees do not know just how long their assets will need to last. Investment managers either remained ignorant of these risks or were otherwise comfortable allocating assets while treating these risks as distant and low-priority concerns.

Meanwhile, those favoring insurance (safety-first) believe that contractual protections are reliable and that staking your retirement income on the assumption that favorable market returns will eventually arrive is emotionally overwhelming and dangerous. The insurance side is clearly more concerned with the implications of market risk than those favoring investments, believing that even with a low probability of portfolio depletion, a retiree gets only one opportunity for a successful retirement. At the very least, they say, essential income needs should not be subject to the whims of the market. The safety-first school views investment-only solutions as undesirable because the retiree retains all the longevity and market risks, which an insurance company is in a better position to manage.

Today, the value provided by risk pooling is becoming better understood by investment managers as retirement income planning has emerged as a distinct field within financial services. This is happening as traditional sources of risk pooling, such as company pensions and Social Security, play a reduced role and retirees look for ways to transform their 401(k) savings into sustainable lifetime spending. Employers now tend to contribute to various defined-contribution pensions like 401(k)s, where the employee accepts longevity and investment risk and must make investment decisions. 401(k) plans are not pensions in the traditional sense, as they shift the risks and responsibility to employees rather than employers. In the transition from defined benefit to defined contribution, people are not getting as much access to risk pooling as they used to.

Without the relative stability provided by earnings from employment, retirees must find a way to convert their financial resources into a stream of income that will last the remainder of their lives. Wealth management has traditionally focused on accumulating assets without applying further thought to the differences that happen after retirement. To put it succinctly, retirees experience reduced capacity to bear financial market risk once they have retired. The standard of living for a retiree becomes more vulnerable to enduring permanent harm as a result of financial market downturns. It is now clear that the financial circumstances facing retirees are not the same as for preretirees, calling for different approaches from traditional investment advice for wealth accumulation.

A mountain-climbing analogy is useful for clarifying the distinction between accumulation and distribution, as the goal ultimately of climbing a mountain is not just to make it to the top; it is also necessary to get back down. The skillset required to get down a mountain is not the same as that needed to reach the summit. In fact, an experienced mountain climber knows that it is more treacherous and dangerous to climb down a mountain. On the way down, climbers must deal with greater fatigue, they risk falling farther and with greater acceleration when facing a downslope compared to an upslope, and the way our bodies are designed makes going up easier than coming down.

Exhibit 1.1 The Mountain Climbing Analogy for Retirement

The retirement phase, when you are pulling money from your accounts rather than accumulating wealth, is much like descending a mountain. The objective of a retirement saver is not just to make it to the top of the mountain, which we could view as achieving a wealth accumulation target. The real objective is to safely and smoothly make it down the mountain, spending assets in a sustainable manner.

Seeking efficiencies and protections to better support sustainable spending is a primary focus for this book. When we properly consider the range of risks introduced after retirement, it is difficult to overcome the conclusion that the integrated strategies preferred by safety-first advocates, which combine investments and insurance, support more efficient retirement outcomes that better support spending and legacy and help retirees to make it more safely down the mountain.

◉ The Retirement Researcher Manifesto

As I have attempted to summarize the key messages and themes that have underscored my writing and research going into this book, I find that the following eight guidelines serve as a manifesto for my approach to retirement income planning. It is helpful to start with these guidelines because this book is ultimately about how to implement these guidelines in practice.

Play the long game

A retirement income plan should be based on planning to live, not planning to die. A long life will be expensive to support, and it should take precedence over assuming one will not live long. Fight the impatience that could lead you to choose short-term expediencies carrying greater long-term cost. This does not mean, however, that you sacrifice short-term satisfactions to plan for the long term. Many efficiencies can be gained from a long-term focus that can support a higher sustained standard of living.

Retirees must still plan for a long life, even when rejecting strategies that only help in the event of a long life. Remember, planning for average life expectancy is quite risky—half of the population outlives their expectancy. Planning to live longer means spending less than you otherwise would. Developing a plan that incorporates efficiencies that will not be realized until later can allow more spending today in anticipation of those efficiencies. Not taking such long-term, efficiency-improving actions will lead to a permanently reduced standard of living.

Do not leave money on the table

The holy grail of retirement income planning is finding strategies that enhance retirement efficiency. I define efficiency as follows: if one strategy allows for more lifetime spending and a greater legacy value for assets relative than another strategy, then it is more efficient. Efficiency must be defined from the perspective of how long you live. Related to the previous point, a number of strategies can enhance efficiency over the long term (but not necessarily over the short term) with more spending and more legacy.

Use reasonable expectations for portfolio returns

A key lesson for long-term financial planning is that you should not expect to earn the average historical market returns for your portfolio. Half of the time, realized returns will be less. As well, we have been experiencing a period of low interest rates, which unfortunately provides a clear mathematical reality that at least bond returns are going to be lower in the future. This has important implications for those who have retired. (These implications are relevant for those far from retirement as well, but the harm of ignoring them is less than for retirees.) At the very least, dismiss any retirement projection based on fixed 8 or 12 percent returns, as the reality is likely much less when we account for portfolio volatility, inflation, and a desire to develop a plan that will work more than half the time.

Be careful about plans that only work with high market return

A natural mathematical formula that applies to retirement planning is that higher assumed future market returns imply higher sustainable spending rates. Bonds provide a fixed rate of return when held to maturity, and stocks potentially offer a higher return than bonds as a reward for their additional risk. But a *risk premium* is not guaranteed and may not materialize. Probability-based retirees who spend more today because they are planning for higher market returns than available for bonds are essentially "amortizing their upside." They are spending more today than justified by bond investments, based on an assumption that higher returns in the future will make up the difference and justify the higher spending rate.

For retirees, the fundamental nature of risk is the threat that poor market returns will trigger a permanently lower standard of living. Retirees must decide how much risk to their lifestyle they are willing to accept. Assuming that a risk premium on stocks will be earned and spending more today is risky behavior. It may be reasonable behavior for the more risk tolerant among us, but it is not a behavior that will be appropriate for everyone. It is important to think through the consequences in advance.

Build an integrated strategy to manage various retirement risks

Building a retirement income strategy is a process that requires determining how to best combine available retirement income tools in order to meet retirement goals and to effectively protect against the risks standing in the way of those goals. Retirement risks include longevity and an unknown planning horizon, market volatility and macroeconomic risks, inflation, and spending shocks that can derail a budget. Each of these risks must be managed by combining different income tools with different relative strengths and weaknesses for addressing each of the risks. There is no single solution that can cover every risk.

Approach retirement income tools with an agnostic view

The financial services profession is generally divided between two camps: those focusing on investment solutions and those focusing on insurance solutions. Both sides have their adherents who see little use for the other side. But the most efficient retirement strategies require an integration of both investments and insurance. It is potentially harmful to dismiss subsets of retirement income tools without a thorough investigation of their purported role. In this regard, it is wrong to describe the stock market as a casino or to dismiss annuities or permanent life insurance as expensive and unnecessary.

For the two camps in the financial services profession, it is natural to accuse the opposite camp of having conflicts of interest that bias their advice, but each side must reflect on whether their own conflicts color their advice. On the insurance side, the natural conflict is that insurance agents receive commissions for selling insurance products and may only need to meet a requirement that their suggestions be suitable for their clients. On the investments side, those charging for a percentage of assets they manage naturally wish to make the investment portfolio as large as possible, which is not necessarily in the best interests of their clients who are seeking sustainable lifetime income and proper retirement risk management. Meanwhile, those charging hourly fees for planning advice naturally do not wish to make their recommendations so simple that they forego the need for an ongoing planning relationship. It is important to overcome these hurdles and to rely carefully on what the math and research show. This requires starting from a fundamentally agnostic position.

Start by assessing all retirement assets and liabilities

A retirement plan involves more than just financial assets. The retirement balance sheet is the starting point for building a retirement income strategy. At the core is a desire to treat the household retirement problem in the same way that pension funds treat their obligations. Assets should be matched to liabilities with comparable levels of risk. This matching can either be done on a balance sheet level, using the present values of asset and liability streams, or it can be accomplished on a period-by-period basis to match assets to ongoing spending needs. Structuring the retirement income problem in this way makes it easier to keep track of the different aspects of the plan and to make sure that each liability has a funding source. This also allows retirees to more easily determine whether they have sufficient assets to meet their retirement needs or if they may be underfunded with respect to their goals. This organizational framework also serves as a foundation

Exhibit 1.2	**Basic Retirement Assets and Liabilities**	
	Retirement Balance Sheet	
	Assets	**Liabilities**
	Human Capital • Continuing Career • Part-time Work	Fixed Expenses (Longevity) • Essential Living Needs • Taxes • Debt Repayment
	Home Equity	Discretionary Expenses (Lifestyle) • Travel & Leisure • Lifestyle Improvements
	Financial Assets • Checking Accounts • Brokerage Accounts • Retirement Plans	
	Annuities & Life Insurance	Contingencies (Liquidity) • Long-Term Care • Health Care • Other Spending Shocks
	Social Capital • Social Security • Medicare • Company Pensions • Family & Community	Legacy Goals (Legacy) • Family • Community & Society

for choosing an appropriate asset allocation and for seeing clearly how different retirement income tools fit into an overall plan.

Exhibit 1.2 provides a basic overview of potential assets and liabilities to consider.

Distinguish between technical liquidity and true liquidity

An important implication from the retirement balance sheet view is that the nature of liquidity in a retirement income plan must be carefully considered. In a sense, an investment portfolio is a liquid asset, but some of its liquidity may be only an illusion. Assets must be matched to liabilities. Some, or even all, of the investment portfolio may be earmarked to meet future lifestyle spending goals. Curtis Cloke describes this in his Thrive University program for financial advisors as allocation liquidity. Retirees are free to reallocate their assets in any way they wish, but the assets are not truly liquid because they must be preserved to meet the spending goal. Assets cannot be double counted, and while a retiree could decide to use these assets for another purpose, doing so would jeopardize the ability to meet future spending. In this sense, assets are not as liquid as they appear.

This is different from free-spending liquidity, in which assets could be spent in any desired way because they are not earmarked to meet existing liabilities. True liquidity emerges when there are excess assets remaining after specifically setting aside what is needed to meet the household liabilities. This distinction is important because there are cases when tying up a portion of assets in something illiquid, such as an income annuity, may allow for the household liabilities to be covered more cheaply than could be done when all assets are positioned to provide technical liquidity.

In very simple terms, an income annuity that pools longevity risk may allow lifetime spending to be met at a cost of twenty years of the spending objective, while self-funding for longevity may require setting aside enough from an investment portfolio to cover thirty to forty years of expenses. Because risk pooling and mortality credits allow for less to be set aside to cover the spending goal, there is now greater true liquidity and therefore more to cover other unexpected contingencies without jeopardizing core spending needs. Liquidity, as it is traditionally defined in securities markets, is of little value as a distinct goal in a long-term retirement income plan. It must be true liquidity to count.

◉ The Retirement Income Challenge

The process of building a retirement income strategy involves determining how to best combine retirement income tools to optimize the balance between meeting various retirement goals and effectively protecting those goals from retirement risks. Building an optimal strategy is a process, and there is no single right answer. No one approach or retirement income product works best for everyone. Different people will approach the problem in different ways, as some will feel affinity for solutions connected with managing withdrawals from an investment portfolio, while others will begin from a desire to build income guarantees. The objective becomes to flesh out the details for how each income tool could contribute, quantify the advantages and disadvantages of different strategies, and determine how to best combine the income tools into an overall plan that can best meet goals and manage risks.

Financial Goals for Retirement

It is important to clarify the goals for a retirement income plan, as different income tools are better suited for different goals. Retirement plans should be customized to each person's specific circumstances. Each retiree should seek to meet specific financial goals in a way that best manages the wide variety of risks that threatens those goals. The primary financial goal for most retirees relates to their spending: maximize spending power (lifestyle) in such a way that spending can remain consistent and sustainable without any drastic reductions, no matter how long the retirement lasts (longevity). Other important goals may include leaving assets for subsequent generations (legacy) and maintaining sufficient reserves for unexpected contingencies that have not been earmarked for other purposes (liquidity). Lifestyle, longevity, legacy, and liquidity are the four Ls of retirement income.

Changing Risks in Retirement

It is important to understand from the very outset how changing risks are primarily what separate retirement income planning from traditional wealth management. Retirees have less capacity for risk, as they become more vulnerable to a reduced standard of living when risks manifest. Those entering retirement are crossing the threshold into an entirely

Exhibit 1.3

Retirement Risks

- Reduced earnings capacity
- Visible spending constraint
- Heightened investment risk
- Unknown longevity
- Spending shocks
- Compounding inflation
- Declining cognitive abilities

foreign way of living. These risks can be summarized in seven general categories, listed in Exhibit 1.3.

Reduced earnings capacity

Retirees face reduced flexibility to earn income in the labor markets as a way to cushion their standard of living from the impact of poor market returns. One important distinction in retirement is that people often experience large reductions in their risk capacity as the value of their human capital declines. As a result, they are left with fewer options for responding to poor portfolio returns.

Risk capacity is the ability to endure a decline in portfolio value without experiencing a substantial decline to the standard of living. Prior to retirement, poor market returns might be counteracted with a small increase in the savings rate, a brief retirement delay, or even a slight increase in risk taking. Once retired, however, people can find it hard to return to the labor force and are more likely to live on fixed budgets.

Visible spending constraint

At one time, investments were a place for saving and accumulation, but retirees must try to create an income stream from their existing assets—an important constraint on their investment decisions. Taking distributions amplifies investment risks by increasing the importance of the order of investment returns in retirement.

It can be difficult to reduce spending in response to a poor market environment. Portfolio losses could have a more significant impact on the standard of living after retirement, necessitating greater care and vigilance in response to portfolio volatility. Even a person with high risk tolerance (the ability to stomach market volatility comfortably) would be constrained by his or her risk capacity.

The traditional goal of wealth accumulation is generally to seek the highest returns possible in order to maximize wealth, subject to risk tolerance. Taking on more risk before retirement can be justified because many people have greater risk capacity at that time and can focus more on their risk tolerance. However, the investing problem fundamentally changes in retirement.

Investing during retirement is a rather different matter from investing for retirement, as retirees worry less about maximizing risk-adjusted returns and worry more about ensuring that their assets can support their spending goals for the remainder of their lives. After retiring, the fundamental objective for investing is to sustain a living standard while spending down assets over a finite but unknown length of time. The spending needs that will eventually be financed by the portfolio no longer reside in the distant future. In this new retirement calculus, views about how to balance the trade-offs between upside potential and downside protection can change. Retirees might find that the risks associated with seeking return premiums on risky assets loom larger than before, and they might be prepared to sacrifice more potential upside growth to protect against the downside risks of being unable to meet spending objectives.

The requirement to sustain an income from a portfolio is a new constraint on investing that is not considered by basic wealth maximization approaches such as portfolio diversification and modern portfolio theory (MPT). In MPT, cash flows are ignored, and the investment horizon is limited to a single time period such as a year. This simplification guides investing theory for wealth accumulation. When spending from a portfolio, the concept of sequence-of-returns risk (the order that market returns arrive) becomes more relevant, as portfolio losses early in retirement will increase the percentage of remaining assets withdrawn to sustain an income. This can dig a hole from which it becomes increasingly difficult to escape, as portfolio returns must exceed the growing withdrawal percentage to prevent further portfolio depletion. Even if markets subsequently recover, the retirement portfolio cannot enjoy a full recovery. The sustainable withdrawal rate from a retirement portfolio can fall below the average return earned by the portfolio during retirement.

Heightened investment risk

As we just discussed, retirees experience heightened vulnerability to sequence-of-returns risk when they begin spending from their investment portfolio. Poor returns early in retirement can push the sustainable withdrawal rate well below that which is implied by long-term average market returns.

The financial market returns experienced near the retirement date matter a great deal more than retirees may realize. Retiring at the beginning of a bear market is incredibly dangerous. The average market return over a thirty-year period could be quite generous, but if one experiences negative returns in the early stages when spending begins, withdrawals can deplete wealth rapidly, leaving a much smaller remainder to benefit from any subsequent market recovery, even with the same average returns over a long period of time. What happens in the markets during the fragile decade around the retirement date matters a lot.

The dynamics of sequence risk suggest that a prolonged recessionary environment early in retirement without an accompanying economic catastrophe could jeopardize the retirement prospects for particular groups of retirees. Some could experience much worse retirement outcomes than those retiring a few years earlier or later. It is nearly impossible to see such an instance coming, as devastation for a group of retirees is not necessarily preceded or accompanied by devastation for the overall economy.

Unknown longevity

The fundamental risk for retirement is unknown longevity, which is summarized in the question, How long will your retirement plan need to generate income? It is the risk of running out of assets before running out of time. The length of retirement could be much shorter or longer than the statistical life expectancy. A long life is wonderful, but it is also costlier and a bigger drain on resources. Half of the population will outlive their statistical life expectancy, and that number is only increasing as scientific progress increases the number of years we can expect to live. For some retirees, the fear of outliving resources may exceed the fear of death. This can create a paralyzing effect on retirement spending.

When determining longevity, it may seem natural to base calculations on the aggregate US population, but clear socioeconomic differences have been identified in mortality rates. Higher income and wealth levels and more education each correlate with longer lifespans. This may not be a matter of causation (i.e., more income and education cause people to live longer), but perhaps an underlying characteristic leads some people to have a more long-term focus, and that, in turn, may lead them to seek more education and practice better health habits. The very fact that you are reading this somewhat technical tome on retirement income suggests you probably have a longer-term focus and can expect to live longer than the average person. In this case, mortality data based on population-wide averages will underestimate your longevity.

Not everyone will live longer, as unfortunate accidents and illnesses will inevitably befall some along the way. But in a statistical sense, my average reader will live longer than the average person.

The American Academy of Actuaries and the Society of Actuaries created the Longevity Illustrator (www.longevityillustrator.org) to help users develop personalized estimates for their longevity based on a few questions about age, gender, smoking status, and an overall assessment of health. It is a free and simple-to-use resource. Exhibit 1.4 provides its output for sixty-five-year-old males and females based on their health assessment and smoking status.

In a probability-based world, the available means for an individual to manage longevity risk is to choose a conservative planning horizon for which there is a sufficiently low probability to outlive. This will require spending less so that available assets can be drawn out for a longer period of time. The probability of surviving to advanced ages is low. Individuals must determine how low a level of spending they are willing to accept today in their effort to plan for a longer life and better ensure that they will not deplete their assets before death.

For example, a nonsmoking sixty-five-year-old female in average health who is willing to accept a 10 percent chance for outliving her financial plan would want her plan to work to age ninety-nine. For a male with the same characteristics, age ninety-seven corresponds to accepting the same amount of longevity risk.

Exhibit 1.4

Planning Ages for Sixty-Five-Year-Olds from the Longevity Illustrator

	Males					
	Nonsmoker			Smoker		
Health Classification Chance of Survival	Excellent	Average	Poor	Excellent	Average	Poor
90%	72	71	70	68	68	67
75%	80	78	76	73	72	71
50%	87	85	83	81	78	76
25%	94	92	90	88	85	83
10%	98	97	95	94	91	89

	Females					
	Nonsmoker			Smoker		
Health Classification Chance of Survival	Excellent	Average	Poor	Excellent	Average	Poor
90%	75	74	72	70	69	68
75%	83	81	79	76	75	73
50%	90	88	86	84	82	80
25%	96	94	93	92	89	87
10%	101	99	97	97	95	93

Source: The Longevity Illustrator, www.longevityillustrator.org.

In 1994, William Bengen chose thirty years as a conservative planning horizon for a sixty-five-year-old couple when he discussed sustainable retirement spending. But as mortality improves over time, this planning horizon is becoming less conservative, especially for nonsmokers in reasonable health.

The Society of Actuaries (SOA) also produced the 2012 Individual Annuity Mortality tables that I think will appropriately reflect the situation for my readers. Compared to the Longevity Illustrator numbers shown in Exhibit 1.4, the individual annuity mortality table corresponds with data for nonsmokers in average to good health. And this data set provides mortality rates at all ages, making it useful for supporting the annuity calculations in this book. This mortality data is specifically for annuity purchasers who tend to live longer than average. For instance, those with significant illnesses tend to avoid buying annuities. The data also reflects estimates for future mortality improvements and is not based only on the situation in one year.

Exhibit 1.5 uses this data with mortality improvements projected for a starting year of 2019 to illustrate longevity risk by showing the probability of survival to different ages beyond sixty-five. It also shows outcomes for a

Exhibit 1.5

The Probability of Survival from Age Sixty-Five and the Longevity Risk for a Planning Age of Ninety-Five

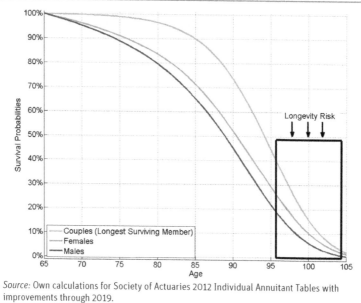

Source: Own calculations for Society of Actuaries 2012 Individual Annuitant Tables with improvements through 2019.

couple's joint longevity. With retirement planning, the trouble is knowing what age to plan for, as this distribution of potential retirement lengths is quite wide. With this data, the probability of a sixty-five-year-old reaching age ninety-five is 23 percent for males, 30 percent for females, and 46 percent for at least one member of an opposite-gender couple. For a couple, thirty years is getting close to being the life expectancy for its longest living member. The probability of outliving a thirty-year time horizon is not insignificant. Longevity risk is the risk of living longer than anticipated and not having the resources to sustain spending for a longer lifetime. It is reflected in the exhibit as if one builds a plan to work through age ninety-five but then lives past this age.

Spending shocks

Unexpected expenses in retirement come in many forms, including:

- unforeseen need to help family members
- divorce
- changes in tax laws or other public policy
- changing housing needs
- home repairs

- rising health care and prescription costs
- long-term care

Retirees must preserve flexibility and liquidity to manage unplanned expenses. When attempting to budget over a long retirement period, it is important to include allowances for such contingencies.

Compounding inflation

Retirees face the risk that inflation will erode the purchasing power of their savings as they progress through retirement. Low inflation may not be noticeable in the short term, but it can have a big impact over a lengthy retirement, leaving retirees vulnerable. Even with just 3 percent average annual inflation, the purchasing power of a dollar will fall by more than half after twenty-five years, doubling the cost of living.

Sequence-of-returns risk is amplified by greater portfolio volatility, yet many retirees cannot afford to play it too safe. Short-term fixed-income securities might struggle to provide returns that exceed inflation, causing these assets to be quite risky in a different sense: they may not be able to support a retiree's long-term spending goals. Low-volatility assets are generally viewed as less risky, but this may not be the case when the objective is to sustain spending over a long time horizon. Retirees must keep an eye on the long-term cumulative impacts of even low inflation and position their assets accordingly.

Declining cognitive abilities

Finally, a retirement income plan must incorporate the unfortunate reality that many retirees will experience declining cognitive abilities, which will hamper portfolio management and other financial decision-making skills. For the afflicted, it will become increasingly difficult to make sound portfolio investments and withdrawal decisions at advanced ages.

In addition, many households do not equally share the management of personal finances. When the spouse who manages the finances dies first, the surviving spouse can run into serious problems without a clear plan in place. The surviving spouse can be left vulnerable to financial predators and other financial mistakes. Survivors often become more exposed to fraud and theft.

While liquidity and flexibility are important, retirees should also prepare for the reality that cognitive decline will hamper the portfolio management skills of many as they age, increasing the desirability of advanced planning and automation for late-in-life financial goals.

⊙ Two Philosophies for Retirement Income Planning

Within the world of retirement income planning, the siloed nature of financial services between investments and insurance leads to two opposing philosophies about how to build a retirement plan. There is an old saying that if the only tool you have is a hammer, then everything starts to look like a nail. This tendency is alive as those on the investments side tend to view an investment portfolio as a solution for any problem, while those on the insurance side tend to view insurance products as the answer for any financial question.

As a basic introduction to these schools, a simple litmus test can be applied. Monte Carlo simulations are often used in financial planning contexts to gain a better understanding of the viability of a financial plan in the face of market and longevity risks. Monte Carlo simulations create randomized series of market returns to test financial plans and their sustainability through various market environments. Suppose a Monte Carlo simulation identifies a retirement plan's chance of success as 90 percent. Both sides of the debate might accept this as the correct calculation from the software, but they will have dramatically different interpretations of what to do with this number.

For probability-based thinkers, a 90 percent chance is a more than reasonable starting point, and the retiree can proceed with the plan. It has a high likelihood of success, and that's enough for them. If future updates determine that the plan might be on course toward failure, a few changes, such as a small reduction in spending, should be adequate to get the plan back on track.

Those identifying with the safety-first school, however, will not be comfortable with this level of risk, focusing instead on the 10 percent chance of failure. They make a distinction between essential expenses and discretionary expenses and seek a solution that practically eliminates the possibility of failure for meeting essential expenses. Jeopardizing success, they say, is only reasonable for discretionary expenses.

Financial service professionals and retirees should understand which school they most identify with and to what extent their own thinking might incorporate views from each school. Consumers of the financial services profession must understand whether they and their advisor are speaking the same language. Advisors able to communicate effectively from both sides will be more likely to deliver successful retirement income outcomes by being able to tailor comfortable plans for their clients.

The Probability-Based School of Thought

How much can retirees withdraw from their savings, which are invested in a diversified investment portfolio, while still maintaining sufficient confidence that they can safely continue spending without running out of wealth for the length of retirement?

In the early 1990s, William Bengen read misguided claims in the popular press that average portfolio returns could guide the calculation of sustainable retirement withdrawal rates. If stocks average 7 percent after inflation, then plugging a 7 percent return into a spreadsheet suggests that retirees could withdraw 7 percent each year without ever dipping into their principal. Bengen recognized the naïveté of ignoring the real-world volatility experienced around that 7 percent return, and he sought to determine what would have worked historically for hypothetical retirees at different points. He used data extending back to 1926 for US financial markets for his research, which introduced the *concept of sequence-of-returns risk* to the financial planning profession.

The problem he set up is simple: a new retiree makes plans for withdrawing some inflation-adjusted amount from his or her savings at the end of each year for a thirty-year retirement period. For a sixty-five-year-old, this leads to a maximum planning age of ninety-five, which Bengen felt was reasonably conservative. What is the highest withdrawal amount as a percentage of retirement date assets that, with inflation adjustments, will be sustainable for the full thirty years? He looked at rolling thirty-year periods from history (1926 to 1955, 1927 to 1956, etc.). He found that with a 50/50 asset allocation to stocks and bonds (the S&P 500 and intermediate-term government bonds), the worst-case scenario experienced in US history was for a hypothetical 1966 retiree who could have withdrawn 4.15 percent at most. That is if distributions are taken at the end of each year. More realistically, if distributions are taken at the start of each year, this sustainable withdrawal rate falls to 4.03 percent.

Thus was born what is known as the *4 percent rule.*

Bengen's work pointed out that sequence-of-returns risk will reduce safe, sustainable withdrawal rates below what is implied by the average portfolio return over retirement. Its popularity has coalesced into what we are calling the probability-based approach.

The probability-based approach is based closely on the concepts of maximizing risk-adjusted returns from the perspective of the total portfolio. Asset allocation during retirement is generally defined in the same way as during the accumulation phase—using modern portfolio theory (MPT) to identify a portfolio on the efficient frontier in terms of single-period trade-offs between risk and return. Different volatile asset classes that are not perfectly correlated are combined to create portfolios with lower volatility. The efficient frontier identifies the asset allocation combinations with the highest probability-weighted arithmetic average return (often called *expected return* in finance literature) for an acceptable level of year-by-year volatility (often called *risk*). Investors aim to maximize wealth by seeking the highest possible return given their capacity and tolerance for volatility over a specific time horizon.

For retirement planning, spending and asset allocation recommendations from the efficient frontier are based on historical or Monte Carlo simulations of failure rates in order to mitigate the risk of wealth depletion inherent in drawing down a portfolio of volatile assets. The failure rate is the probability that wealth is depleted before death or before the end of the fixed time horizon which stands in for a maximum feasible lifespan. Asset allocation decisions are generally guided by what can minimize the failure rate in retirement. Advocates of the probability-based approach take this as license to use more aggressive asset allocations in retirement.

Advice from Bengen and subsequent studies is to have a stock allocation between 50 and 75 percent, but as close as possible to the higher end. Probability-based advocates are generally more optimistic about the long-run potential of stocks to outperform bonds and provide positive real returns, so investors are generally advised to take on as much risk as they can tolerate in order to minimize the probability of plan failure. This school of thought was the focus of my book *How Much Can I Spend in Retirement? A Guide to Investment-Based Retirement Strategies.*

The Safety-First School of Thought

The safety-first school of thought was originally derived from academic models of how people allocate their resources over a lifetime to maximize lifetime satisfaction. Academics have studied these models since the 1920s to figure out how rational people make optimal decisions. In the retirement context, the question to be answered is how to get the most lifetime satisfaction from limited financial resources. It is the basic question of economics: how to optimize in the face of scarcity? More recently, Nobel Prize winners such as Paul Samuelson, Robert Merton, Franco Modigliani, and William Sharpe have explored these models.

Safety-first arrives from a more academic foundation, so it is often described with mathematical equations in academic journals. As a result, it has been slow to enter the public consciousness. The safety-first approach is probably best associated with Professor Zvi Bodie from Boston University, whose popular books such as *Worry-Free Investing* and *Risk Less and Prosper* have brought these ideas alive to the public. Michael Zwecher's *Retirement Portfolios* is also an excellent resource written for financial professionals about this school of thought.

Advocates of the safety-first approach view prioritization of retirement goals as an essential component of developing a good retirement income strategy. The investment strategy aims to match the risk characteristics of assets and goals, so prioritization is a must.

Prioritizing goals has its academic origins in the idea of utility maximization. As people spend more, they experience diminishing marginal value with each additional dollar spent. The spending required to satisfy basic needs provides much more value and satisfaction to someone than the additional spending on luxuries after basic needs are met. Retirees should plan to smooth spending over time to avoid overspending on luxuries at the present and then being unable to afford essentials later.

In developing Modern Retirement Theory, financial planner Jason Branning and academic M. Ray Grubbs created a funding priority for retiree liabilities. Essential needs are the top priority, then a contingency fund, funds for discretionary expenses, and a legacy fund. They illustrate these funding priorities with a pyramid. Building a retirement strategy requires working from the bottom to properly fund each goal before moving up to the next.

There is no consideration of discretionary expenses or providing a legacy until a secure funding source for essentials and contingencies is in place.

The purpose of saving and investing is to fund spending and other goals during retirement. Safety-first advocates move away from asset allocation for the investment portfolio to broader asset-liability matching, which focuses more holistically at the household level and emphasizes hedging and insurance along with investing for upside. In simple terms, hedging means holding individual bonds to maturity, and insurance means using annuities and life insurance as solutions for longevity and market risk.

With asset-liability matching, investors are not trying to maximize their year-to-year returns on a risk-adjusted basis, nor are they trying to beat an investing benchmark. The goal is to have cash flows available to meet spending needs as required, and investments are chosen in a way that meets those needs. Assets are matched to goals so that the risk and cash-flow characteristics are comparable. For essential spending, Branning and Grubb's Modern Retirement Theory argues that funding must be with assets meeting the criteria of being secure, stable, and sustainable. In this regard, another important aspect of the investment approach for the safety-first school is that investing decisions are made in the context of the entire retirement balance sheet. This moves beyond looking only at the financial portfolio to consider also the role of human and social capital. Examples of human and social capital include the ability to work part-time, pensions, the social safety net, and so on.

An important point is that volatile assets are seen as inappropriate for basic needs and the contingency fund. Stated again, the objective of investing in retirement is not to maximize risk-adjusted returns, but first to ensure that basics will be covered in any market environment and then to invest for additional upside. Volatile (and hopefully, but not necessarily, higher returning) assets are suitable for discretionary expenses and legacy, in which there is some flexibility about whether the spending can be achieved.

Asset allocation, therefore, is an output of the analysis, as the entire retirement balance sheet is used, and assets are allocated to match appropriately with the household's liabilities. Asset-liability matching removes the probability-based concept of safe withdrawal rates from the analysis, since it rejects relying on a diversified portfolio for the entire lifestyle goal.

In fact, the general view of safety-first advocates is that there is no such thing as a safe withdrawal rate, such as the 4 percent rule, from a volatile portfolio. A truly safe withdrawal rate is unknown and unknowable. Retirees only receive one opportunity to obtain sustainable cash flows from their savings and must develop a strategy that will meet basic needs, no matter the length of life or the sequence of postretirement market returns and inflation. Retirees have little leeway for error, as returning to the labor force might not be a realistic option. Volatile assets like stocks are not appropriate when seeking to meet basic retirement living expenses. Just because a strategy did not fail over a historical period does not ensure it will always succeed in the future.

The idea is to first build a floor of low-risk, contractually protected income sources to serve basic spending needs in retirement. The floor is built with Social Security and any other defined-benefit pensions, and by using financial assets to do things such as building a ladder of TIPS or purchasing an annuity with lifetime income protection. Not all of these income sources are inflation adjusted, and you need to make sure the floor will be sufficiently protected from inflation, but this is the basic idea.

The objective for retirement is first to build a safe and secure income floor for the entire retirement planning horizon, and only after that does one include more volatile assets that provide greater upside potential and accompanying risk. Once there is enough flooring in place, retirees can focus on upside potential with remaining assets. Since this extra spending (such as for nice restaurants, extra vacations, etc.) is discretionary, it will not be the end of the world if it must be reduced at some point. The protected income floor is still in place to meet basic needs no matter what happens in the financial markets. With this sort of approach, withdrawal rates hardly matter.

● The Road Ahead

Retirement plans can be built to manage varying risks by strategically combining different retirement income tools. Our discussion of tools will focus on meeting spending and legacy goals with the intention of preserving some true liquidity to serve as reserves for spending shocks. The book navigates through the tools for building a retirement income plan with the basic ordering in mind: bonds, stocks, insurance. The first option is to use individual bonds to build a retirement income bond ladder that locks in desired spending at targeted dates. The bond yield curve determines how much can be spent in this way. To spend more than bonds can support, the second option is to rely on a diversified investment portfolio to provide higher returns by earning a risk premium above bonds. The third option is to pool longevity and market risks by using annuities and life insurance.

Fixed-Income and Individual Bonds

A starting point for retirement income is to hold fixed-income assets to their maturity to protect assets for upcoming retirement expenses. Holding bonds to their maturity can keep the retiree from selling them at a loss, which may help alleviate sequence-of-returns risk. Individual bonds do not provide longevity protection, however. And while they may provide technical liquidity, selling them early to use for other contingencies could result in capital losses as well as the loss of assets that had been earmarked to cover future spending. Traditional bonds will be exposed to inflation risk, but Treasury Inflation-Protected Securities (TIPS) can be used to lock in the purchasing power of money in real terms. We investigate bonds further in Chapter 2.

Total-Return Investment Portfolios (Risk Premium)

Making systematic withdrawals from a well-diversified investment portfolio is a common way to obtain retirement income. Systematic withdrawals do not protect a retiree from longevity risk or sequence-of-returns risk and may only protect from inflation risk when asset returns can keep up with inflation. This approach has its benefits, such as the potential to keep the nest egg growing to leave a large inheritance, as well as provide a sense of technical liquidity that could become true liquidity if markets perform well. A total-return approach is particularly vulnerable to declining cognitive abilities, as it requires complex financial decision-making to manage distributions and investments. It is the foundation of the probability-based approach. We review the process of determining sustainable spending with a volatile investment portfolio in Chapter 3.

Annuities (Risk Pooling)

Annuities with lifetime income protections can provide an effective way to build an income floor for retirement. Annuities, as opposed to individual bonds, provide longevity protection by hedging the risks associated with an unknown retirement length. Annuities can be real or nominal, fixed or variable, and income payments can begin within one year or be deferred to a later age. Social Security and the traditional defined-benefit pensions still offered by some employers may also be treated as annuities providing lifetime income protection as well.

The simplest type of annuity is an income annuity. We introduce these in greater detail in Chapter 4. There are also countless types of annuities can be used for many different purposes, including reasons unrelated to providing lifetime income.

With our focus in this book on retirement income, though, there are two additional annuity types we consider in detail. These include deferred variable annuities with lifetime income provisions, which are the subject of Chapter 5, and fixed index annuities (a newer name for equity index annuities) with lifetime income provisions, which are the subject of Chapter 6. Unlike income annuities that solely focus on protecting lifetime income, these other annuity types provide various combinations of lifetime income, liquidity, and upside growth potential.

Life Insurance (Risk Pooling)

Permanent life insurance is another tool that can play a role in a retirement income plan. In Chapter 7, we focus on whole life insurance and discuss briefly about variable and index life insurance as well. Whole life insurance provides a death benefit and a guaranteed cash value, both of which can be used in different ways to help support a lifetime financial plan. We focus on four potential roles for life insurance, including meeting a legacy goal with less assets, providing the comfort and support to also use an annuity with lifetime income protections, using the cash value of the life insurance as a volatility buffer asset to help manage sequence risk, and treating the cash value as a fixed-income alternative that may provide competitive returns on an post tax basis, especially if life insurance is desired in the preretirement period.

Product Allocation

Retirement income planning is not an either/or proposition. In the final two chapters, we step away from the notion that either investments or insurance alone will best serve retirees. Each tool has its own advantages and disadvantages. An entire literature on product allocation has arisen, showing how a more efficient set of retirement outcomes can be obtained by combining investments with insurance in the form of partial annuity strategies.

Deciding whether to annuitize, when to annuitize, how much to annuitize, and whether to build a ladder of annuities over time are all important questions. Annuities protect from longevity and sequence-of-returns risk, and they can protect from inflation risk if a real annuity is purchased. Because income continues automatically, they also provide protection for cognitive decline. David Laibson, a professor at Harvard University, refers to income annuities as "dementia insurance."

Chapter 8 focuses on issues about including income annuities into an overall retirement income plan. Chapter 9 provides a deeper comparison of different types of annuities in terms of their tax treatment, credit risk, and additional provisions for upside and liquidity. We also provide tips on distinguishing good and bad annuities, as well as criteria for choosing an annuity type.

Further Reading

Bengen, William P. 1994. "Determining Withdrawal Rates Using Historical Data." *Journal of Financial Planning* 7 (4): 171–180.

Bodie, Zvi, and Michael J. Clowes. 2003. *Worry-Free Investing: A Safe Approach to Achieving Your Lifetime Financial Goals.* Upper Saddle River, NJ: Financial Times Prentice Hall. [http://amzn.to/2mWqdUG]

Bodie, Zvi, and Rachelle Taqqu. 2012. *Risk Less and Prosper: Your Guide to Safer Investing.* Hoboken, NJ: John Wiley. [http://amzn.to/2sjgBFT]

Branning, Jason K., and M. Ray Grubbs. 2010. "Using a Hierarchy of Funds to Reach Client Goals." *Journal of Financial Planning* 23 (12): 31–33.

Zwecher, Michael J. 2010. *Retirement Portfolios: Theory, Construction, and Management.* Hoboken, NJ: John Wiley. [http://amzn.to/2uOcbRA]

CHAPTER 2

Fixed-Income Assets

For standard investment approaches, bonds are generally treated as a diversifying asset class that can help to reduce portfolio volatility. The standard investing philosophy for accumulation does not really consider how the nature of risk changes upon retiring. In short, it uses modern portfolio theory to choose an asset allocation strategy that includes bonds as part of a total-returns investment portfolio. Bonds, with their lower expected returns and volatility, provide a way to reduce the portfolio's overall volatility to an acceptable level while still maintaining a sufficient overall portfolio return.

Asset allocation in this framework is generally determined in terms of assets-only considerations to build a diversified portfolio with the highest expected return for the accepted level of risk. To the extent that retirement income needs are considered, it is generally to find an asset allocation that will minimize the probability of failure for the financial plan. Looking back to William Bengen's original work in the 1990s about sustainable spending rates, the best worst-case historical spending rates could be achieved with an overall bond allocation of 20 to 65 percent. He also found that intermediate-term US government bonds provided a sweet spot in terms of return and volatility trade-offs, keeping worst-case historical spending rates at the highest possible level.

As a pure building block for retirement income, though, we may think of holding individual bonds to maturity to provide the desired cash flows to fund annual expenses on an ongoing basis throughout retirement. In this method, maturing bonds and bond coupon payments provide a steady and known stream of contractually protected income to meet planned expenditures. There will not be capital losses if bonds are not sold prior to maturity.

A retirement income bond ladder is the natural starting point for building a retirement income strategy. It can neutralize market-related risks for the retirement income plan, though it still exposes the retiree to longevity risk, as it is possible to outlive the end-date chosen for the bond ladder. If one seeks to spend more than the bond yield curve can support for a given ladder length, the two options are to seek a risk premium through stock market investments, or to pool longevity risk through insurance products. In this chapter, we lay the foundation for understanding how the retirement income bond ladder works as a baseline for a retirement income strategy.

○ Understanding How Bonds Work

Before we can discuss bonds in depth, it is important that we establish a common understanding of what bonds are and how they work. As a starting point, a bond is a contractual obligation to make a series of specific payments on specific dates. Typically, this includes interest payments made on a semiannual basis until the maturity date and the return of the bond's face value. Bonds are issued by both governments and private corporations to raise funds, and they are purchased by investors seeking an investment return on their capital.

Treasuries are issued by the US government. Technically, treasuries with maturities of a year or less are called *bills*, while those with maturities of more than a year up to ten years are called *notes*. *Bonds* typically refers to treasuries with maturities of more than ten years. In my discussion, I will use the term bond generically to represent these cases. Bank CDs also function as a type of bond in terms of providing specified cash flows at specified dates, though they are not traded on secondary markets.

Bond interest rates—both coupon rates and the yields subsequently provided to investors—are determined by the interaction of supply and demand for the bonds as they continue to be traded. An increase in demand—such as that triggered by a "flight to quality" when investors are panicked by the falling prices of risky assets—will push up the price of these bonds. Conversely, a stretched government seeking to raise funds through an increasing supply of new bond issues will reduce the price of bonds.

Newly issued bonds are sold on the primary market, but many go on to be traded on secondary markets. A bond that sells at par value can be purchased for the same price as its face value. Bonds may also sell at a premium (higher than face value) or discount (lower than face value). Bond prices are quoted in terms of bid and ask prices. *Bid* is the price the bond can be sold for, and *ask* is the price at which it can be purchased. The difference in prices is the spread made by the party helping conduct the exchanges between buyers and sellers. Household investors will experience lower bid and higher ask prices than reported in newspapers because the newspapers report the wholesale prices for institutions placing trades in excess of $1 million.

Rising interest rates will lower prices for existing bonds, so the subsequent return to the new purchaser can match the higher returns available on new bonds with higher interest rates. Conversely, lower interest rates will increase the price existing bonds can sell for. If sold at their face value, these older bonds offer higher returns than newly issued bonds, and their owners will want to hold them. An agreeable selling price can only be found if the bond sells at a premium, and then the new purchaser receives a subsequent return on their purchase price that is in line with newly issued bonds. The price of a bond on the secondary market will fluctuate in the opposite direction of interest rates.

In the universe of bonds, there is not one single interest rate. Differences in interest rates among bonds reflect several factors:

- the time to maturity for the bond (longer-term bonds will experience more price volatility as interest rates change)
- the credit risk of the bond (bonds that are more likely to default on their promised payments are riskier and will have to reward investors with higher yields)
- liquidity (bonds that are more actively traded may offer lower yields as investors will demand an additional return premium for sacrificing iquidity)

- the tax status of the bond (municipal bonds from state and local government agencies are free from federal income taxes and thus offer lower interest rates)

Bonds may also feature other options that affect the price an investor is willing to pay. For instance, if the bond is *callable* (meaning the issuer retains the right to repay it early if interest rates decline), the potential capital gains are reduced, which in turn lowers the price investors are willing to pay.

US government treasuries are generally seen as having the lowest credit risk, and they will generally offer lower yields than corporate bonds with the same maturity date. They are less likely to default and create problems for borrowers to receive what is owed. They are backed by the full faith and credit of the US government. Treasuries are also free from state and local taxes.

In recent years, financial innovation has led to the creation of many new types of fixed-income instruments with varying risk and return potential, but the retirement income planning discussion here is about using traditional government or noncallable (face value cannot be repaid early) high-quality corporate bonds to support a retirement income strategy.

● Bond Pricing 101

As a bond provides a contractual right to a series of future payments received at specified points of time, the price for a bond is simply the present discounted value of the future cash flows. The face value of a bond will be repaid at maturity.

A *zero-coupon bond* provides only a bond's face value, and it will be sold at a discount to the face value in order to provide a return and compensate for the risks related to holding it. A *coupon bond* provides the face value at maturity in addition to a series of coupon payments (often on a semiannual basis) until the maturity date. The *coupon rate* is contractually defined as a percentage of the face value.

The *yield to maturity* is the internal rate of return an investor will earn by holding a bond to maturity and receiving its cash flows. The yield to maturity for a new investor differs from the coupon rate whenever the bond sells for a different price than its face value.

Exhibit 2.1 provides a simple example to understand the pricing process for bonds. The bond being considered is a ten-year coupon bond with a face value of $1,000 and a coupon rate of 3 percent. In this simple example, one coupon payment of $30 (3 percent of $1,000) is made at the end of each year for ten years to the bond's owner(s) on those dates, and the face value is paid in full at the end of the tenth year. These can be seen in the exhibit's Cash Flows column. The next three columns provide the discounted value of these cash flows for different interest rates: 3 percent, 3.5 percent, and 4 percent. When the discount rate is 3 percent, we see that the total discounted cash flows add to $1,000, which is the same as the face value. This is an important point: When the interest rate is the same as the bond coupon rate, the price of a coupon bond will match its face value.

Let's be clear about what the discounted value of the payments means. In year ten, for instance, the discounted value of the payment with a 3 percent interest rate is $766.42. Imagine placing this amount in a bank account that earns an annually compounded 3 percent return each year. After ten years, it will grow to be $1,030, which is the amount of the cash payment provided in year ten. In other words, an investor would need to set aside $766.42 today in order to have $1,030 in ten years if the funds grew at a 3 percent annually compounded return.

If interest rates in the economy are 3.5 percent, then an investor would not be willing to pay $1,000 for this bond that provides only 3 percent coupon payments. The investor would prefer a new bond that presumably is now offering a 3.5 percent coupon. To entice an investor to purchase the bond in this exhibit, the bond would have to be sold for a lower price. In a competitive and active market, bonds with the same maturity and risk characteristics must offer the same potential return for both parties to agree to a trade. In this case, the future cash flows are discounted at 3.5 percent, and the sum of these discounted cash flows (and potential selling price) is $958.42.

Whoever owns the bond is entitled to the predefined cash flows of $30 per year plus $1,000 more in the final year. These cash flows do not change with interest rates. What changes is the selling price of the bond. For an investor who pays $958.42 for the bond, the yield to maturity received by the investor on this smaller investment is 3.5 percent. Note that a 0.5 percent increase in interest rates reduced the selling price of the bond by 4.2 percent. If the investor sold the bond, the return received by the previous owner is defined in terms of any coupon payments received less the capital loss associated with the interest rate rise. Increasing interest rates lower the prices for existing bonds. The same phenomenon is also shown for an interest rate of 4 percent. In this case, the bond's price would have to be set at $918.89 to adequately entice an investor. The 8.1 percent price reduction provides a yield to maturity of 4 percent to the new purchaser that then matches the overall higher interest rate in the economy.

The yield to maturity can differ from the coupon rate as bonds are bought and sold at prices other than face value, exposing the investor to *interest rate risk*—the risk that a bond price will fall due to rising interest rates.

Coupon rates are one of the most confusing aspects of bonds for people to understand. When the bond is issued, it pays a set coupon rate. For a

Exhibit 2.1

Basic Pricing for a Ten-Year Coupon Bond

| Coupon Rate: | 3% |
| Face Value: | $1,000 |

		Discounted Cash Flows		
	Interest Rates	3%	3.5%	4%
Year	Cash Flows			
1	$30.00	$29.13	$28.99	$28.85
2	$30.00	$28.28	$28.01	$27.74
3	$30.00	$27.45	$27.06	$26.67
4	$30.00	$26.65	$26.14	$25.64
5	$30.00	$25.88	$25.26	$24.66
6	$30.00	$25.12	$24.41	$23.71
7	$30.00	$24.39	$23.58	$22.80
8	$30.00	$23.68	$22.78	$21.92
9	$30.00	$22.99	$22.01	$21.08
10	$1,030.00	$766.42	$730.19	$695.83
Bond Price:		$1,000.00	$958.42	$918.89
Price Change:		0.0%	-4.2%	-8.1%

regular Treasury bond, if the coupon rate is 3 percent and face value is $1,000, then the bond pays coupons of $30 per year. Usually these are paid semiannually—two coupon payments of $15 in this case. Note that the coupon rate never changes. Interest rates can change, but that will affect the yield, not the coupon rate. If interest rates rise, then the price the bond can be sold at will decrease, raising the underlying yield to maturity to match the increasing interest rate. But if I buy a $1,000 face value bond on the secondary market for only $700 and it has a 3 percent coupon, it is important to understand that my coupon income will be based on 3 percent of $1,000, not 3 percent of $700. Though this may seem basic and simple as I explain it, it has proved to be a major source of confusion.

The *yield* is the yield to maturity based on the ask price paid by the investor—the return the investor would get for buying the bond today and holding it to maturity. If the ask price matches the face value, then the yield will be the same as the coupon. If the ask price is higher, then the yield will be less than the coupon, and if the ask price is lower, then the yield will be higher than the coupon. Why? This gets back to the point I was stressing before about how the coupon rate never changes. The bond provides a promise for a fixed set of payments. It pays all the fixed coupon amounts and repays the face value at the maturity date. These payments do not change. But bonds can be sold and resold on secondary markets prior to the maturity date. If I pay $900 for a bond providing a fixed set of promised payments, then I'm going to get a higher return on my $900 investment than if I paid $1,100 for the same set of promised payments. Lower ask prices imply higher yields, and vice versa.

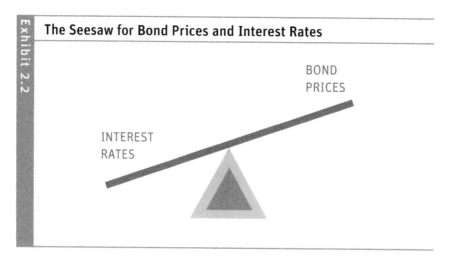

Exhibit 2.2

The Seesaw for Bond Prices and Interest Rates

BOND PRICES

INTEREST RATES

○ Bond Duration

Bond prices are sensitive to interest rate changes, and bond duration is a measure of just how sensitive. For instance, in Exhibit 2.1, an increase in interest rates for the simple bond from 3 percent to 4 percent caused the bond's price to fall by 8.1 percent. This bond has a duration of 8.1, meaning that a 1 percent rise in interest rates leads to an 8.1 percent drop in price. The bond duration is measured in years, and the weighted-dollar average for the time when the cash flows are received in this example is 8.1 years.

Exhibit 2.3 uses the same basic setup as Exhibit 2.1 to provide more insight about how bond prices relate to interest rates and time to maturity. Again, the basic scenario is that we have purchased a bond with a $1,000 face value and 3 percent annual coupon payments. The current interest rate for a comparable bond is also 3 percent. Sometime shortly after purchase, interest rates change, with the exhibit showing new potential interest rates from 1 to 5 percent. The exhibit shows the new price that bonds with different maturities could sell for after the rate change. The bottom

Exhibit 2.3

Bond Prices and Interest Rates

Current Bond Value:	$1,000
Coupon Rate:	3% (annual)
Current Interest Rate:	3%

New Interest Rate: New Bond Price

Years to Maturity	1.0%	1.5%	2.0%	2.5%	3.0%	3.5%	4.0%	4.5%	5.0%
1	$1,020	$1,015	$1,010	$1,005	$1,000	$995	$990	$986	$981
5	$1,097	$1,072	$1,047	$1,023	$1,000	$977	$955	$934	$913
10	$1,189	$1,138	$1,090	$1,044	$1,000	$958	$919	$881	$846
20	$1,361	$1,258	$1,164	$1,078	$1,000	$929	$864	$805	$751
30	$1,516	$1,360	$1,224	$1,105	$1,000	$908	$827	$756	$693

New Interest Rate: Percent Change for Bond Price

Years to Maturity	1.0%	1.5%	2.0%	2.5%	3.0%	3.5%	4.0%	4.5%	5.0%
1	2.0%	1.5%	1.0%	0.5%	0.0%	-0.5%	-1.0%	-1.4%	-1.9%
5	9.7%	7.2%	4.7%	2.3%	0.0%	-2.3%	-4.5%	-6.6%	-8.7%
10	18.9%	13.8%	9.0%	4.4%	0.0%	-4.2%	-8.1%	-11.9%	-15.4%
20	36.1%	25.8%	16.4%	7.8%	0.0%	-7.1%	-13.6%	-19.5%	-24.9%
30	51.6%	36.0%	22.4%	10.5%	0.0%	-9.2%	-17.3%	-24.4%	-30.7%

section of the exhibit shows the percentage change in price resulting from the rate change. Here we can clearly see how bond prices move counter to interest rates, and how price fluctuations are more dramatic for longer-term bonds, demonstrating their higher duration. At the extreme, the thirty-year bond would experience a capital *gain* of 22.4 percent if interest rates *fell* by 1 percent, and a 17.3 percent capital loss if interest rates *rose* by 1 percent. Price risk increases with time to maturity. If interest rates rose to 5 percent, the capital loss for a thirty-year bond would be 30.7 percent—comparable to a significant stock market drop. Despite their reputation as reliable and predictable, bonds can be risky.

While more complex bonds can have some unusual duration properties, the basic noncallable coupon and discount bonds we consider for a retirement income plan define duration in a straightforward way. A bond's duration is essentially the effective maturity of a bond—an average of when the bond's payments are received, weighted by the discounted size of those cash flows.

A zero-coupon bond provides one payment at the maturity date, so its duration is the same as the time to maturity. The further away the maturity date, the higher the bond's duration, making it more sensitive to interest rate changes. A coupon bond will have a shorter duration than the time to the maturity date because coupon payments are received before the maturity date. Higher coupon rates push relatively more cash flows sooner, which otherwise lowers the duration for a bond with the same maturity date. Also, lower interest rates mean the future cash flows from a bond are discounted less relative to nearer-term cash flows, and so bond duration increases when interest rates are low. An implication for this point is that our low-interest-rate environment increases the interest rate risk for holding bonds, as a rate increase can result in a bigger capital loss.

An observant reader of Exhibit 2.3 might note that duration is not symmetric. For a thirty-year bond, a 1 percent increase in interest rates to 4 percent results in a capital loss of 17.3 percent, while a 1 percent decrease in interest rates to 1 percent results in a capital gain of 22.4 percent. The duration measure works best for small interest rate changes because it is a linear approximation to a shape that is curved. The term *convexity* describes price sensitivity to interest changes more precisely. Bond prices are more sensitive to rate decreases (prices rise more) than to equivalent rate increases (prices fall by less). These differences are accounted for by the fact that changing interest rates also impact duration. The duration for a given bond rises as interest rates fall and future cash flows are discounted by less. But for a household retiree, duration provides a close enough approximation to this relationship, and only those with a greater interest in the mathematics of bond pricing should worry about further adding bond convexity to their discussion.

Though somewhat technical, this discussion of bond duration is important because the concept also applies to retirement spending liabilities and, therefore, the ability to meet retirement goals. Retirement spending has a duration that can be defined in the same way as an effective maturity for those cash flows. It is an average of when expenses must be paid, weighted by the size of the discounted values of those expenses.

Individual bonds have a duration. A bond fund, which is a collection of bonds, also has a duration equal to the average duration of each holding weighted by its proportion in the fund. Retirement liabilities have a duration, too. If the duration of the bonds and the spending liabilities can be matched to the same value, then the retiree has immunized his or her interest rate risk. Rising interest rates would lower the value of bond holdings, but rising rates also lower the present value of the future spending obligations. When durations are the same, both the asset and liability values are reduced by the same amount, and the retiree remains equally well-off in terms of the ability to meet liabilities. This is the meaning of immunizing interest rate risk. If the durations do not match, then the retiree is exposed to interest rate risk.

◉ Treasury Inflation-Protected Securities (TIPS)

In discussing retirement liabilities, it is also important to address the issue of inflation and how to think about bonds when they are meant to fund a liability that grows with the consumer price index. Fortunately, this is now practical as the United States began issuing Treasury Inflation-Protected Securities (TIPS) in 1997. Backed by the full faith and credit of the US government and assurances that inflation cannot eat away at their value, TIPS provide a risk-free asset for US-based investors.

The face value and coupon payments for TIPS are both indexed to keep pace with inflation and preserve purchasing power, and their yields are quoted in real inflation-adjusted terms. Whenever positive inflation (as opposed to deflation) is expected, real yields will be less than the nominal yields quoted on traditional (i.e., not inflation adjusted) bonds. As an approximation:

real interest rate = nominal interest rate – expected inflation rate

Nominal interest rates are determined by compensation expected to keep pace with inflation plus a real rate of return for the investor. Supply and demand affect bond prices and interest rates. Real interest rates can be negative.

Investors may expect a positive nominal return on their investment (otherwise, there is no reason to invest), but that return may not be able to keep pace with inflation. Unlike traditional bonds, TIPS yields are quoted as real interest rates.

Their nominal yields are not known in advance because they depend on the subsequently realized inflation experience. Conversely, we know nominal yields for traditional bonds, but their real yields can only be known after observing the realized path of inflation up to the maturity date.

Inflation adjustments for TIPS are linked to the Consumer Price Index for All Urban Consumers (CPI-U). These adjustments are tracked in terms of the *accrued principal*, which is a unique term for TIPS. Accrued principal is the inflation-adjusted value of the initial face value since the TIPS was issued. For TIPS, inflation adjustments are realized by having the coupon rate be paid on the value of the accrued principal, not the nominal initial face value.

As well, at the maturity date, the investor receives the accrued principal back, not the nominal face value. A real coupon rate is paid on an inflation-adjusted amount, and an inflation-adjusted amount is returned at the maturity date.

If there is deflation, the accrued principal can decrease, but it is protected from falling below its initial par value. This means that TIPS on the secondary markets with lower accrued principal will be able to provide better protection from a deflationary episode, other factors being the same.

Otherwise, deflation that is not significant enough to cause the accrued principal to fall below its initial par value will hurt TIPS relative to traditional bonds. Generally, the purpose of TIPS is to provide protection from unexpectedly high inflation, and buying TIPS with a lower relative accrued principal is a secondary consideration when choosing specific TIPS to purchase.

It is important to note that TIPS are purchased in nominal dollars. On the secondary market, the ask price for TIPS is quoted in real terms, represented as a percentage of the inflation-adjusted accrued principal. The price paid is the ask price times the accrued principal divided by 100.

TIPS notes and bonds have been issued since January 1997. Until mid-2002, each auction for TIPS of the various maturities provided an initial real yield above 3 percent. Lucky investors in 1998 and 1999 could have purchased thirty-year TIPS yielding close to 4 percent and yields on ten- and twenty-year TIPS exceeded 4 percent in 1999 and 2000. Since this time, TIPS yields have fallen.

An auction for a five-year note held in October 2010 made headlines as the real yield dipped below zero (to -0.55 percent) for the first time. Purchasers of those issues locked in yields that will not keep pace with inflation. Though surprising at the time, negative yields for TIPS have become the norm in recent years until the flattening of the yield curve in 2018 brought shorter-term TIPS yields above 0 percent again.

In 2003, Zvi Bodie and Michael J. Clowes published the book *Worry-Free Investing: A Safe Approach to Achieving Your Lifetime Financial Goals*, in which they argued that typical retirement-oriented investors should rely primarily on TIPS for their retirement savings. Of course, other financial assets should be included in retirement portfolios, but, they said, only once you have enough savings (after accounting for any income expected from Social Security and other defined-benefit pensions) to cover your planned retirement expenditures without these riskier assets. In an interview in the February 2010 issue of *Journal of Financial Planning*, Bodie confirmed his continued endorsement of this strategy. He also indicated that his personal retirement portfolio is 100 percent in TIPS.

TIPS tend to be the preferred choice in academic approaches to retirement income, assuming that spending needs grow with inflation. But not everyone agrees. First, there are issues to consider related to how TIPS provide adjustments for the Consumer Price Index for All Urban Consumers (CPI-U). The CPI-U does not match the actual inflation experience of any individual household purchasing a different basket of goods. The Bureau of Labor Statistics has also created an experimental CPI for the elderly that suggests their consumption basket cost may grow at a faster overall rate. It is also safe to assume that the spending of many households will not keep pace with inflation in retirement as their consumption basket changes over time. TIPS are presented by some as the perfect hedge for the retirement spending liability, but that is only true if a retiree's spending grows at the same rate as the CPI-U.

Another reason TIPS are not universally adored is that while they are exempt from state and local taxes (like all treasuries), the inflation adjustments provided for their coupon payments and principal are taxable at the federal level. This tax will need to be paid on an ongoing basis for the inflation adjustments on the accrued principal, even though you won't see a penny of it until the maturity date. Calculating taxes for this "phantom income" can be especially complex, so many retirees prefer to hold their TIPS in qualified retirement accounts.

Another negative is that TIPS tend to have a higher duration than traditional treasuries because of their lower real coupon rates and because the cash flows received from TIPS will weigh more heavily toward payments with bigger inflation adjustments made closer to the maturity date.

Michael Zwecher suggests in his 2010 book *Retirement Portfolios* that he is not dogmatic about seeking inflation protection. He views the higher yield on traditional bonds as a premium for writing a call option on inflation. As indicated, traditional bonds lose out when inflation is unexpectedly high. Some retirees may be willing to accept this risk in return for the higher yield that traditional bonds provide otherwise. This could be especially true of households who are not as exposed to this inflation risk either because their spending will not keep pace with inflation or because they have inflation protection from other assets like Social Security.

Overall, there is no single answer to the choice of TIPS versus traditional treasuries. I tend to lean toward TIPS as a default choice, but individual circumstances could certainly warrant a more mixed approach. Individuals who can live comfortably on their inflation-adjusted Social Security benefit, for instance, may have little need for TIPS.

The Yield Curve and Break-Even Inflation

Understanding the relationship between bond risk and time to maturity and duration of a bond provides the basis for understanding the bond yield curve. The yield curve shows the yields to maturity for a series of bonds—typically US Treasury bonds—with the same credit quality but different maturity dates, along with the term structure for interest rates.

Exhibit 2.4 provides an example of the yield curve for Treasury Bonds and for TIPS on May 1, 2019.

Bonds with more distant maturity dates typically offer higher interest rates than bonds with earlier maturity dates. This is not always the case, but in the exhibit, we do see this effect, even though it is more muted than usual. For treasuries, a thirty-year treasury was yielding 2.92 percent while a five-year treasury was yielding 2.31 percent, for instance. Likewise, with TIPS the real yield for a thirty-year maturity was 0.95 percent, compared with 0.48 percent for a TIPS with a five-year maturity.

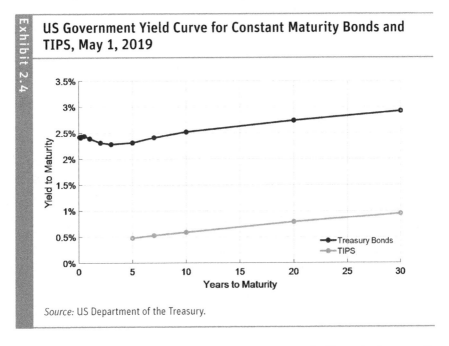

Exhibit 2.4

US Government Yield Curve for Constant Maturity Bonds and TIPS, May 1, 2019

Source: US Department of the Treasury.

Longer-term bonds experience bigger price fluctuations as interest rates change. When interest rates increase, the price of existing bonds on the secondary market falls in order to calibrate the yield investors will receive from owning existing bonds with the yields being offered by newly issued bonds at the higher interest rates. Bonds that mature sooner are less exposed to this price risk. Thus, shorter-term US Treasury securities are generally considered to be among the lowest-risk investment assets when annualized volatility represents the measure of risk, which means they tend to be offered at a lower yield. Higher yields accompany longer-term bonds, as investors need an added incentive to accept the higher price risks.

The shape of the yield curve is molded by two theories. First, expectations theory suggests that the shape of the yield curve should be reflected by beliefs about future short-term interest rates. For example, investing in bonds over ten years can be done in two ways:

1. Buy a ten-year bond, or
2. Buy a one-year bond and then reinvest in a new one-year bond after one year, continuing with a succession of ten one-year bonds.

For markets to be in balance, these two strategies should offer the same expected return to an investor, meaning that the combined impact of one-year rates over ten years should match the rate for a ten-year bond. An inverted yield curve where short-term rates exceed long-term rates can be understood as a clear expectation that short-term interest rates will fall in the future. Since interest rate fluctuations are extremely difficult to predict, the expectations theory alone would probably leave the average yield curve relatively flat.

The other theory to determine yield curve shape is the liquidity preference theory, which suggests a need for a risk premium to be offered for longer-term bonds to account for their increased interest rate risk and price volatility, as discussed. Longer-term bonds are less liquid, as well, since this price risk could force them to be sold at a loss if an unexpected expense arose. With this risk premium added to the expectations theory, the typical or neutral shape for the yield curve becomes upward sloping.

With TIPS, we now have a better idea of market expectations for future inflation, though I would not call it perfect. TIPS offer a break-even inflation rate, defined as the difference in yields on the same maturity of traditional treasuries and TIPS. TIPS yields may not reflect the true underlying real interest rate because they have a few other components built into their pricing, such as a premium for their relative illiquidity as they represent a smaller market than treasuries, and a potential additional premium for the protection they provide against unexpected high inflation.

Despite the other factors of TIPS pricing, the difference between Treasury and TIPS rates for the same maturity represents a reasonable market estimate of future inflation expectations. Exhibit 2.5 uses the same data as in Exhibit 2.4 to find this difference.

Again, we see with the thirty-year maturity that treasuries yield a nominal 2.92 percent. Its real yield is unknown and depends on realized future inflation. Meanwhile, a thirty-year TIPS offers a real yield of 0.95 percent. Its nominal yield is unknown, as it also depends on realized future inflation. The difference between these yields is the implied break-even inflation rate: 1.97 percent, or approximately 2 percent. Without a liquidity or inflation-protection premium, this represents the market's equilibrium estimate of future inflation. Over the next thirty years, the markets have priced in expectations for inflation of about 2 percent.

If realized annual inflation exceeds 2 percent over the next thirty years, then TIPS will outperform treasuries. But if inflation falls short, TIPS will

Exhibit 2.5

US Government Yield Curve and Implied Break-Even Inflation, May 1, 2019

Maturity	Treasury Yield	TIPS Yield	Implied Break-Even Inflation Rate
1 Year	2.39%	n/a	n/a
5 Years	2.31%	0.48%	1.83%
10 Years	2.52%	0.59%	1.93%
20 Years	2.74%	0.79%	1.95%
30 Years	2.92%	0.95%	1.97%

Source: US Department of the Treasury.

underperform. If enough traders thought inflation would be higher than this, they would *buy* TIPS and *sell* treasuries, raising the price of TIPS today, and giving us lower TIPS yields, higher treasury yields, and a larger break-even inflation rate. Such trading would continue until the market reaches the equilibrium we observe.

Traditional bonds are priced around the objective of getting a return that exceeds expected inflation. If inflation is unexpectedly high, then the real return on nominal bonds is less. TIPS, on the other hand, keep pace with higher inflation because it triggers a higher nominal return above their underlying real interest rate. Essentially, TIPS provide protection from unexpected inflation. They outperform treasuries when inflation exceeds the implied break-even inflation rate.

This is a valuable attribute when spending is expected to grow with inflation. Traditional bonds outperform if inflation is unexpectedly low. Low inflation also makes it easier to meet retirement spending goals, so this outcome is less in need of protection. Retirees generally get more use from insurance that protects from *high* inflation, making TIPS a more natural candidate for retirement portfolios. In short, TIPS provide retirees with reliable, inflation-adjusted income that will maintain its real purchasing power.

○ Laddering with Individual Bonds

Duration matching is not straightforward for bond funds when shares of the bond fund must be sold to meet ongoing retirement expenses. If rates have risen, shares of the bond fund may need to be sold at a loss, with more shares sold to meet a given spending objective. This triggers sequence risk and locks in losses. Immunization only works if interest payments can be reinvested at a new higher interest rate to compensate for capital losses. But not all the funds are fully reinvested when a spending goal is met, so reinvestment risk and interest rate risk do not get neutralized. The return on remaining assets would need to be even higher to keep the retirement liability funded. Immunization is harder when there is also a spending goal to support.

A more practical approach is to use individual bonds in a retirement income plan. A retirement income bond ladder can be structured so the cash flows provided through coupons and maturing face values will provide a steady and known stream of contractually protected cash flows for the ongoing expenditure needs in retirement. Cash flows from the bonds are matched to fund desired expenses at desired dates. Interest rate risk can be ignored for the retirement expenses that have been matched with these dedicated assets. Sequence risk is reduced because there is less risk of assets being sold at a loss. Rebalancing may be required in terms of extending the length of the bond ladder as time passes to cover future expenses, but the complexities involved in an ongoing effort to match durations can be better avoided.

Retirement income bond ladders generally take the form of Treasury bonds to minimize the possibility of default risk. For a household retiree, maximizing investment returns is not the goal; the goal is to meet expenses. Paper losses on individual bonds do not have to be realized if the bond is held to maturity. While the retiree misses out on the opportunity to buy the bond at a lower price later, this cannot be known in advance. It is always unfortunate to buy bonds and then see the price drop due to rising rates. But if the initial purchase allows the retiree to meet his or her retirement objective, then it is a successful purchase, no matter what interest rates subsequently do.

Retirees who realize that it is nearly impossible to predict interest rate fluctuations can take comfort in knowing that individual bonds allow them to enjoy retirement and ignore subsequent interest rate fluctuations. Ignoring interest rate fluctuations is not possible with a bond fund strategy that has to make frequent adjustments to the portfolio's duration in order to immunize against interest rate risk.

The difference between a traditional bond ladder as an accumulation tool and a retirement income bond ladder is that with a traditional ladder, the cash flows received as coupons and face value are *reinvested* to purchase new replacement bonds at prevailing prices that extend the ladder and keep its length relatively constant over time. With a retirement income bond ladder, the cash flows received are spent on planned retirement expenses. A retirement income ladder will naturally wind down if other assets from outside the ladder are not used to extend it further as time passes.

As we have discussed, changing interest rates lead, in turn, to capital gains or losses for investors. For professional bond traders, rising interest rates would be a serious problem for someone who had just purchased a long-term bond. Most traders have no intention of holding bonds to maturity and will realize capital losses on the subsequent sale. Interest rate increases might also force retirees owning bond funds into a position of selling shares at a loss in order to meet retirement expenses. For a bond portfolio that is not fully immunized, this triggering of sequence-of-returns risk can create irreparable harm for retirees.

I would argue that it is much easier for a retiree to ignore unrealized capital losses on an individual bond than for a professional trader or retiree needing to sell bond shares to meet expenses because the individual bond is bought with the purpose of being held to maturity to provide a desired amount of spending at that date.

Exhibit 2.6 quantifies this point. If interest rates are at 3 percent when a thirty-year bond is purchased, but then subsequently rise permanently from 3 percent to 4 percent during the first year the bond is held, the retiree is sitting on an unrealized capital loss for the next twenty-nine years. After one year, the bond price falls to $838, representing a 16.2 percent loss. Nevertheless, the bond continues to pay its 3 percent coupon payments and at maturity will repay the $1,000 face value. As the maturity date slowly approaches, the unrealized losses slowly dissipate. The bond price gradually returns to match its face value. The full recovery will happen at the maturity date when the final cash flows are received as expected. In this way, a household investor can be justified in ignoring those unrealized capital losses on the bond, as they will not be realized if the bond is held to maturity.

It is important to provide a caveat that this analysis is easier to think about with TIPS because with traditional bonds interest rate increases could result from increases in inflation that would reduce the purchasing power of the bond at maturity.

A full thirty-year bond ladder could be created with the idea of generating lifetime income. One might seek more than thirty years, but Treasury bonds with maturities past that are not available. A thirty-year bond ladder does not *truly* provide lifetime income. The bond ladder would be spent down

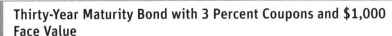
Exhibit 2.6

Thirty-Year Maturity Bond with 3 Percent Coupons and $1,000 Face Value

Ongoing Price of Bond if Interest Rates Stay at 3 Percent and if Interest Rates Rise to and Stay at 4 Percent

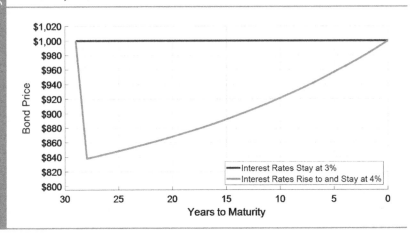

entirely by year thirty, creating a problem for someone still alive in year thirty-one. For this reason, not all assets should be used to construct such a ladder. It is important to set something aside for unplanned contingencies and the prospect of living longer than thirty years. For unplanned expenses, while the bond ladder is liquid, selling portions of it to meet unexpected expenses directly means sacrificing some of the assets earmarked for later retirement spending. Also, retirees selling individual bonds prior to their maturity dates face interest rate risk, as a rise in interest rates would force capital losses to be realized in these cases. For someone considering a thirty-year retirement income bond ladder, it is important to also take a serious look at income annuities as a cheaper and more secure way to generate lifetime income.

As for the mechanics of selecting bonds and building a bond ladder, I discuss this in greater detail in my book *How Much Can I Spend in Retirement?* For the present book, the focus is on comparing other strategies that seek higher returns than bonds, and so simplifying the bond piece can be justified. The level of sustainable spending calculated using a full bond yield curve ends up being quite close to the level of spending determined assuming a flat yield curve at the level of a long-term average interest rate. With the bond yield curves shown in Exhibit 2.4, sustainable spending with a flat 3 percent yield curve for treasuries or a flat 1 percent yield curve for TIPS are reasonably good approximations for the sustainable spending available from the full yield curve.

Exhibit 2.7 provides reasonable approximations for sustainable spending in retirement as it relates to a bond interest rate (or, as we develop in Chapter 3, a fixed return for an investment portfolio) and a retirement longevity assumption. For a sixty-five-year-old with $1 million, the exhibit shows sustainable spending levels given both returns and longevity. The returns can express either nominal or real returns. If nominal returns, then the spending numbers would also be nominal and would not adjust for inflation. If the returns are real, however, then spending numbers are also real and would grow with inflation.

If the retiree sought to buy a retirement income bond ladder through age ninety-five using Treasury bonds, the 3 percent yield curve assumptions suggests that the sustainable spending amount is $49,533. Again, because this is an assumption about nominal bond yields, this spending amount would not growth with inflation. As inflation is generally a positive number, real returns are less than nominal returns. With real returns the initial spending level would be less but would grow with inflation. With the 1 percent TIPS yield curve assumption, sustainable spending through age ninety-five is $38,364 plus inflation.

Exhibit 2.7

Sustainable Spending for a Sixty-Five-Year-Old with $1 Million of Assets as Based on Fixed Portfolio Returns and Longevity

		Fixed Return					
		0%	1.0%	2.0%	3.0%	4.0%	5.0%
Planning Horizon (Age)	70	$200,000	$204,000	$207,998	$211,995	$215,988	$219,976
	75	$100,000	$104,537	$109,144	$113,816	$118,549	$123,338
	80	$66,667	$71,410	$76,299	$81,327	$86,482	$91,755
	85	$50,000	$54,867	$59,958	$65,258	$70,752	$76,422
	90	$40,000	$44,957	$50,216	$55,755	$61,550	$67,574
	95	$33,333	$38,364	$43,774	$49,533	$55,606	$61,954
	100	$28,571	$33,667	$39,218	$45,184	$51,517	$58,164
	105	$25,000	$30,154	$35,839	$42,002	$48,580	$55,503
	110	$22,222	$27,431	$33,245	$39,597	$46,406	$53,583

The fixed return assumptions could be treated as bond yields, in which retirement income is based on building a ladder of individual bonds. In this case, the yield would reflect the average yield from the bond ladder if the yield curve was not otherwise flat. These returns could also reflect the return assumptions for a diversified investment portfolio. In this case, these returns would reflect the net return assumption after working through the series of factors described in the next chapter.

A thirty-year TIPS ladder is as close as we can get to a real-world safe withdrawal rate for thirty years of inflation-adjusted spending. The exhibit shows that at current interest rates, this number is less than 4 percent of the initial retirement date assets. Spending more from an investment portfolio is based on a hope that a higher return arrives to sustain a higher spending rate. This is risky. It is important to note that with this bond ladder, nothing will be left at the end of the thirtieth year. The calculation is risk free for thirty years, but the possibility of living beyond thirty years must be considered. A TIPS ladder does not hedge longevity risk. Longevity risk can only be managed by assuming a more conservative planning age with a lower probability to outlive, and then spending less to stretch the asset base out over a longer retirement horizon.

Further Reading

Bodie, Zvi, and Michael J. Clowes. 2003. *Worry-Free Investing: A Safe Approach to Achieving Your Lifetime Financial Goals.* Upper Saddle River, NJ: Financial Times Prentice Hall. [http://amzn.to/2mWqdUG]

Pfau, Wade. 2017. *How Much Can I Spend in Retirement: A Guide to Investment-Based Retirement Income Strategies.* McLean, VA: Retirement Researcher Media. [http://amzn.to/2xLgXGC]

Zwecher, Michael J. 2010. *Retirement Portfolios: Theory, Construction, and Management.* Hoboken, NJ: John Wiley. [http://amzn.to/2uOcbRA]

CHAPTER 3

Stocks and Diversified Investment Portfolios

When the objective for an asset base is to fund a specific stream of spending on a year-by-year basis for a known length of time, the least risky way to do this is to build a bond ladder. As long as the securities do not default, bond ladders provide the intended cash flows to match spending liabilities at the appropriate dates. If spending grows with inflation, TIPS will provide protection from a higher than expected inflation experience. Conversely, traditional bonds will work for spending that does not grow with inflation, or that otherwise grows at a fixed rate that is known in advance.

As a quick reminder, the problem with trying to determine a sustainable spending rate from an investment portfolio is that retirees must manage a differing set of risks when deciding how much to spend.

The three basic risks for retirees are longevity risk, market risk, and spending shocks. Longevity risk relates to not knowing how long one will live and, therefore, how long wealth must last. Market risk relates to the possibility that poor market returns deplete available wealth and reduce the sustainable standard of living. Spending shocks are surprise expenses from outside the planned budget, such as for long-term care and major health expenses, which require a pool of contingency assets beyond what are being used to support the expected portion of living expenses. Retirement will be cheaper with some combination of a shorter life, strong market returns, and few spending shocks. But retirement could become quite expensive when a long life is combined with poor market returns and significant spending shocks.

Retirees face longevity risk and spending shocks. They do not know how long they will live, and they must manage unanticipated retirement expenses. With each additional year the cost of retirement grows. If they misestimate their longevity, a bond ladder will be depleted before the end of retirement. A bond ladder is an inefficient way to manage longevity risk, as the only option is to assume an exceptionally long retirement and to spend less to stretch out the asset base. As well, spending shocks create the risk that assets meant for future lifestyle must be sold and spent early, and this reintroduces interest rate risk and the potential for capital losses on the bonds sales.

This book is about comparing two methods that aim to generate higher returns than bonds in order to reduce the overall cost of retirement. We compare two other ways to manage these longevity and spending shock risks: risk pooling and the risk premium. This chapter focuses on the risk premium, or the idea that stocks will outperform bonds over reasonable lengths of time, and the additional growth potential of stocks can more easily support a lifetime spending goal than bonds alone. While the risk premium brings market risk back into the mix, the idea is that this risk is sufficiently low, and the diversified portfolio will work better for managing the overall combination of retirement risks.

Investors facing a situation of wishing to fund specific spending amounts will often seek to create a diversified portfolio including riskier components such as stocks. The intention is to seek additional growth for assets to support a greater spending amount than bonds can provide, and to otherwise lay a foundation to support spending for longer periods than planned. Investment growth could also provide contingency funds to help cover unanticipated spending shocks. This chapter explains the basis and pitfalls of the probability-based approach that relies on the stock market as a key tool for funding retirement.

◉ Overview of Stocks and the Stock Market

Stocks provide an ownership stake in a company. They provide access to company earnings based on its future performance. Companies can pay dividends to their stockholders to return profits to the owners, or they could reinvest profits into the firm to lay the foundation for better performance and even larger dividends to owners in the future.

The stock price can be driven up when investors anticipate stronger future performance than previously anticipated, and this can serve as a source of capital gains for stocks owners who sell shares. However, there are no contractual protections to receive either capital gains or dividends. In the ownership structure, stockholders are residual claimants, meaning that their rights to receive firm earnings or assets fall behind most other claimants like bond holders or lenders. Companies could underperform relative to expectations, and the stock price could decrease in anticipation of a reduced ability for the company to pay dividends in the future. The returns from a stock over a specified holding period are the dividend payments it makes plus any capital gains or capital losses. For owners having to sell shares after a price decline, stocks could underperform relative to bonds.

The value of a stock can be estimated as the present value of its anticipated future dividend payments. This relates to our bond pricing discussion, as bonds can be priced as the present value of their future cash flows. Except that, again, there are no promises supporting anticipated dividends. Projections of company performance can change over time, leading to fluctuations in stock prices. With this price volatility, funding retirement expenses by selling stocks can be risky as stock prices may be in decline at the time they need to be sold, requiring more shares to be sold to meet an expense.

Mutual funds and exchange-traded funds (ETFs) provide a simple way for household investors to diversify across a broad range of company stocks. These same investment vehicles exist for bonds as well. With stocks, these investment vehicles provide a collection of stocks that help to reduce the individual risks of companies by diversifying across a broader range of companies. By limiting exposure to individual companies, this also limits exposure to that company's specific risks. If company specific risks are independent from one another, then this diversification leaves investors exposed to the overall systematic market risk for the collection of stock holdings, while diversifying away from the company-specific risks so that overall volatility is less.

Our analysis treats stock and bond investments in terms of overall index returns, which implies that the funds in question are index funds. Index funds are passively managed holdings of the components in a market index, and they are generally offered with lower expenses than mutual funds driven by active management decisions about which companies to hold. Actively managed funds attempt to outperform the overall market either by identifying and selecting mispriced securities or by forecasting broad market trends.

Actively managed funds may charge higher fees in part to pay investment managers and researchers to select securities they believe will outperform the overall market index. Whether such active management can provide increased returns net of the investment management fees and taxes, after accounting for the fund's risk relative to the overall market, is a subject of continued debate. Generally, though, the conclusion of academic research is that there is no reason to believe than an actively managed fund will outperform an index fund when considered net of investment fees, taxes, and risk. Investment fees tend to be higher for active funds to compensate a larger team of individuals working to select stocks, and active funds tend to generate high taxes through their turnover of investments that passes capital gains to the fund owners on an ongoing basis even if shares are not sold.

In a market equilibrium, higher return investments must be viewed as riskier in terms of there being greater volatility in the returns. If higher returning investments were not viewed as riskier, demand would increase and the price would be pushed up immediately, reducing the potential returns for subsequent owners.

This is the basis for the efficient market theory, which says that stock prices incorporate all of the known information regarding market performance. New information about a stock is processed quickly through price adjustments. Good news, reflecting better future performance prospects, will lead those with the information to purchase the stock immediately, driving its price up, and vice versa. Current prices reflect the aggregate expectations of all market participants. An implication of this is that stock price movements should follow a random walk as new information, either good or bad, will arrive in a random and unpredictable manner. An implication of stock prices quickly incorporating information from all market participants into their prices is that it is not feasible to systematically beat the market through active decision-making. A lower cost passive strategy based on index funds capturing the broad-based returns for different asset classes can capture the overall market returns in the least costly and most tax efficient manner when market prices behave efficiently.

Passive strategies can be supported with less fees because they are not paying analysts, and the reduced turnover of holdings helps to manage transaction costs and creates greater tax efficiency by avoiding the realization of capital gains. Regarding taxes, index funds can be more efficient because they have less turnover for the assets held, which in turn can help reduce the creation of short-term capital gains that are taxed at income tax rates. At the very least, actively managed funds introduce another type of risk called tracking risk, which relates to how the returns might vary from the index returns over time. Because our analyses are based on assumptions for market indices, it is easier to think about our investments as index funds rather than actively managed funds.

◉ Historical Market Returns

The primary subject of this book is comparing the risk premium with risk pooling as a source of funding for retirement goals. An important step is to first make clear what the risk premium is and how it relates to an investment portfolio. Fundamentally, investors prefer certainty to uncertainty. A bond provides a known yield with contractual protections helping to ensure that its return is realized if held to maturity. Stock returns are more uncertain, as they depend on the future performance of the company as well as on changing investor perceptions about the company.

If a stock offered the same average return as bonds, but with greater volatility around that average, the typical risk averse investor would not be willing to purchase it. Risk averse individuals are willing to pay more to receive certainty, so less-volatile assets should have lower expected returns. To accept risk, investors will seek a higher expected return over time than they could receive from more reliable bonds. That higher expected return represents the risk premium. Stocks can generally be expected to outperform bonds over time, but such outperformance is not predictable and there can be reasonably long stretches in which stock returns lag bonds.

A good starting point for understanding the historical returns for different asset classes is with Morningstar and Ibbotson Associates data. They have compiled US financial market returns since 1926 in their *SBBI (Stocks, Bonds, Bills, and Inflation) Yearbook*. This data is usually the source for calculating average historical market performance and creating assumptions for future portfolio returns. We can use this data as a starting point for understanding about historical stock performance.

Exhibit 3.1 provides historical averages and volatility for different market indices in this dataset for both nominal and real terms. With this dataset, small-capitalization stocks have offered the most return potential along with the most volatility. Their simple average arithmetic return was 16.2 percent during this time period in nominal terms, with a standard deviation of 31.6 percent.

Arithmetic mean returns are calculated by adding up all the annual returns from the historical data and then dividing by the number of years in the data set. The standard deviation is a measure of volatility in terms of the degree of fluctuations experienced around the average outcome. Approximately, two-thirds of the historical returns fell within the range of 31.6 percent more or less than the average of 16.2 percent. That range is -15.4 percent to 47.8 percent. The remaining one-third of historical returns were even more extreme in either direction. Volatility reduces the predictability for realized returns. When thinking of risk as volatility, we generally care most about the risk for losses, but if market returns are symmetric around an average, then using standard deviation will work just as well.

While the arithmetic mean represents the average historical growth rate over a single year, it does not reflect the growth rate over a longer period. The average compounded return represents the growth rate over multiple years, and it is always less than the arithmetic mean for any volatile asset. Increased asset volatility causes the compounded return to fall by even more relative to the arithmetic return. For long-term investors, it is the compounded return that matters.

To understand this volatility effect on compounded returns, realize that positive and negative returns do not create a symmetric impact on wealth. Negative returns must be followed by even larger positive returns to get back to the initial point. For instance, a 50 percent drop requires a 100 percent gain to get back to the starting point. For this reason, wealth will grow at a lower compounded rate than the arithmetic average. Compounded returns take a larger haircut as the volatility of returns increases. With the high volatility of small-capitalization stocks, the compounded return was 11.8 percent, a full 4.2 percent less than the arithmetic average. The 11.8 percent return reflects the fixed growth rate for the asset class that supported its cumulative return over the entire historical period.

Next in the chart are large-capitalization US stocks, as represented by the S&P 500 index since its creation in the 1950s, and a more general index of large companies in the years before that. The arithmetic average for large-capitalization stocks was 11.9 percent (roughly 12 percent, which is why that number is used on occasion as an estimate for stocks returns) with a standard deviation of 19.8 percent (roughly 20 percent). The volatility impact was such that these stocks grew over time at an average compounded rate of 10 percent.

Moving to bonds, Morningstar data shows that since 1926, the average return from intermediate-term government bonds was 5.2 percent with a standard deviation of 5.6 percent. With the lower volatility, the compounded return is only slightly less at 5.1 percent. For long-term government bonds, annual returns averaged 5.9 percent with volatility of 9.8 percent, and long-term corporate bonds averaged 6.3 percent with volatility of 8.4 percent. The observation that corporate bonds enjoyed higher returns than long-term government bonds with less volatility is an anomaly about the usual link between risk and reward. But these are after-the-fact numbers and may not reflect investor attitudes about risk. Corporate bonds are usually considered to be riskier than government bonds due to their credit risk regarding potential defaults. Meanwhile, thirty-day Treasury bills averaged 3.4 percent with volatility of 3.1 percent. These different bond asset classes have varying return and volatility characteristics.

Among the universe of bond fund choices, retirement income studies generally show the most favorable results with intermediate-term government bonds. They provide an appropriate balance between seeking higher yields while also maintaining lower volatility to avoid jeopardizing the spending goals for the portfolio. Including more types of bonds, such

Exhibit 3.1

Summary Statistics for US Financial Market Annual Returns and Inflation, 1926–2018

Nominal Returns

	Arithmetic Average Return	Average Compounded Return	Standard Deviation
Small-Cap Stocks	16.2%	11.8%	31.6%
Large-Cap Stocks	11.9%	10.0%	19.8%
Long-Term Corporate Bonds	6.3%	5.9%	8.4%
Long-Term Government Bonds	5.9%	5.5%	9.8%
Intermediate-Term Government Bonds	5.2%	5.1%	5.6%
30-Day Treasury Bills	3.4%	3.3%	3.1%
Consumer Price Inflation	3.0%	2.9%	4.0%

Real (Inflation-Adjusted) Returns

	Arithmetic Average Return	Average Compounded Return	Standard Deviation
Small-Cap Stocks	13.0%	8.7%	31.0%
Large-Cap Stocks	8.8%	6.9%	19.8%
Long-Term Corporate Bonds	3.4%	3.0%	9.4%
Long-Term Government Bonds	3.1%	2.5%	10.8%
Intermediate-Term Government Bonds	2.3%	2.1%	6.6%
30-Day Treasury Bills	0.5%	0.4%	3.8%

Source: Own calculations from *SBBI Yearbook* data available from Morningstar and Ibbotson Associates.

as corporate bonds, long-term bonds, or short-term bills, can be justifiable for reasons other than maximizing the sustainable spending rate from a portfolio.

The chart also shows that inflation historically averaged 3 percent with a 4 percent standard deviation. With the low volatility, the compounded inflation rate was only slightly less at 2.9 percent. This leads us into the second part of Exhibit 3.1, providing the real historical returns after removing inflation. Real returns put the analysis on a consistent basis over time so that the long-run spending plans may be discussed in terms of today's purchasing power. Focusing on two of the asset classes in the table that are most relevant to our subsequent discussion, if we remove the effects of inflation from the compounded returns, historically the S&P 500 provided an inflation-adjusted compounded return of 6.9 percent, and it was 2.1 percent for intermediate-term government bonds. The respective arithmetic real returns were 8.8 percent and 2.3 percent.

◉ Modern Portfolio Theory

Before shifting into further discussion about whether these historical numbers provide the most appropriate assumptions for future market performance, it is worth understanding how to choose an asset allocation and put together an investment portfolio while assuming that these historical numbers are the right ones to use. The more basic point is that any assumptions can be used. Once a set of assumptions are agreed upon, how is an investment portfolio asset allocation determined as based on those assumptions? With efficient markets, this asset allocation decision among the available asset classes becomes the most important driver of overall portfolio returns and volatility, rather than trying to select individual securities or predict overall market movements.

In the 1950s, Harry Markowitz created Modern Portfolio Theory (MPT), which has served as the foundation for how wealth managers build investment portfolios for their clients. Harry Markowitz won the Nobel Prize in Economics in 1990 for this work. It provides a framework for choosing an asset allocation under a specific set of assumptions that wealth managers have traditionally accepted as being a reasonable starting point for households.

His fundamental insight was to show why investments should not be treated in isolation, but rather in terms of how they contribute to the risk and return of the overall portfolio. A very volatile individual investment might help to reduce overall portfolio volatility if its price movements tend to be in the opposite direction of the rest of the portfolio. This is diversification. Prior to Markowitz, portfolio managers seemingly did not realize this on a widespread basis, as they viewed their job was to choose what they felt are the very best individual securities, with each considered on a standalone basis. In their view, diversification would only reduce the potential for outsized returns.

Modern Portfolio Theory is a single-period model. It does not reflect how households are making decisions over multiple periods of time. It also does not include any spending constraint. It is an assets-only model about how to achieve efficient diversification, or to find the best tradeoff between portfolio returns and volatility. For the inputs, a user decides on the universe of asset classes to consider, and then decides on an average arithmetic return and standard deviation for each asset class, as well as the cross correlations for returns between each of the asset classes.

While we have discussed arithmetic average returns and standard deviations, correlations have not yet come up. The correlation coefficient between two asset classes measures their degree of co-movements. It ranges from -1 (move precisely in opposite directions) to one (move precisely in the same direction). If the correlation coefficient is zero, this means that the two asset classes move independently from one another. The lower the correlation coefficient, the greater the reduction in the portfolio volatility when the two asset classes are combined. With low correlations, the volatility of the portfolio can be less than the volatility of any of its component asset classes. Exhibit 3.2 provides an example of these inputs as based on the historical returns from the Morningstar data.

With these historical numbers we can see that movements in small-cap and large-cap stocks are closely related, as are the movements between the different types of bonds. But stocks and bonds did not experience close movements with one another, and Treasury bill movements are mostly

Exhibit 3.2

Inputs for Calculating Modern Portfolio Theory's Efficient Frontier as Based on US Financial Market Nominal Annual Returns, 1926–2018

			Correlation Coefficients					
	Arithmetic Average Return	Standard Deviation	Small-Cap Stocks	Large–Cap Stocks	Long–Term Corporate Bonds	Long-Term Government Bonds	Intermed-iate–Term Government Bonds	30-Day Treasury Bills
Small-Cap Stocks	16.2%	31.7%	1	0.79	0.06	-0.10	-0.11	-0.08
Large-Cap Stocks	11.9%	19.8%	0.79	1	0.16	0.00	-0.03	-0.02
Long-Term Corporate Bonds	6.3%	8.4%	0.06	0.16	1	0.89	0.85	0.16
Long-Term Government Bonds	5.9%	9.8%	-0.10	0.00	0.89	1	0.86	0.18
Intermediate-Term Government Bonds	5.2%	5.6%	-0.11	-0.03	0.85	0.86	1	0.48
30-Day Treasury Bills	3.4%	3.1%	-0.08	-0.02	0.16	0.18	0.48	1

Source: Own calculations from *SBBI Yearbook* data available from Morningstar and Ibbotson Associates.

unrelated to the other asset classes except intermediate-term government bonds.

As a next step, Exhibit 3.3 plots the portfolio returns and volatilities for different combinations of the six asset classes as based on their return characteristics shown in Exhibit 3.2. The exhibit shows the portfolio return on the vertical axis and the portfolio volatility on the horizontal axis. Investors would like to move toward portfolios in the upper left-hand corner, all else being the same, as that direction represents portfolios with higher returns and less volatility. The dots reflect the different combinations for these asset classes. The curve that envelops them on the upper-left side is the efficient frontier. It is the asset class combinations offering the highest returns for a given volatility, or the least volatility for a given return. It only makes sense for investors to consider asset allocation combinations from the many combinations reflecting different risk-return characteristics on the efficient frontier.

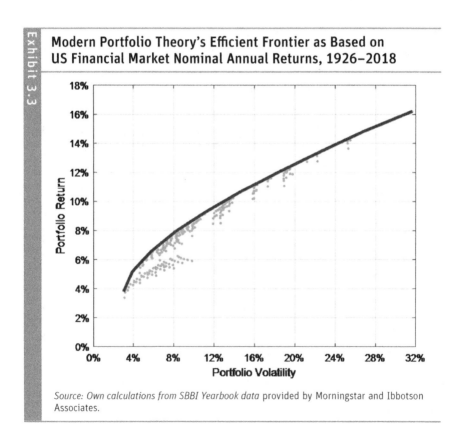

Exhibit 3.3

Modern Portfolio Theory's Efficient Frontier as Based on US Financial Market Nominal Annual Returns, 1926–2018

Source: Own calculations from SBBI Yearbook data provided by Morningstar and Ibbotson Associates.

Efficient frontier diagrams do not actually show the asset allocations of portfolios on the efficient frontier, but this information is also available. Exhibit 3.4 provides an example of ten portfolios on the efficient frontier shown in Exhibit 3.3. These range from the lowest return and volatility combinations to the highest return and volatility combinations. For example, portfolio one is listed with a 3.8 percent return and 3 percent volatility. This portfolio consists of a 91.3 percent allocation to Treasury bills along with small allocations to corporate bonds (7 percent), small-cap stocks (1.3 percent), and large-cap stocks (0.4 percent). Despite small-cap stocks being the most volatile asset class choice, the low correlation of characteristics it shares with other asset classes helps it to play a small role in a low volatility portfolio. The overall portfolio volatility of 3 percent is slightly less than the 3.1 percent volatility of Treasury bills on their own. Then, as we move down the list, we find portfolios with increasing returns and volatilities that contain increasing allocations to stocks and a gradual phase out for Treasury bills and other bonds. The fifth portfolio is the most diversified with an allocation to five of the six asset classes. It provides overall returns of 9.3 percent with a volatility of 11.2 percent.

We now understand that there are serious issues with using MPT to determine investment portfolios for household investors, especially after

Exhibit 3.4

A Selection of Outcomes from the Efficient Frontier as Based on US Financial Market Nominal Annual Returns, 1926–2018

	Portfolio Return	Portfolio Volatility	Asset Allocation					
			Small–Cap Stocks	Large–Cap Stocks	Long–Term Corporate Bonds	Long–Term Government Bonds	Intermediate –Term Government Bonds	30-Day Treasury Bills
1	3.8%	3.0%	1.3%	0.4%	7.0%	0.0%	0.0%	91.3%
2	5.2%	3.9%	4.2%	6.3%	0.7%	0.0%	38.0%	50.8%
3	6.6%	5.7%	7.2%	11.3%	0.0%	0.0%	71.0%	10.6%
4	7.9%	8.2%	13.1%	17.3%	12.4%	0.0%	57.3%	0.0%
5	9.3%	11.2%	19.8%	22.4%	31.2%	15.0%	11.5%	0.0%
6	10.7%	14.7%	29.5%	28.4%	15.1%	27.0%	0.0%	0.0%
7	12.1%	18.5%	40.3%	33.8%	0.0%	26.0%	0.0%	0.0%
8	13.5%	22.6%	51.2%	38.0%	0.0%	10.8%	0.0%	0.0%
9	14.8%	26.8%	68.1%	31.9%	0.0%	0.0%	0.0%	0.0%
10	16.2%	31.7%	100.0%	0.0%	0.0%	0.0%	0.0%	0.0%

Source: Own calculations from SBBI Yearbook data available from Morningstar and Ibbotson Associates.

retirement begins. Harry Markowitz recognized this. After winning the Nobel Prize in 1990, he was asked to write an article in 1991 for the first issue of *Financial Services Review* about how MPT applies to household investors. This article was named, "Individual versus Institutional Investing." In the article, he writes about how he had never thought about the household's investing problem before, and after reflecting on it for an evening, he realized that households face a very different investing problem from the large institutional investors, such as mutual funds, he had in mind when developing MPT. MPT does not teach how individual households should build investment strategies to meet their lifetime financial planning goals.

Namely, and this is really the key for understanding how the retirement income problem differs from the MPT approach, households must meet spending goals over an unknown length of time in retirement. MPT just seeks how to grow wealth over a single time period, such as a year, when there is no need to take distributions from the portfolio. It is an assets-only model. The preretirement wealth accumulation notion that households seek to grow wealth is more closely aligned with MPT, but the retirement income problem is vastly different. There may surely be a relationship between the idea that having more wealth will support more spending, and the idea that building diversified portfolios is still valid, but that relationship is more complicated when it is unknown how long the spending must last and when taking distributions from assets works to amplify the impacts of investment volatility on the retirement income plan.

With sequence risk for portfolio distributions, the extra shares sold to meet a spending goal when markets are down are no longer available to experience the growth of any subsequent market recovery. The point chosen on the efficient frontier can be different when viewed in the context of the household's problem, and there can be a role for annuities or other risk management tools that are not included as asset classes in traditional MPT. Simply, MPT does not account for cash flows or longevity risk. It equates risk with short-term asset volatility rather than with the ability to meet financial goals.

Risk in the context of the household's investing problem is only tangentially related to the volatility or standard deviation of returns. Volatility is important in that it relates to risk tolerance and whether individuals can handle the short-term volatility of their portfolio. If greater volatility leads them to not stick with their financial plan, then this must be incorporated into the asset allocation decision. But more generally, risk for the household relates to the ability to meet financial goals over a long-term planning horizon.

A low-volatility portfolio offering insufficient return potential can ensure failure for the financial plan. This is riskier from the household's perspective than a more volatile portfolio that supports a higher probability of success for the financial plan. A key difference between probability-based and safety-first approaches is that the probability-based approach is more comfortable with accepting greater volatility for higher return potential and an improved chance for success, while the safety-first approach looks for alternatives that do not expose core retirement spending goals to market volatility. The question is ultimately about which is the best way to be able to spend more than a bond ladder can support: to rely on the excess returns expected to be provided by the stock market, or to rely on the power of risk pooling to bring additional spending power to those facing a higher cost retirement.

⊙ The Case for Stocks

The case for using an aggressive investment portfolio with a high stock allocation to fund retirement expenses rests on the idea that it will *probably* work. Stocks are expected to outperform bonds, and if and when that happens, a retiree will be able to spend more from their asset base in retirement.

For example, in a February 2016 *New York Times* column on retiring, David Levine suggested that people treat an all-stock allocation very seriously, saying, "And, so, what I actually say to people who ask my advice is this: Put as much money into the stock market as you can stand. One hundred percent is best, but even if you are very risk-averse, allocate at least 75 percent to stocks."

Exhibit 3.5 shows similar details as Exhibit 3.1 about returns and volatilities for historical US data. But it also highlights more about the differences in returns as one moves up the exhibit to better highlight the idea of a risk premium. These are the historical excess returns that more volatile asset classes provided. Starting from the bottom, historical inflation averaged 3 percent. Short-term Treasury bills provided a historical average return of 3.4 percent, which is 0.4 percent higher than inflation. That represents the short-term real rate of return.

By investing in intermediate-term government bonds, historically one could earn an average 5.2 percent return, which is 1.8 percent more than Treasury bills and 2.2 percent more than inflation. Long-term US government bonds offered another 0.7 percent higher historical return, and long-term corporate bonds offered an additional 0.4 percent on top of the government bonds for a 6.3 percent total return. Moving into stocks, large-capitalization stocks averaged 11.9 percent returns. This was 5.6 percent more than long-term corporate bonds, 6 percent more than long-term Treasury bonds, and 6.7 percent more than intermediate-term treasuries. These are the types of numbers that are often identified as the risk premium, or the expected additional return of stocks over bonds, at least as based on the historical data. As expected, that risk premium is even higher with small-capitalization stocks, which averaged an additional 4.3 percent more than large-capitalization stocks, or, for instance, 11 percent more than intermediate-term government bonds. These risk premia have been identified in terms of their arithmetic averages.

It is also the case that the compounded equity premium would be less than its arithmetic value. For instance, though not shown in the exhibit, large-capitalization stocks outperformed long-term government bonds by 4.5 percent in terms of compounded growth, as compared to the 6 percent difference in arithmetic terms.

These types of comparisons can be made between any of the asset classes in the exhibit, and what these comparisons make clear is that over the entire historical period, stocks have outperformed bonds by a dramatic degree. Those seeking to grow assets in retirement by investing in stocks are relying on these historical relationships to continue in the future.

Advocates for using aggressive investment portfolios as the primary way to fund a retirement plan often will allude to the concept of "stocks for the long run." There is a degree of comfort that an aggressive portfolio will provide sufficient returns in time to maintain retirement sustainability. According to advocates, the long-run growth potential for stocks can be

Exhibit 3.5

The Components of US Financial Market Annual Returns
Stocks, Bonds, Bills, and Inflation Data, 1926–2018

		Component Returns	Total Arithmetic Returns	Standard Deviation
Equity Premium	small-cap stocks	4.3%	16.2%	31.6%
	large-cap stocks	5.6%	11.9%	19.8%
Real Bond Return	long-term corporate bonds	0.4%	6.3%	8.4%
	long-term government bonds	0.7%	5.9%	9.8%
	intermediate-term government bonds	1.8%	5.2%	5.6%
	short-term government bills	0.4%	3.4%	3.1%
Inflation	Inflation	3.0%	3.0%	4.0%

Source: Own calculations from SBBI Yearbook data provided by Morningstar and Ibbotson Associates.

expected to materialize so that the aggressive portfolio can support a higher spending level than bonds alone.

To better understand this probability-based point of view, Exhibit 3.6 plots the historical worst-case annualized nominal returns for large-capitalization US stocks and intermediate-term US government bonds since 1926.

Over shorter holding periods, bonds were less exposed to downside risks. Over one year, for instance, the worst case for bonds was a 5.1 percent drop, while stocks fell by 43.3 percent in their worst year. Over any historical three-year period, bonds provided a positive annualized return. It took fifteen years before stocks historically were always able to provide a positive return. But for holding periods of at least seventeen years, the historical worst-case annualized performance for stocks exceeds that for bonds. Over twenty-year periods, for instance, stocks experienced a worst-case 3.1 percent annualized return, compared to 1.6 percent for bonds. For thirty-year periods, the worst case for stocks was 8.5 percent, compared to 2.2 percent for bonds. And for forty-year periods, stocks' worst performance was an 8.9 percent annualized return, compared to 2.8 percent as the worst for bonds. For historical forty-year periods, even the best case for bonds (8.1 percent) could not beat the worst case for stocks.

Because probability-based advocates have confidence that the historical record provides precedence for what can be expected in the future, this is the basic logic for understanding the view that stocks should be the primary asset to support retirement expenses.

As well, Bill Bengen's work that led to the 4 percent rule-of-thumb for retirement spending is also a historical exploration which shows that higher stock allocations have tended to support more spending with little in the way of additional downside risk. Though not framed this way, Bill Bengen's research is a type of efficient frontier analysis that includes a spending constraint seeking to maximize the amount that could be spent in the worst-case thirty-year period from the historical data. He found

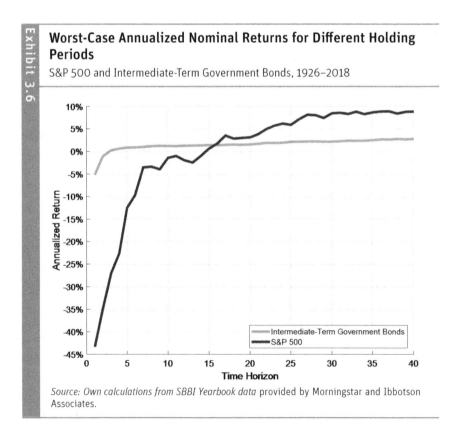

Exhibit 3.6

Worst-Case Annualized Nominal Returns for Different Holding Periods

S&P 500 and Intermediate-Term Government Bonds, 1926–2018

Source: Own calculations from SBBI Yearbook data provided by Morningstar and Ibbotson Associates.

that the highest worst-case spending level could be found for any stock allocation between 35 and 80 percent, and he argued that retirees should attempt to stick with stock allocations in the higher end of the range because this would support additional upside when not in a worst-case retirement scenario.

For historical data, I have confirmed this point in international data as well, showing in my book *How Much Can I Spend in Retirement?* that across the twenty countries in the Global Returns dataset, the highest worst-case spending rate occurred with at least 50 percent stocks in eighteen of the twenty countries. Only in Sweden and Switzerland did the peak worst-case spending level occur with a lower stock allocation.

Noted financial advisor and historian William Bernstein also makes a compelling case for stocks in his e-book *Deep Risk: How History Informs Portfolio Design*. In the introduction, Bernstein begins by offering an operational definition of risk. Risk is the size of real capital loss times the duration of real capital loss. This gets at the idea that it is a permanent, rather than a temporary, loss of capital that that is most damaging to investors. Magnitude and duration of loss are both relevant factors. Mistiming the markets, by buying high and selling low, is the most common method whereby an investor sees this risk manifested, as this is the clearest way to experience a permanent loss of capital. A more disciplined approach to investing is needed to avoid this risk.

This definition allows Bernstein to identify two flavors of risk: shallow risk and deep risk. Shallow risk is the loss of real capital which recovers within several years, while deep risk reflects the permanent loss of real capital. It could be defined, for instance, as a negative real return over a thirty-year period.

It becomes apparent that stocks are risker than bonds with respect to shallow risk, but that the opposite is true with respect to deep risk. Throughout the world in the twentieth century, fixed-income investors have suffered permanent losses in inflationary storms which equity investors were better able to avoid. As Bernstein says, absence of leverage and with sufficient liquidity, retirement savings are not wiped out by too high of standard deviation, but rather by real-world events.

With deep risk, once one has become properly insured to personal vagaries and carefully disciplined with respect to strategy and approach, the four big threats over long horizons are:

1. Severe and prolonged high inflation
2. Prolonged deflation
3. Confiscation
4. Devastation

The remainder of his book focuses on these four risks in terms of what damage they do, how likely they are to happen, and what strategies provide the best chance to mitigate the threat. Relevant here are the probabilities, the consequences of the hardship created, and the costs of protection.

First in terms of the probabilities that each threat will manifest, inflation is high, confiscation is medium, and deflation and devastation are low. Inflation, though high in probability, has a lower cost for protection. It is the most relevant for retirees to worry about, but it is also the least catastrophic for a globally diversified investor. It is the easiest to protect against with international diversification, TIPS held to maturity to match spending needs, delaying Social Security, and an inflation-adjusted annuity. A globally diversified stock portfolio is most effectively protected from the deep risk of inflation, though stocks do exacerbate shallow risk. Meanwhile, unexpected inflation devastates traditional bonds.

Deflation, on the other hand, is the least likely to happen. It is good for bonds and bad for stocks. Solutions include cash, bonds, and international diversification, as well as gold. But using bonds and bills carries a high cost if we experience inflation rather than deflation.

As for confiscation and devastation, the best defenses are holding foreign assets and having a means for escape. He argues that confiscation is a likely deep risk as taxes will likely increase in the future.

Bernstein's conclusion is that the best long-term defense against deep risk is a globally diversified equity portfolio with tilting toward value and precious metals and natural resource companies, TIPS, and potentially some gold and foreign real estate. Because of inflation, bonds become riskier than stocks over long horizons, while shallow risk makes investors with shorter time horizons more vulnerable with stocks. For lifetime financial planning, determining how to transition between deep risk and shallow risk at different points in the lifecycle is one of the greatest challenges facing wealth managers.

Stocks have historically provided a return premium above what is available from holding bonds. This has historically allowed stocks to provide a higher return than bonds. Though this premium is risky and may fail to materialize, many investment analysts are comfortable with the idea that over long time horizons, stocks can reasonably be expected to continue their outperformance.

This does certainly speak to the idea of including a healthy dose of stocks within an overall retirement income strategy, but the question remains about how reliant one should be on the stock market to cover the day-to-day expenses of retirement.

⦿ Caveats about a Primary Reliance on the Stock Market to Fund Retirement Spending

Simple analyses, which look to historical returns as estimates for what retirees should expect in the future, tend to provide an incomplete picture that may overstate the potential for stocks relative to other strategies. We will investigate some of the adjustments that should be made to historical returns to obtain a better idea about the net returns from an investment portfolio on a forward-looking basis. These include accounting for the impacts of volatility on compounded returns, inflation, investment fees, investor behavior, asset allocation, and taxes.

We can also identify stock returns as the sum of inflation, real bond yields, and an equity premium, and we can look to what are reasonable values at the present for these building blocks. Another important matter is to incorporate the idea that most financial planning involves seeking a high probability of success, which requires assuming below average returns, and the necessary reduction to return assumptions is greater when distributions are taken.

While a risk premium must be expected in order to induce investors to position their assets into more volatile investments, there is no reason to necessarily believe that historical excess returns provide the best predictors about the future risk premium. Also, it may take longer than anticipated for returns on stocks to outpace bonds, and retirees who are taking distributions become more vulnerable to this waiting game.

All too often, it seems that examples about retirement planning are based on assumptions that investments will grow at a fixed 8 percent or even 12 percent. While not impossible, the reality is that such return assumptions are overly optimistic, especially for those approaching retirement.

For a lifetime financial plan, the most intuitive way to express a portfolio return assumption is as an inflation-adjusted compounding return. Unfortunately, this is not the most common way returns are expressed. It is more typical to see returns expressed in nominal terms and even as arithmetic numbers that incorrectly reflect long-term growth rates. As well, to understand potential purchasing power, we should make further adjustments for taxes, fees, investor behavior, and asset allocation. A quick review is in order for the steps needed to arrive at a net real compounded return for a portfolio, as well as other adjustments that may be needed to create a properly conservative portfolio return assumption.

Exhibit 3.7

Return Characteristics by Asset Allocation as Based on US Financial Market Nominal Annual Returns, 1926–2018

	Nominal Values			Real (Inflation-Adjusted) Values		
	Arithmetic Average Return	Average Compounded Return	Standard Deviation	Arithmetic Average Return	Average Compounded Return	Standard Deviation
100% Stocks	11.9%	10.0%	19.8%	8.8%	6.9%	19.8%
90% Stocks	11.2%	9.7%	17.8%	8.2%	6.6%	17.8%
80% Stocks	10.5%	9.3%	15.8%	7.5%	6.3%	16.0%
70% Stocks	9.9%	9.0%	13.9%	6.9%	5.9%	14.1%
60% Stocks	9.2%	8.5%	12.0%	6.2%	5.5%	12.3%
50% Stocks	8.5%	8.1%	10.2%	5.6%	5.0%	10.6%
40% Stocks	7.9%	7.5%	8.5%	4.9%	4.5%	9.1%
30% Stocks	7.2%	7.0%	7.0%	4.3%	4.0%	7.8%
20% Stocks	6.5%	6.4%	5.9%	3.6%	3.4%	6.8%
10% Stocks	5.9%	5.7%	5.4%	3.0%	2.8%	6.4%
0% Stocks	5.2%	5.1%	5.6%	2.3%	2.1%	6.6%

Source: Own calculations from SBBI Yearbook data provided by Morningstar and Ibbotson Associates. Stocks are represented by the large-capitalization US stocks and bonds by intermediate term US government bonds.

Exhibit 3.7 shows the historical returns for different asset allocations for portfolios consisting of different combinations of the S&P 500 and intermediate term US government bonds (ITGB). As described with the earlier discussion of Exhibit 3.1, for the period since 1926, Morningstar data reveals that the S&P 500 enjoyed an average (arithmetic) return of 11.9 percent, while intermediate-term government bonds earned 5.2 percent.

Volatility

When simulating long-term financial plans, we also have to account for volatility and the lack of symmetry in outcomes for positive and negative returns, as discussed. We calculate the compounded returns over time to account for this volatility. The S&P 500 compounded return fell to 10 percent, while the compounded return for the less volatile bonds fell only slightly to 5.1 percent. These compounded returns express the growth rate for a portfolio over longer periods, while the larger arithmetic average returns represent the average return only for a single year.

At least one popular radio host likes to imply that his listeners' stock portfolios will grow at 12 percent, but this is a misunderstanding on his part. It is the compounded return, not the arithmetic return, that matters for the long-run growth of a portfolio.

Inflation

Next, we must remove inflation so the numbers allow for a better understanding of purchasing power growth. Real returns will be less because they preserve the purchasing power of wealth over time. Providing the discussion in terms of real returns allows us to plan for the assumption that future spending will grow with inflation. Even low inflation can compound over time into a big impact on purchasing power. Not removing inflation from the calculations can lead to confusion about the purchasing power of future dollars. The real compounded returns fell to 6.9 percent for stocks and 2.1 percent for bonds.

When it comes to inflation, it is important to be consistent about assumptions. If spending is projected to increase with inflation in retirement, then it makes sense to discuss assumptions in real terms. Real returns are lower, but they account for inflation and support a spending need that grows with inflation. Meanwhile, if spending needs are not anticipated to grow with inflation, then discussing the return assumptions in nominal terms is fine. Nominal returns are higher, supporting higher initial spending. That higher initial spending then stays fixed instead of growing with inflation. This means that purchasing power will decline over time, but it can be an appropriate assumption if it matches the actual behavior of retirement spending.

Asset Allocation

The next step is to consider asset allocation. Though many articles about long-term investing will assume 8 or 12 percent returns, this implicitly suggests that the investor holds 100 percent stocks. That will rarely be the case, especially for retirees. Consider, instead, a retiree with a 50/50 portfolio rebalanced annually. For the historical data, Exhibit 3.7 shows that the arithmetic real return was 5.6 percent, and the standard deviation for returns was 10.6 percent. The compounded real return was 5 percent for a 50/50 portfolio.

Exhibit 3.7 provides more details about these adjustments for other asset allocations as well. These numbers make clear about how as the asset allocation shifts from stocks to bonds, the portfolio returns and standard deviations both decrease. Because these numbers also account for correlations between assets, we do also see that the lowest standard deviation occurs with 10 percent stocks instead of 0 percent stocks, despite stocks being more volatile. This is an example about how diversification can reduce portfolio volatility by including different asset classes that do not move entirely in tandem. As retirees often seek to reduce their stock allocation in retirement, it becomes important to base return assumptions on a more bond-heavy portfolio that will have a lower expected return than a high-stock portfolio.

Adjustments for Fees and Performance Relative to Underlying Indices

For some, the 5 percent real return for the 50/50 asset allocation choice might be a properly adjusted starting point for a portfolio return assumption to project retirement outcomes, if this matched the retiree's desired asset allocation. We are getting closer. However, there are further adjustments we could make to this 5 percent number to create a more realistic and useful number for planning purposes. The number could potentially be a bit larger with a more diversified portfolio including international assets, alternative investments, real estate and small-cap stocks. This diversification would primarily serve to reduce portfolio volatility, which can provide a lift for the compounded return. Though it would entail risk, one might also wish to assign a premium to the return assumption to account for a belief that the investment manager can beat the returns on the underlying indices.

On the other hand, the 5 percent return may need to be reduced further to account for any fee drag associated with the management of the underlying investments. The index returns do not account for real-world investment expenses. It is possible to find index funds with low expense ratios, but the expenses for some actively managed funds can exceed 1 percent or even 1.5 percent per year. These are the operating expenses for mutual funds. As well, there can be an additional 12b-1 fee on some mutual funds to help cover marketing and distribution costs for the investment company. These expenses are listed separately from the operating expense ratio and must not be forgotten.

Some mutual funds will also charge a front-end or back-end load as a percentage of the assets when mutual funds are bought or sold. Beyond these explicit expenses, mutual funds may underperform market indices on account of the transaction costs for trading inside the fund and for tax inefficiencies created by fund turnover. In a 2014 article for the *Financial Analysts Journal*, John Bogle estimated that the all-in expenses for actively managed mutual funds could add up to as much as 2.27 percent before adding the tax impact. He estimated the tax impact as an additional 0.75 percent reduction in annual returns.

When these fees are present, they reduce the net returns, approximately, on a one-to-one basis. For instance, if a portfolio was projected to have a 5 percent return before expenses, and investment expenses add up to 2 percent, the investor could expect a net return of about 3 percent. The precise impact is even a bit larger because the expenses apply not just to the principal but also to the growth of the investment.

Adjustments for Taxes

Another issue besetting retirees is that returns will also be affected by tax drag, as ongoing taxes for interest, dividends, and realized capital gains must be paid with the passage of time. The tax efficiency for various types of funds varies, and actively managed funds generally have less tax efficiency than index funds. Morningstar has estimated that taxes for a large-capitalization portfolio like the S&P 500 can reduce annual returns by 0.68 percent. As for bonds, taxes must be paid on the ongoing interest earned by the funds, which could easily reduce returns net of tax by 1 percent or more.

In the John Bogle article just discussed, he estimated the additional tax impact of actively managed funds as reducing returns by 0.75 percent. Indeed, returns net of taxes will be less for households using taxable investment accounts. This aspect must also not be ignored when projecting investment returns for a retirement portfolio.

Adjustments for Investor Behavior

Another concern is whether investors are disciplined enough to stay the course with the investment strategy in order to earn the underlying index market returns. Studies on retirement spending from investment portfolios typically assume that retirees are rational investors who rebalance right on schedule each year to their rather aggressive stock allocations. They never panic and sell their stocks after a market downturn. For many retirees, this may not describe their reality. The behavior gap refers to the concept that investor behavior may cause real individuals to underperform relative to index market returns.

The behavior gap has been estimated, and there is somewhat of a consensus, that individual investors do underperform the overall markets by a couple percentage points per year. For instance, Vanguard's study of Advisor's Alpha identifies the most important factor explaining investor underperformance as a lack of behavioral coaching to help investors stay the course and stick with their plans. They estimate that having the wherewithal to stay the course in times of market stress could add 1.5 percent of additional annualized returns to the portfolios of typical investors. In other words, without behavioral coaching, the typical investor could expect to underperform the markets by 1.5 percent per year due to poor decision-making.

Evolution has designed us not to be effective long-term investors, but rather to seek to avoid short-term dangers. The fields of behavioral finance and behavioral economics have uncovered various biases humans have that are helpful for day-to-day survival, but somewhat maladaptive for long-term investing. A significant body of research is dedicated to detailing these investor behaviors. These are some of the most common behaviors that lead to poor financial outcomes.

Availability Bias/Recency Effect: Using recent or current market behavior to predict future market behavior
The most recent events are always freshest in our minds, and we tend to extrapolate recent events into the future, expecting more of the same. We tend to make long-term decisions based on short-term performance. Large recent market gains lead us to be optimistic about our chances, while market losses have the opposite effect. It takes discipline to overcome these natural tendencies to simplify matters into what can most easily be recalled.

Loss Aversion: Fearing a loss more than you want to make gains
As human beings, we tend to feel that the pain of experiencing a loss is greater than the joy felt by an equivalent gain. This leads to emotional decision-making for financial decisions, as we feel worse about losing relative to a starting point than a symmetric gain from the same starting point. With evolution, this was probably a useful survival tool, but it does not help with investing. It can lead to the avoidance of stocks that require accepting greater short-term volatility (and paper losses) in the effort to achieve upside growth potential and long-term gains. Not recognizing this predisposition can cause people to misjudge their tolerance for risk, making them more likely to bail on their financial plan.

Overconfidence: Believing you know more than other investors
While investment research increasingly points to the difficulty of beating the market—especially after fees, trading costs, and taxes are taken into account—it is natural to believe we know more than everyone else. This is the "Lake Wobegon effect" in practice. As Garrison Keillor relates in *A Prairie Home Companion*, Lake Wobegon is a place "where all the children

are above average." It is all too easy for investors to fall into this kind of thinking. We tend to be too confident in our decision-making around random and uncertain events. This may lead to too much trading and less-than-prudent amounts of diversification.

Hindsight Bias: Thinking you can predict market behavior because you believe you know why past market behavior occurred

In hindsight, market losses may seem to have an obvious or intuitive explanation. We seek to construct a narrative with cause and coherence, such that memories about past events suddenly become straightforward and predictable. This bias can feed into our overconfidence and cause us to believe we will be able to anticipate such market changes the next time around.

Survivorship Bias: Underestimating the risk by ignoring the failed companies

We may underestimate the degree of market risk if we look only at companies still operating today. This misses out on the lessons of many failed companies no longer on the investment radar. It is like thinking a marathon would be easy to run because you watched a bunch of people cross the finish line. You're ignoring all the people who gave up before reaching the end. This can also feed overconfidence.

Herd Mentality: Judging your own success or failure based on that of others

Sometimes the herd mentality can be rationalized. You don't want to miss out on being rich when everyone else is rich, and perhaps being poor is not so bad when everyone else is also poor. But for a long-term investor, following the herd rarely makes sense. It leads to joining the same greed and fear cycle that drives the average investor to buy after markets have already gained and to sell after markets have already dropped.

Ambiguity Aversion: Disliking uncertainty leads to betting on what is known

This behavior drives investors to bet more on what they know than on what they do not know. It has been offered as an explanation for the equity premium puzzle. Stocks have outperformed bonds consistently and by relatively wide margins over time, more so than can be explained by their risks for long-term investors. It may be because investors prefer the short-term safety of bonds, not recognizing the greater long-term growth potential of stocks.

Framing: Reacting differently based on whether the same outcome is presented as a loss or a gain

People's decisions can also be based on how a problem is framed, even if the underlying problem is the same. For instance, asking someone the probability they will live to eighty-five should lead to an answer that is 100 percent less than the probability that they will die by age eighty-five. But framing the problem in terms of dying by eighty-five leads to much less optimism than framing the problem as surviving to eighty-five.

Home Bias and Company Stock: Preferring what is most familiar

Our brains are more comfortable with the familiar. At the extreme, this can lead to disproportionate ownership in one's own company stock, or more simply a bias toward domestic assets over international assets. Both actions lead to a less diversified portfolio and greater exposure to risks that could have been diversified away.

Behavioral Cycle of Investing: Buying high and selling low

Falling markets can be stress-inducing events as we witness our wealth evaporating at a quick pace. This stress can trigger short-term fight-or-flight mechanisms in our behavior that may have helped to avoid day-to-day dangers on an evolutionary basis, but which are not adapted toward sustaining long-term investment success. Market volatility can lead to bad decision-making and to jettisoning well-considered plans. Short-term stress reactions will often involve deviating from the financial plan and selling stocks out of fears for further portfolio losses when historical evidence overwhelmingly suggests it to be wise to stay the course with the plan to build greater long-term wealth. Once a well thought out investment plan is in place, it is frequently better to do nothing in the face of stressful market situations. But this counters human evolution about the way to respond to such situations.

In times of market stress, it is important for retirees to stick with their financial plans and the asset allocation that matches their tolerance for market volatility. Most research about retirement spending from an investment portfolio assumes that investors behave in this rational way.

Unfortunately, investors in financial markets tend to do the opposite of what happens in most other markets: they buy more when prices are high and sell when prices are low. This causes returns to drag behind what a "buy, hold, and rebalance" investor could have earned. To the extent that households fall victim to bad behaviors, the net returns and sustainable spending rates from their investments will be less than otherwise possible.

Adjustments for Current Bond Yields

Another important consideration is that current interest rates are lower than the historical averages. The historical average return is not relevant for someone seeking to estimate future market returns from today's starting point. The general problem with attempting to gain insights from the historical outcomes is that future market returns are connected to the current values for the sources of market returns, rather than to their historical performance.

Returns on bonds depend on the initial bond yield and on subsequent yield changes. Low bond yields will tend to translate into lower returns due to less income and the heightened interest rate risk associated with capital losses when interest rates rise. Decreasing interest rates provide the only mechanism for bond returns to outpace bond yields, but this can only go so far when bond yields already start low.

Exhibit 3.8 demonstrates that, historically, the relationship between interest rates and subsequent bond returns has been tight. The exhibit shows the relationship between bond yields and the subsequent average annualized returns on bonds over the next five years using the Morningstar and Ibbotson Associates Intermediate-Term Government Bond (ITGB) index data since 1926 as a proxy for bonds. Much of the variation in intermediate-term government bond returns over the subsequent five years can be explained by their current yield. The year 2019 began with five-year Treasury yields at 2.5 percent. This is 2.7 percent less than the historical average ITGB return of 5.2 percent. This type of analysis suggests that the most reasonable return assumption for retirements beginning at the start of 2019 is that these bonds will average 2.5 percent returns rather than 5.2 percent returns.

In order to maintain the same risk premium for stocks over bonds, it would be necessary to reduce the return assumption for stocks by the same amount. Even if interest rates were to increase later in retirement, sequence-of-returns risk describes how it is the upcoming returns that matter most, making this adjustment for returns necessary to obtain a more realistic picture about retirement sustainability.

Adjustments for Market Valuations

A common way to estimate stock returns is to add an equity premium to a bond yield. This technique for estimating returns is known as the capital asset pricing model. This model was developed by William Sharpe in the 1960s, and he was awarded a Nobel Prize in economics for his work in 1990 alongside Harry Markowitz.

The model posits that the expected return on a financial asset is equal to a risk-free rate of return plus a risk premium multiplied by a factor showing the relationship between the asset and the overall market portfolio. For an overall market index like the S&P 500, this suggests that its return should be equal to the return provided by low-risk assets like Treasury bonds plus a risk premium to account for the volatility of stocks.

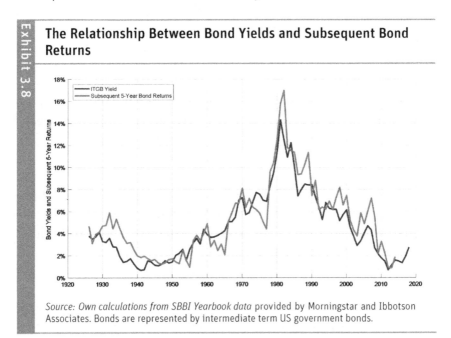

Exhibit 3.8

The Relationship Between Bond Yields and Subsequent Bond Returns

Source: Own calculations from SBBI Yearbook data provided by Morningstar and Ibbotson Associates. Bonds are represented by intermediate term US government bonds.

We have discussed how bond yields are the best predictors for subsequent bond returns. Historically, the S&P 500 outperformed intermediate-term government bonds by 6.7 percent in arithmetic terms. Lower bond yields suggest one reason why stock returns could be less. Adding 6.7 percent to the 2.5 percent bond yield at the start of 2019 would lead to an estimate for stock returns of 9.2 percent, compared to the historical 11.9 percent arithmetic average return. With low bond yields we should also expect lower stock returns as well. Otherwise, stocks would end up providing a higher return premium over bonds than they have historically, and there is little reason to expect a higher risk premium today.

It is also worth addressing estimates of the equity premium. Are the historical excess returns really the best predictors for the future equity premium? An important matter to address is the relationship between the equity premium and the cyclically adjusted price-earnings ratio. When price-earnings multiples are high, markets have historically tended to exhibit mean reversion as relatively lower future returns were realized, and vice versa.

In the mid-1990s, Yale professor and Nobel laureate Robert Shiller popularized the concept of the cyclically adjusted price-earnings ratio (commonly abbreviated either as CAPE or PE10) as being a useful predictor of subsequent stock market returns. The PE10 measure is the stock price divided by the average real earnings on a monthly basis over the previous ten years. A research article published by John Campbell and Robert Shiller in 1998 justifies this measure to remove cyclical factors from earnings, though there is no particular reason to pick precisely ten years other than as an approximation for the length of a business cycle. Today, Robert Shiller provides updated data on the key variables used to calculate PE10 at his website.

Though Robert Shiller focused on the relationship between the PE10 measure and subsequent stock returns, the approach can just as easily be applied to the relationship with the equity premium. The idea with both is that when the PE10 measure is higher, subsequent expected stock returns or their excess returns over bonds should be less.

The historical risk premium can vary based on the historical period under consideration as well as on the choice of stock and bond indices. Robert

Shiller provides freely on his website data for US large-capitalization stock returns, dividends, and earnings, as well as ten-year Treasury bond yields. This data is available since 1871, making it the longest available data series commonly used for retirement income research.

In this dataset, large-capitalization stocks provided an average 5.8 percent higher arithmetic return than ten-year bond yields. This is one way to estimate the equity premium. Exhibit 3.9 parses this historical data in another way, however. It plots the values of PE10 at each historical point against the arithmetic average of the risk premium over the subsequent ten years. The line fitting best through this data shows a negative historical relationship as higher values of PE10 are associated with lower subsequent excess returns for stocks over bonds. To the extent that we view this model as having credible predictive power, it suggests that the best guess for the risk premium over the next ten years from January 2019 is only 1.4 percent, rather than the historical average 5.8 percent. This lower risk premium results from the higher market valuations facing retirees at the present, as PE10 was 28.64 in January 2019, compared to its historical average of 17.0. This projection is well below the historical average because PE10 is well above its historical average.

There is more controversy about the predictive powers of PE10 for stock returns, or their excess returns over bonds, than there is for bond yields to predict bond returns. There are compelling behavioral explanations for why these relationships could remain in the future, but there are also many arguments specifically about the problems with using PE10. For instance, changing accounting standards with regard to how earnings are calculated may be an explanation for why today's PE10 does not properly align with its historical values.

William Bernstein has also written about the paradox of wealth, which is that returns on capital tend to decrease as societies become wealthier. He tracks this trend back to the middles ages. This could explain why we should expect PE10 to center around a higher level than in the past as the returns on capital fall. A related argument along these lines is that low interest rates could also justify a higher value of PE10 than otherwise. Nevertheless, this issue of market valuations exemplifies why it may not always be wise to use historical averages for excess returns to create estimates for the future risk premium.

Exhibit 3.9

The Relationship Between the Cyclically Adjusted Price-Earnings Ratio and the Risk Premium

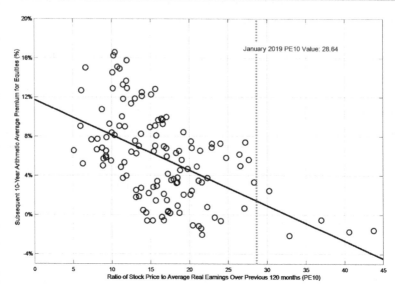

Source: Own calculations with data from Robert Shiller's website (http://www.econ.yale.edu/~shiller/data.htm).

Sustainable spending rates for retirees are intricately related to the returns provided by the underlying investment portfolio. And with sequence-of-returns risk, the returns experienced early on will weigh disproportionately on outcomes. In other words, for those already spending, the assumption that returns will one day normalize to their historical averages is much less relevant than it is for accumulators who will rely on more distant market returns. Current market conditions are much more relevant, making it a mistake to blindly apply a historical average return without further thought.

Adjustments for a Conservative Return Assumption

A simple approach for building a financial plan is to decide on a rate of return for the investment portfolio and to plug that value into a spreadsheet to represent assumed asset growth. Historical data may be used to calculate historical average returns for different asset classes, which are then combined to create the overall portfolio return. This approach is also known as deterministic modeling, as there is no randomness in the future outcome. The same return is obtained each year without variability.

Deterministic approaches are overly simplified because they do not account for volatility and therefore miss the impact of sequence-of-returns risk. The basic approach of assuming a fixed return reflecting the best guess about future market returns leads to a retirement plan with only a 50 percent chance to work. The outcomes are too optimistic and could lead a retiree down an unsustainable path.

The Stock Market's Greatest Hits

We must remember that the stock market is risky and can experience extended downturns for long periods of time.

To get a sense of this, I've tallied up all the cases of stock market drops greater than 50 percent in inflation-adjusted terms for the twenty-one developed-market countries included in the Dimson, Marsh, and Staunton Global Returns Dataset, 1900–2017. This dataset provides total returns for stocks, long-term government bonds, short-term government bills, and inflation on an annual basis since 1900. These calculations are based on annual data, and the drawdowns from peak to trough may be even bigger with monthly data, had that data been available. The data provides total market returns, which includes reinvested dividends. Though World War I and II account for some of these significant market drops, there are still plenty of other examples from more peaceful times.

Exhibit 3A.1 shows the country name, years (beginning of the first listed year to end of the second listed year), and the percentage drop in real terms for the stock market over that period. I also provide the year that the real stock market value would again exceed the level prior to the market drop, as well as the number of years it took for this to happen. The United States experienced two significant drops of this nature, with recoveries happening in seven and ten years. The implication of the chart is that stock market drops can be steeper than what the United States has experienced, and the subsequent recoveries can take longer as well.

Exhibit 3A.1

The Stock Market's Greatest Hits

	Time Period	Market Drawdown	Year Market Returned to Predrawdown Level	Wait Time (Years)
Australia	1970–74	–66%	1985	(15)
Austria	1914–25	–96%	2003	(89)
	1947–50	–83%	1960	(13)
	1962–68	–61%	1989	(27)
	2007–08	–61%	Still Waiting	
Belgium	1914–18	–80%	1927	(13)
	1929–34	–69%	1972	(43)
	2007–08	–51%	2015	(8)
Canada	1929–32	–55%	1935	(6)
Finland	1917–21	–85%	1935	(18)
	1943–48	–73%	1959	(16)
	1974–77	–62%	1983	(9)
	1989–91	–60%	1996	(7)
	2000–02	–61%	Still Waiting	
	2008	–53%	2016	(8)
France	1943–50	–88%	1985	(42)
	1962–1980	–50%	1985	(23)
Germany	1914–31	–84%	1958	(44)
	1948	–91%	1955	(7)
	2000–02	–58%	2007	(7)
Ireland	1973–74	–63%	1985	(12)
	2007–08	–75%	Still Waiting	
Italy	1913–21	–68%	1924	(11)
	1944–45	–85%	1959	(15)
	1974–77	–74%	1985	(11)

Exhibit 3A.1

The Stock Market's Greatest Hits (continued)

	Time Period	Market Drawdown	Year Market Returned to Predrawdown Level	Wait Time (Years)
Japan	1943–47	–98%	1969	(26)
	1990–02	–70%	Still Waiting	
Netherlands	2000–02	–52%	2017	(17)
New Zealand	1987–90	–73%	2003	(16)
Norway	1917–21	–74%	1935	(18)
	1974–78	–73%	1985	(11)
	2008	–54%	2016	(8)
Portugal	1920–1924	–71%	1936	(16)
	1974–1978	–94%	1987	(13)
	1988–1992	–64%	1997	(9)
	2008–2011	–51%	Still Waiting	
South Africa	1919	–52%	1923	(4)
Spain	1936–50	–84%	1996	(19)
	1974–82	–55%	1955	(22)
Sweden	1974–82	–68%	1936	(19)
	2000–02	–54%	2006	(6)
Switzerland	1915–20	–73%	1927	(12)
	1973–74	–56%	1985	(12)
United Kingdom	1973–74	–71%	1983	(10)
United States	1929–31	–61%	1936	(7)
	1973–74	–52%	1983	(10)

Source: Own calculations from Dimson, Marsh, and Staunton Global Returns Dataset (1900–2017). Of the twenty-one countries in the dataset, only Denmark avoided having an entry in the exhibit.

Monte Carlo simulations provide an alternative that is now widely used in financial planning software. Simulations are used to develop sequences of random market returns fitting predetermined characteristics, in order to test how financial plans will perform in a wider variety of good and bad market environments. The use of Monte Carlo tools has increased considerably over the past decade, which can likely be attributed to lower computing costs, increased recognition that returns are random, and desires to provide more robust financial plans. A thousand or more simulations could be created to test the robustness of a retirement plan in many market environments.

Monte Carlo simulations can be created for different asset classes or for an overall portfolio. With the asset class approach, one defines the arithmetic average return, the standard deviation for that return, and the correlations with other asset classes. Random draws are then taken from statistical distributions sharing these characteristics. By combining the arithmetic mean with volatility, the resulting simulated returns will display the appropriate compounded return over time. Historical data is commonly used to set these input characteristics. Most financial planning software works in this way.

With Monte Carlo based financial planning software, retirees generally focus on building a plan that achieves a high probability of success, such as 80 or 90 percent. This implicitly means the underlying assumed return is below average. But when thinking in terms of a fixed return assumption, we usually consider what we view as the best guess for future returns. Again, the best guess only implies a 50 percent chance for success. Half of the time, the realized return will be higher and half the time it will be less. In order to have a conservative fixed return assumption, we must further scale down from our best guess estimate. This is a point which many investment management professionals have not internalized into their thinking, as they are conditioned to using their idea about average returns as the input.

Implied fixed investment returns are usually not shown with Monte Carlo simulation output in financial planning software, but they do exist underneath the hood. We can reverse engineer their values. So which implied portfolio fixed return supports a 90 percent chance for success? The implied return will be lower than the average return input for the simulation, and I find support for appropriate portfolio return assumptions in the postretirement period to be more conservative than in the preretirement period.

Consider three scenarios:

1. An individual investing a lump-sum amount for thirty years
2. An individual saving a fixed percentage of a constant inflation-adjusted salary at the end of each year over a thirty-year accumulation period
3. An individual withdrawing the maximum sustainable constant inflation-adjusted amount from a portfolio at the start of each year over a thirty-year retirement period

Exhibit 3.10 provides the distribution of results for these simulations. These simulations are based on a standard 50/50 portfolio using historical Morningstar data for the S&P 500 and intermediate-term government bonds. For the portfolio, Exhibit 3.7 revealed that the real arithmetic average return was 5.6 percent, with a 10.6 percent standard deviation. This leads to a real compounded return of 5 percent.

For the lump-sum investment, the numbers represent the distribution of average compounded returns over 100,000 thirty-year periods. For the accumulation phase, the distribution of outcomes is for the internal rate of return for the final wealth accumulation when making thirty annual contributions. For the retirement phase, the distribution of results is for the internal rates of return on the portfolio when withdrawing the maximum sustainable amount over a thirty-year period with distributions taken at the start of each year.

The accumulation and distribution phases are dollar-weighted returns, instead of simple time-weighted returns for the lump-sum investment, because they account for cash inflows or outflows over time. Whenever there are cash flows, the ordering of returns matters because returns at different times will impact different amounts of net asset flows. This is the source of sequence risk.

In all three cases, the median return was close to 5 percent, with slight variations for accumulation and retirement based on the timing of the cash flows. This matches the observation that with an expected growth rate of 5 percent, the portfolio achieves at least a 5 percent growth rate only half of the time, as the probability the median return can be achieved is only 50 percent. When choosing a number to plug into a spreadsheet, a conservative retiree might be more comfortable using something like the return in the 25th percentile—or even the 10th—of the distribution. These lower return numbers would correspond to 75 or 90 percent probabilities of success, respectively, for a financial plan created with planning software.

Exhibit 3.10 provides the implied fixed returns at other percentiles of the distribution as created through this reverse-engineering process. With the lump-sum investment, the compounded real return at the 25th percentile is also 3.7 percent. For an accumulator, the 25th percentile return is 3.7 percent, while it is 3.3 percent for the retiree. Higher success rates are connected with lower portfolio returns, since the return hurdle must be exceeded by the portfolio for the financial plan to be successful. At the 10th percentile, realized compounded real returns were 2.6 percent for the lump-sum investment, 2.4 percent for the accumulator, and 2 percent for the retiree.

Exhibit 3.10

Distribution of Compounded Real Returns over 30 Years

Monte Carlo Simulations for a 50/50 Asset Allocation

Based on SBBI Data, 1926–2018, S&P 500 and Intermediate-Term Government Bonds

	Lump Sum	Accumulation	Retirement
1st Percentile	0.7%	0.2%	-0.1%
5th Percentile	1.9%	1.6%	1.3%
10th Percentile	2.6%	2.4%	2.0%
25th Percentile	3.7%	3.7%	3.3%
Median	5.0%	5.1%	4.9%
75th Percentile	6.3%	6.5%	6.6%
90th Percentile	7.5%	7.8%	8.2%
95th Percentile	8.2%	8.6%	9.2%
99th Percentile	9.6%	10.1%	11.2%
Mean	5.0%	5.1%	5.0%
Std. Deviation	1.9%	2.1%	2.4%

Source: Own calculations with 100,000 Monte Carlo simulations for thirty-year periods. Portfolio returns are lognormally distributed with a 5.6 percent arithmetic real return and 10.6 percent standard deviation.

These numbers are naturally lower to provide a greater chance of success, and sequence-of-returns risk pushes these numbers even lower for accumulators and retirees. The volatility of outcomes increases as we transition from a lump sum (standard deviation of 1.9 percent) to accumulation (2.1 percent) to retirement (2.4 percent). This trend represents growing sequence risk.

Individuals accumulating or spending assets will have different experiences than someone using a lump-sum investment. Accumulation effectively places greater importance on the returns earned late in the career when a given return impacts more years of contributions. This is sequence-of-returns risk as it applies in the accumulation phase. With greater importance placed on a shorter sequence of returns, we should expect a wider distribution of outcomes.

As for retirement, the impacts are even bigger as sequence risk further amplifies the impact of investment volatility. Retirees experience heightened sequence-of-returns risk when funding a constant spending stream from a volatile portfolio. A portfolio decline causes withdrawals to become a larger percentage of remaining assets. This digs a hole for the portfolio that can be difficult to escape. The distribution of internal rates of return during retirement will be even wider because of the heightened importance placed on the shorter sequence of postretirement returns. A conservative retiree seeking a return assumption for retirement should use a lower value than for preretirement.

In this discussion, I am tackling Monte Carlo from a different direction—using Monte Carlo simulations to calculate a fixed average growth rate for the portfolio. Those fixed returns could then be used in a deterministic planning analysis to determine outcomes with a greater chance to succeed. Conservative investors will want to work with lower assumed returns, implying a need to save more today. The exhibit provides insight about appropriately conservative adjustments for return assumptions.

Not only does sequence risk widen the distribution of outcomes in retirement, but retirees also experience less risk capacity. With less time and flexibility to make adjustments to their financial plans, retirees who experience portfolio losses after leaving the workforce can experience a devastating impact on remaining lifetime living standards.

This is another reason why individuals may want to use different return assumptions pre- and postretirement. For example, a conservative individual might be willing to use the 25th percentile return during accumulation (calibrated to a 75 percent chance for success) but only the 10th percentile during retirement (90 percent chance). If the individual were comfortable with the arithmetic real return and volatility of 5.6 percent and 10.6 percent, this would suggest using a 3.7 percent compounded real return assumption in the spreadsheet for accumulation and a 2 percent compounded real return assumption in the spreadsheet for retirement.

Because of sequence-of-returns risk, conservative investors will want to use lower fixed-return assumptions than just the compounded return assumed for a lump-sum investment. Sequence-of-returns risk is relevant for both the accumulation and retirement phases. Assumed returns should be lower in both cases. The impact is even greater for retirement. Conservative individuals will not want to use the expected return for their portfolios when developing lifetime financial plans. This is a really important point to remember and internalize when working in environments that require a fixed-return assumption without an accompanying volatility.

⊙ Determining Sustainable Spending from an Investment Portfolio in Retirement

Determining the sustainable spending rate from a diversified investment portfolio in retirement requires making decisions about longevity and market returns. The final section in this chapter provides an opportunity to integrate this discussion in order to obtain a better sense about sustainable distributions from an investment portfolio in retirement.

Rather than blindly applying something like the 4 percent rule-of-thumb for portfolio distributions, we can create a more realistic analysis using the process described in this section. This process provides sustainable portfolio distributions that are calibrated to the retiree's longevity risk aversion (see callout box) and accepted risk for outliving the investment portfolio.

Looking ahead, we also seek to develop market return assumptions that can be applied to the pricing of annuities, with regard to the bond yield curve, fees, and other related assumptions, so that we are able to compare investments and annuities on an equal footing.

Exhibit 3.11 brings together the factors that determine portfolio return assumptions as outlined in this chapter. To derive generalized stock and bond returns, we start with the components of portfolio returns: inflation, real bond yield, and a risk premium for stocks relative to bonds. First, the inflation assumption is 2 percent, which is based on the current break-even inflation rates between traditional Treasury bond and TIPS as was shown in Exhibit 2.5.

Next, the assumed real bond yield and return is 1 percent. This is based on the current TIPS yield curve also seen in Exhibit 2.5. When building a bond ladder for retiree income, the average yield for the ladder matches closely to the long-term TIPS rates, which are approximately 1 percent. Sustainable spending is approximated quite well by assuming a flat yield curve at the long-term interest rate as compared to pricing a bond ladder based on the entire yield curve. As our focus is on comparing the risk premium to risk pooling, we simplify the analysis for bonds by assuming a flat yield curve with a 1 percent real yield. When inflation is included, the yield curve is flat with a 3 percent nominal yield. These two values become the assumed gross arithmetic returns for bonds.

As for stocks, I assume a risk premium of 6 percent. This matches the historical risk premium for the S&P 500 over long-term US government bonds (as our yield curve, again, is based on a long-term bond to reflect the average yield from a retirement income bond ladder) as shown in Exhibit 3.5. Implicitly, then, stocks are represented by the S&P 500. Adding the historical equity premium to the bond returns, we obtain an assumed 9 percent nominal arithmetic return and a 7 percent real arithmetic return for stocks. Interest rates are lower today, and the financial markets expect inflation to fall below its historical averages, which is why our return assumptions end up lower than their historical values.

The next step in Exhibit 3.11 is to adjust these gross returns to account for all of the various factors we discussed. While the portfolio diversification and alpha factor could increase returns, the other factors listed (fees, investor behavior, taxes, and above average market valuations) would generally lead to lower net returns. For the baseline assumptions to be

Longevity Risk Aversion and Choosing a Planning Age

With the probability-based approach, what planning age should a retiree choose when building a retirement income plan?

This is a personal decision to be based partly on objective characteristics: gender, smoking status, health status and history, family health history, and other socioeconomic characteristics that correlate with mortality. It is also based on an individual's answers to more subjective questions: how do you feel about outliving your investment portfolio, and what would be the impact on your standard of living if you outlived your portfolio?

Moshe Milevsky coined the term *longevity risk aversion* to describe the emotions related to how one feels about the possibility of outliving one's investment portfolio in late retirement. Beyond the objective information available about mortality, longevity risk aversion is what will drive a retiree's decision about an appropriate planning age. Those with greater fear of outliving their wealth will seek to build a financial plan that can be sustained to a higher age for which there is a sufficiently low probability to outlive.

Longevity Risk Aversion

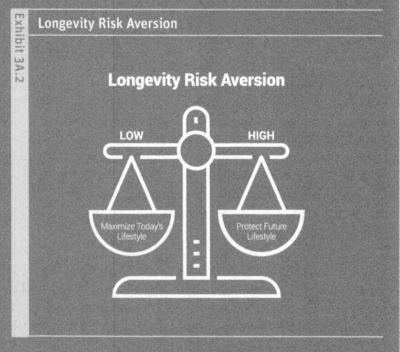

To understand longevity risk aversion, consider which of these statements resonates more with you.

1. To get the most enjoyment out of retirement, it is optimal to frontload spending and to enjoy a higher standard of living while one is still able to do so.

2. The thought of needing to significantly reduce my living standard or burdening my children at an advanced age is sufficiently alarming that I would rather maintain a more conservative lifestyle today to better protect against this possibility.

Answering #1 implies lower longevity risk aversion, while answering #2 implies high longevity risk aversion. With low longevity risk aversion, the focus is on maximizing today's lifestyle. With higher longevity risk aversion, the focus shifts to protecting lifestyle in the future.

An individual's longevity risk aversion determines how he or she will evaluate the trade-off between how a higher planning age improves the chances that a plan will work and how it reduces the sustainable spending amount in retirement. For example, a sixty-five-year-old female who is willing to accept a 10 percent chance for outliving her financial plan may decide to base her planning on surviving to age 100.

For retirees who are self-managing their longevity risk, the idea is to choose a sufficiently long time horizon that one is unlikely to outlive, then ensure that one's plan can work for this long. Those with greater longevity risk aversion, which is the fear of outliving their resources, will seek a higher planning age with a lower probability to outlive. Individuals pick planning ages that are sufficiently conservative to reflect their personalized concerns about outliving their wealth. These factors will feed into the decision about which planning age to use in Exhibits 3.12 to 3.14.

used for investments in this book, we will give the benefit of the doubt to investments and assume no adjustments for these various factors. This also justifies the assumption of fair annuity pricing at the beginning of the next chapter. As will be seen in later chapters, the case for using risk pooling to support retirement income is quite strong even when we do not reduce net portfolio returns for investments. As such, in Exhibit 3.11 we assume that the net returns for stocks and bonds match their gross returns.

The next steps in Exhibit 3.11 are to decide the standard deviation assumptions for the asset classes as well as the asset allocation for the portfolio, and to then combined these details to create overall net return and volatility assumptions for the portfolio. In this example, I assume a standard deviation of 20 percent for stocks. This closely matches the historical volatility for the S&P 500, which Exhibit 3.1 shows was 19.8 percent for both nominal and real returns.

As for bonds, I assume a 0 percent standard deviation. This simplifies the fixed-income yield curve and inflation to be unchanging over time. It also means that bond yields and bond returns are the same. Since total returns for a bond portfolio are volatile, this assumption requires explanation. I am eliminating interest rate risk from the analysis, as there is no possibility for fluctuating interest rates to create capital gains or losses for the underlying bond portfolio. If interest rates rise, the value of a fixed-income portfolio declines, but the present-value cost of funding a future spending goal also decreases. If the duration of the bond portfolio matches the duration of the spending liability, then interest rate fluctuations have offsetting effects on the asset and liability sides of the retirement balance sheet and interest rate risk is hedged.

Alternatively, we could think of our retiree as holding individual bonds to maturity, which means that any capital gains or losses from interest rate fluctuations would not be realized as the bonds reach maturity and provide their face value as a source of retirement spending for that year.

This simplification about fixed income does not meaningfully impact the decision between investments and insurance; it simply lets us focus more directly on the equity risk premium and insurance risk pooling without also having to further worry about fluctuating interest rates. Bond holdings may be riskier for households not using asset-liability matching than implied by our analysis, which would disadvantage an investment strategy using bonds relative to an annuity. Insurance companies do use asset-liability matching so as to not be forced to sell assets at a loss.

Exhibit 3.11

The Building Blocks of Portfolio Returns

	Stocks	Bonds
Components of Arithmetic Returns		
Inflation	2.0%	2.0%
Real Bond Return	1.0%	1.0%
Risk Premium	6.0%	—
Gross Nominal Arithmetic Return	9.0%	3.0%
Gross Real Arithmetic Return	7.0%	1.0%
Further Adjustments:		
Investment Management Fees	0.0%	0.0%
Portfolio Diversification / Alpha	0.0%	0.0%
Investor Behavior	0.0%	0.0%
Taxes	0.0%	0.0%
Market Valuations	0.0%	0.0%
Net Nominal Arithmetic Return	9.0%	3.0%
Net Real Arithmetic Return	7.0%	1.0%
Standard Deviation of Returns	20.0%	0.0%
Asset Allocation	50.0%	50.0%

Portfolio Characteristics

Portfolio Nominal Arithmetic Return	6.00%
Portfolio Nominal Compounded Return	5.5%
Portfolio Real Arithmetic Return	4.00%
Portfolio Real Compounded Return	3.5%
Portfolio Standard Deviation	10.0%

Source: Own calculations and assumptions as described in the text.

Using the portfolio return and volatility assumptions determined in Exhibit 3.11, we then reverse engineer fixed return assumptions and sustainable spending levels for a desired retirement time horizon and targeted probability of success. The investment portfolio is modeled using 100,000 Monte Carlo simulations for these portfolio returns, assuming a lognormal distribution.

Exhibit 3.12 presents the implied compounded real returns for different planning horizons and probabilities of success. As these are real return factors, they would support inflation adjusted spending. The arithmetic average portfolio return is 4 percent real with a standard deviation of 10 percent. However, for deciding on a fixed return assumption, one must account for the likelihood of success they seek for the spending plan in terms of both a planning horizon and probability of success. For instance, if the retiree sought a 90 percent chance that portfolio distributions could be sustained through age ninety, this would imply an assumed fixed real growth rate for the portfolio from the 10th percentile of outcomes at 0.5 percent.

We should make a few observations about this 0.5 percent return value. First, it is less than the assumed 1 percent real return from holding bonds. In other words, to achieve the desired success rate from the diversified portfolio, one ends up assuming a lower return, and therefore a lower spending amount, than bonds could ensure. The flip side of this, though, is that 90 percent of the time the retiree could expect to earn a higher effective return than this number and may even be able to grow their wealth throughout retirement as they otherwise are spending less than would have been feasible. Conversely, the bond ladder would lock-in the 1 percent real return throughout retirement without a chance for upside.

The other interesting aspect is to note that the fixed return assumption increases for longer retirement horizons, as it is 0.8 percent for planning through age ninety-five and 1 percent (matching the bond yield) for planning through age 100. The reason that returns increase with the time horizon is because to sustain spending for longer, the spending amount must decrease, which reduces the impact of sequence-of-returns risk.

This concept is seen more clearly in Exhibit 3.13, which provides the corresponding spending numbers for the returns in the previous exhibit. Returning to the same example, if the retiree seeks a 90 percent chance

Exhibit 3.12

Fixed Rates of Return Assumptions for a Sixty-Five-Year-Old
Reverse Engineered Inflation-Adjusted Compounded Returns for Retirement

	Planning Horizon (Age)				
	85	**90**	**95**	**100**	**105**
Worst Case	-5.9%	-5.0%	-4.2%	-3.7%	-3.3%
5th Percentile	-0.6%	-0.2%	0.1%	0.3%	0.5%
10th Percentile	0.2%	0.5%	0.8%	1.0%	1.1%
25th Percentile	1.7%	1.9%	2.0%	2.1%	2.2%
Median	3.4%	3.4%	3.4%	3.4%	3.4%
75th Percentile	5.3%	5.1%	4.9%	4.8%	4.8%
90th Percentile	7.0%	6.7%	6.4%	6.2%	6.1%
95th Percentile	8.1%	7.7%	7.3%	7.1%	6.9%
Best Case	19.2%	18.7%	18.3%	17.9%	17.5%
Std. Deviation	2.7%	2.4%	2.2%	2.1%	2.0%

Source: Own calculations with 100,000 Monte Carlo Simulations for a 50/50 portfolio of stocks and bonds. These calculations are based on the net portfolio returns shown in Exhibit 3.11. The portfolio's real arithmetic return is 4% and standard deviation is 10%.

that spending lasts to age ninety, they would choose from the 10th percentile of spending outcomes. That is $42,633 of annual inflation-adjusted spending. To sustain spending through age ninety-five with the same success rate, spending would need to reduce to $37,194. This is a 3.72 percent withdrawal rate from retirement date assets, and it would be the number that corresponds to the 4 percent rule-of-thumb with these market expectations for a thirty-year retirement. If sustainability with 90 percent success was instead sought for thirty-five years through age 100, then the annual spending number falls further to $33,418. Again, it is because the spending amount decreases that the return assumption can increase; the lower spending rate reduces the exposure to sequence-of-returns risk and reduces the impact of investment volatility in the retirement plan.

Retirement spending goals are often expressed in terms of inflation-adjusted spending numbers. This is what the 4 percent rule-of-thumb assumes. But as we move the discussion toward annuities, many annuities will protect a fixed amount of spending without inflation adjustments. It is not appropriate to compare the payout rate for a fixed annuity payment to the sustainable distribution rate from an investment portfolio that assumes inflation-adjusted spending. As such, Exhibit 3.14 repeats this analysis using the nominal portfolio return assumptions from Exhibit 3.11, which include a 6 percent return and a ten percent standard deviation.

When the returns are nominal rather than real, it means that the spending numbers are nominal instead of real. They will start at higher values but will not grow for inflation. Returning to the same example, seeking 90 percent success through age ninety-five allows fixed spending of $47,746, which is 28.4 percent more than the corresponding $37,194 inflation-adjusted spending number from the previous exhibit. Again, this spending starts at a higher value but stays fixed rather than growing over time. If we compare to the pricing for an annuity providing fixed payments, then it

Exhibit 3.13

Sustainable Spending for a Sixty-Five-Year-Old with $1 Million of Assets
Reverse Engineered Inflation-Adjusted Sustainable Spending Amounts for Retirement Retirement

	Planning Horizon (Age)				
	85	**90**	**95**	**100**	**105**
Worst Case	$26,488	$20,318	$16,590	$14,033	$12,146
5th Percentile	$46,965	$38,870	$33,642	$30,051	$27,468
10th Percentile	$50,985	$42,633	$37,194	$33,418	$30,660
25th Percentile	$58,305	$49,440	$43,700	$39,692	$36,781
Median	$67,445	$58,079	$51,954	$47,702	$44,601
75th Percentile	$77,865	$67,998	$61,527	$57,027	$53,797
90th Percentile	$88,291	$77,965	$71,249	$66,603	$63,186
95th Percentile	$95,088	$84,616	$77,649	$72,783	$69,338
Best Case	$166,254	$159,535	$155,514	$152,157	$148,989
Std. Deviation	$14,717	$13,979	$13,480	$13,123	$12,863

Source: Own calculations with 100,000 Monte Carlo Simulations for a 50/50 portfolio of stocks and bonds. These calculations are based on the net portfolio returns shown in Exhibit 3.11. The portfolio's real arithmetic return is 4% and standard deviation is 10%.

is the numbers in Exhibit 3.14 that provide the most directly comparable values.

To plant the seed for where this analysis is heading, in Exhibit 4.1 from the next chapter, I calculate that the lifetime fixed payout for a $1 million premium to a life-only income annuity for a sixty-five-year-old female is $57,800 per year. That number can be directly compared to those shown in Exhibit 3.14, since in both cases we are discussing nominal spending that does not grow with inflation. Suppose this individual is considering an investments solution for retirement and will use a 50/50 asset allocation to stocks and bonds and agrees with the net return assumptions for which this example is based.

Suppose further that she seeks a 90 percent chance that her portfolio will last to age ninety-five. In this case, she would use the 10th percentile

Exhibit 3.14

Sustainable Spending for a Sixty-Five-Year-Old with $1 Million of Assets
Reverse Engineered Fixed Sustainable Spending Amounts for Retirement

	Planning Horizon (Age)				
	85	90	95	100	105
Worst Case	$30,136	$26,347	$22,923	$19,862	$18,473
5th Percentile	$56,420	$48,687	$43,727	$40,394	$38,082
10th Percentile	$60,794	$52,781	$47,746	$44,369	$41,996
25th Percentile	$68,756	$60,421	$55,167	$51,635	$49,163
Median	$78,707	$70,049	$64,580	$60,900	$58,353
75th Percentile	$89,821	$80,818	$75,142	$71,335	$68,691
90th Percentile	$100,899	$91,636	$85,810	$81,861	$79,140
95th Percentile	$108,001	$98,510	$92,538	$88,571	$85,823
Best Case	$184,786	$175,766	$169,443	$166,628	$164,791
Std. Deviation	$15,818	$15,308	$14,988	$14,785	$14,654

Source: Own calculations with 100,000 Monte Carlo Simulations for a 50/50 portfolio of stocks and bonds. These calculations are based on the net portfolio returns shown in Exhibit 3.11. The portfolio's nominal arithmetic return is 6% and standard deviation is 10%..

assumption for age ninety-five, which allows spending of $47,746 per year. Because this amount is less than the annuity provides, it means she would need more assets to support the same amount of spending as the annuity while preserving the degree of comfort she desires for meeting her retirement income goal. In this case, she would require 21 percent more assets, or $1.21 million devoted to spending from the investment portfolio to comfortably match the amount of spending that the annuity could provide with $1 million.

These discrepancies would become even larger if she were even more longevity risk averse. For instance, if she sought a 95 percent chance that her portfolio would last to age 100, she could only spend $40,394 annually. In this case, her nest-egg would need to be 43 percent larger, or $1.43 million, in order to match the protected lifetime spending level afforded by $1 million in the annuity.

On the other hand, if she were less longevity risk averse, it is possible that investments would let her spend more than the annuity with the caveat that the chances of outliving the investment portfolio would increase accordingly. For instance, if she sought a 75 percent chance that her assets would last to age ninety, then she could spend $60,421 from the portfolio, which is larger than the $57,800 that the annuity could support from the same underlying asset base.

These comparisons will become important later in the book when we discuss how to integrate the retirement asset base to build retirement income strategies that can more efficiently meet the various financial goals of retirement. But before that, we must introduce risk pooling and how annuities and life insurance can also serve as potential tools in a retirement income plan. We will now shift from the risk premium to risk pooling.

Further Reading

Bengen, William P. 1994. "Determining Withdrawal Rates Using Historical Data." *Journal of Financial Planning* 7 (4): 171–180.

Bernstein, William J. 2012. *The Ages of the Investor: A Critical Look at Life-Cycle Investing (Investing for Adults).* Efficient Frontier Publications. [http://amzn.to/2s495L2]

Bernstein, William J. 2013. *Deep Risk: How History Informs Portfolio Design.* Efficient Frontier Publications. [https://amzn.to/2XCsX7E]

Bogle, John C. 2014. "The Arithmetic of 'All-In' Investment Expenses." *Financial Analysts Journal* 70 (January/February).

Campbell, John Y., and Robert J. Shiller. 1998. "Valuation Ratios and the Long-Run Stock Market Outlook." *Journal of Portfolio Management 24 (2): 11–26.*

Kinniry, Jr., Francis M., Colleen M. Jaconetti, Michael A. DiJoseph, and Yan Zilbering. 2014. "Putting a Value on Your Value: Quantifying Vanguard Advisor's Alpha." Vanguard Research Paper. https://www.vanguard.com/pdf/ISGQVAA.pdf

Levine, David A. 2016. "How Much of Your Nest Egg to Put Into Stocks? All of it." *New York Times* (February 13): p. B4.

Markowitz, Harry M. 1991. "Individual versus Institutional Investing." *Financial Services Review* 1 (1).

Milevsky, Moshe A., and Huaxiong Huang. 2011. "Spending Retirement on Planet Vulcan: The Impact of Longevity Risk Aversion on Optimal Withdrawal Rates." *Financial Analysts Journal* 67 (2): 45–58.

Pfau, Wade. 2017. *How Much Can I Spend in Retirement: A Guide to Investment-Based Retirement Income Strategies.* McLean, VA: Retirement Researcher Media. [http://amzn.to/2xLgXGC]

CHAPTER 4

Income Annuities (Risk Pooling)

For those seeking to spend more in retirement than the bond yield curve can support, the alternative to seeking risk premium through an aggressive asset allocation is to pool risk through insurance. Income annuities are the simplest type of insurance products which trade a lump-sum payment for protected lifetime income. The ability to convert a portion of assets (as it is not an all-or-nothing decision) into a guaranteed income stream is a fundamental retirement income tool which contrasts with an investment portfolio in terms of the advantages and disadvantages for managing retirement risks.

We start our discussion of annuities with the income annuity because it is the most straightforward and easy-to-understand way to convert a pot of money into a guaranteed stream of spending for life. This chapter focuses specifically on income annuities, also known as immediate annuities, single-premium immediate annuities (SPIAs), deferred income annuities (DIAs), or longevity insurance. The next chapters will expand the discussion to include other types of more complex annuities that are also able to offer lifetime income protections.

Risk pooling and mortality credits are the driver of value from an income annuity. The annuitant accepts the risk of dying early and receiving fewer payments from the annuity in exchange for the ability to continue receiving payments for a very long time in the event of a long life. By pooling longevity risks with a collection of individuals, an income annuity allows its owners to spend assets as though they will earn fixed-income returns and live to their life expectancy. Those who end up living beyond their life expectancy will have their continuing benefits subsidized by those who die before life expectancy.

With an income annuity, one is essentially offering to leave part of the premium on the table for others in the risk pool in the event of an early death, in order to receive the protection of maintaining an ongoing income stream through subsidies from others in the event of a long life. While this clearly benefits the long-lived, we can also conclude that it benefits the short-lived as well by allowing them to enjoy a higher standard of living than they might have otherwise been comfortable supporting from an unguaranteed investment portfolio. This can allow for more spending and a more satisfying retirement experience compared to those self-managing longevity risk by spending less and then leaving too much behind at death.

This risk pooling capability can be an attractive proposition when longevity is unforeseeable. With investing approaches that exclude risk pooling and the mortality credits it can provide, greater spending conservatism is otherwise needed to stretch assets out over a potentially long retirement and in the face of a potentially poor sequence of market returns. Risk pooling can provide a cheaper (in terms of being able to earmark fewer assets for the purpose) and more efficient method for supporting a retirement income goal. This can also leave the remaining assets to be more focused on growth, which can even help to support a greater net legacy over time.

Income annuities also provide peace of mind and other psychological benefits for retirees. Retirement income is no longer dependent upon the vagaries of the stock market and its daily fluctuations. Annuity owners could possibly even live longer because of the reduced stress they face with funding their retirement, and also perhaps because they want to make sure they get their money's worth from the annuity by drawing from rather than contributing to that risk pool.

⊙ Menu of Income Annuity Features and Options

As a first step to understanding annuities, we consider basic questions about how income annuities work, as well as what options are available.

Who is covered by an annuity?

There are a few terms relevant to know about how annuities are structured. The contract owner is the one who buys and makes decisions about an annuity contract. The annuitant is the person or persons on whose age and survival is used to determine annuity payments. The contract owner is often also the annuitant, but this does not necessarily have to be the case. The beneficiary is the one who will receive any death proceeds, such as a cash refund, after the annuitant passes away.

When do income payments start?

Income annuities can be either immediate or deferred. An immediate annuity begins income payments within one year of the purchase date, while a deferred income annuity does not begin payments until at least one year after the purchase date. A deferred income annuity purchased at retirement with income beginning at age eighty or eighty-five is also referred to as longevity insurance.

After the Treasury Department updated regulations in 2014 to facilitate the use of longevity insurance inside retirement plans, longevity insurance is now also known as a qualified longevity annuity contract (QLAC). In practice, deferred income annuities are used less as a form of longevity insurance and more for prepaying retirement and removing market risk in the pivotal preretirement years. In such a case, one might purchase a deferred income annuity at age fifty-five, for instance, for income to begin at sixty-five.

Do income annuities cover one life or two?

True to their name, single life income annuities only cover one person's life. With such an annuity, income payments continue until the annuitant's death. A joint life annuity, on the other hand, continues payments for as long as at least one of two annuitants survives.

Often joint annuities are set up for two spouses, but marriage is not a requirement for two annuitants to be included on a joint life contract. Since payments are expected to last longer when two lives are covered, the joint protection comes at the cost of a lower initial payout rate. A joint life and 100 percent survivor annuity provides the same payment as long as one annuitant is alive. With a joint life and 67 percent survivor annuity, the payment would reduce by 33 percent upon the first annuitant's death, allowing for a higher initial payment level.

What are the different flavors of payouts?

A life-only income annuity is the Platonic ideal, offering the highest payout and the most mortality credits. Payouts are highest because the purchaser is taking the most "hit by a bus risk"—the common fear of signing an annuity contract and then being hit by a bus and killed on the way out of the office. Life-only annuities are popular with academics because acceptance of this risk makes more funds available to the longer-surviving members of the risk pool, allowing one to buy protected lifetime income at the lowest possible cost. In practice, many annuity buyers will be uncomfortable with a life-only annuity.

A variety of other flavors will lower the payout rate but may otherwise make the income annuity a more palatable choice. By offering less mortality credits to the risk pool because you want some protection for your beneficiary in the event of an early death, you should, in turn, expect to receive less mortality credits back from the risk pool in the event of a long life. This is the nature of the trade-off that results in a lower payout rate for added protections. Other flavors of annuities that lower the payout rate in exchange for protections to the beneficiary in the event of an early death include:

- Lifetime with ten-year period certain annuity: Pays for life. If the annuitant dies before ten years is up, the beneficiary continues receiving payments for the full ten years. These period-certain guarantees can also be arranged for any number of years, such as five, fifteen, or twenty.
- Cash refund provision: Provides a cash refund of the difference to the beneficiary if an annuitant dies before the owner receives cumulative payments from the annuity that sum to the initial premium.
- Installment refund: Works very similarly to the cash refund, except beneficiaries receive the difference as continued annuity payments

in installments until the full premium has been returned, rather than receiving a onetime refund.

- Period certain: An income annuity does not require a lifetime provision. It may just make payments for a set period of time. This works the same way as building a bond ladder and can be an alternative to individual bonds when considering retirement income bond ladder strategies.

Are payments fixed or do they grow over time?

There are generally three options regarding income annuity payments.

- Fixed or level income annuity: These annuities will pay the same amount on an ongoing basis for as long as the contract requires. The purchasing power of the income payments will decrease over time as there is no adjustment made for inflation.
- COLA: A cost-of-living adjustment (COLA) provision allows payments grow at a fixed compounding rate each year. For instance, if I decide that 3 percent is a reasonable assumption for future inflation, I might choose a COLA of 3 percent with the intention of preserving the purchasing power for my annuity income. If realized inflation ends up being higher, I will lose purchasing power over time, but purchasing power would increase if realized inflation ends up being lower. COLAs can only approximate the inflation experience in retirement.
- CPI: One could add a provision that the income growth rate of the annuity payments precisely matches the Consumer Price Index (CPI). When inflation is low, income grows more slowly, as do living costs for the retiree. When inflation is high, income grows more quickly to better support the increasing cost of living. CPI-adjusted income annuities hedge inflation risk in the same manner as TIPS. Not many companies are currently offer CPI-adjusted income annuities, and so the pricing may not be competitive.

The CPI option could still be attractive for someone who is particularly worried that inflation will be higher than the markets expect. A CPI-adjusted income annuity really is the closest thing we have to a risk-free asset for retirement income. With these annuities, it is also important to check the contract carefully about whether there is a cap on the inflation adjustment. For instance, with a cap of 6 percent, even if inflation is 9 percent in any given year, income payment will only grow by at most 6 percent. This limits the attractiveness for an individual who is really concerned about high inflation in the future.

The Popularity of Different Income Annuity Options and Flavors in Practice

CANNEX (www.cannex.com) is a Toronto-based company that provides a popular platform for learning about annuity pricing. They provide frequent reports about the types of searches being made by distribution companies and financial advisors that could potentially result in an annuity sale. Their CANNEX Survey Experience covering 2018 provides a lot of insight about the types of single premium immediate annuities and deferred income annuities that are popular in the US market. Here are some insights from this report.

The average age for when the premium will be paid on quotes generated for primary annuitants is 66.6. By gender, it is 67.6 for females and 66.0 for males. For primary annuitants, 1.73 percent are age 45 or less, while 3.63 percent are over age 85. When we look further at immediate or deferred annuities, the average age for primary annuitants looking at immediate annuities is 68.5. It is 61.5 for those considering deferred annuities (income begins at least 13 months later).

73 percent of quotes will have payments begin within one year (immediate annuities), while the other 27 percent of quotes have income begin in more than one year. For deferred income annuities, the length of the deferral period is relatively evenly distributed from one year to more than twenty years. We can note that longevity insurance is not a particularly popular annuity use, as only 6.2 percent have deferral periods in excess of ten years, and only 1.8 percent of quotes have deferral periods in excess of 15 years.

For joint annuities, 93.6 percent have a nonreducing payment upon the death of the first annuitant. This is a joint and 100 percent survivors benefit annuity. For the small remaining percentage, about half of the remainder will have the annuity payment reduce by 50 percent upon either the first death or the death of the person identified as the primary annuitant.

As for the annuity flavor, the most popular option is to include a cash refund provision (47 percent) in the event of an early death. The next most popular option is life with ten years of certain payments (16.6 percent), followed by a life-only guarantee (14.4 percent). Other period-certain options with some traction include five years (6.1 percent) and twenty years (4.8 percent). The installment refund accounts for 3.9 percent of quotes. The remaining 6.5 percent of quotes reflect other various period-certain options.

Nonqualified taxable accounts will be the source of annuity funds with 58 percent of quotes, while the other 42 percent of quotes are for various tax-qualified retirement plans.

Monthly payments are sought 81.5 percent of the time, with annual payments 18 percent of the time, and only 0.5 percent seek payment frequencies other than these two choices.

When a quote with a premium is provided, the average premium was $288,155 for immediate annuities and $248,755 for deferred annuities. Meanwhile, for those seeking the cost of providing a specific payment, the average annual income sought was $35,745 for immediate annuities and $36,670 for deferred annuities.

As for fixed or growing payments, 95.7 percent of quotes are for fixed payments. Only 0.2 percent of quotes are for CPI-adjusted income annuities, while 4.1 percent include different COLA options. The most popular COLA options are 2 percent (1.9 percent of quotes) and three percent (1.3 percent of quotes).

Putting this all together to create a baseline scenario for our income annuity discussions, a few ideas that we can gain from the CANNEX survey include that sixty-five is a reasonable age to consider an annuity, joint annuities should have nonreducing benefits, cash refund and life-only income annuities are both viable options, the majority will buy an annuity with taxable assets, both immediate and deferred income annuities are popular in practice, and fixed-income annuities without COLAs or other income growth are by far the most commonly used choice.

Those seeking inflation protection specifically from the annuity should go with options two or three. It is important to recognize, though, that increased future payments mean a lower initial payout rate. I will return to this issue of how to approach the management of inflation risk in Chapter 8.

● Annuity Pricing 101

How are income annuities priced? It is not as hard as one might think, as the basic recipe requires just three ingredients:

1. Mortality rates (which vary by age and gender) impact how long payments will be made. Younger people will have longer projected payout periods, which means that payout rates must be lower.
2. Interest rates impact the returns the annuity provider can earn on the underlying annuitized assets. Higher interest rates imply higher payout rates because the insurance company will be able to earn more interest on the premiums in their general account supporting the annuity payments.
3. Overhead costs relate to extra charges an annuity provider seeks to cover business expenses and to manage risks related to the accuracy of their future mortality and interest rate predictions.

Pricing for a Life-Only Income Annuity

Exhibit 4.1 provides a simple example to illustrate the basic pricing dynamics for an *actuarially fair* income annuity. This is an annuity without any overhead costs, and it assumes the underlying projections for mortality and fixed-income returns are correct. I use the capital market expectations I described in Chapter 3, of which the relevant aspect is that I assume the bond yield curve is flat at a nominal 3 percent interest rate. For this example, we consider a sixty-five-year-old female who is offered $10,000 of spending per year as long as she lives. Since we are using a nominal bond yield curve, this spending is fixed. The income annuity is life-only, so payments stop at death. How much is this protected lifetime income stream objectively worth?

Finding how much the annuity is worth requires inputs for investment returns to be earned on the premium financing these payments, and the survival probabilities to each subsequent age. Our example calculation

Exhibit 4.1

Calculating the Cost of a $10,000 Income Stream for a Sixty-Five-Year-Old Female (Life Only)

Discount Rate: 3.00%

Age	Income	Discount Factor	Discounted Value of Income	Survival Probabilities	Survival-Weighted Discounted Value
65	$10,000	100.0%	$10,000	100.0%	$10,000
66	$10,000	97.1%	$9,709	99.4%	$9,646
67	$10,000	94.3%	$9,426	98.7%	$9,302
68	$10,000	91.5%	$9,151	98.0%	$8,965
69	$10,000	88.8%	$8,885	97.2%	$8,637
70	$10,000	86.3%	$8,626	96.4%	$8,315
71	$10,000	83.7%	$8,375	95.5%	$8,000
72	$10,000	81.3%	$8,131	94.6%	$7,691
73	$10,000	78.9%	$7,894	93.6%	$7,389
74	$10,000	76.6%	$7,664	92.5%	$7,093
75	$10,000	74.4%	$7,441	91.4%	$6,801
—	—	—	—	—	—
95	$10,000	41.2%	$4,120	30.2%	$1,245
96	$10,000	40.0%	$4,000	25.7%	$1,029
97	$10,000	38.8%	$3,883	21.5%	$835
98	$10,000	37.7%	$3,770	17.5%	$660
99	$10,000	36.6%	$3,660	14.0%	$512
100	$10,000	35.5%	$3,554	10.8%	$384
101	$10,000	34.5%	$3,450	8.1%	$280
102	$10,000	33.5%	$3,350	5.9%	$199
103	$10,000	32.5%	$3,252	4.1%	$135
104	$10,000	31.6%	$3,158	2.8%	$89

Cost of Annuity (Sum of Survival-Weighted Discounted Values): **$172,915**

Annuity Payout Rate: **5.78%**

Source: Survival Probabilities are calculated from the Society of Actuaries 2012 Individual Annuitant Mortality Tables with improvements through 2019.

includes some simplifications. With a typical upward-sloping yield curve, payments coming sooner would earn less interest, and later payments would grow at a faster rate. Additionally, many annuity providers will likely seek higher returns than Treasury bonds offer by including high-quality corporate bonds with higher yields to compensate for slightly higher default risk. Annuity providers may also be using more refined mortality data that is better connected to their customer base.

I also assume the full year of spending arrives at the start of each year, rather than having income arriving on a more typical monthly basis. But the simplifications here will capture the concept of annuity pricing well enough.

The 3 percent bond yield and return acts as a discount rate to reduce the value needing to be set aside today for the future $10,000 payments. For instance, the exhibit indicates that at age seventy-five, the discount factor is 74.4 percent. The interpretation is if I put $7,441 in the bank today, and it grows at an annual 3 percent compounding interest rate for the next ten years, I can expect these assets to grow in value to $10,000 by my seventy-fifth birthday. If I was building a bond ladder, this is the amount I would need to invest into a ten-year zero-coupon bond to provide that $10,000 payment.

The process is the same for the $10,000 payment provided at each age. The later payments are received, the more time they have to compound and grow, requiring less to be set aside today to fund those payments.

The next columns are what differentiates an income annuity from a retirement income bond ladder. For a bond ladder, the total cost is the sum of the Discounted Value of Income column, which is $238,082 through age 104. Annuity owners obtain a discount on the bond ladder pricing because the survival probabilities to each subsequent age indicate whether these payments will need to be made. Any one individual is either alive or dead. But for a large pool of individuals representing the customer base of the annuity provider, the company can rely on the law of large numbers to evaluate what percentage of customers will remain alive at each subsequent age. This is risk pooling.

The data from the Society of Actuaries suggests that a sixty-five-year-old female has a 91.4 percent chance of living to seventy-five. An annuity provider can expect 91.4 percent of their sixty-five-year-old female customers to be alive and receiving income at seventy-five. The company does not know who specifically from among their customers will be alive and receiving payments, but they can be pretty confident with their planning that 91.4 percent of their customers will be alive.

When we multiply this percentage by the discounted value of the funds needed to provide the $10,000 payment at seventy-five, we see that the annuity company plans $6,801 for the cost of providing this payment at age seventy-five. This is the survival-probability weighted discount factor, and the same process is followed for each age. For another example, a $10,000 payment at age 100 requires $3,554 to be set aside today with a 3 percent interest rate for the purposes of an individual building a bond ladder. Given that there is a 10.8 percent chance for the sixty-five-year-old female to reach age 100, the annuity provider further multiplies this amount by the survival probability so that the expected costs for a $10,000 survival-contingent payment is only $384. A sixty-five-year-old female need only pay $384 today for a guarantee to receive $10,000 at age 100 if she accepts that receiving the payment is contingent upon her surviving to that age.

When we add survival-weighted costs by age, we see that the total expected cost to provide $10,000 of annual spending to a sixty-five-year-old female, at least through age 104, is $172,915. If this dollar amount represents the premium charged, then the payout rate on the annuity is the $10,000 income it provides divided by this cost. The payout rate is 5.78 percent. Note that this is also 27 percent less than the cost of the bond ladder. The bond ladder costs more, with the benefit that the bond ladder supports some legacy if retirement lasts less than the full ladder length. But the bond ladder does not provide any additional longevity protection beyond the end date of the ladder as assets are fully depleted at that time. With the income annuity, that longevity protection can be provided with 27 percent less funds.

Pricing for an Income Annuity with Period-Certain Payments

We can also consider a few more examples to better understand how this model for annuity pricing can be applied to different annuity flavors. For instance, what happens to the price of this annuity if we guarantee that income will be provided for at least ten years, even if the annuitant does not live that long? This type of provision may be desired for someone worried about an early death.

Practically speaking, to provide ten years of certain income, the only adjustment needed in Exhibit 4.1 is that the Survival Probabilities become 100 percent for the first ten years of payments. The annuitant does not become immortal, but from the perspective of the actuaries who are pricing this annuity, payments must be made regardless of the annuitant's survival status.

Mathematically, there is a 100 percent chance the first ten payments will be made. This raises the cost of the first ten payments. But because there was already a high probability that the annuitant lives for at least ten years, the increase in cost will be relatively minor. The ten-year period-certain provision raises our hypothetical annuity's cost from $172,915 to $175,738. The increased cost lowers the payout rate (which is the initial $10,000 income divided by the cost) from 5.78 percent to 5.69 percent. The reduction in payout rate reflects the reduction of mortality credits that the annuity purchaser has offered to the other participants in the risk pool by requiring that payments are received for at least ten years.

Pricing for an Income Annuity with a Cash Refund Provision

An income annuity with a cash refund is priced in a similar way, though the math becomes a bit more complex. For each age, we must also consider the probability that this age represents the age of death for the annuitant in order to calculate the probability that the cash refund will be provided to the beneficiary at that age. The probability of death is the difference between the survival probability for the next year and the survival probability at the start of the current year. The refund amount declines with age as payments are received and is discounted by the factor for that age.

Exhibit 4.2 shows the more complex set of calculations for pricing an income annuity with a cash refund provision. A cash refund provision for the original life-only annuity from Exhibit 4.1 would raise the cost from $172,915 to $185,784. Its cost is $12,869. The increased cost lowers the payout rate from 5.78 percent to 5.38 percent. Calculating the $185,784 premium requires an iterative process because the cost of the cash refund cannot be known without knowing the payout rate that determines the cash refund amount. But the payout rate cannot be known without knowing the cost of the cash refund.

The basic method to solve for this is to slowly raise the premium level up from the life-only amount until reaching the point where the guess for the premium amount matches the estimated premium from the calculations for the cash refund. In this example, it happens when the premium reaches $185,784.

The trade-off for the cash refund is that while the owner could receive the highest income with a life-only income annuity, he or she can alleviate fears about not living long enough to fully receive back the premium amount through annuity payments by adding the provision which will create an opportunity for the beneficiary to receive this difference in the event of the annuitant's early death. A life-only income annuity offers the highest payout to provide compensation for accepting the risk of an early death. The cash refund means one is contributing fewer mortality credits to the risk pool and should therefore expect to receive fewer mortality credits back in return. This happens through a lower payout rate.

Academics who study income annuities generally suggest a life-only income to fully maximize the income-producing power, with legacy goals covered through other means. But these sorts of period-certain or refund provisions are quite popular in practice, as noted with the overview of Cannex searches. Psychologically, for many it is too difficult to overcome the perceived lack of fairness with a life-only income annuity in which one could die shortly after paying the premium and then receive back little in return.

Pricing for an Income Annuity with Cost-of-Living Increases

Another income annuity option we can price is an annuity offering a cost-of-living adjustment (COLA). Using a COLA requires a minor adjustment to what was shown in Exhibit 4.1. If the COLA is 2 percent, then rather than having a fixed income of $10,000 each year, the annuity instead provides an income which grows by 2 percent each year. If income starts at $10,000 at age sixty-five, it becomes $12,190 at age seventy-five, $14,859 at age eighty-five, and so on. Naturally, having the ability to receive more income over time will raise the overall cost of the income stream.

Exhibit 4.2

Calculating the Cost of a $10,000 Income Stream for a Sixty-Five-Year-Old Female (Life with Cash Refund)

Discount Rate: 3.00%

Age	Income	Discount Factor	Survival Probabilities	Survival-Weighted Discounted Value	Probability of Death	Cumulative Income Received	Refund Amount	Survival-Weighted Discounted Refund
65	$10,000	100.0%	100.0%	$10,000	0.64%	$10,000	$175,784	$1,131
66	$10,000	97.1%	99.4%	$9,646	0.68%	$20,000	$165,784	$1,087
67	$10,000	94.3%	98.7%	$9,302	0.71%	$30,000	$155,784	$1,050
68	$10,000	91.5%	98.0%	$8,965	0.76%	$40,000	$145,784	$1,015
69	$10,000	88.8%	97.2%	$8,637	0.81%	$50,000	$135,784	$981
70	$10,000	86.3%	96.4%	$8,315	0.87%	$60,000	$125,784	$943
71	$10,000	83.7%	95.5%	$8,000	0.93%	$70,000	$115,784	$900
72	$10,000	81.3%	94.6%	$7,691	0.99%	$80,000	$105,784	$853
73	$10,000	78.9%	93.6%	$7,389	1.06%	$90,000	$95,784	$802
74	$10,000	76.6%	92.5%	$7,093	1.14%	$100,000	$85,784	$747
75	$10,000	74.4%	91.4%	$6,801	1.22%	$110,000	$75,784	$690
—	—	—	—	—	—	—	—	—
95	$10,000	41.2%	30.2%	$1,245	4.49%	$310,000	$0	$0
96	$10,000	40.0%	25.7%	$1,029	4.22%	$320,000	$0	$0
97	$10,000	38.8%	21.5%	$835	3.99%	$330,000	$0	$0
98	$10,000	37.7%	17.5%	$660	3.53%	$340,000	$0	$0
99	$10,000	36.6%	14.0%	$512	3.18%	$350,000	$0	$0
100	$10,000	35.5%	10.8%	$384	2.68%	$360,000	$0	$0
101	$10,000	34.5%	8.1%	$280	2.19%	$370,000	$0	$0
102	$10,000	33.5%	5.9%	$199	1.79%	$380,000	$0	$0
103	$10,000	32.5%	4.1%	$135	1.33%	$390,000	$0	$0
104	$10,000	31.6%	2.8%	$89	2.81%	$400,000	$0	$0

Survival-Weighted Present Discounted Value of Income:	$172,915
Survival-Weighted Present Discounted Value of the Cash Refund:	$12,869
Total Cost of Income Annuity:	$185,784
Annuity Payout Rate:	5.38%

Note: Survival Probabilities are calculated from the Society of Actuaries 2012 Individual Annuitant Mortality Tables with improvements through 2019.

In this case, the cost for a 2 percent COLA increases the life-only annuity price from $172,915 to $219,460. While we must remember that income increases over time with this provision, the payout rate for the initial income amount falls from 5.78 percent to 4.56 percent. With a lower payout rate, but 2 percent annual payment growth, the income payment in year thirteen would finally match the initial income payment for the level version if the same premium amount was applied to each contract. It takes twenty-four years before the cumulative payments received are the same with each contract. The trade-off is whether to accept a lower initial income in order to gain the ability to have income grow over time, or to just annuitize less assets to receive the same initial income amount that does not otherwise grow.

By backloading annuity payments, a COLA provision actually increases the amount of mortality credits received. Payments become larger at the time that survival probabilities are less. Nonetheless, income annuities with COLAs are not at all popular in practice. The Cannex survey showed that 95.7 percent of searches were for level payments with no COLAs or CPI adjustments. I believe this is justified. Rather than building in cost-of-living adjustments into the annuity at a higher premium, I do think it makes sense to annuitize less today for the same initial income. Other remaining assets can then be invested to provide a source of inflation protection. Later in retirement, some may find that ongoing expenses are not growing, and so they still have sufficient protected income. Meanwhile, for those who find that inflation is chipping away at the purchasing power of their income annuity, it is always possible to revisit the annuity decision and make another purchase to increase reliable income. I will address this point in greater detail in Chapter 8.

Pricing for Longevity Insurance

Another option is to treat the income annuity as longevity insurance. This involves, for instance, paying for a deferred income annuity at age sixty-five and not receiving payments until a much higher age, such as eighty or eighty-five. With a life-only version of longevity insurance, this really leverages the power of mortality credits, as the costlier nearer-term annuity payments that are more likely to be made have been removed from the calculus.

In Exhibit 4.3, the income provided between ages sixty-five and eighty-four is $0. Annuity payments begin at age eighty-five. The long period for annuitized assets to grow and earn interest combined with the lower probabilities for surviving to these advanced ages results in the annuity cost being dramatically lowered to $32,444. Compared to the immediate life-only income annuity, the cost for guaranteed income has fallen by 81 percent. The payout rate from this annuity is the income divided by the cost, which has grown to 30.8 percent.

Longevity insurance is a unique tool for retirement income considering the relatively small amount of assets required to support such distant spending needs. This allows retirees to better plan for a fixed horizon until income from the deferred annuity begins.

In practice, deferred income annuities are more commonly used to prepay for retirement income, not as longevity insurance. For instance, a fifty-five-year-old might purchase a deferred income annuity which will begin income at sixty-five. We have already determined that the cost of a life-only income annuity at sixty-five is $172,915. If a fifty-five-year-old female wanted to provide lifetime income starting at sixty-five, we could further discount the price in two ways—by the ability to earn interest for ten years before income starts and by the probability that the fifty-five-year-old will live to sixty-five.

The discount factor for ten years of investment growth at 3 percent is 74.4 percent. The same mortality data also reveals a 96.6 percent chance that the fifty-five-year-old lives to sixty-five. Multiplying these two factors by $172,915 gives us a premium of $124,274 for a deferred income annuity purchased at fifty-five. This represents an 8.05 percent payout rate.

Pricing for an 85-Year-Old Female

We looked at longevity insurance as it applies to a sixty-five-year-old female purchasing a deferred income annuity with income starting at eighty-five. We may also consider the alternative of just waiting until age eighty-five and then buying an immediate annuity. During those twenty years, interest rates and mortality tables can change in unexpected ways, which will impact the future pricing calculations.

Calculating the Cost of a $10,000 Deferred Income Stream for a Sixty-Five-Year-Old Female Beginning at Age Eighty-Five (Longevity Insurance, Life Only)

Discount Rate: 3.00%

Age	Income	Discount Factor	Discounted Value of Income	Survival Probabilities	Survival-Weighted Discounted Value
65	$0	100.0%	$0	100.0%	$0
66	$0	97.1%	$0	99.4%	$0
67	$0	94.3%	$0	98.7%	$0
—	—	—	—	—	—
83	$0	58.7%	$0	77.9%	$0
84	$0	57.0%	$0	75.3%	$0
85	$10,000	55.4%	$5,537	72.3%	$4,003
86	$10,000	53.8%	$5,375	69.1%	$3,714
87	$10,000	52.2%	$5,219	65.5%	$3,421
88	$10,000	50.7%	$5,067	61.7%	$3,125
89	$10,000	49.2%	$4,919	57.5%	$2,828
90	$10,000	47.8%	$4,776	53.2%	$2,540
—	—	—	—	—	—
100	$10,000	35.5%	$3,554	10.8%	$384
101	$10,000	34.5%	$3,450	8.1%	$280
102	$10,000	33.5%	$3,350	5.9%	$199
103	$10,000	32.5%	$3,252	4.1%	$135
104	$10,000	31.6%	$3,158	2.8%	$89

Cost of Annuity (Sum of Survival-Weighted Discounted Values): $32,444

Annuity Payout Rate: 30.82%

Note: Survival Probabilities are calculated from the Society of Actuaries 2012 Individual Annuitant Mortality Tables with improvements through 2019.

Exhibit 4.3

Exhibit 4.4 shows the calculated cost for this income annuity if we assume that interest rates and mortality data remain the same (an unlikely outcome, of course). An eighty-five-year-old will experience higher mortality rates and a shorter time horizon, reducing the cost of an income annuity at this age. In this case, the premium is $81,054, which raises the payout rate to 12.34 percent.

This payout rate is noticeably higher than that available at age sixty-five, but it is lower than that available with the longevity insurance contract. Longevity insurance contains two key differences: twenty years of asset growth within the contract and the survival-based discount a sixty-five-year-old receives, thanks to her lessened chance of living to eighty-five to receive income.

Waiting until eighty-five to make the purchase means sharing fewer mortality credits with the risk pool. If we discount this $81,054 premium by the 72.3 percent survival probability from age sixty-five and by twenty years of investment growth at 3 percent (a 55.4 percent discount factor), we arrive at the $32,444 premium (after rounding) for the longevity insurance contract.

◉ Payout Rates and Rates of Return for Income Annuities

The pricing of an income annuity is typically described using either the monthly income amount it generates, or as the annual payout rate of the income received as a percentage of the premium amount. For instance, using the example in Exhibit 4.1, an income annuity might offer $481.67 per month for a $100,000 premium. For twelve months, that sums to $5,780, which is 5.78 percent of the initial premium amount. The annuity payout rate is 5.78 percent. I generally describe annuity pricing using this annual payout rate, as the payout rate is directly comparable to a sustainable withdrawal rate from initial retirement date assets for an investment portfolio. Both rates incorporate the idea that principal is spent in addition to any investment returns.

It is important to recognize that the payout rate is not a *return* on the annuity, which may create some confusion. It is wrong to compare the payout rate to an interest rate that involves the subsequent return of principal. For instance, if you can earn 1 percent by holding a CD and 5.78 percent from an income annuity, the income annuity is not almost six times more powerful than the CD.

Exhibit 4.4

Calculating the Cost of a $10,000 Income Stream for an 85-Year-Old Female (Life-Only)

Discount Rate: 3.00%

Age	Income	Discount Factor	Discounted Value of Income	Survival Probabilities	Survival-Weighted Discounted Value
85	$10,000	1.000	$10,000	100.00%	$10,000
86	$10,000	0.971	$9,709	95.56%	$9,278
87	$10,000	0.943	$9,426	90.66%	$8,546
88	$10,000	0.915	$9,151	85.31%	$7,807
89	$10,000	0.888	$8,885	79.53%	$7,066
90	$10,000	0.863	$8,626	73.56%	$6,345
91	$10,000	0.837	$8,375	67.30%	$5,636
92	$10,000	0.813	$8,131	61.02%	$4,961
93	$10,000	0.789	$7,894	54.57%	$4,308
94	$10,000	0.766	$7,664	48.23%	$3,697
95	$10,000	0.744	$7,441	41.80%	$3,110
96	$10,000	0.722	$7,224	35.59%	$2,571
97	$10,000	0.701	$7,014	29.75%	$2,087
98	$10,000	0.681	$6,810	24.23%	$1,650
99	$10,000	0.661	$6,611	19.34%	$1,279
100	$10,000	0.642	$6,419	14.95%	$959
101	$10,000	0.623	$6,232	11.24%	$700
102	$10,000	0.605	$6,050	8.20%	$496
103	$10,000	0.587	$5,874	5.73%	$336
104	$10,000	0.570	$5,703	3.89%	$222

Cost of Annuity (Sum of Survival-Weighted Discounted Values): $81,054

Annuity Payout Rate: **12.34%**

Note: Survival Probabilities are calculated from the Society of Actuaries 2012 Individual Annuitant Mortality Tables with improvements through 2019.

The problem is that the 1 percent number for the CD only represents its interest payments. The principal value is returned at maturity. Meanwhile, a 5.78 percent payout from an annuity includes interest and principal payments (as well as mortality credits—the true source of additional returns beyond that provided by a fixed-income alternative). Principal is being spent as well, and so the comparison to the CD rate is neither fair nor meaningful. The annuity does have a return, but it is less straightforward to calculate.

To know the annuity *return*, it is necessary to know how long the annuitant will live and how many annuity payments will be generated. Or, at least, returns can only be calculated by assuming how long income payments will be received. A longer life means more payments from the annuity, which helps to increase the return it provides. And if the underlying investments in the general account provide a higher return, that feeds into a higher annuity payout rate, which helps to boost the annuity's return more quickly as well. For life-only annuities, returns will be very low early on as relatively little income has been received relative to the premium amount. With enough time, the return can eventually exceed the payout rate.

Annuity returns are determined by the internal rate of return (IRR) on their cash flows. The IRR is a mathematical calculation which looks at the inflows and outflows of money over time and calculates the investment return that would be needed to precisely allow the inflows of funds to grow sufficiently so they can support the subsequent outflows of funds.
For example, suppose one deposits $1,000 into a bank today. In each subsequent year on the anniversary of this bank deposit, the owner withdraws $150 from the bank account. This continues annually until the ninth withdrawal, at which point the bank account balance falls to zero. In total, the owner received $1,350, but these cash flows were received at different points of time. What interest rate must the owner earn on the remaining savings in the bank account to make this stream of nine $150 withdrawals work out as planned? Answering this involves an internal rate of return calculation, and it is the same process we will use to calculate the return on an annuity. Exhibit 4.5 shows how to set up this calculation in Excel. The answer is 6.46 percent. If the bank account provides this annual compounded return on remaining funds, the $1,000 will have sufficient growth to provide the nine $150 payments.

The Insurance Company's General Account

As we discuss the returns from an income annuity, now is a good time to address the underlying investment returns that the insurance company earns by investing the premiums it receives for income annuities. Premiums can be invested until it is time to make the annuity payments. The returns that the insurance company expects to earn do feed into the payout rate offered, with a higher return helping to support a higher payout rate.

When an insurance company receives a customer's premium for purchasing an income annuity, it invests those funds in its general account. General account investments are designed with asset-liability matching in mind. Actuaries have a sense of the insurance company's payment obligations to support annuity payments, life insurance death benefits, and other insurance claims, and their investments are chosen to support these anticipated cash outflows. The general account is highly regulated with respect to the amount of assets to be maintained relative to liabilities and to asset allocation. Assets must be sufficient to fund policy claims after accounting for future premiums and investment returns. General account investments typically include corporate and government bonds, mortgages, loans, a small allocation to equities, and potentially other types of alternative investments.

If we think strictly about returns for the general account and the comparable returns on fixed-income assets that a household could generate on its own, the general account may be able to achieve higher returns than the household.

Regarding the underlying portfolio of assets, the general account of the insurance company is better positioned than the household to manage the risks involved in earning higher fixed-income returns by accepting greater duration, illiquidity, and credit risk. The general account can maintain a longer-term investment focus with assets held to maturity, and with less liquidity required, that can offer higher yields than households could otherwise muster within their own fixed-income portfolios. Because insurance companies generally hold the fixed-income assets to maturity, rising rates will not trigger realized capital losses, but will instead allow new premiums to be invested at a higher rate. As well, insurance companies obtain lower institutional pricing on their trades and can better diversify their holdings among corporate bonds offering higher yields and greater credit risk.

The general account has greater return potential through its ability to invest in longer-term and less liquid assets, and to diversify the credit risk of higher-yielding corporate bonds. Households have less capacity to diversify and manage these risks. Asset values for households are too small, their timeframes are too short, and their liquidity needs are too high to compete with the return potential of the general account. This provides an additional benefit from the income annuity in that its payout is based on a higher assumed investment return than the household could reasonably assume while maintaining the same level of risk for the underlying asset base.

Exhibit 4.5

An Internal Rate of Return Calculation Example

Time Period	Cash Flow
0	-$1,000
1	$150
2	$150
3	$150
4	$150
5	$150
6	$150
7	$150
8	$150
9	$150
Internal Rate of Return:	6.46%

Exhibit 4.6

An Internal Rate of Return Calculation Example (in Reverse)

Investment Return: 6.46%

Time Period	Cash Flow	Account Balance
0	$1,000	$1,065
1	-$150	$974
2	-$150	$877
3	-$150	$774
4	-$150	$664
5	-$150	$547
6	-$150	$423
7	-$150	$291
8	-$150	$150
9	-$150	$0

Perhaps the internal rate of return can be understood more clearly by working in the reverse direction. Suppose I deposit $1,000 in the bank, and it earns an annual interest rate of 6.46 percent. On each anniversary of my deposit, I withdraw $150 from the account. The account balance grows with interest but shrinks with withdrawals. When I take out the $150 withdrawal in year nine, the account balance falls to zero, as expected. Exhibit 4.6 illustrates why the internal rate of return is 6.46 percent.

To understand the distinction between the payout rate and the return on an annuity, we can consider the simple annuity example from Exhibit 4.1 for a sixty-five-year-old female. She purchases a life-only income annuity with a 5.78 percent payout rate. For a premium of $100, a payment of $5.78 is received immediately, and on each anniversary date of the contract an additional payment of $5.78 is received for as long as the annuitant lives.

The returns by age are shown in Exhibit 4.7. Returns start out negative, as cumulative payments fall short of the premium paid. The return crosses from negative to positive with the payment received seventeen years later at age eighty-two. This is seen in Exhibit 4.7. The point at which the return becomes positive is intuitive because with payments starting at sixty-five, the age eighty-two payment is the 17th received, which pushes the total amount of income received to $104.04 (17 x 5.78). This surpasses the initial $100 premium. We have entered the range of positive returns.

With the age eighty-eight payment, the return exceeds 3 percent, which was the assumed return on the underlying assets. Age ninety represents the median life expectancy for a sixty-five-year-old female, and with this payment the return increases to 3.6 percent. Thus, the contract owner has a greater than 50 percent chance that the return on the annuity will exceed the 3 percent return on fixed-income assets because the owner is also receiving mortality credits which are amortized over the life of the annuitant. If the annuitant lives to ninety-five, the return grows to 4.49 percent, and it continues to rise. Eventually, the return will grow to exceed the initial payout rate. This happens sooner when interest rates are higher.

With our 3 percent interest rate, the return does not exceed the payout rate until sometime after age 110, so in this case it is not realistic to discuss the payout rate in the same terms as a rate of return from the annuity. Nonetheless, the most interesting aspect of this analysis is that even before life expectancy, the return from an income annuity exceeds the return from holding a portfolio of bonds without any mortality credits.

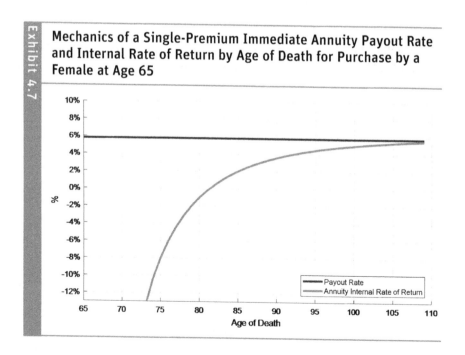

Exhibit 4.7

Mechanics of a Single-Premium Immediate Annuity Payout Rate and Internal Rate of Return by Age of Death for Purchase by a Female at Age 65

Exhibit 4.8 provides returns over time for different flavors of the income annuity example we have used to help illustrate the trade-offs in terms of mortality credits offered and received. The three annuity flavors are the life-only version with a 5.78 percent payout rate, the life with ten-year period certain with a 5.69 percent payout rate, and the life with cash refund version with a 5.38 percent payout rate.

Compared to the life-only income annuity, the two other flavors increase the returns in the event of a short life with the trade-off that the returns are reduced in the event of a long life. For life with ten-year period certain, payments will be provided for at least ten years, even if the annuitant dies before that time. This leads the return for the first ten years to match the return at ten years. Those payments were not life contingent. Then, subsequently, returns grow with the length of life, but since the payout rate is less, the returns over time are also slightly less as well.

As for the income annuity with a cash refund, the return will be zero until the full premium has been repaid because the cash refund covers the difference at earlier ages. The return is zero because cash inflows match cash outflows. Then, after age eighty-two, returns become positive because cumulative payments exceed the premium. The returns continue

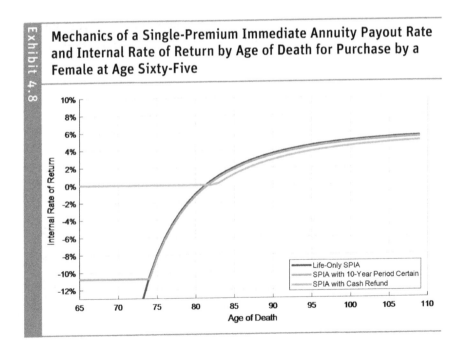

Exhibit 4.8

Mechanics of a Single-Premium Immediate Annuity Payout Rate and Internal Rate of Return by Age of Death for Purchase by a Female at Age Sixty-Five

to grow with age of death, but they always lag the returns for the other two flavors because the payout rate is less. By receiving the protections for a shorter retirement, the annuity owner has offered less mortality credits to the risk pool and therefore receives less mortality credits back from the risk pool in the event of a long life.

○ Money's Worth Measures for Income Annuities

Annuities have a reputation for being a high-fee financial product. Is this reputation deserved? We address this for different types of annuities throughout the book, starting with income annuities. It is a bit complicated to answer this for income annuities because they do not have visible fees. There are no additional fees extracted from the quoted payout rate, as the payout rate is a net number after fees have been deducted internally. Simply, with the internal fees, the quoted payout rate is lower than it could have otherwise been.

Fortunately, we can reverse engineer the fair price for an income annuity without fees and then compare it with real-world annuity payout rates in order to obtain a money's worth measure for the income annuity. We have already seen how to calculate annuity prices. The additional complication relates to making reasonable assumptions for interest rates and mortality rates.

It can be difficult for consumers to get a handle on the sorts of fees and costs that are paid as part of purchasing an income annuity. Some states may place a small tax (ranging from 0.5 percent to 3 percent) on annuity premiums taken from outside retirement plans, but annuity costs are otherwise incorporated into the quoted prices and not explicitly charged from the premium.

Costs are not transparent. For example, a $100,000 premium may be quoted as supporting $600 per month for life. Without any built-in fees, perhaps the fair monthly income could have been $610 or $620. At the same time, perhaps the household could not invest for as much yield as the insurance company or might have an unusually long expected lifespan, such that a more personalized fair monthly income is only $580 or $590. In this case, the annuity provides a great deal. These matters are not transparent unless we are able to calculate the actuarially fair price for an annuity and then compare it to the actual price.

Fortunately, this reverse engineering process lets one estimate the costs built into an income annuity. If an income annuity provides $600 per month, but we simulate that a fair price is to provide $610 per month, then the money's worth of the annuity is $600 / $610 = 0.9836. In this case, the commercial annuity pays 1.64 percent less than the fair price. We could interpret this 1.64 percent as an upfront transaction cost or onetime fee for purchasing the annuity.

In some cases, we may calculate fair annuity payouts as lower than what commercial companies provide, which would lead the money's worth measure to be larger than one, indicating a particularly good deal for the purchaser. These good deals may exist because income annuities tend to be a small part of the insurance company's overall business, and actuaries may be slow in updating their pricing in response to fluctuating interest rates and longevity estimates. It is also possible that the insurance company anticipates earning a higher yield from the general account investments, which could also justify better payout to customers than they could otherwise achieve with their own investments. Alternatively, an individual may enjoy better overall longevity prospects than the average member of the annuity risk pool.

For a more practical real-world example of this, in January 2019, the actual payout rate on a life-only immediate annuity for a sixty-five-year-old female as described in Exhibit 4.1 is 6.52 percent, according to ImmediateAnnuities.com. The payout rate we calculated is 5.78 percent. If our interest rate and mortality assumptions properly reflected the prospects facing the insurance company when making their pricing decision, then this income annuity appears to be a great deal. The actual payout rate of 6.52 percent divided by our estimated payout rate of 5.78 percent is 1.128. We actually get 12.8 percent more income from the commercial annuity than we expected to be able to receive as based on our assumptions. To calibrate the actual payout rate with our mortality data, a flat yield curve of 4.15 percent is needed, instead of the 3 percent used in that exhibit.

Separate from the objective money's worth measure, it is important to also consider the subjective value being received by the annuity owner. For those with longevity risk aversion, the prospects of spending from investments may be such that an income annuity could still support more spending than the retiree otherwise would be comfortable taking from investments. Just because money's worth measures are less than one does not necessarily mean that income annuities are a bad deal.

If retirees value the certainty provided by guaranteed lifetime income, they may value income annuities at more than their fair price. The income annuity provides risk pooling and mortality credits that an individual cannot create on their own. Conservative retirees who are worried about outliving their money and timid about investing aggressively in the stock market could easily decide that they are willing to pay more than the estimated costs derived from these money's worth measures. Because of the certainty of income provided, I might still derive benefit even if the money's worth measure was only 0.7, for instance. If so, then an actual money's worth measure of 0.85, for instance, would be still be attractive.

The general account of the insurance company also has the potential to invest for higher rates while still maintaining a high degree of safety in ways that may not be accessible to the household. We must consider three issues: how much does the retiree value mortality credits, could the retiree earn a 4.15 percent return from their own investments with the same risk level as the annuity, and how does the retiree's personal views about longevity compare with that of the overall risk pool?

Purchasing income annuities can be a win-win situation both for the consumer and the insurance company, as the benefits created through risk pooling are shared between both parties in the transaction. This is the same idea as how one may derive value from owning a mutual fund even after paying the expense ratio because it would not be possible to create such diversification with limited household assets.

More generally, what I have just described is true for any consumer good or service. If a producer can provide the good or service for more cheaply than I could achieve when trying to create it on my own, while still being able to generate a profit through their specialization and economies of scale that I do not have access to, but for a lower price than I value it, then I could derive a net benefit. The transaction is mutually beneficial for both parties. It is important not to forget this fundamental axiom of capitalism applies for insurance as well.

The previous sections explained how to calculate the price for an income annuity. To do a proper money's worth calculation, though, we must be more detailed and specific about the appropriate assumptions to make regarding interest rates and mortality data. What longevity data is most relevant to the annuity owner? How could the owner have invested the premium while maintaining a similar level of market risk if left to his or her own devices? The answers are not clear cut.

Insurance Company Expenses

The annuity provider cannot be expected to offer an income annuity for the actuarially fair price and hope to remain in business. This does not mean that individuals with lesser investment prospects or greater longevity prospects could not find that their personalized money's worth from an income annuity is greater than one. But it does mean that an annuitant with an identical longevity profile as the typical customer and who could invest their assets in an identical way as the insurance company must expect a money's worth measure of less than one. Having the provider stay in business is a natural desire for the purchaser who wants to receive those payments for life. The provider will need to charge more than the fair price to cover business expenses.

Insurance companies face typical business expenses to pay employees and to create a workplace just like any company. As well, insurance companies generally pay a onetime commission of around 2 or 3 percent to the insurance agent on record as having sold the annuity, and this must be covered from premiums. While fee-only financial advisors cannot accept commissions, they could direct a client to purchase an income annuity from a third-party insurance company using the annuity platform from a major online brokerage firm. That brokerage firm might receive a 1 percent commission, and the company supporting the platform might receive a 1 percent commission, for instance.

Additional financial buffers are also needed to protect from the possibility that the insurer has misestimated their risks, as annuity pricing requires long-term projections for interest rates and mortality rates. If interest rates end up lower than expected—or if health improvements accelerate faster and customers live even longer than projected—the actual costs to the insurance companies of providing the guaranteed income will be higher than the estimated costs used to calculate premiums.

Unexpected longevity improvements can be partially offset for an annuity provider who also sells life insurance—systematic increases in longevity mean more claims on annuities but fewer claims on life insurance—but these risks cannot be completely neutralized. As a part of their risk management, the provider needs additional reserves that raise the overhead charge on the annuity and reduce the money's worth measure.

Interest Rate Assumptions

A key question we must consider for determining the money's worth from an income annuity for an individual is to decide whether that individual could invest in the same portfolio and earn the same returns as the insurance company can obtain for its general account. The insurance company may be able to obtain higher investment yields because of its ability to diversify among higher-yielding bonds with greater credit risk, to use asset-liability matching to hold less liquid and longer-term bonds, and to receive institutional pricing on their purchases and to avoid the pricing mark-ups faced by retail investors.

We might consider pricing annuities with Treasury bond yields or corporate bond yields. Corporate bond yields tend to be higher, and higher bond yields will support a higher annuity payout rate. For this reason, simulating annuity prices with corporate bond yields will result in a lower money's worth measure than otherwise. But could an individual create the same type of diversified ladder of corporate bonds at the same cost as the insurance company?

An assumption that could better approximate reality is that insurance companies could earn corporate bond yields on their general account, while households should assume Treasury bond yields for what their fixed-income assets could generate, at least net-of-fees. This assumption will improve money's worth measures and could even lead them to exceed one (i.e. annuity purchasers should not really be worried about fees from the annuity). This outcome is being driven by the differing investment prospects of households and insurance companies when it comes to potential fixed-income returns. For households who truly believe that they could earn higher fixed-income returns on their own, this would reduce the money's worth measures for income annuities.

As well, Jeffrey Brown, Olivia Mitchell, James Poterba, and Mark Warshawsky wrote in their 2000 book *The Role of Annuity Markets in Financing Retirement*, that it is easier for annuity providers to support better pricing relative to other fixed-income assets when interest rates are low and steady. This allows the provider to get a better sense about what future interest rates will be, and if rates tend to rise from their low point then the future pooled assets of the insurance fund will benefit.

In contrast, if interest rates are high and variable, insurance companies may worry about a future rate decrease making it more expensive to fund future payments. They may decide to hold more reserves to help protect assets from this risk. This would mean less competitive pricing for the annuity. Because insurance companies tend to hold the fixed-income assets in their portfolios to maturity, they are less exposed to interest rate risk (needing to lock in capital losses by selling bonds at a loss after interest rates rise) and more exposed to reinvestment risk (it becomes more expensive to buy bonds in the future to cover liabilities if interest rates decrease). Shortly, we will investigate historical and current money's worth measures for annuities, and this may serve as one of the explanations for why money's worth measures are improved at the present.

If the insurance company has better investment prospects than the typical household investor, this can be a way to offset some of the fees of the annuity and to increase their money's worth measures.

Mortality Assumptions

Annuity owners tend to live longer than the average person. In large part, this can be explained by adverse selection, which is the idea that those who purchase annuities tend to have a sense that they may have above average longevity prospects. Those with terminal illnesses will probably not be in the market to buy income annuities.

Annuity customers are more likely to live longer and, therefore, increase the costs to the insurer for providing the lifetime guaranteed payments. Income annuities are not generally medically underwritten, unlike with life insurance, and purchasers will have a better sense about their own longevity than the insurance company. The insurance company must base its pricing on the average mortality of the risk pool, which is its collection of customers. Lower mortality rates lead to increased longevity, which leads to an increased cost for the insurer to guarantee lifetime income.

It is important to be realistic about longevity when determining whether an income annuity is priced fairly. Someone who can reasonably expect to live longer than average should not try to calculate a fair price using population-average mortality. If annuity prices are simulated with mortality rates for the general population, that will cause the money's worth measures to be lower and annuities to look more expensive. This leads to an inappropriate conclusion that the annuity is overpriced.

My readers will tend to display characteristics that are associated with increased longevity, such as higher education levels, more income, greater wealth, and a stronger health focus. When this is the case, money's worth estimates based on mortality tables reflecting the longer lifespans of annuitants are more reasonable to use. The Society of Actuaries data described in Chapter 1 is a reasonable starting point. One cannot expect a payout rate as calculated with the longevity of the average person because the average person does not buy an annuity and is not part of the risk pool.

Longevity Risk Aversion and the Power of Mortality Credits

Finally, there is a subtle psychological point to consider regarding longevity estimates. The previous section sought insight into an individual's objective longevity estimates. In their March/April 2011 *Financial Analysts Journal* article titled "Spending Retirement on Planet Vulcan: The Impact of Longevity Risk Aversion on Optimal Withdrawal Rates," Moshe Milevsky and Huaxiong Huang describe longevity risk aversion as the fear people have about outliving their assets in retirement. This fear is manifested by having individuals behave as though they will live much longer than objective mortality data would suggest. They build financial plans that will last to advanced ages well beyond their life expectancy.

With an investments-only strategy, this longevity risk aversion is manifested through a lower spending rate from investment assets. Because income annuities pool longevity risk, they can help to reduce the worry individuals have about outliving their assets. The income annuity payout is based on objective mortality statistics rather than subjective fears. Annuity payouts stay the same, even for individuals who subjectively worry about a much longer life and who would otherwise spend less from investments.

The case for an income annuity becomes stronger for individuals more worried about longevity. Their retirement spending can be linked to more objective measures of mortality, rather than the lower mortality rates introduced through the psychological fears related to longevity risk aversion. This concept is harder to work into calculations of money's worth measures, except to note that even when money's worth measures are less than one, it does not necessarily mean that an individual is not receiving value from the ability to pool and manage longevity risk.

One way to see this concept applied in practice regards building a financial plan in financial planning software. Someone with longevity risk aversion may choose to build a financial plan through age 100, despite the low probability of living to this advanced age. Adding an income annuity to the financial plan can show improved outcomes in part because the annuity could be worth more than it costs within the financial plan.

The annuity provider calculates the price of the annuity based on objective mortality characteristics that would account for the rarity of living to age 100. But the financial plan assumes that annuity income will be received through age 100, leading the present value of the annuity payments in the financial plan to be greater than the actual purchase price of the annuity. This shows the subtle way in which annuities can create greater value for those who are worried about outliving their assets and therefore plan to live longer than average.

Historical Estimates of Money's Worth Measures

This discussion has provided the backdrop for considering actual money's worth measures. First, we look at past academic estimates, and then I update estimates for the present. Researchers Jeffrey Brown, Olivia Mitchell, James Poterba, and Mark Warshawsky provided an investigation of money's worth calculations in a 1999 article that was subsequently republished in their book, *The Role of Annuity Markets in Financing Retirement*. This article created the concept of money's worth measures as a tool for understanding the implicit costs for an income annuity.

To give one example from their analysis of 1995 data, they found that for a sixty-five-year-old couple with a joint and 100 percent survivor's life-only annuity, the money's worth measures were as follows based on the assumptions used:

- With population-wide mortality table and the Treasury yield curve: 0.868
- With population-wide mortality table and the Corporate yield curve: 0.792
- With the annuitant mortality table and the Treasury yield curve: 0.929
- With the annuitant mortality table and the Corporate yield curve: 0.841

As should be expected from our previous discussion, the annuity is priced most attractively when using the annuitant mortality table and assuming that the underlying funds are invested in Treasury bonds. As noted, while this scenario does make the income annuity look the best, it is worth considering that this may be the most appropriate and fairest set of assumptions for readers to use when deciding on the value of the income annuity.

In this case, the 0.929 value means that the pricing on the commercial annuity provides 92.9 percent of the income that could be expected from a fair priced annuity. By using the annuitant mortality table, the impact of adverse selection has been removed from the calculations, so that the 7.1 percent difference represents the cost or fee for the annuity that covers company expenses, the build-up of additional reserves for risk management, and company profit. As we have noted, the insurance company is likely generating a better outcome than this estimate because of its ability to invest in higher yielding assets than Treasury bonds, but we assume that the household does not have access to such opportunities after accounting for fees and the level of risk.

Next, when using the Treasury yield curve with population-wide mortality, the money's worth ratio is 0.868. The further difference of 0.061 (or 6.1 percent) can be attributed to the impact of adverse selection in the annuity purchasing population: annuity purchasers do tend to live longer than the average person and pricing must reflect this. While this number would be more appropriate for the typical person with average longevity prospects, the typical person reading this book will experience better longevity prospects than average. This calculation is less relevant for my readers.

As well, when switching to higher yielding corporate bonds relative to Treasury bonds, the money's worth measures decline because the higher yielding corporates would support more income on an actuarially fair basis. With the annuitant mortality table and the corporate yield curve, the money's worth measure is 0.841, implying an internal charge of 15.9 percent. While this number better reflects what the insurance company is expected to obtain from the sale, this does not account for the additional difficulty and credit risk that would be assumed by an individual trying to purchase the same corporate bond ladder to fund retirement income.

The final number in the table, for the population-wide mortality table and the corporate yield curve, is 0.792. This is the lowest money's worth measure, implying an internal charge of 20.8 percent. But it is not particularly relevant for my readers. It would be the prospects facing an average American who could obtain the higher net-returns from corporate bonds during retirement.

Current Estimates of Money's Worth Measures

We now update money's worth measures to January 2019. Exhibits 4.9 and 4.10 show money's worth measures for life-only immediate annuities and longevity insurance. For the real-world commercial income annuities, payout rates were obtained from www.ImmediateAnnuities.com on January 10, 2019. The premium amount is $100,000. Purchases are assumed to be made in Georgia, which is a state that does not tax annuity premiums. Joint annuities assume full continuation of benefits for the survivor. Prices reflect the best available offer on that date from among insurance companies with at least an A credit rating.

For the simulated annuity prices, mortality data is based on cohort life tables from the Social Security Administration. These cohort life tables are provided for birth years in intervals of ten years, and the assumed birth year at each age is rounded accordingly to use the closest available life table.

Unlike the more common Social Security period tables, these cohort tables reflect assumed mortality improvements over time. But they are for the general population rather than the subset of annuity purchasers. Though annuity purchasers mostly enjoy greater longevity, use of the annuitant mortality tables leads to money's worth measures much greater than one, suggesting that annuity companies are either not expecting Society of Actuaries data to apply, or they have not otherwise updated their mortality data to reflect these longevity improvements. Interest rate assumptions are based on the yield curve for Treasury strips as of the start of 2019. For payments beyond thirty years, the thirty-year yield is projected to apply at subsequent maturities.

Exhibit 4.9 provides results for life-only immediate annuities purchased at different ages for couples (joint), males, and females. Payout rates are first shown for commercial annuities offered through ImmediateAnnuities. com. Next, I provide simulated annuity payout rates for the mortality and interest rate assumptions described. These simulations provide my effort to calculate an actuarially fair price for the annuity. Finally, money's worth measures are shown. They represent the ratio of the payout rate on the commercial annuity divided by the payout rate on the simulated annuity. If the ratio is larger than one, we can conclude that the commercial annuity provides a good deal relative to the actuarially fair pricing (which should not happen on a regular basis). A ratio smaller than one allows us to observe an estimate for the implicit costs built into the prices of commercial annuities, noting our philosophical points regarding how to make a fair comparison. The difference reflects both the impacts of adverse selection and the costs of business and risk management for the annuity provider.

For life-only immediate annuities, we can observe several trends. First, money's worth measures decrease with age and tend to be the highest for couples, followed by females, and then males.

These observations reflect the idea that money's worth measures are larger when average remaining longevity is higher. Income guarantees are riskier for insurance companies at advanced ages because longevity risk increases. While remaining longevity is shortened with age, the range of potential lifespans around the average widens on a relative basis with age.

Exhibit 4.9

Estimated Money's Worth for Life-Only Immediate Annuities in January 2019

		Age in January 2019						
		55	60	65	70	75	80	85
Payout Rate, Commercial Annuity	Joint	5.09%	5.38%	5.80%	6.38%	7.31%	8.86%	11.14%
	Male	5.65%	6.16%	6.83%	7.80%	9.29%	11.60%	15.53%
	Female	5.50%	5.93%	6.52%	7.37%	8.69%	10.60%	13.93%
Payout Rate, Simulated Annuity	Joint	4.17%	4.52%	4.98%	5.62%	6.57%	8.02%	10.26%
	Male	4.74%	5.24%	5.92%	6.89%	8.35%	10.61%	14.16%
	Female	4.57%	5.04%	5.65%	6.50%	7.76%	9.72%	12.77%
Money's Worth	Joint	1.2200	1.1896	1.1641	1.1353	1.1123	1.1044	1.0855
	Male	1.1926	1.1740	1.1533	1.1322	1.1120	1.0936	1.0967
	Female	1.2020	1.1769	1.1541	1.1342	1.1201	1.0898	1.0913

Notes: Payout rates for commercially available income annuities were accessed at www.ImmediateAnnuities.com on January 10, 2019. See text for simulated annuity assumptions.

One year of additional life has a much bigger impact when the insurance company expects a person to live five more years as compared to twenty more years. Insurance companies must set aside more reserves to cope with this risk, which reduces the money's worth measures.

As well, these money's worth measures are larger than one. This requires comment, as we must deal with the philosophical issues and potential disagreements around the appropriate assumptions to be used for the purpose of calculating actuarially fair pricing for income annuities. We cannot expect money's worth measures to remain greater than one in equilibrium as that would cause insurance companies to consistently lose money. Consumers should not expect to receive the entire value of risk pooling, just as they do not receive the entire value from their investments after accounting for fees. But at the present pricing appears reasonable from the consumer's perspective if we suppose that the investment alternative for the consumer is treasuries.

Next, Exhibit 4.10 provides corresponding results for longevity insurance, in which a sixty-five-year-old purchases a life-only income annuity that will begin paying income at a later age ranging from sixty-five (for comparison) to eighty-five. These money's worth measures are also greater than one and peak at age seventy-five.

The assumptions I used to reflect money's worth were based on what consumers might be expected to manage when investing on their own when not taking advantage of the more diversified and higher-yielding asset base held by the insurance company. To the extent that insurance companies can earn more than Treasury bonds on the invested premiums, this would effectively lower the money's worth measures from their perspective, helping to ensure their sustainability. But because consumers cannot invest that way on their own, such matters are not relevant when trying to investigate money's worth from the consumers perspective and to decide whether income annuities provide a good deal.

◉ The Annuity Puzzle: Other Issues Impacting the Annuity Decision

This discussion has been fairly positive with regard to the role of income annuities as a retirement income tool. My explanations follow standard

Exhibit 4.10

Estimated Money's Worth for Longevity Insurance (Life Only) in January 2019

		Longevity Insurance for 65 Year-Old, Age that Income Begins				
		65	70	75	80	85
Payout Rate, Commercial Annuity	Joint	5.80%	7.87%	11.53%	16.81%	not avail.
	Male	6.83%	9.95%	15.95%	25.38%	44.90%
	Female	6.52%	9.00%	13.79%	21.28%	36.47%
Payout Rate, Simulated Annuity	Joint	4.98%	6.53%	8.99%	13.24%	21.85%
	Male	5.92%	8.20%	12.09%	19.42%	35.93%
	Female	5.65%	7.69%	11.09%	17.24%	30.39%
Money's Worth	Joint	1.1641	1.2050	1.2825	1.2698	not avail.
	Male	1.1533	1.2129	1.3194	1.3068	1.2497
	Female	1.1541	1.1696	1.2438	1.2340	1.2000

Notes: See notes provided with Exhibit 4.9.

Social Security as an Annuity

With this discussion of income annuities, it is worthwhile to provide a reminder that Social Security is also an income annuity. Social Security retirement benefits are provided for life. As a government-backed, inflation-adjusted monthly income for life, Social Security benefits help to manage longevity risk, inflation risk, and market risk. Social Security also provides survivor benefits. Social Security is generally one of the largest assets on the retirement balance sheet. For a high-earning couple, the present value of lifetime Social Security benefits could exceed $1 million.

Retirement benefits can begin as early as age sixty-two, but the benefits grow with delay credits through age seventy for those willing to wait. If one views the lost benefits from ages sixty-two to sixty-nine as a premium to buy a larger annuity income starting at seventy, delaying Social Security can be viewed as the best annuity money can buy. By delaying Social Security for those eight years, the lifetime subsequent Social Security benefit will be 76 percent larger, implying a payout rate higher than private insurance companies are able to provide.

Delaying Social Security should be the first step for anyone considering income annuities as part of their retirement income plan. Starting Social Security early and buying an income annuity is inefficient. The first step to including annuities in a retirement income plan is to delay Social Security benefits, at least for the high earner in a couple. Then a decision can be made about whether even more protected income is desirable for the financial plan.

academic theory regarding income annuities and their role in pooling longevity risk and providing mortality credits. Without this risk pooling, retirees must be needlessly conservative in their spending to ensure they still have something left if they live well beyond their life expectancy.

For this reason, economists have long wondered why people do not make greater use of income annuities as retirement income tools. Often cited in connection with this bafflement are Menahem Yaari's research from 1965 about spending for an uncertain lifetime, and Franco Modigliani's Nobel Prize acceptance speech addressing the subject in 1985.

In *The 7 Most Important Equations for Your Retirement*, Moshe Milevsky described this mystery in the words of Wharton professor Solomon Huebner, the founder of The American College, who first defined the basic puzzle in the 1930s:

> The prospect, amounting almost to a terror, of living too long makes necessary the keeping of the entire principal intact to the very end, so that, as a final wind-up, the savings of a lifetime, which the owner does not dare to enjoy, will pass as an inheritance to others. In view of these facts, it is surprising that so few have undertaken to enjoy, without fear, the fruits of the limited competency they have succeeded in accumulating. This can be done only through annuities ... Why exist on $600, assuming 3 percent interest on $20,000, and then live in fear, when $1,600 may be obtained annually at age sixty-five, through an annuity for all of life and minus all the fear?

The annuity puzzle, as defined by academic economists, regards why income annuities are not more widely used. Numerous explanations have been offered, some more legitimate than others. One obvious starting point for resolving the puzzle is that many retirees may wish to build a legacy. Maximizing personal spending is not the only goal. The desire to leave a legacy may be a strong deterrent from annuitizing for those who have not fully thought through the implications of different alternative approaches that do not include annuities. When not accounting for the other retirement liabilities that must be funded, it is easy to conclude that investments can support the largest legacy. We explain the problem with this conclusion in Chapter 8.

It is important to also think about the dual impacts of investment volatility. One might expect the uncertainty of investment returns to motivate greater annuity use as a protection, but there could be another countervailing force at work. Income annuities remove downside risks, but they also eliminate upside for those assets. The annuity decision carries a sense of finality as one is forever removing the possibility of picking the next winning stock and striking it rich. For hopeful retirees, that loss of potential financial betterment can be a deal breaker. It is important to remember, though, that an annuity is not an all-or-nothing decision.

What's more, real-world annuities will have overhead charges as insurance providers must cover expenses, make a profit, and account for adverse selection and misestimation risks. These costs reduce payout rates and the potential gains from annuitization. Nonetheless, as we have discussed, the fees built into income annuities do not appear as large as may be commonly thought.

In addition, the standard economics model does not ascribe importance to the idea that retirees may value the ability to maintain flexibility and control over their financial wealth. Preferences, needs, and circumstances may change, so holding off on making the irreversible decision to annuitize holds value for many. The extra control may be partly an illusion, since retirees face spending needs that must be met and risks of wealth depletion that must be mitigated. Nonetheless, the behavioral need to feel like one is in control is important. Income annuities may create the perception that one is losing control over their hard-earned assets.

Another possible behavioral explanation is the feeling of being poorer after annuitization because of the resulting noticeably lower remaining account balance. This confuses total wealth with the spending power available from that wealth, but it can exert a powerful psychological influence on decisions. Individuals rarely like to see a drop in the value of their financial assets. It is not fun to see $1 million on a financial statement one month and $800,000 the next. Visually, this is what happens with the purchase of an income annuity. The lump-sum paid for the lifetime income protection is removed from the financial portfolio, even though the lifetime income stream is an asset whose present value could be included on the more complete retirement balance sheet. It is not common for individuals to think in these holistic terms.

Curtis Cloke provides a descriptive visual about this behavioral thinking: he calls it the "Scrooge McDuck effect." Envision Scrooge McDuck diving into his vault of gold coins. He loves to touch and feel his money. This is what we are describing. People like seeing a big number on their financial statements and do not want to see that number reduced—even if they can envision no plausible case where they would need to have full liquidity for all their financial assets.

Perhaps related to this point, surveys have shown that people have a difficult time thinking through the mathematics of translating between lump-sum amounts and lifetime income streams. They may grossly underestimate the value of lifetime income. One million dollars may sound like a lot, but people are much less impressed to hear this might only sustain an annual inflation-adjusted income of around $30,000 to $40,000. As such, individuals may think that $30,000 of lifetime annual income is only worth $300,000, for instance, even though the reality is that this income is worth much more.

Often, retirees may also be thinking about annuities framed in terms of a gamble on the possibility of a long life, rather than as a risk reduction measure aimed at improving that possible long life. Retirees can more easily visualize being run over by a bus after signing the contract than they can being old and without income. They view this as unfair, thinking that the insurance company wins at their expense, instead of the other members of the risk pool. Another helpful technique is to use age-progression software to create a picture of one's future self, which can help make longevity risk more concrete. In this regard, people may underestimate their life expectancies, calibrating from birth rather than their current age, and not realizing they may live significantly longer than average. Insurance exists to protect us from bad outcomes, but annuities provide insurance against a generally good outcome: living an unexpectedly long time. Emphasizing a break-even age one has to reach for an annuity to provide higher returns misses the point about their insurance value. This mind-set leads to undervaluing lifetime income and a reluctance to annuitize.

It also turns out that framing annuities as an investment makes them less attractive. A study by Jeffrey Brown, Jeffrey Kling, Sendhil Mullainathan, and Marian Wrobel asked two different groups of randomly selected individuals a question with only a very slight twist in the way the question was worded for each group. They found that 70 percent of respondents would annuitize to obtain $650 of monthly spending for life, compared to only 21 percent who annuitize to obtain a guaranteed monthly return of $650 for life. The same concept with only a slight change in how it was framed led to a very different result.

Another matter is that Social Security already provides an inflation-adjusted annuity which may fulfill basic needs for many retirees. The basic formulation of the annuity puzzle assumes no other outside income sources beyond financial wealth, but Social Security provides such inflation-adjusted lifetime income support. For middle class households, the present value of those Social Security benefits may be larger than the financial portfolio, suggesting that the household already has sufficient reliable income. Individuals have a clear need to set aside a certain amount of financial assets to serve as a contingency fund to cover uncertain and potentially large future medical and long-term care expenses. With Social Security in place, many retirees may not have enough additional financial assets to practically consider an annuity.

Many individuals may also worry about the long-term viability of annuity providers and may view the annuity guarantee as anything but a sure bet. Mistrust of the annuity provider could be related both to (a) whether the provider is taking on too much risk and may be unable to fulfill its promises, or (b) whether incomprehensible fine print exists within the annuity contract that is detrimental to their interests. Fear that a systemic crisis could overwhelm annuity providers and state guarantee associations is common. Such concerns are probably overstated, but they create real fear. Chapter 9 covers this matter in greater depth.

Looking ahead, variable and index annuities with income guarantee riders were designed to overcome some of the behavioral concerns mentioned. They provide liquidity to reduce the finality of the decision, upside potential to keep that hope alive, the ability to keep the contract value of the annuity visible as a financial asset, and the ability to leave a death benefit to the estate. We consider these in upcoming chapters.

Further Reading

Brown, Jeffrey R., Olivia S. Mitchell, James M. Poterba, and Mark J. Warshawsky. 2001. *The Role of Annuity Markets in Financing Retirement*. Cambridge, MA: The MIT Press. [http://amzn.to/2FMOggk]

Brown, Jeffrey R., Jeffrey R. Kling, Sendhil Mullainathan, and Marian V. Wrobel. 2008. "Why Don't People Insure Late Life Consumption: A Framing Explanation of the Under-Annuitization Puzzle." NBER Working Paper No. 13748.

Hegna, Tom. 2011. *Paychecks and Playchecks: Retirement Solutions for Life.* Acanthus Publishing. [https://amzn.to/2K8bcKp]

Milevsky, Moshe A. 2013. *Life Annuities: An Optimal Product for Retirement Income.* Charlottesville, VA: Research Foundation of CFA Institute. [https://amzn. to/31qj2Vo]

Milevsky, Moshe A. 2012. *The 7 Most Important Equations for Your Retirement.* Hoboken, NJ: Wiley. [http://amzn.to/2x2glw2]

Milevsky, Moshe A., and Huaxiong Huang. 2011. "Spending Retirement on Planet Vulcan: The Impact of Longevity Risk Aversion on Optimal Withdrawal Rates." *Financial Analysts Journal* 67 (2): 45–58.

Modigliani, Franco. 1986. "Life Cycle, Individual Thrift, and the Wealth of Nations." *American Economic Review.* 76 (3): 297–313.

Yaari, Menahem E. 1965. "Uncertain Lifetime, Life Insurance, and the Theory of the Consumer." *The Review of Economic Studies.* 32 (2): 137–150.

CHAPTER 5

Variable Annuities

Variable Annuities Caveat

In this discussion of variable annuities, I am mostly making an implicit assumption that the annuity is competitively priced. Fees reflect what is needed to support the guarantees provided by the insurance company and to keep the company profitable. But fees are not excessive such that the value to the consumer is eliminated.

It must be noted that not all variable annuities are created equal. As will be discussed, they are complex financial instruments, and that complexity can hide a lack of competitiveness in the pricing of individual products. A variable annuity that is pitched along with a free dinner presentation is possibly not the type of financial product I have in mind. One should tread carefully. Due diligence and a comparison with other annuity options is needed to make sure that the product is priced fairly and will behave in the way that the purchaser understands it to behave. I do not want the "bad" annuities out there to free-ride off of my explanations about the potential positives that can be created by "good" annuities.

Generally, the most efficient means for balancing protected income and investment upside is to combine life-only income annuities with aggressive stock portfolios. However, this requires a degree of investor self-control and long-term focus that may be difficult to achieve in practice. It requires accepting both the loss of liquidity as annuity assets disappear from the portfolio balance, as well as accepting a very aggressive asset allocation for what remains on the portfolio statement.

As a means for accommodating the concerns of real-world retirees, deferred variable annuities and fixed index annuities with lifetime income protections have developed as a compromise between downside protection and upside potential. We will cover variable annuities in this chapter and fixed index annuities in the next chapter.

Owners continue to see the annuity assets remain on their financial statements as part of the overall portfolio balance. As well, those assets maintain exposure to market upside that is not provided within an income annuity. This provides a behavioral benefit that makes the retiree more comfortable in considering a safety-first strategy incorporating risk pooling. The appeal to retirees is based on the combination of downside protection with a protected income stream, upside growth potential through their underlying investments (or links to investment indices in the case of fixed index annuities), and maintaining liquidity for the underlying assets, while also offering the potential for tax-deferral when compared with taxable investments.

For variable annuities, retirees can see their account values, they can continue to invest in funds (technically called variable insurance trusts, but similar to mutual funds) within the annuity subaccounts, and any funds remaining at death are generally available to beneficiaries as a death benefit, all while ensuring protected income for life.

Lifetime income provides insurance against outliving assets in retirement, resulting from a combination of either living too long and/or experiencing poor investment returns. As well, there are situations when variable and index annuities might help to achieve more efficient outcomes in retirement in terms of providing a better combination of spending and legacy. These relate to asset allocation and whether it may change when an income guarantee is in place. Income guarantees provide greater relative benefit to retirees who are either willing to invest more aggressively because of the guarantee, or who would otherwise be uncomfortable using stocks in retirement.

Those who accept the notion that the income guarantee increases risk capacity, and are willing to use a more aggressive asset allocation than otherwise both inside and outside of the annuity, could find that the additional exposure to the stock market equity premium more than offsets the annuity fees when markets perform well in retirement. The guarantee would also prove valuable if it otherwise stops retirees from panicking and selling stocks after a market drop. And when markets perform poorly, by paying an insurance premium for the income protection, one should anticipate depleting the underlying asset base sooner than with a lower-cost, investments-only strategy. But the annuity still includes a lifetime guarantee to support retirement spending after assets deplete, which is not the case with an investments-only approach. Investments-only strategies might last a bit longer, but spending stops completely once those assets are gone.

Second, variable and index annuities could create better outcomes for those who would simply use a lower stock allocation no matter the chosen retirement strategy, but who are unwilling to sacrifice the liquidity foregone with an income annuity. With a low stock allocation, investment assets are more likely to deplete, and again, the annuity provides the opportunity to continue with income for life even after the contract value of assets is gone. Without exposure to the risk premium, the contract value of underlying assets is more assured to deplete in the event of a long retirement. With investments-only, asset depletion ends the ability to spend, but an income guarantee assures this continued spending ability for life.

It is not possible to make any overall conclusions for or against variable annuities and fixed index annuities with income riders, as this depends on the personal preferences of individuals about the issues of upside and downside, the desire for liquidity, and the types of asset allocations which would be used both with and without the income guarantee in place. But there will certainly be cases when retirees can derive value from these types of annuities. After providing a quick summary of various annuity types, we explore this story first for a deferred variable annuity.

◉ Overview of Annuity Types

This chapter is about how the lifetime income protections available through deferred variable annuities can support a retirement income goal through risk pooling and mortality credits. The next chapter adds fixed index annuities. We have already considered immediate and deferred income annuities. It is worthwhile to start by stepping back to describe the universe of available annuities more completely.

A fundamental component for the definition of an annuity is that it is a contract which can be structured to provide a series of payments from the insurance company, either for life or for a fixed period. However, today there are many annuities where this payment aspect is downplayed. As the tax code in the United States provides tax advantages for annuities, other forms of annuities have evolved with a greater emphasis on providing tax-deferred growth for the assets in the annuity with a de-emphasis on their income-generating abilities. But any annuity must provide a method for being annuitized into a series of payments.

Two broad classifications for annuities exist: fixed and variable. Simply, fixed annuities credit interest to the underlying assets in the annuity at a fixed rate (which can change over time), while variable annuities position the premiums into subaccounts that allow for investments into different funds earning a variable rate of return. Fixed annuities pool assets in the insurance company's general account, while variable annuities hold assets in separate individual investment subaccounts. Since variable annuities behave more like investments, those selling them need to be properly licensed in most states to sell both insurance and investments.

This definition about fixed and variable annuities can be confusing. First, income annuities are fixed annuities, but they do not show an underlying account balance to which interest is credited. Rather, the insurance company determines the payout rate based, in part, on the interest it projects to earn on the underlying premiums held in its general account.

Second, fixed index annuities can be structured to credit interest based on the performance of a volatile investment index. This can make them sound more like a variable annuity, but technically it is just a matter that fixed interest is being credited as based on outcomes for a volatile index. They provide principal protection. Unlike a variable annuity, fixed index annuities do not provide subaccounts in which investments are made. They only credit interest based on the performance of an associated index. An exception to this classification is variable index annuities, which operate more like fixed annuities but do not provide principal protection unless an additional optional rider is included. Finally, variable annuities could include subaccount options that provide fixed returns in the same manner as a fixed annuity, but the distinction is that variable annuities position the assets in investment subaccounts, unlike fixed annuities that hold them as part of the insurance company's pooled general account.

One other potentially confusing way to classify annuities is whether they are immediate or deferred. The confusion relates to the idea that this classification is not related to when guaranteed income begins, but rather to when the act of annuitization takes place. Some deferred annuities could provide income immediately through structured lifetime payments, while some immediate annuities may defer income payments. For the former, the variable annuities and index annuities with income riders that we discuss are both types of deferred annuities, even if guaranteed distributions start immediately. The reason they are still called deferred annuities in this case is that technically the contract does not annuitize until the contract value of the underlying assets has fallen to zero.

Because the lifetime income rider supports lifetime income in the same manner as an income annuity, I tend to become a bit lazy about this distinction regarding when technical annuitization takes place, colloquially suggesting that annuitization happens when guaranteed distributions begin rather than when the contract value reaches zero. Again, even if guaranteed distributions begin immediately from a deferred variable annuity with an income rider, the annuity is not technically annuitized until the value of the assets in the underlying subaccounts have been depleted, and so we are talking about a deferred variable annuity.

Meanwhile, the income annuities discussed in Chapter 4 are immediate annuities. The act of annuitizing the assets takes place at the time the premium is paid. There is no liquidity for the underlying premiums past that stage. "Immediate" immediate annuities begin income payments within one year of annuitization, while deferred immediate annuities begin income payments at least one year past annuitization. In Chapter 4, I used the alternative name of deferred income annuity to avoid the seeming contradiction of terms within the name "deferred immediate annuity." But it is not really a contradiction because the immediate part of the name refers to immediate annuitization, and the deferred part of the name refers to the delay in starting the annuitized payments.

It is worth mentioning a few other annuities that could play a role in a retirement income plan, before digging into the discussion of deferred variable and fixed index annuities.

Deferred Fixed Annuities

Deferred fixed annuities (DFAs), or multiyear guaranteed annuities (MYGAs) may be used as an accumulation tool in the years leading up to retirement. They are the annuity equivalent of holding CDs or other shorter-term fixed-income investments to a targeted maturity date. These annuities are deferred because they do not require immediate annuitization. Though all annuities offer an ability to annuitize the assets into a stream of payments, this may not be the priority for most DFA purchases. Rather, the objective is to seek competitive after-tax fixed-income returns for assets.

When choosing between bonds, CDs, and deferred fixed annuities, there are several differences to emphasize. First, deferred fixed annuities provide protection from interest rate risk. Unlike a bond fund or individual bonds not held to maturity, deferred fixed annuities do not experience losses if interest rates rise. Principal is protected and secured, providing a way to take risk off the table in the pivotal years before retirement.

Second, deferred fixed annuities offer the ability to seek corporate bond yields held in the insurance company's general account, relative to treasuries, without being unduly exposed to the credit risk of individual companies. Insurance company general accounts provide similar diversification to a bond fund.

Finally, a deferred fixed annuity offers tax deferral, unlike bonds held in taxable accounts that face ongoing taxes on their interest. Tax deferral is only relevant when the annuity is purchased outside of a qualified retirement plan. With this combination of volatility protection, higher yields, and tax deferral, deferred fixed annuities may provide a higher net return than households could achieve with other fixed-income choices. As for disadvantages, deferred fixed annuities may have penalties or withdrawal charges due on distributions taken before the end of the annuity's withdrawal charge period, which can mean that they offer less flexibility than bonds for covering unplanned expenses requiring liquidation before maturity.

Investment-Only Deferred Variable Annuities

Deferred variable annuities were originally created in the 1950s in the United States as a tax-deferred vehicle for accumulating assets. They grew in popularity after the Tax Reform Act of 1986 limited the opportunities for tax-deferred savings in qualified retirement plans. Though every annuity, by definition, must include a means to convert into a guaranteed income stream, the attractiveness of early variable annuities related to their ability to defer taxes rather than to generate income.

This may be the reason that annuities and pensions evolved as two distinct words in American English. If not for the tax code, the terms should be indistinguishable. Both were meant to serve as sources of lifetime income with the only practical distinction being perhaps that annuities were sold through commercial providers rather than being a benefit offered by employers or the government.

In the 1990s, the emergence of income guarantee riders for deferred variable annuities brought their income-generating potential back to the forefront and the chapter will be focusing on these shortly.

Nonetheless, even more recently there has been a movement to bring back the traditional deferred variable annuity with low costs and de-emphasized guarantees as a way to provide tax deferral for those investors who have already filled the tax-deferred space in their qualified retirement plans and still seek to invest further in tax-inefficient asset classes that may generate ordinary income and short-term capital gains, such as bonds, actively managed stock funds, alternative assets, and real estate investment trusts. To benefit from tax deferral, it is vital that the annuity costs are less than the tax deferral benefits.

Regarding lifetime income, if it is later desired, the owner might investigate exchanging the annuity assets into a new annuity with better guaranteed income provisions. This can be done as a 1035 exchange in the tax code. Assets are exchanged into a new annuity without triggering a taxable event at that time.

Though these investment-only variable annuities are liquid, investors must remember that the tax deferral advantages provided by the government for certain tax-qualified investments like these may be accompanied by the need to pay taxes and an additional 10 percent penalty on distributions taken before the age of 59.5. The government provides tax benefits to encourage retirement savings and will take back these benefits and penalize those using the tools for different purposes.

There are exceptions that can allow earlier distributions without penalties. When penalties are not applied, gains are still taxed at income tax rates. This includes long-term capital gains or other qualified dividends that would have been taxed at a lower rate inside of a taxable account. It would generally be unwise to hold stock index funds and other tax-efficient investments inside variable annuities. Tax-inefficient investments are taxed at income tax rates anyway.

When considering an investment-only variable annuity, be sure to consider the investment options available, the explicit costs for the annuity, and whether 12b-1 fees are included to increase the expense ratios on the offered underlying funds. These 12b-1 fees are marketing and distribution fees from the fund that can be incorporated into the expense ratio. If the variable annuity includes 12b-1 fees, this would represent an additional cost to weigh for those with other investment opportunities that do not include such fees.

Immediate Variable Annuities

The main variable annuity discussion in this chapter will be about deferred variable annuities. Immediate variable annuities do also exist, and they do work differently. They do provide lifetime income protections. However, while academics tend to like the concept of immediate variable annuities, they are quite rare in practice. This rarity is why they are not featured more heavily here.

Briefly, immediate variable annuities provide a guaranteed income for life, but the amount of income provided over time varies based on the returns to an underlying portfolio of assets and how these returns compare to an assumed interest rate for the contract. Owners buy annuity units with the premium, and these annuity units generate a variable amount of income over time. They provide a way for someone to have a lifetime income, but to accept some risk about the level of this income. If markets underperform relative to the assumed interest rate, the amount of guaranteed income decreases. But market outperformance relative to the assumed interest rate will increase guaranteed income.

Each annuity unit provides a guaranteed lifetime income, it is just unclear what this income amount will be per annuity unit until market performance for the underlying annuity subaccounts is realized.

⦿ Deferred Variable Annuities

Deferred variable annuities with income guarantee riders have gained popularity as a retirement income tool providing behavioral solutions for the annuity puzzle. Retirees are not always comfortable seeing the premiums disappear from their portfolio balances when buying income annuities that convert a lump-sum premium into a protected lifetime income. Many features of a variable annuity could be replicated by combining an income annuity with an aggressive investment portfolio, but both of those choices can be tough for retirees to accept.

A deferred variable annuity can provide a palatable alternative. Its appeal to retirees is based on its combination of downside protection with a lifetime income stream, upside growth potential through its underlying investments, and maintaining liquidity for the underlying assets, while also offering the potential for tax-deferral when compared with taxable investments. Retirees can see their account values, they can continue to invest in funds within the annuity subaccounts, and any funds remaining at death are available to beneficiaries as a death benefit. These features can provide a happy compromise leading to a palatable way for retirees to take advantage of risk pooling as a part of their retirement income plan.

Nevertheless, the features and workings of deferred variable annuities with income riders can be rather complex. Prospectuses about variable annuities can be hundreds of pages long. Frankly, this is an area where I wish variable annuity providers would simplify matters by adopting standardized features that are easier to understand and compare. But because there are many moving parts to a variable annuity, and because consumers tend to latch on to certain characteristics and downplay other important characteristics, we find ourselves in a situation in which different providers seek to tweak the characteristics of their product offerings in ways that will better appeal to consumers while adjusting other less salient features in a less attractive direction.

This process often leads to greater overall complexity. It also means that not all variable annuities are created equal and some will perform better than others. An important caveat for this discussion is that I generally describe competitively priced variable annuities, and that is not a description fitting all products on the market.

For those just starting to investigate deferred variable annuities, complexities relate to understanding how the income guarantee works and how its fees are structured. A few key terms include the contract value of assets, the guaranteed benefit base, the possibility of step-ups, and the rollup rate applied during the deferral period. Different companies will use different names for these features and some translation from the terms I use may be necessary when looking at a specific product.

A guaranteed lifetime withdrawal benefit rider supports an income for life at a fixed withdrawal percentage (based on the age when distributions begin) of the guaranteed benefit base. The guaranteed benefit base is a hypothetical amount used to calculate the guaranteed withdrawals. It initially equals the premium paid into the annuity, which is also the initial contract value for the assets. Over time, the contract value of assets can rise or fall depending on realized investment returns and as fees and distributions are taken from the asset base. On any contract anniversary, if the contract value of the underlying assets has reached a new high watermark and exceeds the guaranteed benefit base, that base is stepped up to the new high watermark value. This increases the subsequent amount of guaranteed income. If the retiree does not take out more than the guaranteed withdrawal amounts, guaranteed withdrawals never decrease, even if the account balance falls to zero. One exception to this is that some companies market a feature that allows for higher distributions when assets remain and lower distributions after assets deplete. The contract may be terminated at any point with the contract value of the remaining assets, net of any potential surrender charges, returned to the owner. During the deferral period before distributions begin, a variable annuity may also offer a guaranteed rollup rate to increase the benefit base automatically over time if the value of the underlying contracted assets has not otherwise grown larger on its own.

I'll aim to provide a big picture overview of the key features to understand when trying to figure out how a variable annuity works and when trying to compare different variable annuity options. This will hopefully prepare you with a list of questions to ask to make sure you understand the variable annuity contract under consideration. This discussion fits into four general categories: how do guarantees grow during the deferral period, how are guaranteed withdrawals determined and how can they grow during the distribution period, what is the death benefit, and how does the insurance company manage the risk it creates by offering the guarantee?

Deferral Period

We begin with the growth process for the guaranteed benefit base during the deferral or accumulation period before distributions begin. This growth is important because it is subsequently used to determine the amount of guaranteed lifetime income provided by the annuity. The deferral period can be skipped if the retiree wants lifetime distributions to begin immediately.

Deferred variable annuities with income guarantee riders generally support the ability to lock-in a guaranteed growth rate on the benefit base during the accumulation period before guaranteed distributions begin, including the ability to define the benefit base as the high watermark of the contract value of the underlying assets on anniversary dates over the history of the rider. This benefit base is a hypothetical number used to calculate the amount of guaranteed income paid during the withdrawal phase. It is distinct from the contract value of assets, which is what the owner could access based on actual account growth net of fees and any surrender charges.

For example, if the rollup rate for the benefit base is an annually compounding 6 percent, the value of the benefit base would double in approximately twelve years. The benefit base could be even larger if the contract value grew larger on the relevant dates when this is checked. Conversely, the actual contract value of the underlying assets will be determined by market performance. After the twelve-year accumulation period has passed, if the market has underperformed and the value of the benefit base is significantly higher than the contract value of the underlying assets, then the income guarantee is "in the money." The benefit base is larger than the contract value. In such a case, the owner may wish to continue paying for the rider and to receive the guaranteed income as calculated on this higher benefit base.

On the other hand, if markets performed well during those twelve years, the contract value of the underlying assets may be close to or the same as the value of the benefit base. In this case, the retiree may consider whether it is worthwhile to begin taking distributions with the income guarantee, to have the contract value of the underlying assets returned to an unprotected investment portfolio, or to exchange into a different annuity with better withdrawal opportunities for the contract value.

Generally, the benefit base can grow at the higher of either a guaranteed rollup rate or the high watermark achieved through investment growth of the contract value for the underlying assets held inside the annuity. But the interaction of these two possibilities can get confusing. I'll talk about both rollups and step-ups, which are not interchangeable terms. Rollups are a guaranteed minimum growth rate for the benefit base, and step-ups are increases for the benefit base triggered when the contract value of the underlying assets in the annuity subaccounts have grown to achieve a new high watermark value. Let's start with the rollup rate.

What is the guaranteed rollup rate for the benefit base? Is it a compounded rate or simple rate?

To begin, we can consider a rollup rate that is applied annually on the contract anniversary for when the annuity was opened. If a variable annuity offers a 5 percent guaranteed compounded rollup rate during the deferral period, then the benefit base supported by a $100,000 premium would grow to $127,628 after five years (100,000 x 1.05 ^ 5) and to $162,890 after ten years (100,000 x 1.05 ^ 10).

If this were instead a 5 percent simple growth rate, then 5 percent of the initial premium would be added to the benefit base after each year, leading to $125,000 after five years and $150,000 after ten years, for instance. The longer the deferral period, the more opportunity a compounded rollup rate has to move ahead, with growth on past growth, relative to a simple rollup rate on the initial premium. For instance, with these numbers provided, we can see that a 5 percent compounded growth rate would beat a 6 percent simple growth rate after ten years, as the latter would have only growth to $160,000.

Exhibit 5.1 provides an example of $100,000 placed into a variable annuity at age fifty-five which offers a 5 percent annual compounded growth rate on the benefit base. As mentioned, after ten years, the benefit base has grown to $162,890. If the contract value of the underlying assets never grew to exceed this guaranteed rollup rate when checked on the relevant dates, then this would reflect the benefit base for the annuity.

It is worth emphasizing that the guaranteed rollup rate is not a guaranteed investment return. It does not apply to the contract value of assets. It only applies to the benefit base used to calculate guaranteed income amounts. This detail is a constant source of confusion for individuals.

When are rollups vested into the benefit base?
Most commonly, the rollup rate is applied annually on the anniversary date for when the contract went into effect, and this is also when the benefit base would be vested at the new higher value. That is the case illustrated in Exhibit 5.1.

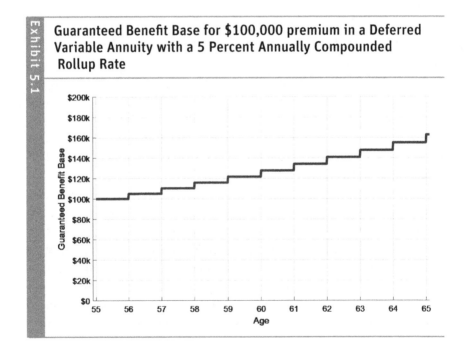

Exhibit 5.1

Guaranteed Benefit Base for $100,000 premium in a Deferred Variable Annuity with a 5 Percent Annually Compounded Rollup Rate

Some variable annuities will apply the rollups on a more frequent basis, such as daily, monthly, or quarterly. With compounding, more frequent rollups can provide an edge because there is more opportunity for interest to accumulate on interest. However, the question remains about when the rollups become vested. More frequent rollups might still only vest on the contract anniversary date. The only reason this could be a problem is for someone seeking to begin distributions midyear. Even though rollups are more frequent, if they do not vest until the anniversary date, then the benefit base will not yet be higher when calculating the income guarantee. Withdrawals before the anniversary date would not factor in any of the potential growth for the year.

How long does the guaranteed rollup rate last? Does it have any other features?

Guaranteed rollup rates for the benefit base generally end once guaranteed distributions from the contract have commenced. As well, in cases where those distributions do not begin for a long period of time, the rollup rate may only last for a certain number of years.

Some variable annuities may have other guaranteed growth features as well. For instance, one might see a bonus applied to their initial premium, such that the initial benefit base is higher than the premium. Another possibility could be that the benefit base is guaranteed to double after a certain number of years if underlying contract value growth did not otherwise jump far enough ahead of the guaranteed rollup rate to have independently caused this.

How frequent are the step-ups to the benefit base? When are they applied?

Another reason that the benefit base can increase is because the contract value of the underlying assets has grown to achieve a new high watermark that exceeds the value of the guaranteed benefit base provided through rollups. We must consider how frequently these new high watermark step-up possibilities are checked for the benefit base and when they vest. Most commonly, these step-ups are applied for contract value growth on an annual basis at the contract anniversary date. If the contract is worth more than the guaranteed benefit base on the contract anniversary date, then the benefit base is adjusted upward to match the contract value at this time. In these cases, if the contract value reached a new high watermark earlier in the year but then dropped by the anniversary date, the higher earlier value would not matter. Only the value on the designated dates is used to determine if a new high watermark has been achieved.

Naturally, the ability to apply step-ups on a more frequent basis, such as daily, monthly, or quarterly, is valuable to the annuity holder. It creates more opportunities for growth in the contract value to achieve new high watermarks for the benefit base. When these step-up opportunities are applied more frequently than on an annual basis, it is important to also know about when they vest. If they do not vest until the anniversary date, then this can again create issues for those seeking to begin distributions midyear if a new high watermark for the benefit base has not yet vested to increase the guaranteed income.

How does the rollup rate interact with step-ups?
A final consideration for deferrals is how the rollup rate reacts to step-ups for the benefit base. What happens when the contract value achieves a new high watermark above the guaranteed rollup rate? There are two basic options. The rollup rate might only be applied to the original premium, or it may stack on top of new high watermarks achieved through asset growth. The latter case is more advantageous to the annuity owner. The easiest way to understand this is with an example.

Exhibit 5.2 provides such an example for a $100,000 premium placed into a variable annuity with a ten-year deferral period that offers a 5 percent annual compounded rollup rate that is vested on each contract anniversary as in Exhibit 5.1. The contract value for the underlying annuity assets is also shown in the exhibit. The growth of the contract value was chosen for this example to more clearly illustrate the difference for stacking the rollup rate on step-ups. The contract value trails the guaranteed rollup rate until age fifty-nine when a very large market return pushes the contract value well above the benefit base. This market growth creates a step-up to the new high watermark for the benefit base. Then the contract value subsequently declines and trails the benefit base for the remainder of the deferral period. With that step-up at age fifty-nine, there are two ways that the rollups may respond. Without stacking, the rollup continues to apply only to the original premium and the benefit base stays at the high watermark level achieved at age fifty-nine until age sixty-three when the cumulative rollups once again allow the benefit base to grow. In this example, the benefit base at age sixty-five ends up at the same $162,890 value. There was a temporary period between ages fifty-nine and sixty-three where the benefit base was larger, which could have been beneficial if the owner decided to begin lifetime distributions earlier than planned, but it otherwise does not impact the amount of guaranteed income if distributions begin at sixty-five.

We can observe how stacking leads to a much better outcome in this example. With stacking, once the new high watermark was achieved at age fifty-nine, the rollup rate begins to be applied to this new high watermark, rather than only being applied to the original premium. This allows for greater subsequent growth of the benefit base at the rollup rate from that new high watermark. In this example, stacking allowed the benefit base to grow to $194,477 at age sixty-five. This stacking has laid a foundation for 19 percent more guaranteed lifetime income from the annuity.

Distribution Period

The deferral period ends once guaranteed lifetime distributions commence. We have entered the distribution period. Guaranteed income will be set using an age-based guaranteed withdrawal or payout percentage rate applied to the value of the benefit base. The guaranteed withdrawal rate

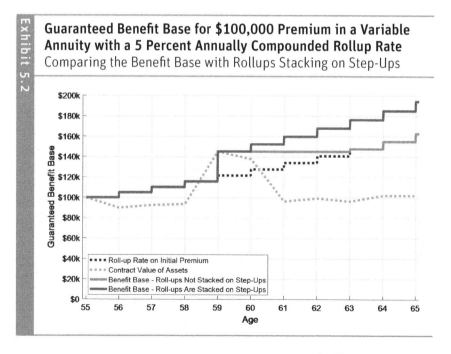

Exhibit 5.2

Guaranteed Benefit Base for $100,000 Premium in a Variable Annuity with a 5 Percent Annually Compounded Rollup Rate
Comparing the Benefit Base with Rollups Stacking on Step-Ups

- Roll-up Rate on Initial Premium
- Contract Value of Assets
- Benefit Base - Roll-ups Not Stacked on Step-Ups
- Benefit Base - Roll-ups Are Stacked on Step-Ups

multiplied by the benefit base sets a guaranteed distribution amount supported for life, even if the contract value of the underlying assets is depleted. Guaranteed distributions may even increase through step-ups if new high watermarks are reached for the underlying asset base on the designated dates when this is checked.

What are the guaranteed withdrawal rates?

For deferred variable annuities with income riders supporting a guaranteed lifetime withdrawal benefit, the guaranteed withdrawal rates or payout rates are most typically based on the age that lifetime guaranteed distributions begin, and on whether the distribution is taken by a single individual or by a couple. These payout rates can vary between companies and even for different versions of variable annuities offered by the same company. The rates are set at the time of the contract and would not change for that contract holder, though over time the rates may change for new purchases.

For a simple example, a company might offer the following payout rates to single individuals based on the age that lifetime withdrawals begin: 4.5 percent for ages fifty-nine to sixty-four, 5 percent for ages sixty-five to sixty-nine, 5.5 percent for ages seventy to seventy-nine, and 6.5 percent for ages eighty and over. For couples, payout rates would generally be 0.5 percent less (so, 4.5 percent at sixty-five, for instance) and would be based on the age of the younger person. For couples, another possibility could be that the payout rates remain the same as for singles, but that a higher fee is charged to support the guarantee over the longer expected joint lifetime. Variable annuity payouts generally do not make a distinction between genders, which would provide benefit to longer living women relative to men.

The payout rates on variable annuities at different ages will generally be less than the payout rate offered by an immediate annuity purchased at the same age (although this is not always true, as it may occasionally be possible to find variable annuities with larger income guarantees than an immediate annuity). This can be expected since the variable annuity continues to provide liquidity for the underlying assets and the potential for upside growth in the guaranteed income. However, the question remains about how much less the payout rate is for a variable annuity relative to an income annuity.

Exhibit 5.3 provides an example, showing the payout rates on immediate annuities for couples at different ages alongside the payout rates on the hypothetical variable annuity just described. The immediate annuity payout rates were collected from ImmediateAnnuities.com on January 15, 2019, and they include a cash refund provision to match closer with the death benefit provisions of the variable annuity. The gaps in provided income can be quite large. Payouts are closest after the variable annuity payout increase at age seventy when the immediate annuity provides 25 percent more income, and they are the farthest apart at age seventy-nine when the immediate annuity offers 58 percent more income. We will return to this issue later when we delve into how to think about the upside potential of a variable annuity.

Next, we consider the joint impacts of rollup rates and payout rates on the amount of guaranteed income the annuity can support. When it comes time to begin taking guaranteed withdrawals, it is worthwhile to investigate whether applying the contract value of the annuity assets to a higher payout rate possibly available from other annuities could result in more guaranteed income than applying a potentially lower payout rate to the annuity's benefit base.

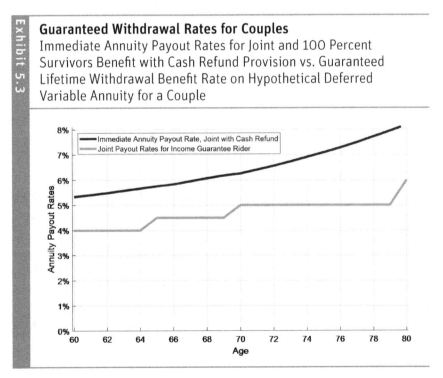

Exhibit 5.3

Guaranteed Withdrawal Rates for Couples
Immediate Annuity Payout Rates for Joint and 100 Percent Survivors Benefit with Cash Refund Provision vs. Guaranteed Lifetime Withdrawal Benefit Rate on Hypothetical Deferred Variable Annuity for a Couple

For instance, consider a variable annuity with a $1 million benefit base and a 4.5 percent payout rate at the current age. If a different annuity is offering a 5 percent payout at this age when the owner wishes to start income, then the owner would be better off exchanging to the other annuity if the contract value is greater than $900,000 (as that would guarantee more than $45,000 of annual income), but remain with the existing annuity if the contract value is less than $900,000 (as $45,000 is guaranteed from the benefit base).

Moshe Milevsky has described the separate presentation of rollup rates and guaranteed withdrawal rates as telling consumers the temperature in Celsius when individuals can only make sense of temperatures provided in Fahrenheit. In this case, what a retiree will understand is the amount of income guaranteed by the annuity (Moshe does take the guaranteed income a step further and translates it into an equivalent investment return that can be more directly compared to the returns offered by other investment opportunities).

It may not be immediately obvious to someone whether an annuity with a 5 percent rollup rate and 5 percent withdrawal rate is better than an annuity with a 4 percent rollup rate and a 6 percent withdrawal rate. The answer also depends on how long the deferral period lasts before income begins, as longer deferral periods will increase the relative importance of the rollup rate and shorter deferral periods mean one should instead focus more on the withdrawal rate.

Exhibit 5.4 provides more clarity on how to better understand the intricacies of rollup rates and withdrawal rates for someone placing a $100,000 premium into a variable annuity and deferring for ten years before distributions begin. For instance, with the example in the previous paragraph, a 4 percent rollup and 6 percent withdrawal rate support $8,861 of guaranteed annual lifetime income, which is quite a bit more than the $8,144 provided by the 5 percent rollup and 5 percent withdrawal combination. The former provides more guaranteed income, which is the whole point of a lifetime income guarantee. To be clear, fees and investment opportunities also matter in determining upside potential, but for now we stick to only considering guaranteed income levels if no step-ups are ever realized.

Individuals considering variable annuities may tend to focus on the guaranteed rollup rate. They may even misunderstand it to mean a guaranteed return on their investment or contract value, rather than a guaranteed return on a hypothetical benefit base that is then used to calculate guaranteed income. This creates room to maneuver, as companies can raise the headline rollup rate that receives the attention while more subtly reducing the subsequent withdrawal rates attached to the benefit base. This avoids being on the hook to support a higher guaranteed income level that one might otherwise expect with a higher rollup rate.

Another example of this from the exhibit, for instance, is that a 6 percent rollup and 4.5 percent withdrawal combination provides less income ($8,059) than a 5 percent rollup and 5 percent withdrawal combination ($8,144). If consumers are confused and only focus on which annuity provides the higher rollup rate, then they may miss out on the opportunity to achieve the highest guaranteed income for their premium dollars.

Exhibit 5.4

Guaranteed Income Supported by a $100,000 Premium with a Ten-Year Deferral Period Before Income Begins

| | Rollup Rate | Withdrawal Rate | | | | |
		4.0%	4.5%	5.0%	5.5%	6.0%
Compounded	4.0%	$5,921	$6,661	$7,401	$8,141	$8,881
	4.5%	$6,212	$6,988	$7,765	$8,541	$9,318
	5.0%	$6,516	$7,330	$8,144	$8,959	$9,773
	5.5%	$6,833	$7,687	$8,541	$9,395	$10,249
	6.0%	$7,163	$8,059	$8,954	$9,850	$10,745
	6.5%	$7,509	$8,447	$9,386	$10,324	$11,263
	7.0%	$7,869	$8,852	$9,836	$10,819	$11,803
Simple	5%	$6,000	$6,750	$7,500	$8,250	$9,000
	6%	$6,400	$7,200	$8,000	$8,800	$9,600
	7%	$6,800	$7,650	$8,500	$9,350	$10,200
	10%	$8,000	$9,000	$10,000	$11,000	$12,000

At a more extreme level, it is also important to monitor whether the guaranteed rollup rate is presented as a compounding growth factor with growth also available on past growth, or whether it is a simple growth factor with growth only provided on the original premium. A simple 5 percent rollup rate on a $100,000 premium for ten years would grow the benefit base to $150,000, while a compounded growth rate would bring the benefit base to $162,890. This does make a difference. We can observe in Exhibit 5.4, for instance, that a 10 percent simple growth rate with a 4 percent withdrawal provides less income ($8,000) than a 6 percent compounded growth rate with a 4.5 percent withdrawal ($8,059). It is important to focus on the guaranteed income provided by the rollup and withdrawal factors, rather than trying to make some determination in isolation about which combination of factors *sounds* better.

Many consumers misinterpret the guaranteed growth rate on their benefit base as a guaranteed investment return, not realizing that it is the combination of a growth rate on the benefit base and the withdrawal rate applied to the benefit base that determine the level of guaranteed income. These two factors cannot be disentangled. A higher rollup rate combined with a lower payout rate does not necessarily leave consumers in a better position.

Are there cases when the amount of guaranteed income can be decreased?

Generally, if an annuity contract states that a guaranteed income level remains for life then this is the case as long as distributions do not exceed the guaranteed levels. But some annuity providers make clear that there is an option to receive more income when assets remain, if they are willing to reduce the amount of guaranteed income they will receive after the contract value of annuity assets has been depleted. For instance, rather than offering a 5 percent guaranteed payout for life, the contract may stipulate that distributions are guaranteed to be allowed at 7 percent of the benefit base until the contract value of assets has been depleted, and then the level of guaranteed income drops to 3 percent of the benefit base (a 57 percent reduction). This approach makes a distinction between maximum allowed withdrawal amounts (7 percent) and protected income payments (3 percent).

At the surface, this sort of structure may not sound very appealing. The purpose of having the guarantee in place is to protect income if the contract

Types of Living Benefits

Throughout this book, I am describing lifetime income protections for deferred annuities as guaranteed lifetime withdrawal benefits (GLWB). These are quite common today and are a reasonable default for discussing a living benefit.

There are a few other types of living benefits to be aware of as well. They were more popular in the past, and they continue to survive in limited form at the present. First, the guaranteed minimum income benefit (GMIB) promises access to a particular age-based payout rate with the benefit base when the contract is annuitized. The GMIB is similar to a GLWB, except that the GMIB requires annuitization, while the GLWB begins a lifetime income while maintaining the deferral status for the annuity. Second, a guaranteed minimum accumulation benefit (GMAB) promises that the contract value grows to a minimum value. It is not linked to a lifetime income. Third, the guaranteed minimum withdrawal benefit (GMWB) guarantees that the return of principal or the value of the benefit base can be distributed through systematic withdrawals. It does not guarantee a lifetime income beyond this.

The unique features of the GLWB used primarily in this book are that it does support a lifetime income and it does not require annuitization to receive the lifetime income.

value of assets has been depleted, and this approach does guarantee less income. Advocates of this structure would argue, though, that the higher initial withdrawal rate for the annuity means that less assets can be moved to the annuity to achieve the same level of initial income. This allows more to remain within the investment portfolio held outside the annuity.

If distributions are also taken from the nonannuity investments, they can be less, which will help to preserve the nonannuity portion of the portfolio. This could serve to support additional income later in retirement from unguaranteed sources and it may be an appealing way to achieve benefits from having guaranteed income sources while committing less assets to the annuity.

What is the distinction between lifetime distributions and nonlifetime distributions?

Variable annuities generally make a distinction between distributions that are covered by the lifetime income guarantee rider, and onetime distributions that are not covered by the guarantee. Nonlifetime distributions may be allowed before guaranteed income begins. That distinction is important, as it would generally allow rollups to continue, as rollups mostly end once guaranteed distributions begin. As well, nonlifetime distributions beyond the guaranteed level are allowed after the guaranteed distributions begin, but this will reduce the subsequent guaranteed distribution amounts proportionately.

One further note is relevant here. Some income guarantees allow for market value adjustments or earnings-sensitive adjustments which allow the owner to temporarily take a higher guaranteed distribution. These would generally be structured to allow for larger distributions during periods when the markets are experiencing gains.

How are guarantees affected if a distribution larger than the guaranteed amount is taken?

If excess distributions beyond the guaranteed level are taken, they will reduce the subsequent guaranteed distribution amount. Different mechanisms may be used to make these adjustments, but the general idea would be that the guaranteed distribution level would reduce proportionately by the amount of the nonguaranteed distribution as a percentage of the remaining contract value of assets.

In addition to a desire to have a larger onetime distribution, required minimum distributions may trigger the need for an excess distribution when the annuity is held inside of a qualified retirement plan. If the contract is still within the period that surrender charges apply, most companies will make an exception not to charge on distributions specifically meant to meet this tax requirement. But if lifetime distributions have begun, any excess distribution needed to cover required minimum distributions (RMDs) will generally result in the proportional reduction to the subsequent lifetime income guarantee. Retirees may look to take the RMDs from other qualified assets rather than from the annuity assets.

How are rollups and step-ups affected after lifetime distributions begin?

Typically, variable annuities end their guaranteed rollup provisions once guaranteed lifetime distributions commence. Step-up opportunities do continue for the guaranteed benefit base whenever the underlying contract value of assets reaches a new high watermark on the relevant dates. When step-ups can happen more frequently than annually, then the usual process is that on the contract anniversary date there is a look-back to determine the high watermark on the relevant dates over the past year and any step-up is then vested at this time. Then, applying the guaranteed withdrawal rate to the higher benefit base at the anniversary date will allow for larger subsequent lifetime guaranteed withdrawals. It is important to keep in mind that step-ups will become less likely after distributions begin because it will require the contract value to achieve new high watermark values net of distributions and fees.

Typically, the age when guaranteed lifetime distributions begin will determine a guaranteed withdrawal rate from the benefit base that remains in place for life. The withdrawal rates do not increase with increasing age when new age bands are entered. But some annuity providers may include provisions to increase payout rates over time.

One possibility is that if a step-up brings the benefit base to a higher level again at a later age, the owner may be able to apply the higher payout rate at that age to the new high watermark for an even bigger increase in income. Another possibility is that as each age band when a higher payout rate is reached, the company may check if applying that payout rate to the account value will support an increase in income, and if so, may then reset the guaranteed income level to this higher value. This could happen without reaching a new high watermark if the contract value is close enough that income would increase with the higher payout rate for the new age band.

Death Benefits

The standard death benefit for a deferred variable annuity is the greater of the contract value of any remaining assets at death, or the total premiums paid less distributions received by death. It is provided to the beneficiary. In addition to optional withdrawal benefit riders (also called living benefits), many deferred variable annuities also offer optional death benefit riders that create an opportunity for more than the standard death benefit. One should look carefully at these as they could be counterproductive for those focusing on getting the most guaranteed income from their variable annuity. For instance, a common death benefit rider could support a death benefit equal to the full value of the annuity premiums if at least one dollar remains in the contract by an advanced age. One must consider whether it is a wise choice if the focus is otherwise placed on maximizing the spending power afforded by an income guarantee.

With our focus on maximizing spending power, we maintain a willingness to deplete the underlying contract value for assets. But to keep the death benefit, the contract value must stay above $0, which could create complications because the income guarantee could never be activated if the death benefit is to be maintained. Such a death benefit could be more worthwhile for individuals who are not seeking to get the most possible value out of their income guarantee, such as a strategy to pay RMDs from the underlying assets while preserving their initial value as a death benefit. Generally optional income benefit and death benefit riders should not be combined because they serve different purposes.

Another optional death benefit guarantee may set the death benefit at the higher of either the initial premium, the contract value, or the benefit base, but then reduce the death benefit for any distributions taken. It would not be worthwhile to pay extra for this when focused on taking distributions. Some retirees may consider these death benefit options as an alternative to permanent life insurance (especially when no longer insurable) if generating income is not the primary focus for this portion of the asset base. Also, later in retirement if the sequence risk issue did not materialize and the retiree is in good shape, the focus may start to shift toward passing wealth to the next generation with minimal need for further distributions, and a variable annuity with an additional death benefit rider can be an option to consider in this circumstance. This emphasis on legacy as the primary goal falls outside our scope. With our analysis, we do seek to not needlessly sacrifice legacy, but the focus is on maximizing sustainable retirement spending in the most efficient manner in order to indirectly also support legacy.

Managing Risks for the Income Guarantee

Providing a guaranteed lifetime withdrawal benefit is a risky endeavor for the insurance company. The insurance company must manage both longevity and market risk, as they are obligated to provide lifetime income payments at the guaranteed level if the underlying assets held within the annuity have been depleted. The greater the investment volatility and the higher the guaranteed withdrawals that the insurance company allows, the greater is the cost for creating a risk management framework to support that guarantee. Companies have several methods for managing these risks. First, companies can create a strong culture of financial performance and risk management. This may help to create an edge in obtaining efficiencies around supporting the guarantees in the least costly way. It may be hard to distinguish much in this regard between the leading insurance companies other than to assess their strength and size, as well as their past performance with supporting income guarantees during market downturns. Especially as the income guarantees on variable annuities are not covered by the state guarantee associations protecting fixed annuities, one must take care to choose a company that is likely to be around and be able to support the guarantees it offers.

Beyond the company's culture and approach to risk management, insurance companies generally have the following levers for managing the risks around supporting a lifetime income guarantee:

- Supporting a lower guaranteed income amount
- Choosing high-quality managers for the investment subaccounts
- Limiting the volatility allowed within the investment subaccounts, either by capping the allowed stock allocation (investment choices are each labeled as risky or not risky, the allowed percentage of risky investments is capped) or by requiring the use of volatility-controlled investment funds or cash positions within the subaccounts
- Increasing the fees for the variable annuity and the income guarantee rider to provide more reserves and to support the purchase of more financial derivatives to hedge the risk created by market volatility

For the first point, we have already discussed how the insurance company can use different rollup, step-up, and payout features to help better control the amount of guaranteed income it is contractually obligated to support. Companies may reduce their obligations by encouraging consumers to only focus on one detail such as a guaranteed rollup rate. Guarantees can be weakened by using a lower rollup rate, by less frequently vesting the rollups, by not stacking roll ups on step ups, or by connecting the benefit base to lower distribution rates. But this sort of approach may only go so far as it relies on behavioral mistakes by purchasers to focus on only one lever of the income machine. Companies seeking to provide competitive levels of guaranteed income must seek to manage these accepted risks through investment controls and fees.

What are the investment options and constraints for the variable annuity subaccounts?

The risk to the insurance company for supporting an income guarantee grows as the contract value declines and falls further away from the guaranteed benefit base. The insurance company maintains the responsibility to continue funding the guaranteed income levels if the underlying portfolio depletes. And so, as the contract value of remaining assets falls relative to the guaranteed benefit base used to determine income, risk to the insurance company increases. Insurance companies would like to keep the contract value strong and close to the benefit base so that they are less exposed to the costs of providing the lifetime income guarantee.

The ability to invest more aggressively is a clear advantage provided to the retiree by an income guarantee, and this is a risk that must be managed by the insurance company offering the guarantee. Investing aggressively creates more upside potential for the retiree. Investment growth that leads to step-ups means both a larger benefit base and a larger contract value for assets. Retirees then only experience a portion of the downside risk. Market losses will reduce the contract value, but the income guarantee will provide spending power if the assets deplete through a combination of portfolio losses and distributions. The income guarantee behaves as a type of put option on the stock market, as it supports upside growth while reducing the potential harm to the lifetime standard of living resulting from market losses.

Ultimately, while the underlying contract value of assets remains positive, retirees are spending their own money. The insurance company pays from its own resources when the contract value depletes. Contract value depletion is what triggers annuitization, and that is why these are classified as deferred annuities.

Insurance companies can try to control this exposure to market volatility and capital losses either by limiting the total allocation allowed to risky assets, by choosing less volatile funds to be included as part of the subaccount options, or by directly managing the amount of volatility exposure through volatility-managed investment funds or dynamic asset allocation that automatically shift assets away from equities at times of market stress.

Variable annuities will vary by their depth of investment offerings and by the constraints placed on these offerings. Most will provide funds from a variety of leading mutual fund companies. Insurance companies tend to carefully select and manage the fund choices within their annuities with an eye to finding good performers. The insurance companies are incentivized to avoid underperforming or poorly managed funds because this could cause contract values to be depleted more quickly, forcing the insurance company to make good on its guarantees.

As for constraints, the simplest is to create a maximum allowed allocation to risky investment such as stocks. Annuity holders may have investing freedom for choosing among the funds within the annuity universe, but they would be restricted from increasing the overall risky allocation above some limit such as 60 or 70 percent. Some companies will also require that 10 percent of premiums remain in a secured value account that earns a fixed interest amount based on short-term interest rates.

Another trend is to use volatility-managed funds, which automatically reduce the stock allocation to keep a consistent volatility level if volatility rises in the markets. Some companies may require the use of these type of funds or may otherwise require that a portion of the assets within the annuity be held in a cash account with minimal volatility.

What are the fees associated with the variable annuity?

While I discussed a variety of ways that insurance companies manage the risks around supporting lifetime income guarantees, fees are the headline mechanism for managing the guarantee risk. Fees can be used to purchase financial derivatives and support other forms of risk management for the guarantee.

Deferred variable annuities generally have several types of ongoing fees. The first relate to the underlying funds expenses that would be included with any mutual fund investment. The only issue to consider here is whether the funds within the subaccounts have elevated fees due to the inclusion of 12b-1 fees in their expense ratios, and whether investment options available to the individual outside of the variable annuity also include 12b-1 fees as well. These fund fees are charged on the contract value of underlying assets and would end if the contract value depletes.

The second type of fee relates to mortality and expense charges for the insurance company. These fees help to support the risk pooling needs of the insurance company as well as basic annuity death benefits (such as the return of the contract value or the total premiums paid into the annuity not yet received as distributions, whichever is higher) and also help to cover the costs of business and to support the profit needs of the company. These fees are also generally charged on the contract value of assets. The annuities may also have a small fixed annual fee as well, at least for accounts with lower balances.

A third type of fee that may exist temporarily are contingent deferred sales charges (or surrender charges) for those seeking nonlifetime distributions above the allowed level in the early years of the contract. Surrender charges receive much of the criticism related to the fee levels for variable annuities.

Variable annuities are liquid in that they may be surrendered with the contract value returned as an excess distribution above the guaranteed distribution level. But in the early years of the contract, surrender charges may limit the portion that can be returned without paying a fee. For instance, surrender charges could work on a sliding scale basis starting at 7 percent in the first year the annuity is held, and then gradually reducing by 1 percent a year down to zero after the seventh year that the annuity is held. In this case, after the seventh year the surrender charges end, and the contract value will be fully liquid in all subsequent years.

The purpose of these charges is to help the insurance company offset the large fixed costs involved in setting up a new annuity contract that can otherwise only slowly be offset through the ongoing mortality and expense charges of the annuity over longer periods. The largest of these fixed costs is the commission paid to the adviser selling the variable annuity. Surrender charges would not be charged on any guaranteed lifetime distributions, and often variable annuities allow free annual withdrawals of up to 10 percent of the assets before surrender charges begin. Surrender charges may also be waived for required minimum distributions when held in qualified retirement plans.

Newer variable annuities designed for noncommission advisors will generally have lower fees in part because the advisor will charge for their service separate from the annuity rather than being paid through the annuity. There is no longer an upfront commission to be paid by the insurance company. Mortality and expenses fees should also be less for these no-commission variable annuities since a portion of the fees is no longer siphoned off to pay the advisor.

Rightly, the insurance company can offer these annuities as a lower-cost option to consumers. However, consumers must monitor whether ongoing charges from their financial advisor taken from outside of the annuity may offset the lower costs within the annuity. Financial advisors will be paid somehow, such that while shifting these fees from being collected within the annuity to moving directly to the advisor outside the annuity will reduce the internal costs to the annuity, it may or may not reduce the overall costs for financial tools and advice for the end consumer. There are exceptions, but variable annuities are rarely sold directly to consumers; most variable annuity sales require the involvement of a financial advisor. One final point here is that by lowering the internal costs to the annuity, there is a greater opportunity to obtain step-ups and more lifetime income from the annuity.

Finally, optional riders providing living benefits through a lifetime withdrawal guarantee or a stronger than standard death benefit guarantee require an additional ongoing charge. The rider is charged while the contract value remains positive. Rider charges end after the account is depleted and the guaranteed benefits continue to be made with insurance company resources.

Rider charges can be confusing because they may be charged in three different ways. The most expensive option is to have the rider charged on the benefit base. As the contract value approaches $0, this will increase the rider cost as a percentage of remaining assets and work to deplete the contract value more quickly. Two other options include charging the rider on the contract value of assets and charging the rider on a declining benefit base equal to the benefit base less cumulative guaranteed withdrawals. Charging on the contract value could be more expensive in scenarios with market upside and strong growth for the contract value, while charging on the declining benefit base could be more expensive if the contract value declines quickly and if there is a long deferral period.

For these optional riders, it is clearly worthwhile not to pay for riders that you do not intend to use. It is often counterproductive to pay for strong income guarantees and strong death benefits on the same variable annuity because these benefits are often at odds. It is also important to keep in mind that most variable annuity contracts allow provisions for these fees to be increased (or decreased) and one should take note of the maximum possible charges allowed by the contract.

With these various fees, it is possible that total variable annuity fees could add up to three to 4 percent. This, along with surrender charges, is how variable annuities have developed a reputation as being a high-cost financial product.

The message about fees is worth digging into further, as it presents one of the biggest objections made to variable annuities. Variable annuities have generally come under attack for the higher internal costs relative to an unprotected investment portfolio. But it is important to frame the issue of variable annuity fees in terms of the potential value the variable annuity can provide to a retirement income plan. Variable annuities may have higher ongoing charges than nonannuity investment portfolios, but a portion of those fees are to pay for the assurance of a lifetime income in the face of longevity and market risk.

It may be easiest to think about the fee issue by comparing to simple income annuities. Income annuities do not include transparent fees, as has been noted. The fees are internal to the product and the payout rate is provided on a net basis. Money's worth measures can be used to back out the implied fees for an income annuity. But if we frame the income annuity in the same way as a variable annuity, we would conclude that the income annuity has a 100 percent fee in its first year to provide the guaranteed lifetime income. Once an income annuity is purchased, assets are relinquished to the insurance company and will be inaccessible at any point in the future when the annuitant remains alive (there could be a cash refund provision at death). There is no contract value.

In contrast, the variable annuity provides liquidity. Variable annuity liquidity allows for the guarantee to be ended at any time and remaining assets can be returned. Excess distributions are allowed with a proportional reduction to the guarantee. The fee drag will work to gradually reduce the contract value over time rather than eliminating it immediately.

In practice, we do not describe the income annuity as having a 100 percent fee. Rather, we focus on the role its guaranteed income can play in the overall financial plan. Variable annuities maintain a contract value which has a higher cost associated with it, but the focus should be on how many assets must be earmarked for different retirement goals. With risk pooling, an income rider may allow fewer assets to be earmarked to meet retirement spending needs and that is where its value lies. A variable annuity with an income rider is then able to pay a guaranteed income for life based on a fixed percentage of the hypothetical benefit base. The most compelling aspect of the variable annuity is that even in cases when the contract value of the underlying assets has been depleted, the income guarantee will continue to pay for the lifetime of the annuitant.

More broadly, in the context of the retirement income plan, focusing on the internal costs of a variable annuity is not the best way to frame the problem we are attempting to solve. Is an investments-only strategy with lower internal fees preferable if its approach to managing longevity and sequence risk means that the retiree must either spend less or delay financial independence because it is necessary to earmark a larger overall asset base to ensure that retirement spending goals can be covered? That is the context in which to assess fees: can they support better outcomes through risk pooling that reduce the overall costs of the plan in terms of the asset base required to meet the financial goals of retirement?

Income Guarantees, Risk Capacity, Upside Potential, and Asset Allocation

If one maintains the same asset allocation both inside and outside of the variable annuity, then the additional fees for a variable annuity can be expected to deplete the underlying value of the assets more quickly than if they were held in an unprotected investment account with lower fees.

However, this outcome changes if one accepts the notion that having an income guarantee in place can support using a higher stock allocation within a variable annuity. In this case, when markets do well in retirement, the additional exposure to the risk premium can more than offset the higher costs of the variable annuity to allow for greater overall growth in assets. If markets perform poorly in retirement, the additional costs within the variable annuity could cause it to deplete assets sooner than otherwise. But with poor returns, the investments-only portfolio will be on track to depletion shortly thereafter.

With the variable annuity assets, at least, the income guarantee continues to support spending after the contract value depletes. With investments-only, spending power ends. Over time, variable annuities with income guarantees could have lower remaining wealth (due to fees) or higher remaining wealth if the guarantee moves someone to accept a higher stock allocation and stocks perform well.

The assumptions made about asset allocation for guaranteed funds and unguaranteed funds are incredibly important. It is natural that retirees with income guarantees will feel more comfortable accepting a more aggressive asset allocation, and ideally one should compare approaches using the asset allocations a retiree would choose for both a guaranteed and unguaranteed approach. This will be individual specific. Moshe Milevsky and Vladyslav Kyrychenko have provided research based on over one-million variable annuity policy holders showing that those with optional income guarantees were willing to have about a 5 percent to 30 percent higher stock allocation than those without guarantees on their variable annuities. For instance, someone willing to hold 40 percent stocks without a guarantee may increase their stock allocation to between 45 percent and 70 percent (if allowed) with an income guarantee in place.

Having the income guarantee supported with actuarial bonds increases the risk capacity of retirees, as their retirement standard of living is less vulnerable to a market downturn. This can provide the capacity to use a higher stock allocation when a guarantee is in place, both inside and outside of a variable annuity. Inside because the income guarantee protects income on the downside while still offering upside potential. Outside because the income guarantee reduces the harm created if portfolio assets are depleted. Risk capacity is greater.

A retiree may be willing to invest more aggressively within the variable annuity than with an investments-only strategy. The variable annuity owner has the upside potential to grow the asset base and increase guaranteed income with a higher stock allocation, while knowing at the retirement income is protected and sustainable even if the market is performing poorly in the pivotal early years of retirement.

The income riders on variable annuities provide the ability to receive mortality credits, which can reduce the asset base required to support a lifetime spending goal. The rider fees paid for the income guarantee provide insurance that the spending will be protected in case someone experiences a combination of either living too long or experiencing sufficiently poor market returns that they outlive their underlying investment assets and cannot sustain an income for life.

A higher variable annuity fee may provide stronger protections, or it may provide more upside potential. Retirees seek to evaluate variable annuities along the tradeoff between what can provide the most certainty for the least cost to potential upside opportunities.

In evaluating a variable annuity guarantee, it is important to first start with the level of guaranteed income it provides if no upside is ever achieved. This can be compared with the guaranteed income from an income annuity offering a cash refund, since this is the most comparable to the standard death benefit for variable annuities. The difference in payouts between the two better relates to the cost of upside and liquidity while alive. Most frequently, the variable annuity guaranteed withdrawal rate will be less than an income annuity. The differential reflects the guaranteed income one would give up to receive the upside potential and liquidity in the contract.

With the investment options and annuity features, how likely is it that the contract value can grow, and how important is it to the retiree to maintain the liquidity provided by the contract for those assets? About liquidity, we must remember that it may not be true liquidity if those assets are earmarked for income because excess distributions beyond the guaranteed amount will reduce the subsequent amount of guaranteed income provided. But if a retiree values this liquidity nonetheless, then comparing the amount of guaranteed income lost to provide the liquidity (and upside) help to quantify the tradeoff for the decision between income annuities and deferred variable annuities with income guarantees.

Marketing Approaches for Income Guarantees

We have outlined many factors that impact deferred variable annuity performance: rollup rates and the frequency of their vesting, as well as how long they are applied, step-ups and their frequency, whether rollups stack on step-ups, guaranteed withdrawal rates, death benefits, investment choices, allowed asset allocation and the range of investment offerings, use of volatility-managed strategies, fees for the variable annuity and the optional riders and what they are applied to, and so on.

What approach can provide the most certainty to the retiree about guaranteed income while costing the least in terms of opportunity for upside growth? Companies tend to take a particular marketing approach toward framing their annuity products as the better option for retirees. They may focus on a few of these aspects and downplay others. With so many levers and possibilities, it is difficult to say which is best. Companies with better financial policies and strength could offer a better overall product, but at some level we should expect that among the best companies there may not be that much underlying difference, net of costs. There will be an associated cost for the risk accepted by the insurance company, and this will not vary too much among companies. In the end, the decision may ultimately center around choosing a strong company providing an approach and story that makes the retiree feel the most comfortable.

The most salient features for marketing variable annuities are the arms races that develop around which company is providing the highest rollup rates and/or guaranteed withdrawal rates. Companies may be strong on both, but without being the highest for either, can struggle to make their message heard. But they may also focus on what really matters: showing how their combination of rollup and withdrawal rates support more guaranteed income than the competitors along the lines of the discussion with Exhibit 5.1. Another position used here is to offer a higher initial guaranteed withdrawal rate on the condition that guaranteed income decreases if the contract value depletes, such as starting with allowed withdrawals equal to 7 percent of the benefit base but reducing withdrawals to 3 percent of the benefit base after contract depletion.

Along these lines, purchasers should remember to remain cautious and not necessarily pick the company offering the highest guarantees. Financial strength is important, and the company with the highest guarantee may have mismanaged its risk. Weaker companies may not have properly hedged their risks and the guarantees may not be sustainable.

Another marketing angle is to be the provider with more frequent step-up opportunities. The consumer receives value if step-ups can be locked in daily, rather than annually, as it increases the probability for step-ups to happen and for new high watermarks to be achieved. The contract anniversary is not always the date with the highest market level over the previous year. It is even better for owners if these step-ups can immediately vest and can have the rollup rate stacked on them.

Another approach is to be the provider offering the most investment freedom. While remaining competitive with the other means for reducing risk, a company may place emphasis on maintaining an open investment architecture with no limits on the stock allocation and no requirements that any sort of volatility-management approach be included for the underlying asset base. Arguably, this allows a retiree to choose an asset allocation appropriate to their situation rather than to the risk management needs of the insurance company.

Finally, companies could focus on providing the lowest costs for their guarantees, though this is not necessarily a key focus for any company.

Offering a low cost alone is not the point, as the strength of the guarantees will also probably be less. The issue is more about what variable annuity offers the most value for its cost. Supporting a stronger guarantee is more costly, and paying a higher cost is not necessarily bad for a guarantee that provides greater value to the retiree.

Further Reading

Milevsky, Moshe. 2009. "Annuity Analytics: What is a Guaranteed Rate Really Worth?" Research Magazine (August).

Milevsky, Moshe A., and V. Kyrychenko. 2008. "Portfolio Choice with Puts: Evidence from Variable Annuities." Financial Analysts Journal, Vol. 64, No. 3 (May/June), p. 80–95.

CHAPTER 6

Fixed Index Annuities

Fixed Index Annuities Caveat

In this discussion of fixed index annuities, which use to be called equity indexed annuities, I am mostly making an implicit assumption that the annuity is competitively priced. Internal costs reflect was is needed to support the guarantees provided by the insurance company and to keep the company reasonably profitable. But costs are not excessive such that the value to the consumer is eliminated. As well, I assume value is created because the annuity has a clear role to play in the financial plan and is not being sold by an unscrupulous financial advisor only to generate a commission.

It must be noted that not all fixed index annuities are created equal. As will be discussed, they are complex financial instruments, and that complexity can hide a lack of competitiveness in the pricing of individual products. A fixed index annuity that is pitched at a free dinner presentation is more likely not the type of financial product I have in mind, especially if it is misused.

One should tread carefully. Due diligence and a comparison with other annuity options is needed to make sure that the product is fairly priced and will behave in the way that the purchaser understands it to behave. I do not want the "bad" annuities out there to free-ride off of my explanations about the potential positives that can be created by "good" annuities.

A fixed index annuity (FIA) with an optional guaranteed lifetime withdrawal benefit (GLWB) shares many similarities with its variable annuity (VA) counterpart. Both are deferred annuities that may take advantage of rollup rates and step-up opportunities to increase guaranteed income. Both provide guaranteed withdrawal rates. Both also provide tax deferral benefits outside of qualified retirement plans. FIAs may also have surrender charges on excess distributions taken in the early years of the contract beyond the free withdrawal allowances provided. The following discussion assumes familiarity with the content about variable annuities from the previous chapter because there are so many similarities between the two. Here I will emphasize the differences.

Where fixed index annuities are most different from variable annuities is the underlying mechanism for asset growth. VAs allow for the direct investment of premiums into subaccounts. FIA premiums are added to the general account of the insurance company and credit interest to the owner based either on a fixed return or on the performance of a linked market index. FIAs offer index-linked interest, but they are not invested directly into the underlying index. They simply pay interest to the owner using a formula linked to the performance of the index.

With FIAs, the credited interest (or returns) can be structured more precisely in terms of controlling downside and upside exposures. Many FIAs will protect principal in the sense that 0 percent interest is credited even if the underlying index declines significantly in value. To obtain this protection, FIA owners should expect to receive only a portion of any positive gains experienced by the index. These types of structured outcomes can lead to a different investing experience that could have implications for retirement income planning and sequence-of-returns risk. Overall, FIAs may generally reduce the potential volatility of the underlying contract value relative to a variable annuity. On the spectrum of risk, index-linked FIAs fall in between fixed annuities with a fixed interest rate and variable annuities with volatile subaccount investments.

FIAs also differ from VAs in that, as with an income annuity, FIA fees tend to be structured internally to the product such that there are no observable fees to reduce the contract value. Fees can be kept internal because they are based on a spread, like other banking products. The insurance company earns more from investing the premiums than it pays to the owner. As with income annuities, it is also possible to reverse engineer and estimate the internal costs for the FIA, though this process does get more complicated, as will be explained.

FIAs do not have mortality and expense charges and they do not invest in funds such that there are no investment fees. Internal fees are reflected through the limits placed on the upside growth potential. Of course, upside growth potential must be limited in order to support the downside risk protections. The internal fees for the FIA just mean that upside growth potential is less than it could have been if the insurance company did not need to cover its expenses and profit needs.

At the same time, though, households may not be able to earn the same rates of returns on their funds as an insurance company that obtains institutional pricing on trades, better diversification, and longer-term investment holding periods. It is not always the case that households could easily replicate on their own what the FIA provides as an accumulation tool.

The exceptions to the lack of external fees include that FIAs may still have a surrender charge schedule in the early years for excess distributions. This is done to allow the insurance company to invest the premium in longer-term assets and to cover the company's fixed expenses for providing the annuity. These surrender charges will gradually disappear for long-term owners. As well, any optional lifetime income benefits or enhanced death benefits added to the contract have observable fees that will be deducted from the contract value. Though otherwise protected, the contract value of the FIA could decline on a net basis after accounting for optional rider expenses.

Another key difference from VAs is that, related to their potential to protect principal, fixed index annuities may also be emphasized as an accumulation tool in the preretirement transition years to help lock-in a wealth accumulation target at the retirement date with a high probability. The FIA can be treated as an asset class alongside stocks and bonds, but with the unique property that it protects from downside losses. After accounting for its tax deferral, the question becomes whether it provides enough upside exposure to compete with other fixed-income investment opportunities on a risk-adjusted basis. For these accumulation uses, the optional lifetime income benefit may not be emphasized.

In other applications, though, the FIA can be discussed alongside other annuities providing lifetime income as a tool to better manage longevity and market risk and to meet a retirement spending goal with less earmarked assets. For some FIAs, using an income rider may be required.

This chapter continues by explaining in greater detail how interest is credited to FIAs, how the insurance company determines the terms it offers for the FIA, how FIA returns behave in relation to stocks and bonds, and other details about understanding how an FIA can function as a retirement tool.

● Crediting Interest with an Annual Reset One-Year Term Point-to-Point Crediting Method

We start with considering how interest is credited to fixed index annuities, since this is the area that differs the most from variable annuities. Since FIAs are fixed annuities, crediting interest is the technical term for the returns generated by the contract value. As with variable annuities, it can be difficult to provide a standard explanation for how these returns are calculated on FIAs. Almost countless methods are used in practice and there is a trend to increase the complexity of the methods used. The discussion here cannot be comprehensive, but I will try to provide enough of a general understanding of the main options found in practice.

FIAs will generally provide options to either credit interest at a fixed rate, or as based on the performance of an external index. The amount of interest received depends on both the index and the crediting method chosen.

Perhaps the most common FIA design is to credit interest through one-year point-to-point crediting with a cap and an annual reset. At the end of each yearly term on the anniversary date of the contract, the interest-crediting formula uses the index gain for that year (the price return for the index over the one-year term) to credit interest. A floor of 0 percent is protected, and full participation is provided for upside gains up to a cap rate. The cap rate can be changed, subject to a minimum allowed value, and is redetermined in advance of each new annual term starting on contract anniversary dates. This is a necessary feature to account for the market conditions surrounding the ongoing costs for creating the FIA protections.

Digging deeper, we must consider the index used with the FIA. Insurance companies generally offer access to different index options as well as a fixed interest option. Contract owners can often combine these options in any way they choose and can change the allocations at the start of each new term. Common index choices include the S&P 500 for large capitalization US stocks, or the MSCI EAFE index that provides representation for international stocks. Companies may also offer other index options seeking lower volatility, such as an effort to pick a subset of less volatile stocks from the wider S&P 500. Lower volatility can help to support better parameters that link returns to the interest credited. Increasing complexity may also be found with dynamic allocation options that will vary the allocations based on predetermined formulas which adjust to volatility. To keep this discussion manageable, I will describe the S&P 500 as the index of choice for an index-linked FIA. It is a commonly used index in practice and matches the general assumption throughout much of this book that the stock market is represented by large capitalization US stocks.

Another important matter must be addressed regarding the index. As mentioned, annuity premium dollars are not actually invested in the underlying index. Rather, the insurance company is purchasing financial derivatives that provide a return based on the index performance (more on this shortly). An implication of this process is that interest-crediting is not based on the total returns from the underlying index. Dividends are generally excluded from the calculations. Only the price returns (capital gains or capital losses) play a roll. This is an important detail because, historically, dividends have been an important part of the total return for the S&P 500.

For the Morningstar data on S&P 500 returns from 1926 through 2018, the compounded growth rate for the S&P 500 was 10 percent. However, with dividends excluded, the price returns were only 5.8 percent. It is the latter number that matters for determining FIA interest.

The dividend issue requires extra caution because there is a tendency to confuse this point in the marketing literature for some fixed index annuities. As will be discussed, FIAs should be considered as a potential alternative to other fixed-income assets, but some marketing literature emphasizes that an FIA can beat its corresponding stock index, suggesting higher returns with less risk. The comparison may be in terms of the cumulative growth for FIA assets relative to the S&P 500 from some starting date, with the idea being that the FIA provides a greater wealth accumulation at the end. While it is possible for an FIA to outperform its linked stock index occasionally, especially if the time period included significant market downturns that let the FIA shine, this should not be expected as a typical outcome.

The problem is that marketing comparisons are made in terms of comparing the FIA returns against the price returns of the S&P 500 with dividends excluded. That comparison might be justified since the FIA performance is based on the price returns. But I find it misleading because if an individual were comparing an FIA with a corresponding stock index mutual fund or ETF, the corresponding fund would provide total returns including dividends. It will be more difficult for an FIA to beat the total return performance of the corresponding index than to just beat the price returns.

I have found that the compliance departments of insurance companies are usually quite strict and take great care to properly disclose matters and to avoid misleading consumers. And while such marketing literature does provide small-print disclosures that the price index is being used instead of a total returns index for the investment alternative, I can only imagine that the vast majority of individuals reading the marketing piece would overlook, or not otherwise understand, this vital detail. It may lead individuals to believe that FIAs can reliably outperform the stock market without accepting the downside risk of the stock market.

Again, the joint combination of downside protection along with a portion of upside may occasionally be adequate to outperform the associated index, but FIA owners should not expect this to happen regularly, as it would defy the financial maxim that there is no such thing as a free lunch in terms of earning higher returns without taking on greater risks.

As for credited returns, FIAs provide downside protections with limited upside potential as based on the performance of the linked index. For instance, having a floor of 0 percent on credited interest ensures that if the index experiences a loss during the contract term, the contract value of the FIA is protected from loss. Even bond funds have downside risk for capital losses when interest rates rise. FIAs are usually structured to avoid such losses. Because there is a cost for creating protection for the contract value against a loss when the index declines in value, one should not expect to receive the full upside potential from the index. FIAs do not provide a way to get the returns from the stock market without accepting the risk of the stock market.

With the chosen index, interest crediting will generally be based on a formula that can include floors, caps, participation rates, spreads, and, less commonly, buffers. To explain these basic features, it helps to have a basic annuity design. We will consider an *annual reset one-year term point-to-point crediting method.*

Though it is a mouthful, an annual reset one-year term point-to-point crediting method is probably the most straightforward and intuitive way to understand and use an FIA. Allowing for longer term lengths to also be included in this category, it is likely the most common as well. The one-year term and the point-to-point method means that the changes in the index values on one-year contract anniversaries will be used to calculate interest. Annual point-to-point looks at the change in the index at two different dates, one year apart. The term could be longer, such as three, five, or seven years. Whatever the term length, it is the cumulative change in the index value over the term that is relevant for crediting interest. The term length is also important because at the end of each term, the insurance company may change these parameters (such as caps or participation rates) used to calculate interest for the following term.

As for the annual reset design, this reflects how interest crediting calculations start fresh for each term. If the index lost 10 percent in the previous term and credited 0 percent interest for that term, it is only the new point-to-point change for the current term that matters to calculate the new term's interest. In other words, there is no need for cumulative gains to make up for previous losses when the annual reset provision is included.

Regarding interest calculations, the first step is to identify the *floor* on returns. This provides protection from downside risk and is generally a key feature of FIAs, except for ones using a buffer approach instead. The floor provides a minimum value that credited interest cannot fall below. Typically, it is 0 percent in order to provide full downside protection, but it could be less or more. If the floor is less than zero, then the annuity is technically a variable index annuity and maintains most characteristics of the FIA except that it is also regulated as a security because it can experience losses. If the index price return is less that this floor value, the interest credited will instead be equal to the floor.

In terms of how an FIA works, a simple way to think about the downside protection with the guaranteed floor is that the insurance company buys enough bonds with the annuity contract value that the growth of that portion with interest will match the original contract value at the end of the term. Suppose the yield on the insurance company's general account is 4 percent, and I have $100 as a contract value in my FIA. Simplifying with an annual interest payment assumption, if the insurance company invests $96.15 in bonds, this amount will grow to $100 in a year with the 4 percent interest. The $96.15 investment fully protects my principal and creates a 0 percent return floor. It also leaves $3.85 for the insurance company to use for both covering their needs and providing upside potential.

Note that if the floor is less than 0 percent, the amount of bonds needed to guarantee it would be less. For instance, if the FIA (or, technically, a variable index annuity in this case) guaranteed that returns will not be less than -2 percent, then $98 must be protected. That would require $94.23 growing at 4 percent, leaving $5.77 to be used for other purposes. Conversely, the floor return could be positive. With yields of 4 percent, the guaranteed floor could not be greater than 4 percent because sufficient assets are not available to guarantee a higher return. It requires the full $100 to guarantee a 4 percent return when yields are 4 percent.

Let's return to the 0 percent floor example, which takes $96.15 to protect if the general account assets are yielding 4 percent. No financial product is truly free. But many FIAs can be marketed as no-cost as there are no external fees quoted on the product. FIAs do not charge for mutual fund expenses or a mortality and expense charge on the contract value in the same way that a variable annuity does. But fees will be accounted for internally. Fees can only be observed by comparing the upside potential an FIA provides after creating its downside protection to the actuarial fair upside potential possible if there were no internal charges to the contract value.

Fortunately, there is a simple way in practice to observe the yields on FIAs net of the internal fees for a participating company. We may not know the gross returns for the insurance company investments, but we can know the net amount after fees as based on the FIA's one-year fixed return option not linked to an index. In this example, suppose the insurance company separately offers a guaranteed fixed return option of 2 percent for the current term. It must be yielding more than this to cover its expenses and profit motives. With a 2 percent fixed return, it takes $98.04 to protect principal (or $100 to guarantee 2 percent growth). The $98.04 to protect principal, when it is based on the guaranteed fixed return option offered by the FIA, implies that the combined cost to support the floor and cover company expenses is $98.04. The remaining $1.96, which is the difference in the floor protection cost at the assumed general account gross yield, less the floor protection costs based on the net yield offered by the company's fixed interest option, is the options budget that remains to seek the upside growth for the FIA when it is linked to a volatile market index instead of accepting a fixed return.

Related to what the household can do on its own, that internal fee may be less on a net basis than what it seems. This is because the insurance company can earn higher returns from its fixed-income holdings than a household could independently achieve. The insurance company can receive institutional pricing for its purchases as a type of size discount, and its asset-liability matching emphasis allow for diversified long-term holdings. The insurance company can seek higher return premiums relative to a household from holding assets with longer maturity dates, greater credit risk, and less liquidity than a household can generally justify. Households using an FIA in place of holding bonds in taxable accounts can also benefit from the tax deferral aspect of the FIA.

The next step is to see how upside potential develops through a *participation rate*. The insurance company can use the remaining funds to buy a one-year at-the-money call option on the S&P 500 index. This is a financial derivative that provides its owner with the right, but not the obligation, to buy shares of the S&P 500 at the option's strike price. The option is at-the-money if the strike price matches the current value of the index.

Suppose the S&P 500 index is currently at 1000, and the insurance company buys a call option to purchase the index at 1000 after a one-year period. If the index has declined in value at the end of the year, the insurance company will not exercise its option to buy the index at the now higher strike price. The option expires, worthless. With the bond, the contract value was protected at $100 and no additional upside is received because the credited interest linked to the index is $0. This represents the principal protection of the FIA.

However, if the S&P 500 index price has increased in value at the end of the year through capital gains (not including reinvested dividends), then the insurance company exercises the option to buy the S&P 500 at the now lower strike price. What happens in practice is that the shares are not actually purchased, but the call option owner receives a payment equal to the gain in the index relative to the strike price from the seller of the call option. For example, if the index ended the year at 1060, it experienced a 6 percent price return, and this gain is received by the insurance company. The gain can then be credited to the contract value of the annuity.

The assumed $1.96 left in this example is probably not enough to buy a call option on a full share of the S&P 500. Suppose, for example, a one-year call option costs $3.50. In this case, the $1.96 options budget represents 56 percent of the call option price. This means that the index annuity could offer a 56 percent participation rate on the upside from the S&P 500 price return. The FIA could offer a protective floor through bond purchases with the potential to receive 56 percent of the upside growth through the call option purchase with the remaining funds. If the S&P 500 price return was 4 percent, for instance, then the annuity would be credited with a 2.24 percent gain. Owning a bond and a call option on the index allows the insurance to guarantee a minimum interest value while also offering upside exposure to the index.

As an alternative, FIA owners might seek to maintain an ongoing participation rate of 100 percent. One way that this can be accomplished is by introducing a cap on interest that can be credited. To create 100 percent upside participation, the insurance company could also sell call options on the S&P 500 to provide additional funds beyond the $1.96. This would support buying more of the at-the-money call option. In our simple example, to provide 100 percent participation, the insurance company would like to buy a full call option costing $3.50. It needs to raise an additional $1.54 to do this. Call options become cheaper as the strike price increases since the market would need a bigger gain before any payment from the option is due. There will be a strike price that would support call option pricing at $1.54. The key is to find what this value is. It would then serve as the cap for the current term of the FIA. The insurance company sells a call option at a higher strike price to raise additional funds in order to buy a full at-the-money call option.

By selling the call option, the insurance company is then on the hook to pay any gains on the index above that strike price to the buyer of the option. Suppose a one-year out-of-the-money call option with a strike price of 1060 is the right level so that the option price is $1.54. The insurance company could sell one call option with the 1060 strike price and then buy the full call option with the strike price of 1000. Then, any gains between 0 percent and 6 percent can be accrued to the contract value with full 100 percent participation. But the gains are capped at 6 percent because any return above that reflects an obligation the insurance company must pay to the owner of the call option it sold.

A subtle detail that must be emphasized is whether the cap is an interest cap or an index cap. I have been describing an interest cap, which is more advantageous to the consumer, assuming everything else remains the same.

With an index cap, instead, the amount of the index gain realized is capped before then calculating the amount of interest applied. For instance, suppose an FIA has a 50 percent participation rate and a cap of 10 percent, and the index return is 25 percent. If that cap is an interest cap as we have been assuming, the total interest credited is calculated as 50 percent of 25 percent, which would be 12.5 percent, but it is capped at 10 percent. However, if the FIA instead has an index cap of 10 percent, then 10 percent of the gain is realized for determining interest. With the 50 percent participation rate on the 10 percent index gain realized, credited interest is only 5 percent. This makes a difference and it is important to understand which method is used by the insurance company.

Another method for increasing the participation rate without introducing a cap is to add a *spread* to the FIA interest-crediting formula. Continuing with our same simple example in which we found a 56 percent participation rate, suppose the insurance company could offer a 75 percent participation rate with a 2 percent spread. What this means is that the FIA provides interest of 75 percent of the market gain less 2 percent, but still with the same principal protection in place. In this case, the index would need to experience a 2.67 percent gain before interest is credited because 75 percent of 2.67 percent is 2 percent.

The spread allows for a higher participation rate because it allows for the call option to be purchased with a higher strike price and therefore at a lower cost. In this example, the strike price for the call option can be 2.67 percent higher than its current price because the option only needs pay interest once this level is exceeded to meet the terms of the FIA. In this simplified example, this outcome could have been determined if the price for the call option with that higher strike price is $2.61. Then the options budget allows for 75 percent of an option to be purchased, providing 75 percent of any gains above 2.67 percent.

Another variation on interest-crediting for these one-year point-to-point FIAs is to introduce a *buffer*. But, again, to be clear, this will change the FIA into a variable index annuity (VIA) because principal is not protected. Buffers may reduce downside losses, but they do not provide principal protection. For instance, a VIA that provides a 10 percent buffer would mean that the interest credited is zero percent for any index loss between 10 percent and 0 percent. If the index loses more than 10 percent, then this approach would credit the amount of the loss in excess of 10 percent. For instance, an 18 percent loss on the index would lead to a loss of 8 percent for the VIA, but an 8 percent loss for the index would lead to no loss for the VIA. Accepting this greater downside risk can support more upside potential. But because these types of buffer VIAs do not create a floor for returns, they do not share the same general philosophy about how FIAs are known for providing principal protection.

● Factors Affecting the Parameter Values for Fixed Index Annuities

The previous discussion makes clear that the parameters offered by an FIA (floors, participation rates, caps, spreads, and buffers) will depend in large part on the level of interest rates and the cost of financial derivatives for the associated index. Higher interest rates mean that principal can be protected with less assets, which then leaves more that can be devoted to the options budget used to purchase upside exposure. Participation

Other Fixed Index Annuity Crediting Approaches

The crediting method we have described thus far is a term end-point method with a reset for each subsequent term. We mostly considered an annual point-to-point design but explained that longer terms are also possible. This method only compares the end point to the start point and ignores any gains or losses in between these points.

There are countless other crediting methods also used in practice, although some of these may be quite rare. Jack Marrion and John Olsen provide a more detailed explanation about a wide variety of crediting methods in their book Index Annuities: A Suitable Approach. For the purposes of understanding how FIAs work, I do not think it is necessary to explain other methods in detail, but I recommend the Marrion and Olsen book for those seeking further details. We will consider a few other methods.

Yield spread design
Another possibility is to use a yield spread over the term. Instead of choosing a cap to obtain 100 percent participation rate up to the cap, the insurance company could instead determine the spread that would allow the options budget to provide full participation above the spread. The compounded return over the term is calculated, and then a yield spread is deducted from this to determine the interest that will be credited. In the annual case, if the index returned 7 percent and the spread is 4 percent, then the annuity would be credited with 3 percent interest. If the return is less than the spread, interest credited would match the floor value.

For instance, if the floor is 0 percent, the spread is 4 percent, and the return is 2 percent, then the interest credited is 0 percent. This method could provide more interest than a participation rate when gains are large, but it is likely to be less when gains are more moderate.

High watermark design
Another possibility is to focus on high watermark values during a term to determine interest, but this method is more expensive and is not common.

Rolling average design
Another possibility is a rolling average of index values during the

term. An example of this could be a monthly method to credit interest based on the average value of the index at the end of each month during a longer term such as a year. These averaging methods will moderate the interest credited relative to term end-point methods. Averaging drives the index values toward the middle with both gains and losses, which means that a higher participation rate could be offered than otherwise with everything else being the same.

Monthly sum design
A more extreme and potentially confusing method is called monthly sum. Each month, upside growth has a cap, but there is no monthly floor. At the end of the term, the monthly values are added to determine the interest credited for the term. If the monthly cap is 2 percent, the interest could be as high as 24 percent for a year, but this would be a very rare event. It would require consistent gains of over 2 percent for each month of the year. If the index was up 3 percent each month for eleven months, but lost 25 percent in the twelfth month, then the interest credited for the year is 0 percent, assuming a 0 percent floor. This method's best opportunity to work is to experience steady upward growth without any market dips.

There are other methods as well, and this discussion provides just a taste of the possibilities.

rates can conceivably be higher than 100 percent if interest rates are high enough and the call options are cheap enough. On a related point, it should also be clear that if the owner is willing to accept a lower floor, it would be possible to gain more upside potential since less is needed for bonds and more is available to purchase call options.

The key factors that influence the price of call options were formulized with the Black-Scholes formula in the 1970s. The Black-Scholes formula shows the relationship and factors for determining the price of a European-style call option, which is relevant for FIAs that credit interest on a point-to-point basis. European options can only be exercised at the end date for the option and the price at that time is what matters for determining the value to the option owner. An American option can be exercised at any point before the maturity date and are even more complex to price. But even for

European options, a complex mathematical relationship exists between the factors and the option price (a Nobel prize was awarded to those who figured it out) and the theorem still relies on simplifying assumptions that may not always accurately reflect market option pricing. Nonetheless it can provide a decent approximation. Generally, a call option's price will be based on six factors.

Implied Volatility

The implied volatility of the underlying market index may be the most important factor. Greater index volatility will increase the cost of a call option. Increased volatility creates more possibility that the index price will increase, which would require a larger payoff to the option owner. Implied volatility can be difficult to measure in practice because it depends on future beliefs about how volatile the markets will be. It is typically estimated from calculating the market's recent volatility, with the idea that investors might expect recent volatility to continue at the same pace. For example, one might look to the annualized volatility of monthly stock market returns over the previous year as an estimate of the implied volatility for the purchase of a new option on the index. But this is only an estimate and it may not be precise. Since 1993, the VIX has been available from the Chicago Board Options Exchange as a market estimate of implied volatility for the S&P 500. It can be used as an estimate of implied volatility, but prior to its introduction any estimates of implied volatility will be less reliable. The development of low-volatility index options can be explained, in part because the lower volatility will allow for cheaper option pricing, which in turn supports more advantageous parameters with the upside growth exposure.

Current Index Price

This current price of the index is important with regard to how it relates to the strike price for the associated option.

Option Strike Price

Another important variable is the relationship between the strike price of the option and the current price of the index. The strike price represents the price that the index can be purchased. As the strike price increases relative to the current market price, the option is out-of-the-money and less likely to provide a payoff. Call options only make payment when the index price ends up higher than the strike price. The option will be cheaper with a higher strike price. An at-the-money call option has a strike price matching the current index price. The strike price could be less than the current price (it is in-the-money) which makes it more likely to provide a payoff and more expensive to the purchase. This also explains why an FIA that includes a spread can offer a higher participation rate than otherwise. It allows for the call options purchased with the options budget to have a higher strike price, and therefore less cost.

Risk-Free Interest Rate

The risk-free interest rate is another relevant variable, though it has a smaller impact. It represents the return on a risk-free bond during the interval of the option. With a one-year term FIA, the call option would have a one-year maturity, and the risk-free rate could be approximated with a one-year Treasury rate. Higher interest rates will cause a slight increase in the option price, though this will usually be more than offset by allowing for a bigger options budget to support upside exposure since fewer bonds are needed to protect the principal.

Term to Maturity

A fifth factor is the term to maturity. We mostly spoke of a one-year term, but some FIAs will have longer terms of even seven years or beyond. A longer term does increase the price of the call option, but not on a one-to-one basis. Longer terms can allow for more attractive FIA parameters. In other words, the participation rate can be higher when the terms are longer because the call option price is increasing at a less than linear rate as the term length increases.

Dividend Rate

Finally, if the market index pays a dividend, this becomes a final input for the options price. With this input, the strike price can be entered when thinking in terms of a total return, but then it is reduced by the entered dividend to make the option cheaper in terms of an effective strike price. For example, an index priced at $100 with a strike price of $96 and a dividend yield of 4 percent would create the same call option cost as for an index priced at $100 with a strike price of $100 and no dividend yield. Because dividends could be removed and accounted for separately, it is not mandatory to include the dividend rate as an input for estimating the option price.

It is interesting to also note that the expected return for the index is not one of the factors used to price its call option.

It is also vitally important to understand that the amount of upside potential that can be offered by an FIA will vary over time as interest rates and call option prices change. With an annual reset design, the insurance company must repeat this process each year and will face different interest rates and call option pricing as these variables change values over time. More upside potential is possible with higher interest rates and cheaper call options, and vice versa.

This is the reason why insurance companies maintain the freedom to change the contract parameters (such as the fixed rate, participation rate, cap rate, or spread) at the beginning of each new term, subject to a minimum or maximum value allowed for each parameter within the contract. For those minimum or maximum limits, the boundaries of what the insurance can use may be extreme, such as the potential to cap interest at 0.25 percent for a term. This flexibility is necessary because the insurance company does not know beforehand what the ongoing options pricing and interest rates will be when it is time to renew the process at the start of each new term.

Insurance companies have discretion to change the FIA parameters in a way that would make them less competitive after the fact. A company could offer good introductory parameters on the FIA, but it could change the parameters in an adverse way for subsequent terms in a manner not justified by fair pricing. A company could reduce the options budget so that it keeps more. In comparing FIAs between different companies, it is also important to investigate a company's history regarding changes to its FIA parameters. Does the company have a history of adjusting parameters in an adverse direction, especially during years when surrender charges still applied? If so, this could serve as a red flag about purchasing that company's product.

Some companies will be more effective than others in managing potentially adverse changes from the consumer's perspective. For FIAs with surrender charges, insurance companies will often invest in longer-term bonds matching the length of time that surrender charges remain and will seek as best they can to avoid any adverse change in parameter values before the end of the surrender charge period.

Companies must maintain the right to change parameter values at the start of new terms in order to reflect the realities of changing capital markets, but high-quality companies will make the effort to place the customer's interests first and to not use this nontransparent process to extract additional value from the consumer.

This discussion should also help to make clear why it becomes more difficult in practice to simulate the performance of FIAs. Modeling their performance is more complex than modeling returns for traditional asset classes like stock and bonds. The simplest approach to modeling FIAs is to assume that their current parameters (such as floors, caps, participation rates, and/or spreads) would have applied equally in the past. However, this is not satisfactory because changing market conditions over time would have led those parameters to also be different. As well, many FIAs have just been created recently, and the oldest FIA dates back only to 1995, so that relying on their historical returns or historical parameter values is not an option.

To obtain a better sense about what their past parameters could have been, a more complete model to price FIAs must account for the risk-free interest rate, the broader yield curve and credit spread, internal insurance company costs and the amount available for the options budget, the implied volatility of the underlying index linked to the FIA, and the dividend yield for the underlying index.

Many of these variables are outside the scope of what Monte Carlo simulations would generally include. Some of these variables are not readily observable. In particular, insurance company expenses and assumptions about the performance of their investments, as well as the implied volatility of the stock market are variables that will require assumptions. Simulations of FIA performance will only be as reliable as the underlying assumptions used.

To summarize, the factors affecting the degree of upside participation that can be offered by an FIA include the level of interest rates, the factors affecting options pricing, the strength of the downside guarantee protection, company expenses, company pricing assumptions and whether the company is pricing the FIA to be competitive in the marketplace.

● The Choice of Crediting Method

Before the fact, the various crediting methods available should be approximately equal in terms of long-term performance. Performance after the fact will be different as the actual index return will be translated into different interest credited as based on the crediting method. But before market performance is realized, the different methods are all using the same options budget to purchase financial derivatives that are priced with the same inputs.

Companies face the same market prices for options and interest rates. While companies can be creative about designing their crediting methods, at the end they have to use similar methods to support the guarantees and upside offered. This means that the parameters (such as participation rates, caps, floors, or spreads) will have to be adjusted to match the reality of interest rates and option prices. Different crediting methods are just different ways to bundle these parameters together. One method is not inherently better than another. The different methods just structure the returns of the index differently when calculating the interest to credit. After the index performance is known, there is a crediting method that will have worked best with it.

To better illustrate this, we can consider an example of a one-year point-to-point crediting design with a participation rate or a cap. Is a cap combined with a 100 percent participation rate better than having a lower participation rate but with no cap? Before we know the realized index return, it does not make a difference if both FIAs are priced competitively based on options pricing. But after the fact, one will perform better. The capped FIA will do better when returns are positive but lower, while the participation rate FIA will do better when higher returns are realized. In fact, there is a formula that can determine the break-even return for this calculation. Suppose FIA$_A$ offers a participation rate and FIA$_B$ offers a cap rate. The break-even return needed for A to outperform B is:

$$\frac{100\%}{Participation\ Rate\ for\ A} \times Cap\ Rate\ for\ B$$

With our earlier simple example, we discussed A as having a participation rate of 56 percent and B as having a cap rate of 6 percent. This formula then leads to a break-even return of 10.7 percent. If the price return on the index exceeds 10.7 percent, then the owner is better off with A that offers a lower participation rate but with no cap.

A 15 percent return, for instance, means that A credits an 8.4 percent gain while B's gain is capped at 6 percent. But if the price return falls below 10.7 percent, then the owner is better off with B even though the return is capped at 6 percent. A 10 percent index return, for instance, only credits a 5.6 percent return for A but a 6 percent return for B. If the index gained 5 percent, then A would credit a 2.8 percent gain versus a 5 percent gain credited for B.

Exhibit 6.1 helps to illustrate this. In broader terms, introducing principal protection with a cap leads to the creation of two posts. Returns will tend to fall at either the floor or the cap with fewer returns in between. The

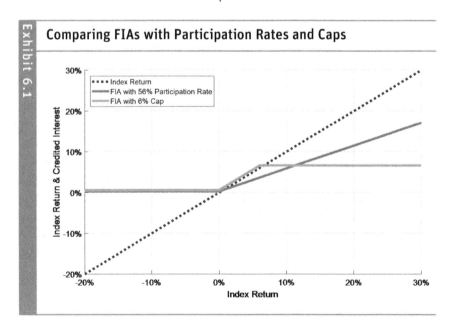

Comparing FIAs with Participation Rates and Caps

Exhibit 6.1

participation rate version without the cap will instead have a broader range of returns above the floor. This may lead it to have higher volatility for the returns, but that is reflected more on the upside, as large positive returns will provide bigger gains for the participation rate version.

For investors who have different beliefs about what future market returns will be, I mentioned how the different crediting methods could provide a benefit based on one's expectations. But to the extent that knowing future market performance is not feasible, one does not need to worry too much about the complexity of various crediting methods. When FIAs are priced competitively, then one cannot easily predict in advance which crediting method will perform best. The choice of a crediting method should be based more on what we are comfortable using.

The annual reset one-year term point-to-point crediting method is relatively easy to understand and is commonly used with FIAs offering lifetime income benefits. Being common, it also has a better opportunity to be found with competitive pricing, as it can be hard to know whether other complex and uncommon crediting methods are offering reasonable pricing.

The key to FIA performance is not so much the crediting method, but the insurance company behind it and how it treats its customers. When resetting parameters at each term, does the company continue to price competitively or keep more for itself. Do they manage their expenses well in order to keep the most available for the options budget? Negative market movements could understandably result in a need to change parameter values in an adverse direction. But a good company will not take advantage of this fact as well as consumer inertia to create worse terms for the consumer upon term renewal.

● Lifetime Income Benefits

FIAs also frequently offer optional lifetime income guarantee benefits in the same manner as variable annuities (VAs). These guaranteed lifetime withdrawal benefits (GLWBs) are what can make FIAs particularly valuable in a retirement income plan. Though the names for different pieces may vary, the discussion from the previous chapter still applies in terms of rollup rates, the potential for step-ups, guaranteed withdrawal rates, and so on. The lifetime guaranteed rates vary by age and are also available for joint contracts at a reduced level or a higher fee. These aspects are all designed to work in similar ways as with a VA. As well, FIAs are deferred annuities. Receiving lifetime income through the optional rider does not formally annuitize the contract while a positive contract value remains.

With these optional income benefits, it is important to emphasize that principal protection for an FIA is on a gross basis and would not apply net of the fees for included optional riders. Principal would be protected in terms of zero interest being credited when the index lost value, but the optional benefit charge would then reduce the value of the principal.

In practical terms, one difference from VAs is that upside potential for step-ups with FIAs may be more limited. The interest crediting method might even prevent the possibility of a step-up during the accumulation period. This could happen when a cap on credited interest is less than the rollup rate, especially when the optional rider fee would reduce the net cap applied. With the distribution phase as well, the capped gains could be less than the guaranteed withdrawal amount plus the rider fee, preventing the possibility for step-ups.

For this reason, greater focus with FIAs should be on the guaranteed income to be generated without necessarily thinking that step-ups will provide much chance to increase this amount, except there are a number of FIAs that automatically increase income over time with a cost-of-living adjustment that does not require a step-up. Certain variable annuities and possibly FIAs that use participation rates instead of caps could provide more upside potential in strong market environments, but caps would limit the ability to benefit from upside.

Some find the idea of using a lifetime income guarantee benefit on an FIA as a bit puzzling. The three reasons to use an income benefit include that one expects to take income from the annuity, there is a possibility of significant decreases in the portfolio value, and there is a possibility of outliving the portfolio. For these three reasons, the second does not apply with an FIA because principal is protected. In the absence of upside, one can calculate with certainty how long the underlying asset base will last with distributions. This is different from a variable annuity in which a market drop could significantly reduce the contract value of the annuity assets and create greater uncertainty about when the contract value may deplete. In this regard, the FIA income protection is more about pure management of longevity risk, not the joint impact of longevity and market risk. The FIA could be viewed as an income annuity that also provides liquidity for the underlying assets.

This naturally leads the comparison of an FIA with an income benefit to an income annuity. The tradeoff is that the FIA should be expected to offer a lower payout rate than an income annuity because it provides liquidity for the asset base and some upside exposure.

However, it is the case that FIA payout rates for their income benefits do occasionally exceed the payout rates on income annuities. Moshe Milevsky wrote a column about this anomaly in 2013 at *Research Magazine*. He found that especially for females, and for long deferral periods before income begins, the FIA payout can beat an income annuity payout. Reasons include that FIA payouts are gender neutral, while females receive a lower payout rate on income annuities since they live longer. As well, with a long deferral period, the insurance company can expect that some FIA owners will lapse and not take the guaranteed distributions from the FIA despite paying for the income rider. This takes the insurance company off the hook for making good on its guarantee, and through competitive pricing some of this benefit is returned to the other owners in the risk pool. With an income annuity, ending the contract is not possible and so there will be no lapsation.

The practical impact of the optional rider fee will be to reduce the contract value a bit more quickly leading to a lower death benefit than otherwise. But with the focus on income rather than accumulation, the rider fee is of secondary importance. The goal is not to find the lowest rider fee, as it would generally support a less generous guarantee, but to find the FIA that offers the most value through lifetime income to the individual for a given rider cost. When the individual survives long enough that the contract value of the FIA is depleted, the benefit continues to support lifetime income.

There is another way that lifetime income benefits can be structured that moves away from the hypothetical benefit base and the rollup rate. This alternative approach also exists for deferred variable annuities, but it is more commonly found with FIAs and so is discussed here.

In the alternate formulation, a lifetime withdrawal percentage, which is still defined by age bands, is determined at the time the income rider is added to the FIA. In this case, it is the age that the benefit is purchased rather than the age that income begins. Then, rather than using a rollup rate with a benefit base, there is a deferral credit that increases the withdrawal rate for each year that the owner defers the start of their lifetime income distributions. When lifetime distributions begin, they are set as a percentage of the contract value at that time, where the percentage is rising over time on account of the deferral credits.

For example, suppose a fifty-five-year-old purchases an FIA that includes this type of income rider. For this contract, the withdrawal percentage when purchased at fifty-five is 4.5 percent, and the deferral credit is 0.3 percent for each year that the individual delays the start of income. The individual plans to retire at age sixty-five, which would provide ten years of deferral. That would mean that the lifetime withdrawal percentage is 7.5 percent (4.5 + 0.3 x 10) of the contract value at that age. In this case, principal is protected only on a gross basis before the rider fee is applied at the end of each year. If the annual rider charge is 1 percent, then in the extremely unlikely event that the index experiences a negative return for all ten years, the rider fee would reduce the contract value on a $100,000 premium to $90,438. With a 7.5 percent withdrawal rate, this provides $6,783 of lifetime income. However, this minimum amount is extremely unlikely to be realized, as it would require ten consecutive years of negative market returns—imagine what this would do to an unprotected investment portfolio—and any upside growth and positive crediting during these ten years would contribute to a higher level of protected lifetime income.

This is just an alternative way to account for potential market growth during the deferral period that can be alternatively applied through a higher payout rate with a deferred income annuity or with a rollup rate for a VA or FIA. As always, rather than getting caught up with thinking about how the different factors interact, it is better to investigate what the guaranteed income level would be at the targeted retirement date, and to then consider whether there are additional reasons to choose an annuity with less guaranteed income, such as the liquidity provisions or the upside growth potential.

◉ Other Fixed Index Annuity Details

Fixed index annuities can be complex financial products, and I will conclude this chapter by discussing some of the other various features one may come across when investigating FIAs.

We begin with surrender charges or, more formally, contingent deferred sales charges. FIAs are meant to serve as long-term tools and surrender charges help the insurance company to invest in longer-term bonds with higher yields and to recover its initial fixed costs for setting up the contract. Surrender charges will only apply to excess distributions in the early years of the contract. As one example, surrender charges might apply during the first seven years of a contract. These charges could start at 8 percent and decrease until they are eliminated entirely after year seven.

There are numerous exceptions that allow one to avoid a surrender charge, including a 10 percent free withdrawal from the contract value for each term. Surrender charges can also be exempted for death benefit payments during the surrender period, or if it is necessary to take required minimum distributions from the contract. As well, there could be exceptions for terminal illness or a nursing home stay, and the allowed benefits for an optional income benefit rider are exempt from surrender charges. Note also that because the government provides special tax treatment for annuities to be used for retirement, a federal income tax penalty may apply for distributions taken before age 59.5.

Someone intending to use the FIA for its long-term income provisions and who has sufficient liquidity elsewhere in the financial plan may even prefer a contract with higher surrender charges. Higher surrender charges, which will not be paid, could support more favorable features elsewhere in the contract.

For distributions subject to surrender charges, a market value adjustment is also applied to protect other annuity owners from capital losses if the insurance company is forced to liquidate bonds at a loss to cover the distribution. The adjustment is based on interest rates and is a way to transfer interest rate risk to the annuity owner. Annuities are meant to be long-term investments, allowing the insurance company to purchase longer-term bonds with higher yields. With excess withdrawals, the insurance company must sell bonds and could realize losses on these sales if rates have risen. The market value adjustment shifts such potential losses to the annuity owner making the withdrawal. Market value adjustments will reduce the contract value further for distributions taken if interest rates have risen, but they could increase the contract value relative to the amount of the distribution if interest rates have declined at the time of the distribution.

An FIA contract will also include a minimum surrender value that overrides surrender charges and market value adjustments if those factors would have resulted in less. An FIA is a fixed annuity instead of a variable annuity because it pays a guaranteed minimum interest rate in this way. The minimum interest rates paid by an FIA may not always be stated explicitly but gets reflected through the minimum guaranteed surrender value of the annuity should one wish to close the annuity contract.

The minimum surrender value implies a guaranteed interest rate that is different from the 0 percent annual floor. This guaranteed minimum surrender value is payable upon a full withdrawal, death, or if the contract value is to be annuitized. As an example, it may be 87.5 percent of the purchase payment at the start. This value then accumulates at a guaranteed minimum surrender value interest rate, but it is reduced for withdrawals and optional rider costs. This minimum surrender value reflects an underlying minimum interest rate that is part of the contract and that is distinct from any floor on credited interest applied on an annual basis. If the floor return was repeatedly realized because of a string of negative index performance, the contract value could be less than this minimum surrender value, and the insurance company would have to credit additional interest to apply retroactively at the time of surrender to meet this obligation. However, with the annual reset design, with just a couple positive index returns, it is likely that the contract value will exceed this minimum guarantee.

To summarize this discussion, for someone seeking to take a full distribution of the contract value, after the surrender period ends the amount is the larger of the contract value or the guaranteed minimum surrender value. During the surrender charge period, the distribution amount is the larger of the guaranteed surrender value (which is not affected by a market value adjustment) and the contract value net of surrender charges and the market value adjustment. The market value adjustment is only applied during the surrender period. These matters could vary slightly if the full distribution is triggered either by death or by annuitizing the contract. To be clear, annuitizing the contract is different from turning on the guaranteed lifetime withdrawal benefit, and most owners would choose the latter.

As well, we have discussed an FIA as providing annual terms. Interest is credited and new parameters are announced at each anniversary date. But there is no particular reason for the FIA term to be one year. It could be longer. The potential appeal of using an FIA with a longer term is that it may be able to provide more upside potential than rolling shorter-term periods. Though the costs of call options increases with the term length, it is not a linear increase. A call option with a two-year term does not cost double of an option that otherwise has the same features but with a one-year term.

Also, less bonds can be purchased because they have more time to grow before needing to match the floor value on interest. This can allow for more participation in the upside after protecting a floor. The other potential attraction for a longer term is that current FIA parameters will be locked in for a longer period before subsequent adjustments take place. This would help if economic trends drive toward less attractive upside opportunities (lower interest rates and more expensive call options). But if conditions improve through higher interest rates and less expensive call options, one would also miss out for longer on taking advantage of these better terms.

Another important caveat about longer terms is that interest is not credited until the end of each term. Any distributions taken before the end of the term, including the death benefit, may not be credited with any partial interest for the term. For instance, an owner who takes a distribution five-years and 364 days into an FIA contract with a six-year term would not receive any credited interest for this period, even if, for example, interest that would credit the account value with 90 percent growth could have been received just one day later on the anniversary date. The contract value would still be the same as at the start of the term.

This aspect requires extra caution when choosing a longer term. One also misses out on the annual reset opportunities to lock in a gain and protect it from subsequent index losses. Some contracts may provide exceptions and credit partial interest in the case the owner seeks to annuitize the contract or if the owner dies and the death benefit is distributed. But this is not the case with all contracts.

Regarding the death benefit, it is typically the remaining contract value or the minimum guaranteed value, whichever is larger. The standard death benefit may be enhanced with optional riders to support a larger amount. An FIA may also offer a premium bonus providing an immediate increase of several percentage points to the initial contract value of assets. One reason this may be offered is to help the insurance company to obtain a longer-term commitment from the consumer, as the bonus will be recaptured for early withdrawals. Bonuses may also be a salient feature that draws attention from consumers. With a premium bonus, individuals must remember that there is no free lunch, as other less salient features would be adjusted in adverse directions in order to support the bonus.

Though this book is focused on retirement income, FIAs are not always used primarily for their income generating optional benefits. Rather, they may be used as an accumulation tool. Fixed index annuities provide protection from interest rate risk and other sources of investment volatility. Unlike a bond fund or individual bonds not held to maturity, they do not experience losses if interest rates rise.

Principal is protected and secured. This can provide powerful behavioral benefits. Fixed index annuities also offer tax deferral, unlike investment assets held in taxable accounts that face ongoing taxes on their growth. Upside may be limited, but protecting principal is where the index annuity has an opportunity to shine relative to other accumulation tools.

FIAs can function as an asset class within an accumulation portfolio to better manage downside risks while still providing participation in the market upside. The ability to better manage downside risks can lay a foundation for either needing less assets to successfully retire, or to be able to enjoy a higher standard of living from a given asset base.

Risk averse households will seek a high probability of success that their financial plan will work, which implicitly leads them to assume a lower rate of return from their investments. This matter was addressed in detail in Chapter 3. By managing downside risks through a more structured approach that creates a floor in which the asset return cannot be negative, a fixed index annuity used within an accumulation portfolio can allow for greater wealth accumulation at lower percentiles of the distribution of outcomes when markets perform poorly. This protection makes it easier to retire successfully in down market environments.

The FIA may serve as a suitable replacement for bonds or other asset classes with a low correlation to the stock market within an accumulation portfolio. Even if the overall portfolio standard deviation increases with the inclusion of an index annuity, the ability to protect from downside losses may serve to reduce risk for the distribution of wealth outcomes. Returns for the index annuity do not follow a traditional bell-shaped distribution.

One final point to include in the general discussion of FIAs is a philosophical question regarding whether we should think about FIAs as a stock-like asset or as a bond-like asset. With a 0 percent floor it has less downside risk than either, but can enough upside be captured with the FIA to beat either stocks or bonds on a risk-adjusted basis? Though the interest they credit is linked to the S&P 500, the returns on FIAs will be closer to bonds than to stocks. However, they are not exactly like bonds either, since principal is protected for FIAs, while bonds can experience capital losses when interest rates rise.

Owners should not think about FIAs as an alternative to owning stocks but rather as another option for fixed-income assets that protects principal and has the potential to outperform bonds when considered net of taxes and fees. With their principal protection, retirees may even consider increasing their stock allocation when replacing bonds with an FIA. One might occasionally observe that the cumulative returns from an FIA exceed the cumulative returns from its corresponding index, but this would have to be triggered by a large market loss in one year that the FIA protects so that its limited upside allows it to jump ahead. This will not be common outcome.

Ultimately, a fixed index annuity offers a tool to securely get assets to retirement by managing market volatility and the sequence-of-returns risk in the pivotal years leading to retirement. This can better set the stage for retirement and for creating more lifetime retirement income from a given asset base. Our focus is on lifetime income, and we will return to the use of FIAs in a retirement income plan when we compare different tools in Chapter 9.

Further Reading

Marrion, Jack, and John Olsen. 2010. *Index Annuities: A Suitable Approach.* St. Louis: Olsen & Marrion, LLC. [https://amzn.to/2WXEBO3]

Milevsky, Moshe A. 2013. "Annuity Anomaly: EIA + GLB > SPIA?" *Research Magazine* (July).

CHAPTER 7

Life Insurance

Thus far, the risk pooling discussion has focused on annuities. Another form of risk pooling for longevity is available through life insurance, and this chapter explores the ways that life insurance can potentially be incorporated into lifetime financial planning. This discussion is mostly about whole life insurance in comparison to term life insurance, but other forms of permanent insurance will be discussed briefly at the end of the chapter.

Whole life insurance can provide a foundation to allow the household to spend more and still be able to provide a bequest, or to increase spending even further by using the cash value as a volatility buffer for the investment portfolio. Whole life insurance can provide a source of funds to support legacy, liquidity, and even long-term care if a rider is added for that purpose. With life insurance playing this role, the retiree may also feel more comfortable using an annuity with lifetime spending protection, which provides the benefits of risk pooling to meet a retirement spending goal using a smaller asset base.

As well, when viewed as an investment, whole life insurance can provide an attractive alternative to holding bonds in an investment portfolio. Premiums are invested in the insurance company's general account, which, as we have discussed, can provide advantages for fixed-income investments relative to what a household can obtain on its own. Life insurance also provides tax deferral for its cash value, and when properly structured, the cash value can be accessed on a tax-free basis during life (meaning that the cash value of life insurance behaves similarly to a Roth

IRA). The death benefit is also provided on a tax-free basis. Because of limits on how much that can be invested into tax-deferred retirement plans, this aspect of life insurance can provide a way to obtain more tax-deferral for savings after exceeding other limits.

That being said, the traditional purpose of life insurance is to provide a death benefit to help support surviving family members or a family business in the event of the policyholder's untimely death. In this context, the amount of life insurance one seeks to hold is what dependents would need to sustain their lifestyle or meet other obligations in the absence of the policyholder being able to contribute to the family through wages or other caretaking. As noted, life insurance can play other roles in a retirement income plan as well. This chapter investigates life insurance from the broader retirement income perspective.

Just as annuities with income guarantees use actuarial science and risk pooling to support a spending level consistent with living to life expectancy, life insurance is also based on actuarial science and provides mortality credits and risk pooling. Life insurance works as the counterpart to lifetime income. While lifetime income protections reduce the cost of funding a long life, life insurance provides higher realized returns to a household in the event of a shorter life. These two contrasting uses of risk pooling can work together effectively in lifetime financial planning.

During the preretirement period, human capital is an important asset for households. Human capital is the present value of all the wages individuals expect to earn during the remainder of their working years. For those with families or other fixed obligations that depend on receiving human capital in the form of those future wages, the life insurance death benefit can serve as a replacement for lost wages in the event of an early death during the working years. We usually think of life insurance as a tool for replacing lost income, but even a homemaker who does not earn wages may consider life insurance to help the household that would then have to pay for more services related to childcare and household management in the event of the homemaker's death.

For this basic human capital replacement framework, one generally does not associate a need for life insurance after retirement begins. The value of human capital approaches zero as the working years end, though those continuing with part-time work in retirement may still be reliant on and need protection for their human capital. Once fully retired, the household subsequently funds lifestyle with assets accumulated during the working years. They have converted their human capital into financial assets.

Term life insurance supports the role of human capital replacement. With term life insurance, one purchases a contract to receive a death benefit should death occur within a certain number of years or by a certain age. The term could be chosen to end once family needs or other financial obligations no longer depend on the future earnings of the worker. A mantra of "buy term and invest the difference" developed in the investing world as the way to approach the life insurance decision. Because the death benefit is temporary with term life insurance, and it also does not include a savings component, term life premiums will be smaller than with other forms of life insurance. For a given pool of funds, this affords a greater remaining amount to be invested after life insurance obligations are met, as long as the individual follows through and invests those additional dollars not spent on life insurance premiums.

For lifetime financial planning, is it really best to pay the smallest amount possible for life insurance in order to invest as much as possible in the financial markets? This chapter puts the concept of "buy term and invest the difference" to the test by investigating whether there are better ways to approach life insurance from the context of comprehensive lifetime financial and retirement income planning. The focus of this chapter is about whether other forms of permanent life insurance should be considered by the household as part of a longer-term retirement strategy that can be set into motion during the accumulation phase. Even though term insurance premiums are lower, this type of life insurance may not always provide the best value in the context of financial planning outcomes related to getting the most spending power and legacy from the available asset base.

I will focus particularly on whole life insurance as an alternative to term insurance. For life insurance, there are natural parallels between different types of insurance products and different types of annuities. Whole life insurance corresponds most closely to income annuities. For both, premiums enter the insurance company's general account and the insurance company invests those premiums with a heavy focus on fixed-income assets and asset-liability matching. Whole life insurance consists of a death benefit and a cash value savings component. A difference between whole life insurance and income annuities is that whole life policies are frequently participating policies that can earn dividends when realized outcomes fair better than the insurance company's conservative pricing projections, while participating income annuities are still relatively rare. Unlike income annuities, whole life insurance is underwritten, and different pricing is available based on health classification.

To conclude the chapter, I will briefly also consider other forms of life insurance that roughly approximate the role of variable and index annuities. These forms of life insurance include variable and index universal life insurance. In the context of retirement income planning, the potential role for these types of insurance policies is to create a source of supplemental retirement income that may provide net benefits when the tax-advantages of life insurance contribute more value that the insurance costs of the policies.

⦿ Term Life Insurance

Term life insurance offers a death benefit if death occurs during the fixed period covered by the contract, when premiums have been paid and the policy remains in force. When not viewing life insurance within the framework of retirement income planning, term life insurance offers the lowest premiums to support the human capital replacement needs of the household. Other types of life insurance are a combination of term life insurance and a savings vehicle. This makes it important to begin the discussion with a clear understanding about how term life insurance premiums are calculated.

Exhibit 7.1 shows the basic mechanics for determining the premium payments required to support a term life insurance policy providing a $500,000 death benefit received on a tax-free basis. The costs of insurance relate to the mortality risk during the period covered by the contract. As such, insurance premiums will vary by age, gender, and health status as determined through the underwriting process. This example is provided for a forty-year-old male using average mortality in the United States for Social Security participants born in 1980 without any assumed underwriting. In practice, nonsmokers in good health will get a more preferred status with lower premiums while others with medical conditions may not even qualify to purchase life insurance. All else being the same, premiums rise with the policy starting age as mortality rates increase. Life insurance is also cheaper for women than for men, since women live longer on average.

As with the previous discussion about how income annuities are priced, Exhibit 7.1 uses a few simplifying assumptions to make it easier to understand the basic structure for how term life insurance works. These simplifications relate to interest rates, mortality and fees. I simplify interest rates to assume that fixed-income assets always and forever earn 3 percent. Interest rates do not change in the future and we do not worry about other fixed-income assets like corporate bonds that may offer higher yields accompanied by greater credit risk. Since interest rates do not change, there is no interest rate risk or reinvestment risk. The insurance company can determine prices knowing with certainty what interest rates will be in the future, so there is no need to accumulate additional reserves to support future claims in the event of an unfavorable fixed-income investing environment.

For mortality data, I use the 1980 Social Security Administration cohort lifetime, which is the closest available life table for current forty-year-olds. This table provides mortality data including projections for the total population of Social Security participants born in 1980. I assume that there is no risk about unexpected changes in mortality so that the insurance company can determine pricing without holding excess reserves to support claims in the event of unfavorable surprises.

This mortality data source is a cohort life table, rather than a period life table. Cohort life tables track mortality for the same individual over time. When a sixty-five-year-old in 2019 turns eighty-five in 2039, his mortality rate at eighty-five will most likely be lower than that of an eighty-five-year-old in 2019. A cohort life table uses projections for future mortality improvements when calculating life expectancies. Even if the projections end up being wrong, they are probably closer to being correct than assuming no mortality improvements at all. Cohort life tables will project longer lives and are surely a better choice for considering longevity when building a retirement income plan. The Social Security Administration also provides cohort life tables for Social Security participants born at different points in the past.

Also, as mentioned, most insurance companies use underwriting to further classify their customers by mortality risk. Some may not qualify for life insurance while others who demonstrate good health and a lower mortality risk can obtain better insurance rates. I assume there is just one life insurance policy for the whole population with the same age and gender, and everyone can qualify without underwriting. This will make my simulated pricing more expensive for those who could otherwise qualify for preferred categories. Another implied assumption is that no one lapses on their insurance policy. All policyholders are assumed to hold onto their policies for their full term.

Finally, I am assuming that the insurance policy provides actuarially fair pricing without expenses deducted for operating the insurance company. This will support direct comparisons in the later analysis between investments and insurance where both are treated as not having fees. Later in the chapter I will describe the implications of changing these assumptions.

The way to understand how premiums are calculated on a term life insurance policy is to recognize that term life insurance is a collection of renewable one-year term policies. Consider that I buy a one-year term policy as a forty-year-old male. Given the mortality data I am using, the insurance company projects that over the next year, 224 forty-year-old males out of 100,000 will die, and this is the number of death benefits that must be paid. The insurance company must collect enough premiums to support these claims. For the population of 100,000 policy holders, this requires charging each participant $1,120 for their one-year of protection providing a $500,000 death benefit to those who die.

Next, suppose I seek protection for two-years instead of one. I still buy the policy at age forty, but I now wish to calculate the cost of protection at age forty-one as well. At age forty, I effectively buy a one-year policy that allows me to renew for the second year without going through additional underwriting. Mortality rates increase with age. But the insurance costs this implies will be partly offset by the fact that there is a smaller pool of survivors from the original pool of policyholders to which the increased mortality rates apply. Of the original 100,000 policy holders, 99,776 remain alive at forty-one and a further 239 of them are expected to die. The life insurance company must collect enough premiums to support these claims. Calculating the premium required today means looking at this cost of insurance in one year, but then further discounting the cost of insurance by the fact that by collecting premiums today, the insurance company can grow that money at the 3 percent rate for one year before it is needed to pay claims. With this discounting, the premium is $1,162. This process continues at each age that coverage is provided. Though not all ages are shown to conserve space, age eighty-seven is the year that the highest number of original policy holders (3,794) are expected to die. Even though mortality rates continue to grow with age, applying them to a dwindling pool of survivors means that the overall number of deaths subsequently declines. At age 100, 754 of the original policy holders are expected to die. The cost of insuring against death between the 100th and 101st birthdays is $640, reflecting the number of deaths among the original policyholders at that age as well as the discounting for the premium paid today that grows at 3 percent for many years before it is used to pay for those death benefit claims.

Summing these insurance costs through age 119, the cost of providing a $500,000 death benefit is $164,927 if paid as a single premium today. This is reflecting the power of compounding interest as well as the role of risk pooling. Death is certain to happen at some point; paying $164,927 today would ensure a death benefit of $500,000 will be paid when death happens. Naturally, the sooner death happens, the higher would be the implied rate of return earned by the policy holder.

Though it is conceivable to buy a permanent term insurance policy as just described, this is not typically how most people approach term insurance. Instead, a term policy may be used in a temporary manner to protect human capital. The cost of a policy, then, is simply the cumulative costs of those one-year term policies for as long as coverage will be maintained.

Consider the case in which someone wishes to have the death benefit protection until reaching an anticipated retirement age of sixty-five. With insurance coverage ending on the 65th birthday, the cost is the sum of the twenty-five one-year policies from age forty through sixty-four. This cost is $40,934. The forty-year-old male could pay this amount today to receive the protection of $500,000 should death happen before age sixty-five. We can gather from the pool of survivors that 87,460 out of 100,000 would still be alive at sixty-five, and so 12,540 members of the pool would have received the death benefit by that time. The premiums of the survivors subsidize the death benefit payments for those who did not make it. This is risk pooling and mortality credits in the life insurance context.

One final matter to consider is that most people do not use this single premium payment method to pay for the term policy. Policyholders typically wish to spread those payments over time. How much should the insurance company charge as an annual premium to cover this term life policy through age sixty-five? To determine this, we can view the shift from a single premium to ongoing premiums as a loan provided by the insurance company to the policy holder. The insurance company needs $40,934 today to fund the term policy expiring at age sixty-five. In effect, the company provides a loan of this amount to the policyholder, and the policyholder pays back the loan over time in the form of annual premium payments. Assuming that the insurance company uses the same 3 percent interest rate for this calculation and that premiums are paid at the start of the year, the matter is to determine the annual premium needed to repay this loan. An annual premium of $2,282 is the solution to this PMT equation:

$$= PMT\ (3\%,\ 25\ years,\ -\$40,934,\ \$0)$$

Regarding taxes, premium payments are made with after-tax dollars and the death benefit is received on a tax-free basis. This taxation structure for term life insurance is most similar to Roth IRAs as gains within the policy resulting from the death benefit being larger than the cumulative premiums paid are not taxed.

If one is thinking about term life insurance, an important policy option to consider for an additional cost is a provision allowing the owner to later convert the policy to permanent life insurance. This option would help to protect from the risk that one later determines a need for additional life insurance coverage but has also incurred a health problem causing him or her to no longer qualify for a new life insurance policy. Such conversion options generally will last for a fixed period or until a particular age.

Exhibit 7.1

Pricing a Term Life Insurance Policy for a Forty-Year-Old Male

Death Benefit: $500,000

Interest Rate: 3%

Age	Discount Factor	Pool of Survivors	Deaths	Discounted Cost of One-Year Term Insurance
40	1.000	100,000	224	$1,120
41	0.971	99,776	239	$1,162
42	0.943	99,537	257	$1,210
43	0.915	99,280	274	$1,254
44	0.888	99,006	291	$1,293
45	0.863	98,715	311	$1,341
46	0.837	98,404	331	$1,385
47	0.813	98,073	346	$1,407
48	0.789	97,727	359	$1,416
49	0.766	97,368	368	$1,410
50	0.744	97,000	379	$1,411
—	—	—	—	—
65	0.478	87,460	1,140	$2,721
66	0.464	86,320	1,239	$2,872
67	0.450	85,082	1,337	$3,011
68	0.437	83,744	1,434	$3,133
69	0.424	82,311	1,529	$3,245
70	0.412	80,781	1,634	$3,366
—	—	—	—	—
99	0.175	3,793	970	$848
100	0.170	2,822	754	$640
101	0.165	2,068	578	$476
—	—	—	—	—
118	0.100	0	0	$0
119	0.097	0	0	$0

Cost of Term Life Policy Through Age 119:	$164,927
Cost of Term Life Policy Through Age 65:	$40,934
Annual Premiums for Term Life Policy Through Age 65:	$2,282

● Whole Life Insurance

Whole life insurance receives its name because it provides the owner with a death benefit for the whole lifetime. It is a form of permanent life insurance. Whole life also includes an accumulation and savings component through its cash value. Whole life insurance may be viewed as a fixed-income investment vehicle that incorporates a permanent death benefit as well. When structured properly, a whole life policy provides a tax-free death benefit and tax-deferred growth for its cash value. There are ways to access the cash value on a tax-free basis as well, as will be discussed. Whole life policies include provisions that guarantee the amount and duration of premium payments. The policy endows at the point that the cash value has grown to equal the amount of the death benefit. Whole life policies are typically designed to endow at either age 100 or age 121. If the policy also matures at one of these ages, then the cash value is paid to the policy holder, with gains in the policy being taxable. Policyholders may prefer to have the policy endow rather than mature, which allows the policy holder to maintain the policy until death so that the cash value can be received as a death benefit without having to pay taxes.

Before digging into the details about how whole life insurance can fit within a retirement income plan, it is worth beginning this discussion with a simple explanation about how to calculate premiums on a whole life policy without extra features. As with term life insurance, the costs for the death benefit are structured as a lifetime series of one-year term policies. But there is one important difference related to cash value accumulation that helps to reduce the insurance costs within a whole life policy over time relative to term insurance.

Exhibit 7.2 provides the mechanics for a whole life policy designed to endow at 100. The death benefit is available when death occurs before age 100. At age 100 the cash value has grown to equal the death benefit and the policyholder could receive the death benefit if still alive, but any gains in the policy would be taxable. If left untouched, the cash value and death benefit can continue to grow with interest and the death benefit could be received at death without triggering a taxable event.

With whole life insurance, there is as a policy cash value that provides a portion and eventually all of the death benefit. The cash value represents the amount that the policy holder could receive by surrendering the policy before death. This is a feature not provided with term life insurance.

The cash value represents an asset for the policy holder and the cost to the insurance company of providing the full death benefit is not the full amount of the death benefit. Rather, it is the difference between the death benefit and the cash value. This is an aspect that helps to reduce the costs of insurance implicit inside the whole life policy over time relative to a term policy. When death occurs, the insurance company only needs to cover the difference between the death benefit and the cash value.

For those needing life insurance for human capital replacement, the ability of whole life to reduce insurance costs through the cash value helps to make cash value growth more competitive relative to buying term insurance and investing the premium difference in bonds. With "buy term and invest the difference," the outside investments have no impact on the cost of insurance. With whole life insurance, the portion of the premium that goes into the cash value is working double-duty by accumulating a return *and* by helping to offset the future costs of the life insurance by reducing the portion of death benefit at risk for the insurance company. A single-premium whole life policy would grow the cash value most quickly to reduce the subsequent costs of insurance within the policy, while policies that extend premium payments out for longer periods would have relatively less prefunding and higher relative insurance costs.

Moving now to Exhibit 7.2, the first four columns are the same as with term life insurance in Exhibit 7.1. The fifth column in the exhibit is different. With term insurance, the insurance company must always support the full death benefit. But with whole life insurance, the insurance company only needs to support the amount of the death benefit that exceeds the cash value in the policy. This column reflects the $500,000 death benefit less the cash value accumulated at the end of the previous year. Now, the amounts shown in the discounted cost of one-year term insurance are impacted by four factors: rising mortality rates with age, the declining number of surviving policy holders, the discount factor on the amount set aside today to fund that future insurance cost, and the declining value of the net death benefit.

Exhibit 7.2

Pricing a Whole Life Insurance Policy for a Forty-Year-Old Male

Death Benefit: $500,000

Discount Rate: 3%

Age	Discount Factor	Pool of Survivors	Deaths	Death Benefit Requiring Insurance	Discounted Cost of One-Year Term Insurance	Premium	Cash Value
40	1.000	100,000	224	$500,000	$1,120	$6,873	$5,926
41	0.971	99,776	239	$494,074	$1,149	$6,873	$11,999
42	0.943	99,537	257	$488,001	$1,181	$6,873	$18,222
43	0.915	99,280	274	$481,778	$1,208	$6,873	$24,603
44	0.888	99,006	291	$475,397	$1,229	$6,873	$31,154
45	0.863	98,715	311	$468,846	$1,258	$6,873	$37,873
46	0.837	98,404	331	$462,127	$1,280	$6,873	$44,770
47	0.813	98,073	346	$455,230	$1,281	$6,873	$51,873
48	0.789	97,727	359	$448,127	$1,269	$6,873	$59,201
49	0.766	97,368	368	$440,799	$1,243	$6,873	$66,776
50	0.744	97,000	379	$433,224	$1,223	$6,873	$74,599
51	0.722	96,621	395	$425,401	$1,214	$6,873	$82,665
52	0.701	96,226	416	$417,335	$1,217	$6,873	$90,971
53	0.681	95,810	442	$409,029	$1,230	$6,873	$99,512
54	0.661	95,368	475	$400,488	$1,257	$6,873	$108,281
55	0.642	94,893	512	$391,719	$1,288	$6,873	$117,282
56	0.623	94,381	554	$382,718	$1,321	$6,873	$126,519
57	0.605	93,827	598	$373,481	$1,351	$6,873	$136,002
58	0.587	93,229	644	$363,998	$1,377	$6,873	$145,743
59	0.570	92,585	693	$354,257	$1,401	$6,873	$155,752
60	0.554	91,892	747	$344,248	$1,424	$6,873	$166,037
—	—	—	—	—	—	—	—
95	0.197	10,545	2,162	$68,010	$289	$0	$444,652
96	0.191	8,383	1,838	$55,348	$194	$0	$457,791
97	0.185	6,545	1,522	$42,209	$119	$0	$471,402
98	0.180	5,023	1,230	$28,598	$63	$0	$485,479
99	0.175	3,793	970	$14,521	$25	$0	$500,018

This leaves two remaining columns to be explained: premium and cash value. They are interrelated. The cash value is an asset of the policy holder. Any premiums paid are first used to pay for the cost of insurance, and the remainder is accumulated as cash value. With our assumptions, cash value also grows at the same economy-wide assumed 3 percent interest rate. The policy in this exhibit is designed to allow premiums to stop after twenty-five years at age sixty-five when the individual is anticipating retirement. The costs of insurance must still be paid; they are deducted from the cash value that is still otherwise growing at 3 percent each year. In this example, the $6,873 premium is specifically chosen so that the cash value grows to match the value of the death benefit at age 100 even after paying all insurance costs. A smaller premium would leave the cash value falling short of the death benefit at age 100, and a higher premium would cause the cash value to reach the death benefit amount too soon.

Though not shown in the exhibit, separate calculations indicate that a single premium of $119,662 at age forty would support the same whole life policy with $500,000 of death benefit coverage and with cash value growing to the value of the death benefit at age 100. Again, the reason the whole life single premium is less than the permanent term insurance premium (which was $164,927) is because of the role the cash value plays in reducing the net amount of the death benefit the insurance company must cover.

Exhibit 7.3 provides a visual representation for the numbers in this whole life example. At the top, the exhibit shows a steady death benefit of $500,000 from age forty to 100. Next, the cash value grows to equal the value of the death benefit at age 100. This example includes premium payments until age sixty-five. By sixty-five, the cash value of $107,380 is higher than the $85,925 of cumulative premiums paid. But it took twelve years for positive returns net of insurance costs to manifest for the cash value. Whole life insurance is not designed to be a short-term strategy. After age sixty-five, the cash value continues to grow net of the continuing insurance costs until the policy endows at age 100.

● Whole Life Insurance in a Lifetime Financial Plan

With this understanding about how life insurance is priced, I can create a simple model to consider four different potential roles for this whole life insurance policy in retirement income planning. First, the death benefit

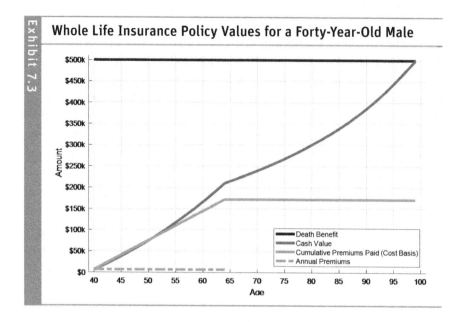

Exhibit 7.3

Whole Life Insurance Policy Values for a Forty-Year-Old Male

for life insurance provides a method to meet a legacy goal using risk pooling and tax advantages that is distinct from preserving investment assets for this purpose. This can allow the retiree to potentially enjoy a higher standard of living in retirement than otherwise possible, while also ensuring that assets have been earmarked to meet the legacy goal.

Second, a permanent death benefit supported through whole life insurance can be integrated into a retirement income plan by helping the retiree to justify the decision to buy an income annuity and to overcome the behavioral hurdles that lead to the annuity puzzle. It can also allow the retiree to purchase a life-only single life annuity that offers the most mortality credits to the risk pool and therefore offers the highest payout rate to the owner. Wealth Building Cornerstones, the firm that developed this strategy, calls it the covered-asset strategy.

The key idea is that the retiree can feel comfortable buying an income annuity because of the understanding that the life insurance death benefit will return the amount spent on the annuity premium to the household at the time of death when annuity payments cease. As opposed to obtaining a form of life insurance for the household through the annuity by adding cash refund provisions or a joint life option, this integrated approach with a separate life insurance policy creates greater flexibility for the household by reducing the required annuity premiums needed to meet a spending goal.

Next, the cash value of whole life insurance also provides a few interesting options for a retirement income plan. Cash value may serve as a volatility buffer to help manage sequence risk in retirement. This strategy was also developed by Wealth Building Cornerstones. Cash value does not experience downside risk for capital losses in the face of rising interest rates. It is guaranteed to grow and can provide a temporary resource to supplement retirement spending rather than being forced to sell portfolio assets at a loss during poor market environments.

Finally, when considered net of fees, taxes, and insurance needs, cash value accumulation within a whole life policy can serve as an alternative and competitive means for investing in fixed-income assets as opposed to using bonds or bond funds within a traditional investment portfolio. We consider each of these four ideas in turn with a case study.

The Case Study

For these comparisons, I create a case study for a forty-year-old married couple with two children who are now constructing a lifetime financial plan. Jerry and Beth have determined that it is time to get serious about retirement and life insurance planning. Jerry is employed and Beth is a homemaker. These gender roles could be switched, but since life insurance is less expensive for women because of their heightened longevity, having the male be the worker is the more conservative case to consider. Jerry is seeking an additional amount of life insurance death benefit equal to $500,000. This, along with his other life insurance, will be adequate to support his family in the event of his death prior to age sixty-five.

Jerry presently has $60,000 saved in a 401(k) plan with his employer, which is invested with an equity glide path strategy representative of a typical target date fund: 80 percent stocks to age forty-five, 65 percent stocks from forty-five to fifty-four, 50 percent stocks from fifty-five to sixty-four, 40 percent stocks from sixty-five to seventy-four, and 30 percent stocks thereafter. He would like to plan for retirement at sixty-five. I will investigate a portion of his assets to be saved in the future that is equivalent to 401(k) employee contribution limits in 2019 with assumed inflation adjustments: $19,000 can be saved each year until age fifty, and then $25,000 thereafter until age sixty-five to account for the allowed catch-up contributions at those ages.

These contribution limits are inflation-adjusted such that real savings are kept the same, but the nominal amounts increase. Because life insurance premiums are fixed without inflation adjustments, the percentage of the savings directed to insurance decreases over time in real terms. Jerry expects to be in a combined 25 percent marginal tax bracket (22 percent for federal taxes and 3 percent for state taxes) in both his preretirement and postretirement years.

For investment returns, I follow the approach explained in Exhibit 3.11 from Chapter 3. Stock returns are simulated with a randomized risk premium above the fixed 3 percent bond yield. That risk premium has a 6 percent average value with a 20 percent volatility. Inflation is fixed at 2 percent annually. This implies a 1 percent real interest rate. Interest rate risk is eliminated from the analysis, as there is no possibility for fluctuating interest rates to create capital gains or losses for the underlying bond portfolio. The risky asset is based on large-capitalization stocks in the United States. Overall, this represents a 9 percent arithmetic average for stocks (7 percent in real terms). The compounded real growth rate for stocks is 5 percent. The investment portfolio is modeled using 10,000 Monte Carlo simulations for investment returns based on these capital market expectations. I assume investors earn these returns net of any investment or advisory fees. As investments are held in tax-deferred accounts, there is no further tax drag to worry about. Investors earn the gross returns and portfolio distributions are taxed as income.

Life insurance is priced using the 3 percent interest rate and the Social Security Administration 1980 cohort life tables for mortality. Pricing for the term and whole life policies was provided in Exhibits 7.1 and 7.2. Income annuities are priced in the same manner using the Society of Actuaries mortality data as explained in Chapter 4, assuming an annual 2 percent cost-of-living adjustment for payments to match the assumed inflation rate. In Chapter 4, the income annuity was priced for females. It offered a 4.56 percent payout rate.

In this case study, we use income annuities for males and couples, and we must also account for the fact that the annuity will not be purchased for twenty-five years. The corresponding payout rates for males and couples with annuities purchased today are 4.83 percent and 3.93 percent, respectively. However, with the longevity improvements assumed by the Society of Actuaries over the next twenty-five years, the male and joint income annuity payout rates at that time are 4.47 percent and 3.75 percent, respectively. These latter numbers are what I use. It makes sense to use different mortality tables to price the life insurance and annuities on account of the different populations that use these financial products. Annuity owners will tend to live longer.

To better understand the impacts of investment volatility on the upside and downside, Monte Carlo simulations are used to create a distribution of outcomes. The exhibits report the 10th percentile, median, and 90th percentile from this distribution. We can interpret the 10th percentile outcome as a bad luck case with poor investment returns. It is possible that retirement outcomes could be even worse, but generally Jerry and Beth could expect better retirement outcomes than seen at the 10th percentile. The median reflects more typical outcomes. It is the midpoint of the distribution, with a 50 percent chance for worse outcomes and a 50 percent chance for better outcomes. These are reasonable outcomes for Jerry and Beth to expect. The 90th percentile is a good luck outcome in which investments perform very well, supporting greater spending and larger account balances.

Note that these results are presented in terms of nominal dollars to avoid reader confusion about why inflation-adjusted dollars are less than nominal dollars. This decision does not impact any comparisons for the relative outcomes between scenarios. However, readers should understand that the purchasing power of a given amount of income or wealth will be less in the future. For today's forty-year-olds, the real purchasing power of money will be about 60 percent of what it is today at age sixty-five, and about 30 percent of today at age 100, assuming 2 percent inflation.

A review of the tax principles used herein is also in order. Investments are made in Jerry's tax-deferred 401(k) plan. This means that taxes are not paid initially on the plan contributions, but any withdrawals from the plan will be subject to ordinary income tax rates. At retirement, Jerry completes a rollover of his 401(k) to a traditional individual retirement account (IRA). This is not a taxable event. With a tax deferred account, the government effectively owns a portion of the account as identified by the tax rate. Taxes are deferred until withdrawals are made.

The investment account values are expressed in posttax terms assuming a 25 percent combined marginal tax rate. Life insurance premiums are paid with posttax funds. No taxes are due on the death benefit, making it a posttax number. As well, a life insurance policy can be arranged so that funds can be borrowed from the cash value without being taxed. When distributions are properly structured, cash value represents a posttax number as well.

If an income annuity is purchased at retirement, this purchase is made with qualified retirement funds in the IRA. The annuity income is then fully taxable at income tax rates as it is received from the qualified account. Because the annuity is purchased in a qualified account, someone seeking to purchase an annuity with funds equivalent to the life insurance death benefit would need to inflate their purchase to account for the differing tax treatment. For example, a nontaxed death benefit of $500,000 is equivalent to $500,000 / (1 - 0.25), or $666,667, in the IRA when the tax rate is 25 percent.

Jerry must decide whether to purchase a term life insurance policy to increase his existing coverage to meet his human capital replacement value for his family, or to otherwise purchase a whole life insurance policy that can serve his additional human capital replacement value need as well as be integrated into his retirement income strategy. From the portion of his annual savings I have outlined, he will pay for life insurance premiums and the taxes to cover those premiums, and the remainder will go into his tax-deferred 401(k) plan.

In all scenarios, I assume that Jerry is directing at least enough to the 401(k) to satisfy the conditions for the highest possible company match, though I do not specifically model any company match when simulating retirement income. More generally, Jerry and Beth may also have other resources in retirement that I am not analyzing. I am modeling the relevant features about how to best make the investment and insurance decisions for the described annual set-asides to meet life insurance needs and to obtain the most desirable retirement outcomes.

Jerry will decide between term life and whole life insurance. The term policy lasts for twenty-five years with a $500,000 death benefit and has an annual premium of $2,282. Taxes on the pretax income required to cover this premium are $761. After paying the term life premium and taxes, he contributes the remaining $15,957 to his 401(k). As mentioned, these savings increase over time with inflation following the employee contribution limit increases on the 401(k), while life insurance premiums remain fixed.

The whole life policy Jerry considers also carries a death benefit of $500,000. The annual premium is $6,873. The policy accrues cash value that can serve as an additional spendable asset for the household and that helps to reduce future insurance costs relative to the term policy. The policy is designed to have premiums paid until age sixty-five. At this age, the policy becomes fully paid up. Subsequent insurance costs are covered by the cash value. The policy endows at age 100 when the cash value grows to match the value of the death benefit. Taxes to cover the whole life premium are $2,291. With a whole life policy, Jerry can contribute $9,836 to his 401(k) at age forty, with that value subsequently growing with the described contribution limits.

An important methodology issue for the case study relates to asset allocation. With a whole life policy, the cash value is a liquid asset contained outside the financial portfolio. It behaves like fixed-income, though it is not exposed to interest rate risk (i.e. the accessible cash value does not decline when interest rates rise). Cash value is not precisely the same as holding bonds in an investment portfolio, as there is not a practical way to rebalance the portfolio between stocks and policy cash value. As well, the premium for an income annuity can be viewed as a fixed-income asset. It is not liquid, but it is repositioning assets into the insurance company general account to support protected lifetime income.

I assume that Jerry will incorporate the cash value of life insurance and any annuity premium into his asset allocation decisions to maintain the overall proportion between stocks and bonds for household assets. For example, if the target date fund calls for a 50 percent stock allocation, then the actual stock allocation Jerry uses will be 50 percent of the sum of the financial portfolio balance, the pretax value of life insurance cash value, and any annuity premium already paid, divided by the portfolio balance.

Though this could conceivably call for a stock allocation of greater than 100 percent when the actuarial bond holdings (annuities and cash value life insurance) are large relative to the financial portfolio, I constrain the maximum possible stock allocation for the financial portfolio to not exceed 100 percent. This higher stock allocation in the investment portfolio can be justified because it is just one part of the asset base and the goal is to maintain a particular stock allocation in relation to overall household assets rather than just to the investment portfolio. This does require the retiree to accept this line of thinking, and this is a topic I will return to in Chapter 8.

Efficiently Funding a Legacy Goal with Whole Life Insurance

The most natural use for permanent life insurance is to fund a legacy goal. Exhibit 7.4 compares the effectiveness of two strategies for meeting a legacy goal during retirement: "buy term and invest the difference" in Scenario 1 and using whole life insurance in Scenario 2. Values are expressed on an after-tax basis with a combined 25 percent tax rate applied to qualified plan distributions and legacy values. The cash value and death benefit from the whole life policy are not treated as taxable assets.

As Jerry and Beth are now getting more serious about their financial planning, they begin to also think about their legacy goals for their children. The couple anchors onto their $500K current life insurance need and believe that an appropriate overall legacy goal would be to leave the children this amount upon Jerry's passing no matter the age. The couple would like to support the highest living standard possible while still maintaining a 90 percent chance that a $500K after-tax legacy goal can continue to be met by age 100. His legacy goal for the investment assets inflates to $666,667 so that the after-tax amount of $500K can be achieved. With permanent life insurance, a substantial safety margin with investments is not needed for legacy.

The question becomes: what is the most efficient way to meet a $500,000 after-tax legacy goal while also being able to support the highest retirement lifestyle from this same pool of assets in a way that does not jeopardize the legacy goal? The couple targets a 90 percent success rate for their financial plan.

If Jerry uses whole life insurance, he can now seek the highest spending rate for his remaining investment assets that maintains a 90 percent chance that the portfolio is not depleted by age 100. He no longer needs to preserve a safety-margin of $667K at age 100 for his after-tax legacy goal to be met with 90 percent confidence. This allows for a higher spending rate from investments. This is the trade-off that we must test empirically: can the couple spend more when using whole life insurance after considering the higher insurance premiums and less 401(k) assets at retirement, but the ability to use a higher distribution rate from investments since there is no longer a need to maintain the safety-margin with investments for legacy?

In Scenario 1, the couple purchases term insurance to provide a death benefit for human capital replacement until age sixty-five. For the remainder of savings, they invest in their 401(k) and use this pot of investment assets to support their spending and postretirement legacy goals.

In Scenario 2, the couple maintains a whole life policy into retirement to cover legacy and invests the remainder in their 401(k) to cover retirement spending. Because the whole life premiums are larger, the couple can generally expect to have less in their 401(k) at retirement. The difference ranges from 17 percent less at the 10th percentile of the distribution to about the same amount at the 90th percentile. Accumulations are generally less because less is invested, but it is possible to accumulate more because of the asset allocation impact in which the cash value is treated as a fixed-income asset, and so the 401(k) asset allocation can be more aggressive in response. The more aggressive asset allocation helps the most when markets perform well. Median 401(k) assets at retirement are $883K in Scenario 1 and $836K in Scenario 2.

Note that if we add the cash value in Scenario 2 to the 401(k) assets, overall wealth is greater because the whole life policy supports lower life insurance costs in the preretirement years, and because taxes will not be paid on the cash value. This outcome alludes to the efficiencies of cash value as a fixed-income investment when life insurance is otherwise needed for the financial plan.

Next, the exhibit shows that the sustainable withdrawal rate is 2.71 percent in Scenario 1 and 3.48 percent in Scenario 2. They are different for two reasons. First, in the second scenario, the asset allocation is more aggressive for investment assets because of the role played by cash value as a fixed-income asset. Second, and more importantly, Scenario 1 requires a substantial safety reserve to support legacy. To meet the legacy goal, Scenario 1 requires a lower spending rate to support a 90 percent chance that remaining assets are not less than the after-tax legacy goal at age 100. The IRA must maintain $667K to support the $500K goal after taxes. In Scenario 2, it is only necessary to maintain a 90 percent chance that investment assets remain above $0 by age 100. Life insurance supports the legacy goal. This allows for a higher distribution rate to be used with investment assets.

The higher distribution rate allows for more spending in Scenario 2 while also meeting the legacy goal. In the median outcome, these assets can support 22 percent more inflation-adjusted spending throughout retirement. At the tenth and 90th percentiles, the percentage increases in spending for Scenario 2 are 7 percent and 29 percent.

Finally, the exhibit shows legacy wealth at age 100. The couple sought a 90 percent chance to meet their legacy goal and we see that approximately $500K is left after taxes in both scenarios at the 10th percentile of the distribution. For the remainder of the distribution, legacy wealth is slightly larger in Scenario 2 despite also supporting more spending. Legacy is 5 percent more at the median and 2 percent more at the 90th percentile. The couple must spend less in Scenario 1 to ensure that investments can support their stated legacy goal.

Nonetheless, with the addition of the death benefit, whole life insurance can consistently support more legacy. Whole life insurance provided the couple a more efficient way to meet the legacy goal, which allows them to enjoy a higher standard of living in retirement with these assets without the tradeoff of a lower legacy when markets perform well in retirement. Scenario 2 is more efficient than Scenario 1 in terms of meeting legacy goals while supporting more spending and legacy.

Though not the case here, in cases when spending is higher and legacy is less, it can be difficult to compare the tradeoff. The last measure of discounted lifetime spending power in the exhibit helps to remedy this. It is the discounted value (at the 3 percent interest rate) of the lifetime spending and age 100 legacy supported by the strategy. We can also observe that Scenario 2 supports more lifetime spending power across the distribution of outcomes.

Exhibit 7.4

Whole Life Insurance for the Legacy Goal

	Scenario 1 Investments + Term Life	Scenario 2 Investments + Whole Life	% change from Scenario 1
Term Life Premiums	$2,282	$0	
Whole Life Premiums	$0	$6,873	
Taxes Paid	$761	$2,291	
Age 40 Remaining Contribution to 401(k)	$15,957	$9,836	

All Subsequent Values are Provided on a Posttax Basis (Assuming a Combined 25% Tax Rate)

Distribution of 401(k) Assets at Age 65

10th Percentile	$541,072	$451,277	-17%
Median	$883,222	$836,288	-5%
90th Percentile	$1,504,396	$1,511,566	0%

Life Insurance Values at Age 65

Cash Value	$0	$210,043	
Death Benefit	$0	$500,000	

Sustainable Spending Rate from 401(k) Assets (with 90% Success)

	2.71%	3.48%	

Distribution of Systematic Withdrawal Income at Age 65

10th Percentile	$14,663	$15,704	7%
Median	$23,935	$29,103	22%
90th Percentile	$40,769	$52,603	29%

Distribution of Legacy Wealth at Age 100

10th Percentile	$506,769	$503,612	-1%
Median	$1,689,769	$1,778,037	5%
90th Percentile	$4,461,739	$4,544,957	2%

Discounted Lifetime Spending Power

10th Percentile	$599,014	$628,048	5%
Median	$1,275,408	$1,455,344	14%
90th Percentile	$2,718,783	$3,089,803	14%

Because investments are used as the source of legacy in Scenario 1, it becomes necessary to remain extra cautious about retirement spending to maintain the desired legacy safety margin for investments. Scenario 2 allows for a higher standard of living in retirement with more inflation-adjusted spending, while still providing the desired confidence that the legacy goal can be met.

Exhibit 7.5 also helps to visualize this process by showing the median spending and legacy across the age range. If the couple's goal is to maximize their standard of living in retirement while still ensuring that their heirs received $500,000 after taxes as a legacy, Scenario 2 accomplishes this more effectively than Scenario 1. As well, the legacy in Scenario 2 has contractual protections, while in Scenario 1 there is still an accepted 10 percent probability that legacy assets will fall below the intended goal.

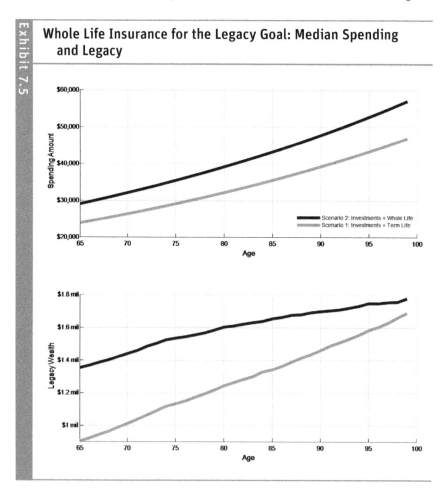

Exhibit 7.5

Whole Life Insurance for the Legacy Goal: Median Spending and Legacy

Across the range of ages, spending and legacy is higher when whole life insurance is used. Whole life insurance can be incorporated into a lifetime financial plan as a more efficient means for meeting a legacy objective, which allows for a higher standard of living to be supported from the remaining assets.

Integrating Life Insurance with Lifetime Income

Another way to use life insurance as part of a lifetime plan is to view the death benefit as the psychological support needed to purchase a life-only income annuity as part of an integrated plan combining investments, whole life insurance, and income annuities. I create three additional scenarios for this investigation:

- Scenario 3 uses the same "buy term and invest the difference" strategy as Scenario 1, but now there is no specific legacy goal to be funded. The couple may spend more aggressively from their investment assets in retirement than in Scenario 1.
- Scenario 4 also uses term life insurance prior to retiring, but the couple will also purchase a joint life income annuity at the retirement date to help support retirement spending.
- Scenario 5 integrates investments with a whole life insurance policy and with a single life income annuity purchased at retirement.

Upon reaching age sixty-five in twenty-five years, Jerry and Beth will consider whether a single-premium immediate annuity (SPIA) might be a worthwhile addition to their retirement income plan. As discussed in Chapter 4, income annuities offer a variety of options regarding whether income starts immediately or is deferred, whether income covers a single life or joint lives, whether there is a certain payment for a set number of years, whether any cost-of-living adjustments will be made to benefits, and whether cash or installment refund provisions are included in the event of an early death.

To simplify our analysis, I consider two basic possibilities: Jerry buys a single life-only immediate annuity at sixty-five on his life, or Jerry and Beth buy a joint life and 100 percent survivor annuity. Both income annuities include a 2 percent annual cost-of-living adjustment that matches the assumed inflation rate, so that the annuity income adjusts to keep the purchasing power consistent throughout retirement. In both cases the annuities are purchased with qualified retirement funds after Jerry has stopped working and completes a rollover from his 401(k) to a traditional IRA.

A male life-only income annuity offers the highest payout rate (the most income) because the buyer offers the most mortality credits to the risk pool by accepting the higher short-term mortality risk. As mentioned in the case study overview, income annuities are priced using Society of Actuaries mortality data and the assumed 3 percent interest rate. With these interest rate and mortality assumptions and with the 2 percent cost-of-living adjustments on the annuity payments, I price a male life-only annuity for a forty-year-old when purchased at age sixty-five at 4.47 percent. The corresponding joint life annuity rate for the couple is 3.75 percent. The single life income annuity provides 19 percent more spending power for a given premium relative to the joint life income annuity.

With the accumulated investment assets, all retirement income in Scenario 3 will be generated with a systematic withdrawal strategy. Jerry seeks annual spending adjustments that match the overall 2 percent inflation rate. The couple uses the highest withdrawal rate possible that keeps investments above $0 by age 100 with a 90 percent probability. This means accepting a 90 percent chance that the spending level can be maintained at the initial amount in inflation-adjusted terms. In Scenario 3, spending from these assets falls to $0 once the portfolio balance depletes.

Scenario 4 shares many similarities with Scenario 3. Jerry uses the same term policy and invests the remainder in a tax-deferred account, leading to the same retirement date wealth accumulation. The difference happens at the retirement date. In Scenario 4, Jerry and Beth purchase a joint life and 100 percent survivorship income annuity with a premium amount equal to up to the pretax equivalent of the death benefit for the whole life policy at age sixty-five. With a 25 percent combined marginal tax rate, the pretax amount to be annuitized is up to $666,667. In simulations where the couple's 401(k) balance has not grown sufficiently to leave at least $100,000 remaining after the annuity is purchased (to provide the couple with a pool of liquid assets to support contingency expenses), then the couple only annuitizes the amount that leaves $100,000 of liquid investable assets (on a pretax basis) after the annuity is purchased.

Though Jerry does not use the whole life policy in this scenario, annuitizing this pretax equivalent amount allows for a proper comparison between Scenarios 4 and 5. After annuitization, the remaining portfolio balance will be utilized for retirement spending using a systematic withdrawal strategy that maintains a 90 percent probability that the account remains above $0 by age 100. The joint life and 100 percent survivor income annuity provides income growing at 2 percent annually for as long as one member of the couple is alive, and any systematic withdrawals will supplement this income for as long as financial assets remain. Portfolio depletion is less drastic in this case, as at least the inflation-adjusted annuity income continues for life.

Next, in Scenario 5 Jerry uses a whole life insurance policy rather than term life insurance. Because of the higher premium, he invests less (starting at $9,836 instead of $15,957) in his 401(k) plan. Second, Jerry buys a male life-only income annuity at sixty-five with the same amount of assets from his retirement portfolio as in Scenario 4. He can now opt for single life instead of joint life because the death benefit from his whole life insurance policy will replace the annuity income stream upon his death.

If desired, Beth could then use part of the death benefit to buy another single life income annuity. As payout rates increase with age, the death benefit should be sufficient to support at least as much annuity income after a few years have passed to account for the lower payout rates for longer-living females. The difference in annuity payout rates (4.47 percent instead of 3.75 percent) allows for 19 percent more income to be generated by the same annuity premium as compared to Scenario 4. Any remaining investment assets will be utilized with a spending rate that supports a 90 percent chance that assets remain by age 100.

Like Scenario 2 in the previous case study, Scenario 5 also treats the cash value as part of the fixed-income allocation and adjusts the stock allocation in the remaining investment portfolio to keep the overall targeted ratio between stocks and bonds at each age. As well, the annuity purchase in Scenarios 4 and 5 is also counted as part of the bond allocation to increase the stock allocation for remaining investment assets. This is important because otherwise, a strategy which combines an investment portfolio with the same asset allocation as before, with a conservatively invested whole life insurance policy and income annuity, would create a more conservative overall asset allocation from the retirement balance sheet perspective. This would reduce growth potential within the strategy.

With these adjustments, I am essentially asking whether the fixed-income component for household assets should be allocated only to traditional bonds or also to actuarial bonds like whole life insurance and income annuities.

Exhibit 7.6 outlines the retirement outcomes for Jerry and Beth. The first part of the exhibit summarizes how they allocate their savings between insurance and Jerry's 401(k) for the three scenarios, as described earlier.

Scenario 3 presents the strategy for buying term insurance and investing the difference in a target date fund. In after-tax terms at retirement, the wealth accumulation ranges from $541K at the 10th percentile to $1.5 million at the 90th percentile, with a median outcome of $883K. With the capital market expectations and asset allocation decisions, the sustainable spending rate that supports a 90 percent chance that assets remain at age 100 is 3.36 percent. This spending rate supports after-tax inflation-adjusted retirement income ranging from $18,180 at the 10th percentile to $50,548 at the 90th percentile, with a median of $29,676.

As for legacy wealth at age 100, it ranges from $3,294 (effectively $0) at the 10th percentile to $3.36 million at the 90th percentile, with a median amount of $1.02 million. Legacy wealth consists of the after-tax value of any remaining financial assets in the investment portfolio and any life insurance death benefit. With Scenario 3, there is no annuitization or death benefit. Investment assets are the only resource to support spending and legacy in retirement.

Scenario 4 also uses term life insurance, but the difference is that partial annuitization takes place with a joint life income annuity at the retirement date. The use of an annuity allows for a slight increase in the distribution rate from investments on account of the higher stock allocation for the investment component in retirement. A joint life income annuity with a 3.75 percent payout rate is purchased with assets of up to $666,667 as described. Before taxes, this supports annuity income of up to $25,000, which reflects $18,750 on an after-tax basis. This is the annuity amount at the median and 90th percentile, but there were insufficient assets at the 10th percentile to annuitize this much and preserve $100,000 for liquidity. This explains the smaller $17,478 amount at the 10th percentile.

Annuity income grows with the same 2 percent cost-of-living adjustment to match the assumed overall inflation rate. A 3.53 percent withdrawal rate is then applied to any remaining investment assets to generate additional retirement income for Jerry and Beth. Scenario 4 supports total income at retirement ranging from $20,125 to $54,205 at the tenth and 90th percentiles, with a median income of $32,278. These numbers are larger than in Scenario 3 (11 percent larger at the 10th percentile, 9 percent larger at the median, and 7 percent larger at the 90th percentile). This demonstrates the potential for mortality credits through the income annuity to pool risk to support more spending relative to an investments-only strategy designed to work with a high probability of success.

With legacy, Scenario 4 generally provides less, at least before accounting for the fact that it provided higher spending. Because partial annuitization with a life-only income annuity removes a significant chunk of investment assets, the distribution of legacy wealth is less able to recover across the distribution of outcomes. By age 100, the investment portfolio is also about to be depleted at the 10th percentile, though annuity income is still available to the couple for as long as they live. Legacy is 8 percent less at the median, and 1 percent more at the 90th percentile. Scenario 4 has taken advantage of only one-type of actuarial bond, creating potential trade-offs when compared with Scenario 3: more retirement income, but less legacy wealth.

Nevertheless, when we evaluate the combined lifetime spending power, we do find that Scenario 4 is more efficient, with increases across the distribution of outcomes. In particular, at the median the 9 percent boost in lifetime annual spending more than offsets the 8 percent drop in legacy on a net basis.

Next, Scenario 5 integrates investments with whole life insurance and income annuities. The value of 401(k) assets at Jerry and Beth's retirement age is less (17 percent less at the 10th percentile, 5 percent less at the median, but about the same at the 90th percentile) than in Scenario 3. Again, this results from less being invested in the 401(k) as more went to the higher whole life insurance premiums, and from the asset allocation in

Exhibit 7.6

Whole Life Insurance Combined with Investments and Income Annuities

	Scenario 3 Investments + Term Life	Scenario 4 Investments + Joint Life SPIA + Term Life		Scenario 5 Investments + Single Life SPIA + Whole Life	
Term Life Premiums	$2,282	$2,282		$0	
Whole Life Premiums	$0	$0		$6,873	
Taxes Paid	$761	$761		$2,292	
Age 40 Remaining Contribution to 401(k)	$15,957	$15,957		$9,836	

All Subsequent Values are Provided on a Posttax Basis
(Assuming a Combined 25% Tax Rate)

Distribution of 401(k) Assets at Age 65			% change from Scenario 3		% change from Scenario 3
10th Percentile	$541,072	$541,072	0%	$451,277	-17%
Median	$883,222	$883,222	0%	$836,288	-5%
90th Percentile	$1,504,396	$1,504,396	0%	$1,511,566	0%

Life Insurance Values at Age 65

Cash Value	$0	$0		$210,043	
Death Benefit	$0	$0		$500,000	

Sustainable Spending Rate from 401(k) Assets (with 90% Success)

	3.36%	3.53%		3.69%	

Distribution of Annuity Income at Age 65

10th Percentile	$0	$17,478		$16,820	
Median	$0	$18,750		$22,350	
90th Percentile	$0	$18,750		$22,350	

Distribution of Systematic Withdrawal Income at Age 65

10th Percentile	$18,180	$2,648		$2,768	
Median	$29,676	$13,528		$12,409	
90th Percentile	$50,548	$35,455		$37,327	

Distribution of Total Income at Age 65

10th Percentile	$18,180	$20,125	11%	$19,587	8%
Median	$29,676	$32,278	9%	$34,759	17%
90th Percentile	$50,548	$54,295	7%	$59,677	18%

Distribution of Legacy Wealth at Age 100

10th Percentile	$3,294	$1,277	about same	$500,000	+++
Median	$1,019,022	$936,733	-8%	$1,485,222	46%
90th Percentile	$3,357,267	$3,402,587	1%	$4,469,206	33%

Discounted Lifetime Spending Power

10th Percentile	$527,035	$582,608	11%	$739,116	40%
Median	$1,210,048	$1,256,909	4%	$1,517,932	25%
90th Percentile	$2,620,572	$2,742,009	5%	$3,268,306	25%

the 401(k) being more aggressive when treating cash value as a bond. The after-tax cash value is $210K at age sixty-five. When adding the cash value to the 401(k) assets, more is obtained at retirement. This results from the tax advantages of life insurance and from the lower internal insurance costs of whole life insurance as cash value reduces the amount of death benefit at risk for the insurance company.

We next consider how much income can be generated by these assets. With partial annuitization through a single life income annuity with a 4.47 percent payout for an amount equal to the death benefit of the whole life policy at age sixty-five, inflation-adjusted annuity income is $22,350 after taxes are paid. The 3.69 percent withdrawal strategy (driven by the more aggressive asset allocation that accounts for the cash value and annuity premium) is then applied to remaining investment assets, generating additional income. Total retirement income at age sixty-five ranges from $19,587 to $59,677, with a median of $34,759. Compared to Scenario 3, retirement income is 8 percent larger at the 10th percentile, 17 percent larger at the median, and 18 percent larger at the 90th percentile.

As for legacy wealth at age 100, Scenario 5 maintains the death benefit of $500K after taxes, which is still available despite investments depleting at the 10th percentile. At the median, Scenario 5 supports legacy wealth of $1.49 million, which is 46 percent larger than in Scenario 3. Of this, $500K is the death benefit and the other $949K is the remaining portfolio balance after taxes. At the 90th percentile, legacy wealth is 33 percent larger than in Scenario 3. Even after accounting for the higher supported spending, legacy wealth is still larger in Scenario 5 in 94 percent of the simulations. Discounted lifetime spending is greater across the distribution of outcomes, reflecting the greater spending and legacy potential of this integrated strategy.

Exhibit 7.7 provides a visualization of these three strategies in terms of median spending and legacy between ages sixty-five and 100. The investments and term life strategy of Scenario 3 supports the least spending, though it does offer the highest median legacy until age eighty-three. After that point, Scenario 5 with the whole life insurance and single life income annuity offers a higher legacy as well as the highest spending across the age range. Scenario 4 with the investments and joint life annuity offers spending that falls between the other two strategies, but legacy is the least as the high level of annuitization leaves too little in the investment portfolio to grow and catch up.

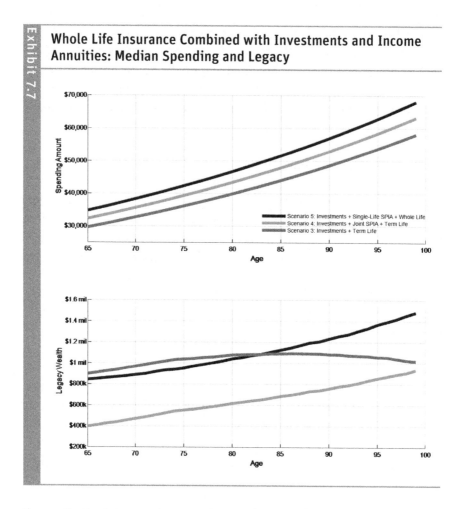

Exhibit 7.7

Whole Life Insurance Combined with Investments and Income Annuities: Median Spending and Legacy

Scenario 5: Investments + Single-Life SPIA + Whole Life
Scenario 4: Investments + Joint SPIA + Term Life
Scenario 3: Investments + Term Life

Generally, the integrated approach provides more legacy wealth while also supporting more retirement income. At the median, Scenario 5 provides 17 percent more lifetime spending and 46 percent more legacy than Scenario 3, with 25 percent growth in overall lifetime spending power. This is the meaning of greater efficiency. The upside growth potential of investments is insufficient to beat a more integrated approach using actuarial science and mortality credits alongside investments.

Adding Whole Life Insurance Cash Value as a Volatility Buffer in Retirement

The next potential use for whole life insurance in lifetime financial planning is using the cash value as a volatility buffer asset to help manage the sequence-of-returns risk for investment portfolio distributions. Retirement spending can be sourced to the cash value after a market downturn to avoid selling portfolio assets at a loss. Returns for buffer assets should not be correlated with the financial portfolio, since the purpose of buffer assets is to temporarily support spending when the portfolio is otherwise down. This attempts to allow for portfolio recovery before distributions from it resume. The cash value of whole life insurance has this characteristic since it is contractually protected from declining in value.

Exhibit 7.8 compares Scenario 3 from before to the new Scenarios 6 and 7. The new scenarios incorporate the volatility buffer strategy in different ways. In Scenario 6, investments are combined with whole life insurance, and the cash value is available to be used entirely as a volatility buffer to help support the portfolio and maximize retirement spending. Scenario 7 maintains investments and whole life insurance while also incorporating a single life income annuity as part of the spending strategy. Scenario 7 follows the previous Scenario 5 except that policy loans from the cash value are also used on a limited basis (so the policy loan balance does not exceed the cost basis by age 100) to bolster retirement spending. Policy loans are taken with the cash value serving as collateral to avoid taxes on these distributions. A conservative (as in higher than the assumed 3 percent economy-wide interest rate) loan interest rate of 5 percent is used to grow the loan balance.

I assume that the whole life policy uses nondirect recognition, which means that there is no adjustment to the growth for the cash value that has been used as collateral for loans. This is a conservative assumption, as policies with direct recognition would support a higher growth rate on the cash value for the loan amount, since the 5 percent loan rate I assume is larger than the 3 percent interest rate earned by assets in the general account. Legacy values at age 100 reflect any remaining investment assets along with the remaining net life insurance death benefit after offsetting cash value policy loans plus accumulated interest.

Scenario 6 allows more aggressive cash value use through policy loans, and I do have to be careful that interest on the loan balance does not push the loan balance over the limit of the available cash value. Such an outcome must be avoided so that taxes are not triggered to be due on all life insurance policy gains in one tax year.

The maximum amount that can be taken from the cash value in any year is the amount that would not grow with 5 percent interest to exceed the slower growing cash value by age 100 (with an additional $5,000 buffer of protection so that the net cash value does not fall entirely to $0). This process ensures that the loan balance growth stays below the cash value, protecting the policy from blowing up. In practice, this outcome can be avoided by monitoring the policy and paying down the loan balance if it is approaching too closely to the total cash value limit. This matter is not a concern for Scenario 7 because the cash value is used on a more limited basis throughout to keep the loan balance less than the policy cost basis by age 100.

The cash value of whole life insurance can be used as a buffer asset to help manage the sequence-of-returns risk exacerbated by taking distributions from a volatile investment portfolio. Maintaining fixed distributions from investments in retirement increases exposure to sequence risk by requiring a higher withdrawal rate from remaining assets when their value declines. Temporarily drawing from the cash value of life insurance has the potential to mitigate this aspect of sequence risk for an investment portfolio by reducing the need to take portfolio withdrawals at inopportune times. By reducing exposure to sequence risk, this can either support more spending or preserve greater overall legacy wealth. Whether or not this strategy will work becomes an empirical question to be tested.

Aggressively using the volatility buffer to support more retirement spending involves making a conscious decision to focus on increasing spending at the potential cost of legacy. The investments-only strategy forces spending to be conservative, feeding instead into a larger legacy because of its inefficient approach for managing longevity and market risk. Nonetheless, limited use of the volatility buffer may not reduce legacy. Though the volatility buffer reduces the net death benefit, the investment portfolio may ultimately grow by more than the reduction to the death benefit, potentially leaving a larger net legacy. This happy outcome can result from the peculiarities of sequence risk and the ability to avoid selling portfolio assets at a loss. The cash value provides a stable income source not impacted by market volatility. Life insurance also receives tax benefits, and the distribution from the cash values can be less since taxes are not paid on the proceeds.

Much of this discussion about using cash value as a buffer asset has a corresponding parallel to opening a line of credit with a reverse mortgage and treating it as a volatility buffer asset. I discuss the latter strategy extensively in my book *Reverse Mortgages: How to Secure Your Retirement with a Reverse Mortgage*. The Sacks and Sacks coordinated strategy from the reverse mortgage book matches how the cash value volatility buffer is typically described by insurance companies. The idea is to spend from cash value in years after a market downturn, while spending from the investment portfolio in years after positive market returns. I will use this same method for deciding when to draw from the cash value as a volatility buffer.

In Exhibit 7.8, Scenario 3 is first repeated to serve as a baseline for comparison. Scenario 3 is the classic "buy term and invest the difference" strategy. Scenarios 6 and 7 switch from term life insurance to whole life insurance and make the cash value available as a volatility buffer. In Scenario 6, the couple spends from the cash value in years after market downturns, as long as the loan balance is not projected to exceed the cash value before age 100 (with an additional $5,000 buffer). In Scenario 7, the cash value is used as a volatility buffer in a more limited way, and a single life income annuity is purchased to merge this aspect of Scenario 5 with a volatility buffer.

Because the cash value provides an additional base of assets to replace some portfolio distributions as well as a fixed-income resource that allows the stock allocation in the investment portfolio to be increased, the initial withdrawal rate for investments increases from 3.36 percent in Scenario 3 to 3.78 percent in Scenario 6, while still maintaining a 90 percent chance that investment assets remain at age 100. Investment holdings at retirement can generally be expected to be lower because of the higher whole life premiums, and this along with the withdrawal rate change leads to inflation-adjusted spending in retirement to change from a 4 percent decrease up to a 13 percent increase across the distribution. The median increase in retirement lifestyle is 6 percent.

Meanwhile, legacy assets are also better supported in Scenario 6 on account of the synergies created by the volatility buffer in managing sequence risk for the investment portfolio. At the median, legacy assets are 28 percent larger at age 100 after already supporting a 6 percent larger lifestyle as well. Across most of the distribution of outcomes, spending and legacy are larger in Scenario 6, as is the discounted lifetime spending power. Whole life insurance used as a cash value volatility buffer can beat "buy term and invest the difference" for a lifetime financial plan initiated by the forty-year-old couple. It is a more efficient strategy.

Moving to Scenario 7, an income annuity is combined with a partial volatility buffer up to the cost basis of the life insurance policy. By age sixty-five, the policy cash value is $210,043. It consists of a cost basis equaling $171,825, which represents twenty-five years of $6,873 annual premiums. Combining the income annuity with the volatility buffer further increases spending relative to Scenario 3 from 11 percent at the 10th percentile to 25 percent at the 90th percentile with a median increase of 21 percent. The withdrawal rate from investments providing a 90 percent chance for success also increases to 4.04 percent because partial annuitization reduces the portfolio size, and the stock allocation increases to offset how the annuity and cash value are treated as bonds. At the median, legacy at age 100 is 34 percent larger as well. Because the cash value was used in a more limited way, the remaining death benefit is still $332K at the 10th percentile. Legacy wealth is larger across the distribution as well, as is the discounted lifetime spending power after accounting for more spending and more legacy.

My personal thought is that Scenario 7 is an appealing way to integrate insurance into a retirement strategy. By limiting cash value use to the policy's cost basis with loan growth, Scenario 7 helps to dramatically reduce exposure to sequence risk and to increase sustainable spending with noticeably less offset to legacy. It also includes the income annuity as an additional risk pooling tool in addition to the remaining life insurance death benefit. For those with a greater emphasis on legacy relative to spending, Scenario 6 with the pure volatility buffer is also a viable choice. Integrating insurance in this manner allows for more efficient retirement income than the traditional buy term and invest the difference strategy found in Scenario 3.

Exhibit 7.9 provides a visual illustration for the median outcome of these strategies by age. Scenario 7 supports the most spending across the age range, but Scenario 6 without the income annuity supports the most legacy across the age range until very late in retirement. Scenario 3 supports the least spending, but it leads to greater legacy than Scenario 7 until about age eighty-five.

Exhibit 7.8

Whole Life Insurance as a Volatility Buffer

	Scenario 3 Investments + Term Life	Scenario 6 Investments + Whole Life Volatility Buffer (Full Use)		Scenario 7 Investments + Single Life SPIA + Whole Life Volatility Buffer (Cost Basis)	
Term Life Premiums	$2,282	$0		$0	
Whole Life Premiums	$0	$6,873		$6,873	
Taxes Paid	$761	$2,291		$2,291	
Age 40 Remaining Contribution to 401(k)	$15,957	$9,836		$9,836	

All Subsequent Values are Provided on a Posttax Basis (Assuming a Combined 25% Tax Rate)

Distribution of 401(k) Assets at Age 65			% change from Scenario 3		% change from Scenario 3
10th Percentile	$541,072	$459,454	-15%	$459,454	-15%
Median	$883,222	$834,603	-6%	$834,603	-6%
90th Percentile	$1,504,396	$1,506,620	0%	$1,506,620	0%

Life Insurance Values at Age 65

Cash Value	$0	$210,043		$210,043	
Death Benefit	$0	$500,000		$500,000	

Sustainable Spending Rate from 401(k) Assets (with 90% Success)

	3.36%	3.78%	13%	4.04%	20%

Distribution of Annuity Income at Age 65

10th Percentile	$0	$0		$17,185	
Median	$0	$0		$22,350	
90th Percentile	$0	$0		$22,350	

Distribution of Systematic Withdrawal Income at Age 65

10th Percentile	$18,180	$17,367		$3,030	
Median	$29,676	$31,548		$13,518	
90th Percentile	$50,548	$56,950		$40,667	

Distribution of Total Income at Age 65

10th Percentile	$18,180	$17,367	-4%	$20,215	11%
Median	$29,676	$31,548	6%	$35,868	21%
90th Percentile	$50,548	$56,950	13%	$63,017	25%

Distribution of Legacy Wealth at Age 100

10th Percentile	$3,294	$14,162	330%	$332,267	9988%
Median	$1,019,022	$1,303,411	28%	$1,361,593	34%
90th Percentile	$3,357,267	$3,743,948	12%	$3,941,638	17%

Discounted Lifetime Spending Power

10th Percentile	$527,035	$507,277	-4%	$699,410	33%
Median	$1,210,048	$1,362,315	13%	$1,507,355	25%
90th Percentile	$2,620,572	$2,939,197	12%	$3,182,914	21%

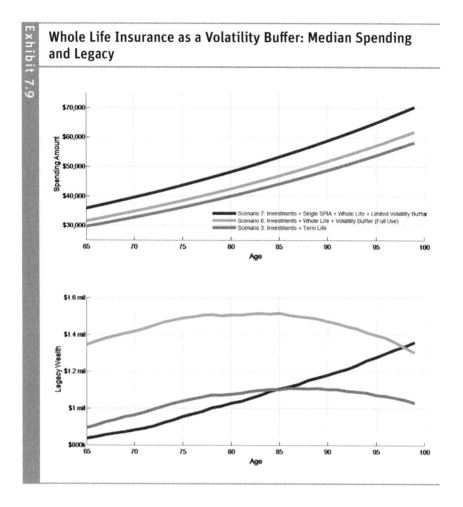

Exhibit 7.9

Whole Life Insurance as a Volatility Buffer: Median Spending and Legacy

Scenario 7: Investments + Single SPIA + Whole Life + Limited Volatility Buffer
Scenario 6: Investments + Whole Life + Volatility Buffer (Full Use)
Scenario 3: Investments + Term Life

Treating Cash Value as a Fixed-Income Investment Choice

Though it requires patience, as it takes time for the initial policy creation costs to be recovered and for cash value to accumulate, long-term investors may find that the long-term net returns on cash value accumulation within a whole life policy may be competitive with the fixed-income returns a household could otherwise obtain from traditional bond investments. This fourth role for life insurance focuses on cash value growth, with the postretirement death benefit serving as an afterthought. In this regard, one might even consider whole life insurance as an alternative source for a temporary death benefit instead of term insurance with the intention to build tax-deferred cash value to later surrender as an alternative to buying term and investing the difference in bonds.

Cash value life insurance provides a way for the policyowner and the insurance company to share the benefits of tax-deferral afforded to life insurance. To be comparable with cash value, the net return on bonds would have to be evaluated as the gross return less investment expenses, taxes, and the term premiums required to purchase an equivalent death benefit for preretirement human capital replacement needs.

The ability for cash value returns to potentially outperform other fixed-income investments relates to several factors. First, regarding the underlying portfolio of assets, the general account of the insurance company is better positioned than the household to manage the risks involved in earning higher fixed-income returns by accepting duration, illiquidity, and credit risk. Actuaries at insurance companies generally can make reasonable estimates about their future claims-related expenses. This allows for a longer-term investment focus with assets held to maturity that can offer higher yields than households could otherwise muster within their own fixed-income portfolios.

The general account is highly regulated with respect to the amount of assets to be maintained relative to liabilities and to asset allocation. Assets must be sufficient to fund policy claims, including death benefits, policy surrenders, and loans, after accounting for future premiums and investment returns.

General account investments typically include corporate and government bonds, mortgages, policy loans, a small allocation to equities, and potentially other types of alternative investments. The general account has greater return potential through its ability to invest in longer-term and less liquid assets, and to diversify the credit risk of higher-yielding corporate bonds. Households have less capacity to diversify and manage these risks. Asset values for households are too small, their timeframes are too short, and their liquidity needs are too high. Policyholders do not have individual accounts within the general account. The account value is aggregated across all policyholders.

The general account of the insurance company is using projections about the inflows of premiums and outflows of benefits and surrenders/loans and is using an asset-liability matching framework so that bonds do not have to be sold at a loss. Because insurance companies generally hold the fixed-income assets to maturity, rising rates will not trigger capital losses, but will allow new premiums to be invested at a higher rate. Any policy dividends should generally be more closely related to interest rate movements, slowly rising after interest rates rise and slowly falling after interest rates fall. Because insurance companies use asset-liability matching, a rise in interest rates allow subsequent bond purchases to be made at higher yields. This stable value aspect of cash value is a key motivator for using it in the volatility buffer strategies.

As well, fixed-income returns must be considered net of taxes. For bonds held in a taxable account, taxes must be paid on the annual interest payments, reducing the compounding growth potential of the assets. Likewise, in a tax-deferred account, taxes must be paid when distributions are made. Cash value within life insurance accumulates on a tax-deferred basis while the asset can potentially also be accessed without needing to pay any additional taxes.

Furthermore, cash value accumulation is already reported net of fees. Fees are internal to the policy and loaded into the stated premium. To be comparable, investment and advisory fees charged on bonds must be incorporated so that bond returns are identified on a net-of-fees basis.

Finally, cash value life insurance also provides a valuable death benefit. If we assume that a preretiree needs life insurance and is considering between term and permanent life insurance, the net returns on a bond portfolio would also need to be reduced to account for the cost of term premiums as a percentage of the whole life premiums. Bond investments could only be made with remaining funds after paying for the term premiums covering the preretirement life insurance need.

The ability for the insurance company's general account assets to earn returns that exceed what households could otherwise obtain, combined with the tax deferral provided by the insurance policy, means that it is possible for life insurance to serve as an attractive long-term fixed-income investment even net of its insurance costs for a lifetime death benefit. It is worth exploring the simple possibility that life insurance cash value can be a viable alternative to include in a household's fixed-income investment portfolio. It is possible for the net returns on cash value to exceed the net returns on other fixed-income investment opportunities.

Exhibit 7.10 provides the details for this analysis. These numbers could be modified to account for different circumstances. I consider the case for a forty-year-old who could either pay a higher premium for whole life insurance to support a permanent death benefit while also growing cash value in the policy, or who could pay a lower premium to support his preretirement death benefit needs with term insurance and then invest the difference between the whole life and term life premiums into a fixed-income portfolio. In this example, I maintain the assumption that interest rates remain fixed at 3 percent, and I do not assume any additional yield premium for investments in the general account relative to what is available to the household on their own. As explained, the insurance company's general account may be positioned to yield higher returns than available to households.

For bonds, the gross yield is 3 percent, but I must account for the impact of taxes, fees, and life insurance needs to determine the net yield. Assuming this individual will remain in the 25 percent tax bracket, the net yield on fixed-income assets must be reduced by 25 percent, or 0.75 percent of the 3 percent bond yield to pay the annual tax bill. As for fees, to be consistent in this example I assume that bonds can be obtained without fees as I do not otherwise charge fees within the insurance policies. Finally, in

Exhibit 7.10	Whole Life Insurance Cash Value as a Fixed-Income Alternative	
	Interest Rate:	**3.00%**
	Additional Yield Premium for General Account:	0.00%
	Bond Portfolio	
	Gross Yield:	3.00%
	Less Taxes (25% Tax Rate):	-0.75%
	Less Investment Fees:	0.00%
	Less Term / Whole Life Ratio ($2,282 / $6,873):	-1.00%
	Net Yield:	**1.25%**

the term life scenario, the premium for term insurance is one-third of the premium for whole life insurance. Assuming this individual seeks life insurance through retirement at sixty-five, only two-thirds of the potential funds are available to be invested into the bond portfolio. This reduces the net returns on bonds by an additional 1 percent. Overall, the net return on bonds in this example has fallen to 1.25 percent.

As for the returns on cash value, the problem is slightly more complex because the insurance costs vary over time (recall the discussion of Exhibit 7.2). The complexity is accounted for by using an internal rate of return calculation. The internal rate of return is the compounded growth rate required on policy premiums to generate the cash value of the policy. These returns can be calculated both for the cash value and for the death benefit. I specifically seek to calculate them for the cash value growth shown in Exhibit 7.2.

Life insurance cash value is not meant to serve as a short-term investment. Exhibit 7.11 tracks the net returns for cash value over the life of the policy through age 100. Cash value returns remain negative until age fifty-one. This is when the cash value amount ($82,665) first exceeds the cumulative premiums paid up to that point ($82,476). It took eleven years. Then, at age fifty-nine, the net returns on cash value exceed those of the bond portfolio for the first time. As time passes, the net returns on cash value continue to grow. They exceed 2 percent at age eighty-two and are 2.27 percent at age ninety-nine. Meanwhile, the life insurance also supports a permanent death benefit.

As for bonds, the death benefit with the term policy ends at age sixty-five. Subsequent net bond returns at age sixty-five could be higher (2.25 percent) if life insurance is no longer used, but this would not cause cumulative net returns to immediately jump to this higher level. If I account for the term premiums that did not enter into the bond portfolio in the same manner that part of the whole life premiums are used to fund the life insurance, I find that the net returns on bonds would trail the cash value returns for life, despite the term strategy not providing a permanent death benefit. Expressing the internal rate of return on the value of the bond portfolio relative to the cash flows used to invest in bonds and pay for term life insurance, the net return on bonds reaches only 1.44 percent at age ninety-nine in this scenario.

With term insurance, there is no cash value to help offset future insurance costs as happens with whole life. This leaves the "buy term and invest the difference" strategy lagging behind permanently. Exhibit 7.11 further shows the net lifetime internal rates of return on the bond investments after also accounting for the term premiums. Bonds do not have an opportunity to catch-up to the permanent life insurance approach even after the term insurance ends and the subsequent net returns become higher in absence of the continuing death benefit.

This analysis has demonstrated the potential for the net returns on cash value to exceed those on other fixed-income assets. It is important to remember that this is accomplished with less risk as well, because cash value is not exposed to interest rate risk. We must also not forget that a permanent death benefit also accompanies this cash value even after age sixty-five. Moving away from our simplified world, comparisons would have to consider the potentially higher returns on the general account, the impacts of fees for both insurance and investments, and the interest rate risk experienced for bond assets.

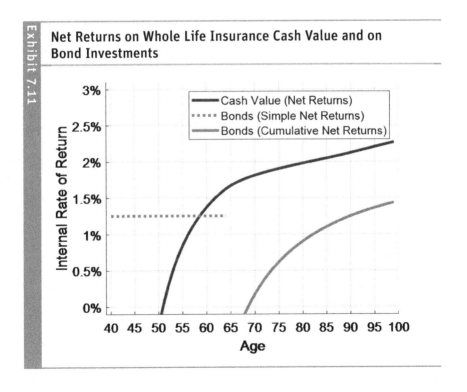

Exhibit 7.11

Net Returns on Whole Life Insurance Cash Value and on Bond Investments

All considered, net cash value returns may be quite competitive with net bond returns, so that even aside from the death benefit, whole life insurance could provide a preferable way to invest in fixed-income assets for the household with a long-term focus.

Additional Considerations for Whole Life Insurance

I described four uses for whole life insurance in retirement income planning using a simplified model that allows for an understanding of the underlying mechanisms at work without being bogged down by additional real-world complexities. This simplified model with interest rates remaining forever fixed and without uncertainty about future mortality rates allowed me to price my own life insurance policies to be compared on an equal basis with investment strategies sharing the same underlying market assumptions. This provides a good foundation for understanding how to compare integrated strategies with life insurance against investments-only strategies. But it is important to explain the additional real-world complexities and how they may impact the previous conclusions regarding the contribution that whole life insurance can provide to a retirement income plan.

The simplified framework in the earlier analyses included the following features of whole life insurance:

- Level premiums that are guaranteed not to increase
- A guaranteed death benefit and guaranteed cash value growth for the policy (guarantees are dependent on the claims paying ability of the insurance company)
- Tax deferral for the cash value growth
- The opportunity to receive the death benefit free from any income or estate taxes
- The ability to surrender the policy for its cash value
- The ability to withdraw funds from the policy on a tax-free basis when structured properly by partially surrendering or borrowing up to the premium paid into the policy, and then taking policy loans against cash value gains

Actual whole life policies have additional features that are too complex to properly simulate cash value and death benefit growth with Monte Carlo simulations, so that the policies can be compared on an equal basis with investments-only strategies. Additional complications include the broader diversification of the investment holdings in the insurance company's general account, the ability for participating policies to pay dividends to policy holders, differences between actual and estimated outcomes for mortality and company expenses and the role played by accumulating reserves for these contingencies, different underwriting categories for life insurance, and whether the company has other business lines that may generate profits returned to policy holders through dividend payments.

Previous sections let us investigate the key issues about the role of whole life insurance without adding these complexities by assuming the mortality and interest rate experience matches expectations and that all retirement income tools are priced fairly and do not include fees.

Exhibit 7.12 summarizes the remaining issues to be discussed around creating more realistic comparisons between whole life and investments. This discussion includes understanding the underwriting process, the options available for whole life insurance, the differences for dividend-paying participating policies and the accumulation of reserves to better cushion uncertainty about the assumptions.

Life Insurance Underwriting

While most annuities do not require underwriting, life insurance is generally underwritten. The life insurance company wants to determine that purchasers do not have health issues which may lead them to expect an earlier age of death. The life insurance company may seek to determine more about your health status with a questionnaire and a physical examination conducted by a qualified medical professional.

Life insurance companies use different health classifications to help match policyholders to their potential health status and longevity. Those determined to be in better health can be expected to live longer and will receive a better health classification that results in lower premium payments. Smokers and those deemed to be in a lower health classification may still qualify for life insurance but will have to pay higher rates for their coverage. Some individuals may have preexisting health conditions that disqualify them from life insurance eligibility. This becomes a risk for waiting to start life insurance coverage, as at some point individuals may

Exhibit 7.12

Additional Considerations for Comparing Whole Life Insurance and Investment Strategies

Reasons Whole Life Insurance Premiums...

Could be Higher	Could be Lower
Insurance companies price policies with higher premiums to also cover company expenses.	Life insurance policies are underwritten. Premiums relate to age, gender, and health classification. Nonsmokers in good health could obtain substantially lower premiums than when pricing policies for the average person.
Premiums must be higher to support additional reserves to cover mispricing related to market returns, mortality, and company expenses. When experience is better than the conservative pricing projections, premiums were too high, and dividends are paid to holders of participating policies as a way to return these excess premiums.	Policies may be priced to endow at age 121 rather than age 100, which lowers premiums as cash value returns play a larger role relative to premiums in supporting policy growth.
Many policies include additional riders such as a waiver of premium to keep the policy in force if the owner becomes disabled, or options to purchase paid-up additions without additional underwriting. Such options provide value that is reflected through higher premiums.	Returns on the insurance company general account may be expected to exceed fixed-income returns available to households.
For whole life insurance, generally being younger is advantageous for starting a policy. The earlier one starts, the more it becomes possible to rely on compounding growth for the cash value rather than to rely on premium payments. Nonetheless, it is possible to wait to later ages to begin a policy, as long as one remains insurable. Premiums will increase with starting age for the policy and with limited-pay policies using shorter premium periods.	Some policyholders will lapse before receiving their death benefits, which reduces costs to the insurance company. This will be reflected through lower insurance premiums.

Other Factors Impacting the Comparisons Between Insurance and Investments

Investments have fees as well, which must be included in scenarios assuming fees on insurance.

Participating whole life insurance policies provide the potential to pay dividends to policyholders, which can be used to purchase paid-up additions that grow the death benefit and cash value.

A term insurance policy with a fixed death benefit is not directly comparable to a participating whole life policy with a growing death benefit.

The tax brackets individuals face pre- and postretirement are important. Those in higher tax brackets will receive relatively more benefit from using a properly structured life insurance policy.

Outcomes for life insurance are dependent upon the solvency of the life insurance company.

In some states, life insurance can provide additional protections from the claims of creditors.

incur a health event that subsequently disqualifies them from obtaining coverage that they could have previously been eligible to receive.

This also suggests the potential value of adding riders to an insurance policy that allow for additional coverage to be purchased later (renewal and convertibility options) without needing to go through the underwriting process again. The earlier examples were based on average longevity numbers; those with better insurance classifications could obtain lower premiums after the underwriting process.

Whole Life Insurance Premiums and Options

Choices exist regarding how long premiums will be paid for whole life policies. For an ordinary whole life policy, premiums are paid for as long as the policy is in force. This means premiums are collected for life or to an advanced age when the policy otherwise endows. Another option is a limited-pay whole life policy in which larger premiums are paid for a fixed number of years so that the policy is fully paid-up by a particular age. A compelling reason for a limited-pay policy would be to ensure that no further premiums would need to be paid after the planned retirement date, for instance. Examples of this option include a twenty-pay policy (the policy is fully paid-up after twenty years of premiums), a ten-pay policy, or even a single-premium policy. The earlier case study used a limited-pay policy in which premiums stopped at age sixty-five.

A potential point of confusion about ordinary life policies is that they may sometimes look like limited pay policies in policy illustrations that assume premiums will eventually be paid by nonguaranteed policy dividends, rather than paying out-of-pocket. For limited-payment policies, premium payments end rather than assuming they are covered through dividends.

Next, while most life insurance policies today have level premiums, it is not strictly a requirement. Level premiums mean that the premium amount stays fixed over time. It is worth considering this aspect further. If one were to buy a new one-year term life policy each year, costs would rise with age to accompany the increasing mortality rates associated with aging. This explains why the quoted level premiums offered by an insurance company will be higher when purchased at later ages.

By choosing a level premium, one is essentially overpaying for the life insurance in the early years of the policy and then underpaying for the insurance in the later years of the policy. The earlier overpayments provide a surplus of funds that are invested by the insurance company and earn interest and are then able to help to subsidize later insurance costs. For whole life insurance, the surplus is reflected through the policy's cash value growth as an asset for the policyholder.

From the policyholder's perspective, this approach for providing level premiums can make sense, which is probably why this structure is so common. The implied returns from life insurance are extremely high in the event of an early death as fewer premium payments support the same death benefit. These implied returns decrease with age as more premiums are paid and the receipt of the death benefit is pushed further away from when the policy started. Level premiums work to help smooth the differential in these implied returns experienced for different ages of death, as they lower the already high returns in the event of an early death but help to boost the returns in the event of a later death.

One important caveat to provide about level premiums is that they do hurt those who lapse on their life insurance policies. By overpaying early on and then surrendering the policy, one loses the opportunity to receive those later insurance cost subsidies. The subsidies instead go to those with participating policies that remain in force. They are received as policy dividends. Indeed, those maintaining their participating whole life policies on a permanent basis do benefit when their counterparts lapse. But level premiums should help to reduce the overall lapsation rates by helping to keep premiums at an affordable level at advanced ages even as insurance costs rise.

Another set of options with whole life policies relate to both the ages that the policy endows and that the policy matures. A whole life policy endows when its cash value grows to match the death benefit. If a policy matures, it means that the individual has lived long enough that they receive the death benefit (or more precisely, the cash value that matches the death benefit) while still alive. Many past whole life policies matured at age 100, which is not necessarily a desirable outcome. By being forced to receive the cash value at that age, it means that any policy gains represent taxable income. For this reason, age 121 has now become a common maturity date for newer whole life policies.

The endowment date and maturity date can be different. A policy that matures at age 121 could endow at age 100 or age 121, for instance. If the policy endows before maturing, different companies have different procedures for what happens. There should no longer be any life insurance costs or premium payments for an endowed policy, but those holding onto the policy may still be able to receive dividends that grow the cash value (which now matches the death benefit). The policyholder may elect to take the cash value of the policy, but this could trigger taxes. Maintaining an endowed policy until death can allow the death benefit to be received with its usual tax advantages. A policy that endows at a younger age will require higher premiums than otherwise because the cash value must grow more quickly to reach the death benefit sooner.

Insurance companies also provide optional riders for life insurance policies for additional benefits and flexibility. Riders providing attractive benefits to policyholders will often require an additional charge that is included in the overall premium paid.

A common rider is the waiver of premium rider for disability. It stops the need to pay premiums without losing any coverage in the event of becoming disabled. This can be an attractive option because otherwise, the lack of income triggered by disability could make it difficult to continue paying life insurance premiums and could force the policyholder to involuntarily lapse on the policy if the household finances become too tight.

Another potential option on a whole life policy is the reduced premium offset. This can allow one to stop making premium payments at some point in exchange for being willing to accept a lower death benefit. It may be an option one would like to implement at retirement as a way to reduce stresses on the retirement income plan caused by paying life insurance premiums after retiring. The reduced premium offset works by using the policy's cash value to buy a single premium permanent life insurance policy at that point in time based on the underwriting and classifications when the policy was first taken out. This option has value because while an individual could always discontinue a policy and receive the cash value, changes in health status may mean that one can no longer qualify for new coverage. The reduced premium offset allows part of the policy to remain in force while stopping the need to pay premiums.

Additional riders can also allow the life insurance policy to help fund long-term care expenses by accelerating access to the death benefit while still alive in order to pay for long-term care. This acceleration of benefits will generally be allowed using the same criteria necessary to also qualify for receiving benefits from traditional long-term care insurance policies.

Another common and important rider provides the option to purchase paid-up additions for the policy. This allows one to add additional out-of-pocket funds to the policy beyond the required premium payments to increase the death benefit and cash value without needing to go through the underwriting process again. This allows the policy holder to expand coverage without having to start a new policy. The additional payments are essentially providing layers of fully paid up or single-premium life insurance. The dividends provided through participating policies could be used as a source of funds to purchase these paid-up additions, and life insurance illustrations may be provided which show dividends being reinvested into the policy in this way.

Finally, life insurance does not have to be based on only one life. A couple could choose a joint life policy that could pay the death benefit based either on the first-to-die or on the second-to-die. The latter option would be noticeably cheaper since joint longevity is greater than for a single individual.

Participating Policies and Dividends

A key difference between the simplified whole life policy I used in the earlier case studies and actual whole life policies is the ability for participating whole life policies to pay dividends. When purchasing a participating whole life policy, the insurance company will provide an illustration about the projected future performance of the policy, including projections about dividends. These illustrations will include both the guaranteed projections for the death benefit and cash value, as well as anticipated levels for dividend payments based on the current dividend scale used by the company. The actual dividends received could end up higher or lower than illustrated, depending on how the factors used to determine dividends subsequently perform.

Because of the conservative nature of the assumptions used to build illustrations, responsible companies provide a greater chance that actual policy performance could exceed even the illustrated values. An aggressive company may produce an illustration that is too optimistic, making it more likely that actual outcomes will lag. For this reason, it is not a good idea to compare policies from different companies based solely on the illustrated outcomes.

Whole life premiums may be higher that shown in my example about policy pricing. Exhibit 7.2 was based on there being no uncertainty about future interest rates and mortality. Because of real-world uncertainty, life insurance premiums build in a degree of extra caution to create reserves as a cushion in case the company's experience deviates too far from its assumptions about investment returns on the general account, mortality rates, and company expenses. Company expenses may include loads to pay commissions, premium taxes, administrative expenses, additional allowances to cover contingencies, and a profit motive. A margin of protection is built-in with a higher premium charged than will probably be necessary.

If those contingencies do not happen, then participating policies return the surplus premiums to the policy holders through dividend payments. Dividend payments are treated as the return of surplus premiums, so the cost basis of the policy is total premiums paid less total dividends received. However, dividends do not reduce the cost basis of the policy if they are returned to the policy through the purchase of paid-up additions or to pay premiums.

One use of dividends is to purchase paid-up additions to increase the cash value and death benefit above the minimum guaranteed levels. Exhibit 7.13 provides an example of a life insurance illustration for an actual policy providing an initial $500,000 death benefit for a forty-year-old male in good health with limited-pay premiums through age sixty-five. For our earlier case studies, the simplified assumptions meant there were no role for dividends. The death benefit and cash value reflected what could be guaranteed by the policy as there was no uncertainty to build reserves against. With dividend paying policies, I must distinguish between the policy's basic guarantees and what the policy could accomplish if dividend payments are received and used to purchase paid-up additions. For this policy, the guaranteed death benefit is $500K, and the policy endows at age 100 when the cash value reaches this level.

Meanwhile, the illustrated death benefit and cash value grow much larger with dividends. The policy still endows at age 100, but the death benefit and cash value by this age have exceeded $2.25 million in the policy illustration based on the company's current dividend scale. Dividends are not guaranteed, and the actual realized performance of the policy could end up being better or worse than the illustrated numbers. If any dividend can be paid, even just once, the policy will provide a better outcome than its guaranteed level. While past performance does not predict future outcomes, the large mutual life insurance companies that have been around since the 1800s are proud of their consistent track records for paying dividends.

Besides using dividends to purchase paid-up additions of coverage, other dividend uses include receiving them as cash payments, using them as a source of funds to pay for insurance premiums, or depositing them in an interest-bearing account with the insurance company.

Mutually owned life insurance companies are owned by the holders of participating policies, as opposed to publicly held companies owned by shareholders. Mutuals can focus on paying dividends to their policy holders rather than to their stockholders. This may give them an edge in providing dividends to the owners of their participating whole life policies.

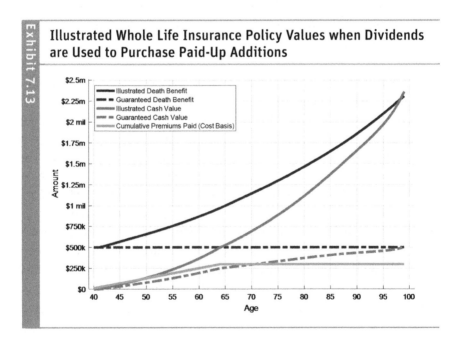

Illustrated Whole Life Insurance Policy Values when Dividends are Used to Purchase Paid-Up Additions

Exhibit 7.13

A final note is that policyholders can request in-force illustrations from the insurance company to show updated trajectories for cash value and death benefit given the realized policy performance as well as for a variety of assumptions around future dividends or future actions around policy loans or surrenders.

○ Variable and Universal Life Insurance

Our discussion of whole life insurance included two critical elements that reduce its risks when incorporated into a retirement income plan. These elements include that premiums are fixed and guaranteed not to increase, and that cash value is guaranteed to grow at a fixed rate. Participating policies can allow for additional upside growth potential for cash value when dividends are paid and are used to purchase paid-up additions, but there is otherwise an underlying guaranteed cash value accumulation in the policy.

These elements are relaxed for other types of life insurance, which include variable life insurance, universal life insurance, variable universal life insurance, and index universal life insurance. These types of insurance policies also combine a death benefit with a cash value accumulation account. Deductions from the cash value are made to cover policy fees and the costs of providing the life insurance death benefit, and the remainder remains invested as an asset for the policy holder. The types of life insurance differ based on how the cash value is invested.

First, variable life insurance shares the similarity with whole life insurance that premiums are fixed and guaranteed not to increase. What differs is that variable life insurance allows policyholders to invest the cash value into subaccounts with investment risk and growth potential through mixtures of stock and bond investments. This creates volatility for cash value; there is greater upside growth potential but also the possibility for losses to be incurred. Policyholders bear market risk with variable life insurance.

The other main type of permanent life insurance is called universal life insurance, and it has several different variations. The primary characteristic of universal life insurance is that premiums are flexible, and their levels are not guaranteed. Premiums may increase beyond what policyholders anticipate or expect. Related to the ability to adjust premium payments, some universal life insurance policies also offer a flexible and adjustable death benefit. For universal life insurance, the Option 1 death benefit works similarly to whole life insurance in that it remains level, and the costs of insurance decline as the cash value increases and reduces the amount at risk for the insurance company. With an Option 2 death benefit, the amount of death benefit at risk for the insurance company remains fixed as the total death benefit is equal to the cash value plus the fixed amount of the death benefit above the cash value.

Fixed universal life insurance credits a fixed interest rate to cash value in a similar manner as whole life insurance. This most basic form of universal life insurance combines a permanent death benefit with tax-deferral and a variable interest rate return for cash value that includes a guaranteed minimum return.

Next, universal life insurance also offers variable and index versions. Variable universal life insurance serves as the life insurance counterpart to deferred variable annuities. Rather than using a fixed savings account, variable universal life allows for diversification of invested premiums across a range of investment options including multiple asset classes. One could potentially invest in 100 percent stocks with a variable universal life policy. Its premiums are not fixed and may require increases to keep the policy in force.

Likewise, index universal life insurance serves as a counterpart for fixed index annuities. Premiums enter into a savings account with returns linked to market indices such as the S&P 500. These policies will include the same types of floors and caps or participation rates as index annuities, which help to control volatility for the assets by giving up some potential upside to provide greater downside protections. For a stock index, performance will be based on price returns with dividends excluded. Index life insurance provides a degree of risk somewhere between fixed and variable universal life insurance. Floors may help to alleviate against the possibility of negative returns than can happen with variable policies.

Though variable and universal life insurance policies could potentially be used in the same manner as discussed for whole life insurance, they may not work as effectively for those purposes, and this is generally not the way that insurance professionals describe using these policies. The death benefit tends to be underplayed, though it could potentially serve to provide a legacy goal or as a backstop to justify the use of an income annuity. As for the volatility buffer strategy, especially with variable life insurance, the policy returns may be correlated with the investment portfolio and render the policies ineffective as a volatility buffer.

Instead, advocates for these forms of life insurance within retirement income planning tend to support using the cash value as a tax-efficient source of supplemental retirement income. For this discussion, it is worth revisiting the tax situation for retirees. There are three potential ways to obtain tax advantages:

1. One could receive a tax deduction for contributed funds, which reduces current taxable income.
2. Gains could accumulate on a tax-deferred basis.
3. The distribution of gains could be obtained free of additional taxes.

It is rare to find a financial tool that offers all three of these advantages. Health savings accounts available to those using qualified high-deductible health insurance plans and when tapping the account to pay for qualifying health expenses are one example.

A traditional IRA or a 401(k) retirement account does provide #1 and #2 as tax advantages, but all distributions from these accounts are then treated as taxable ordinary income. Variable and index annuities provide the second advantage of tax deferral and may serve as a means for obtaining additional tax deferral once retirement account contributions reach their maximum allowed limits. Distributions from these annuities will be taxed as ordinary income.

Meanwhile, there are three general tools that can provide tax advantages #2 and #3. These include Roth IRAs, municipal bonds (on a limited basis), and the cash value and death benefit of life insurance policies. Roth IRAs generally have low contribution limits and income limits for contributions. Once one exceeds these limits, permanent life insurance becomes the primary tool to obtain both tax-deferral and tax-free distributions for after-tax dollars when policies are structured properly with surrender of cost basis and policy loans.

Among life insurance advocates, there are a strain of supporters that focus a great deal on promoting the tax advantages of life insurance to minimize taxes paid in retirement. In explaining their views and approach to retirement income, these advocates first tend to focus on how tax rates are presently at historic lows, and that one should expect much higher tax rates in the future. Higher tax rates should be expected for reasons including currently high levels of government debt and borrowing, future strains to pay promised Social Security and Medicare benefits, and other fiscal and demographic issues centered around how there will be fewer working age members of the population to support the expanding population of retirees. As well, retirees may find that their taxable income does not fall by as much as anticipated due to fewer deductions as the mortgage is paid and children become adults, and as required minimum distributions are applied to the assets held in qualified retirement plans.

These advocates explain that you will be better off paying taxes now at lower rates to avoid paying taxes in the future at higher rates, which naturally leads to advocating for tools that support tax advantages #2 and #3. But Roth IRAs have contribution limits, and one may wish to limit holdings of municipal bonds. This could leave life insurance, with practically unlimited contribution limits, as an important tool for obtaining additional tax-advantages for savings and wealth.

An ideal financial plan for these advocates would involve having just enough saved in qualified retirement plans such as a 401(k) that required minimum distributions do not push these taxable income amounts above the level of standard deductions, then perhaps have some funds in taxable investment accounts from which taxable gains can be drawn without pushing the tax rate out of the 12 percent level (which keeps the tax rate on long-term capital gains at zero), and then taking everything else as distributions out of Roth accounts and life insurance.

One would also take care to try avoiding taxation on Social Security benefits, which are triggered when the modified gross income (including half of the Social Security benefit and interest on otherwise nontaxable municipal bonds) exceeds certain thresholds. One could potentially fund a quite sizable amount of spending power in retirement without having to pay any federal income taxes.

It is important to consider this strategy further because the implications related to volatile cash value returns may reduce the efficiency of this strategy in terms of supporting retirement spending in the same way that trying to maintain a legacy goal with an investment portfolio can force a lower level of spending. The issue is that a larger cash value reserve must be maintained to avoid the possibility that the loan balance from the insurance policy grows larger than the remaining cash value in the policy. Cash value that is exposed to volatile and potentially negative returns requires extreme care to avoid having the accumulated loan balance exceed the total available cash value.

If this happens, it terminates the life insurance policy and the policy gains that have been loaned above the cost basis will subsequently be treated as taxable income in one tax year. This can trigger very adverse tax consequences. As such, care must be taken to not borrow too much of the cash value and to monitor the relative values of the loan balance and the cash value to ensure that the former does not exceed the latter.

To reemphasize, this requires taking precautions to not borrow too much of the cash value to avoid being in the position to have to make payments on the loan balance at a time in late retirement when there may be less flexibility for using remaining investment assets. Especially for variable life insurance, in a down market environment that negatively impacts cash value, it could become necessary to pay down the loan balance to avoid creating a taxable event for the policy gains. Some policies do provide overloan protection riders at an additional cost which can help prevent a policy from lapsing for these reasons.

When comparing variable universal life insurance to an investment account holding the same underlying investment funds, the two strategies are pitting the tax deferral and death benefit protections of the life insurance against the lower costs associated with the investment account that does not have to pay insurance costs and policy expenses, mortality charges, and any potential surrender charges. If the purpose of the policy is to supplement retirement income, then the question really simplifies to whether funds that would otherwise have to be invested in a taxable account could find that the tax advantages of insurance lead to better posttax financial outcomes despite the higher insurance costs.

Modified Endowment Contracts (MECs)

Endowment contracts for life insurance fell out of general use in the 1980s after tax reform removed their tax advantages. Simply, endowment contracts were life insurance contracts in which the cash value could be expected to grow more quickly to reach the value of the death benefit at an earlier age than what is considered as a proxy for the maximum length of life (such as the 100 or 121 ages now commonly used). With a smaller death benefit, cash value could grow more quickly because internal insurance cost will be less. Those using cash value as an investment will wish to keep the cash value as high as possible relative to the death benefit.

Because life insurance receives tax advantages, it is tempting to treat the cash value accumulation as an alternative to traditional investment assets, and to treat the death benefit as an afterthought. The tax-deferral properties of cash value make it very attractive, such that individuals might be looking to use life insurance primarily for its cash value rather than for its death benefit. Tax officials caught onto this. While policymakers believe it is worthwhile to provide tax advantages to encourage life insurance for its death benefit, they did not want these tax advantages to extend to those who were buying life insurance primarily as a tax-advantaged savings vehicle and not for the death benefit.

As such, there are now rules about modified endowment contracts that provide tests about whether a cash value life insurance policy is eligible to receive its tax advantages. For whole life policies, the cash value accumulation test is used. It checks whether the cash value is larger than the net single premium needed to fund the policy's death benefit. The cash value must be less to maintain its tax advantages. A separate guideline premium and corridor test is more common for universal life policies to make sure that they are also not accumulating cash value too quickly relative to the death benefit.

Those policies deemed to have too much cash value accumulation could be deemed to function as modified endowment contracts and would lose their tax advantages. Policy gains become taxable and distributions are treated on a last-in first-out basis so that distributions are taxable gains first before the return of premium. The policies also fall under the same rules for qualified retirement plans that create penalties for distributions taken prior to age 59.5.

These modified endowment contract rules make it important to work with a qualified life insurance professional when using life insurance with a desire to emphasize its cash value properties. Care must be taken to make sure that the policy does not run afoul of the modified endowment contract rules that would eliminate the policy's tax advantages. This could happen at any point within the life of the policy and it requires ongoing monitoring. It is not a onetime matter when the policy is first created.

This is the specific question that Russ DeLibero explored—under my supervision for his PhD dissertation at the American College—in research that we subsequently published called, "Life Insurance as a Retirement Income Tool," in the *Financial Services Review*.

This research looks at a forty-five-year-old who uses a variable universal life insurance policy with a 100 percent stock allocation to accumulate for nineteen years, and then to take supplemental distributions from the policy for the first fifteen years of retirement. Using historical simulations of past stock returns, it seeks to identify a combination of assumed accumulation and distribution rates that could continue to keep the policy in force for an additional twenty-one years through age 100. This is to build in protection that the growing loan balance based on the fifteen years of distributions remains below the cash value until at least age 100.

The policy is designed to provide the smallest death benefit allowed to avoid creating a modified endowment contract, with a focus on maximizing cash value growth by keeping insurance costs as low as possible. The amount of spending the policy can generate that would have worked in 95 percent of the historical rolling periods of data is then compared to a taxable portfolio of stocks to determine the probability that it could keep pace with the life insurance distributions. Because of the 100 percent stock allocation, these strategies are meant to provide a supplemental source of discretionary retirement income rather than serving as a reliable income resource.

This comparison pits the tax deferral and tax-free distribution advantages from the life insurance against the internal life insurance costs and the necessity to remain conservative with distributions to keep the policy in force despite the volatility for the underlying cash value and the growing loan balance. When comparing to assets held within a taxable account, we found that for a policy holder with a preferred no-smoker classification, the probability of success for the investment strategy falls below the life insurance strategy if the qualified dividend and long-term capital gains tax rate exceeds 15 percent.

This happens as well for a standard nonsmoker if the tax rate exceeds 20 percent. The life insurance strategy can be very competitive for assets otherwise held within a taxable account, which is likely the most relevant comparison for most individuals. As for comparisons to assets held in a tax deferred account, it is much tougher for life insurance to keep up due to the need to be conservative with spending to make sure that the policy stays in force. Tax rates would have to rise substantially (such as a postretirement combined marginal tax rate of 55 percent) for life insurance to come out ahead. What this suggests is that these life insurance strategies may have value when compared to holding assets in taxable accounts, but one would probably not wish to divert assets to life insurance from a tax-qualified plan when seeking the most efficient ways to generate supplemental retirement income.

◉ Concluding Thoughts

Contrary to conventional wisdom, there can be a role for permanent life insurance as part of the retirement income plan. This chapter looked at how permanent life insurance may be integrated into lifetime financial planning. To finish the chapter, it is worth emphasizing some caveats about the use of life insurance in order to have a better understanding of the situations when it may be most helpful:

- Including life insurance in a retirement income plan is meant to be part of a long-term strategy. It takes time to accumulate cash value, and surrender charges may apply in the early years to cover the policy acquisition costs for the insurance company. These strategies require patience and a willingness to stick with the plan.
- When using volatility buffer strategies or using cash value in other ways, it is important to continue monitoring the policy to ensure that any loan balance does not exceed the policy's cash value. Such action would trigger a surrender on the policy, making all policy gains taxable. One must monitor the loan balance and pay it down if this becomes a risk either because the interest rate on the loan increases or the cash value is not growing as quickly as anticipated.
- When making plans based on the illustrated growth for the cash value and death benefits, it is important to recognize that the illustrated values are not guaranteed. Actual outcomes could be less or more than illustrated, and the retiree must be comfortable with any actions that may be needed to support the policy if dividends are less than anticipated.

- For those more interested in the tax-deferred growth for cash value than the death benefit, it is important to monitor the MEC status of the contract and to not let the cash value grow too quickly relative to the death benefit.
- Guarantees depend on the credit worthiness of the insurer. Look for companies with strong financial performance as well as low costs. It is important to consider company credit ratings from agencies such as A.M. Best, Fitch, Moody's, and Standard & Poor's.
- Universal life does not have guaranteed premiums. They can be changed.

Further Reading

Copeland, C.W. 2015. *McGill's Life Insurance* (Tenth Edition). Bryn Mawr, PA: The American College Press. [https://amzn.to/2SLlge5]

DeLibero, Russell, and Wade D. Pfau. 2017. "Life Insurance as a Retirement Income Tool." *Financial Services Review.* 26.

Lynch, Kevin M., and Glenn E. Stevick. 2011. *Fundamentals of Insurance Planning* (Fourth Edition). Bryn Mawr, PA: The American College Press.

McKnight, David. 2013. *The Power of Zero: How to Get to the 0% Tax Bracket and Transform Your Retirement.* Boston: Acanthus Publishing.

Pfau, Wade D. 2015. "Optimizing Retirement Income by Combining Actuarial Science and Investments." *Retirement Management Journal.* 5 (2): 15–32.

CHAPTER 8

Fitting Income Annuities into a Financial Plan

Though the discussion in this chapter could be applied to any annuity offering lifetime income benefits, the focus for now returns to income annuities. This is done to keep the discussion more manageable. We will return to the consideration and comparison of different annuity types for an overall product allocation framework in the next chapter. Previous chapters have introduced the role annuities can play in retirement income plans. Here we dig deeper into the why and how.

Income annuities provide bond-like returns with an additional overlay of mortality credits. For someone wishing to spend at a rate beyond what the bond yield curve can support, bond investments will essentially ensure that the plan will fail. Income annuities are *actuarial bonds*. They provide longevity protection which is unavailable with traditional bonds. Retirees receive the bond yield curve plus mortality credits. Income annuities are like a bond with a maturity date that is unknown in advance, but which is calibrated and hedged specifically to cover the amount of spending needed by retirees when they are alive to enjoy it.

Since the insurance company providing the annuity is investing those funds primarily in a fixed-income portfolio, we should view income annuities as part of the retiree's bond allocation. There is less of a need for bonds for the remaining nonannuitized assets. Annuities increase risk capacity because retirement lifestyle is less vulnerable to a market downturn. Also, distributions from the stock portfolio can be lessened, reducing sequence risk and helping to preserve the investment portfolio.

Liquid financial assets can potentially be larger later in retirement with partial annuitization. Legacy is not irreversibly harmed. We provide analysis to demonstrate these points and then dive deeper into questions about how much to allocate to the annuity, how to invest the rest, how to manage inflation risk within the plan, and at what ages to buy annuities and to begin their income.

● The Fundamental Logic of an Income Annuity

The question is why should a retiree hold any bonds in the portion of their retirement portfolio designed to cover retirement spending (longevity and lifestyle goals)? Premiums for the income annuity are invested in bonds (the insurance company adds your premium to its bond-heavy general account) and provides payments precisely matched to the length of time they are needed. Stocks provide opportunities for greater investment growth. Individual bonds can support an income for a fixed period of time, but they do not offer longevity protection beyond the horizon of the bond ladder created. Bond funds are volatile, exposing retirees to potential losses and sequence risk while still not providing enough upside potential to support a particularly high level of spending over a long retirement. Risk pooling with an income annuity can support a higher level of lifetime income compared to bonds. Stocks also offer the opportunity for higher income without any guarantee if stocks can outperform bonds and provide capital gains during the pivotal early years of retirement.

Income annuities can be viewed as a type of coupon bond which provides payments for an uncertain length of time, and which does not repay the principal value upon death. Another way to think about income annuities is that they provide a laddered collection of zero-coupon bonds that support retirement spending for as long as the annuitant lives. Much like a defined-benefit pension plan, income annuities provide value to their owners by pooling risks across a large base of participants. Longevity risk is one of the key risks which can be managed effectively by an income annuity. Investment and sequence risk are also alleviated through the more conservative investing and asset-liability matching approach on the part of the insurance company for the underlying annuitized assets. The payout rates for income annuity assume bond-like returns and longevity is further supported through risk pooling and mortality credits, rather than by seeking outsized stock market returns.

Longevity risk relates to not knowing how long a given individual will live. But while we do not know the longevity for any one individual, the actuaries working at insurance companies can estimate how longevity patterns will play out for a large cohort of individuals. The "special sauce" of the income annuity is that it can provide payouts linked to the average longevity of the participants because those who die early end up leaving money on the table to subsidize the payments to those who live longer. Though it may seem counterintuitive to subsidize payments to others, this act can allow all participants in the risk pool to enjoy a higher standard of living while alive than could be supported with bonds. All participants know that the mortality credits will be waiting for them in the event of a long life.

Meanwhile, sequence risk relates to the amplified impacts that investment volatility has on a retirement income plan that seeks to sustain withdrawals from a volatile investment portfolio. Even though we may expect stocks to outperform bonds, this amplified investment risk also forces conservative individuals to spend less at the outset of retirement, in case their early retirement years are hit by a sequence of poor investment returns. Many retirement plans are based on Monte Carlo simulations with a high probability of success, which implicitly assumes lower investment returns. An income annuity also avoids sequence risk because the underlying assets are invested by the annuity provider, mostly into individual bonds which create income that matches the company's expenses in covering annuity payments.

In hindsight, those who experienced either shorter retirements or who benefited from retiring at a time with strong market returns would have probably preferred if they had not purchased an income annuity. But income annuities are a form of insurance. They provide insurance against outliving assets. In the same vein, someone who purchased automobile insurance might wish they had gone without if they never had an accident. But this misses the point of insurance. We use insurance to protect against low-probability but costly events. In this case, an income annuity provides insurance against outliving assets and not having sufficient spending power late in retirement.

Nonetheless, there is still an important benefit from income annuities even to those who do not make it long into retirement, especially for those who are particularly worried about outliving their assets. That benefit can be seen by comparing it to the alternative of basing retirement spending strictly on a systematic withdrawal strategy from an investment portfolio. In order to self-annuitize, a retiree must spend more conservatively to account for the small possibility of living to age ninety-five or beyond while also being hit with a poor sequence of market returns in early retirement. The income annuity supports a higher spending rate and standard of living than this from the outset. All income annuity participants, both the short-lived and long-lived, can enjoy a higher standard of living while they are alive than they would have otherwise felt comfortable with by taking equivalent amounts of distributions from their investments.

Upon entering retirement, a retiree has several options in terms of allocating between stocks, bonds, and income annuities. Let us consider a simple example with four different approaches. With the basic understanding in place, we can dig in deeper.

Bonds

Suppose a retiree wants to stretch the nest-egg over twenty years and will earn 0 percent returns by investing in bonds. We could assume higher bond returns, but that would simply complicate the math without any loss of generality for this explanation. Since insurance companies also invest in bonds, higher interest rates would increase the annuity payout rate as well. These bonds allow for spending at 5 percent of the initial portfolio balance—the sustainable spending rate—every year of retirement, but it leaves nothing to support spending beyond year twenty.

Income Annuities

Now suppose life expectancy is twenty years and add longevity risk to the equation. Some will not make it twenty years; others will live longer. With the 0 percent returns the annuity provider earns from bonds, the provider could still support this 5 percent spending rate through risk pooling and mortality credits no matter how long a participant lives.

Self-annuitization

Now suppose the retiree self-annuitizes instead by managing this longevity risk without insurance. This requires picking a planning age one is unlikely to outlive. Suppose the retiree decides to plan under the assumption that retirement will last for thirty years. In this case, to spread assets out over thirty years with a 0 percent investment return, the spending rate must fall to 3.33 percent. Note as well, the spending rate could only be 2.5 percent to support wealth lasting for forty years. The longer one wishes for the money to last, the less one can spend. In terms of an unintended legacy, if one did live for twenty years, then a third of the assets would still remain with a thirty-year plan, or half of the assets would still remain with a forty-year plan.

Stocks

Alternatively, one could seek an investment return higher than 0 percent by including stocks. With a fixed annual investment return of 3.1 percent, the retiree could support the 5 percent spending rate for thirty years. With a 4.2 percent investment return, spending could be supported for forty years. The question then centers around how likely it is for the portfolio to earn these higher rates of return through a stock-heavy focus.

Stocks creates risk. Seeking this higher investment return forces the retiree to accept portfolio volatility with a growing allocation to stocks. Spending from investments further heightens sequence risk. A few poor returns early on could easily derail the attempt to support that 5 percent spending rate for as long as the plan targets. Often one might get the higher returns needed to support a bigger spending level in this way, but there is no guarantee that this approach will be successful. The stocks strategy provides greater upside potential for wealth to grow, but it also creates greater downside risk that the retiree cannot meet the spending goal throughout retirement.

Annuitized assets do not provide upside in the sense that a legacy could be left when markets do well, but it also eliminates downside spending risk. The long-lived do receive a form of upside through mortality credits. The effective return from the annuity matches what the stocks needed to earn to support those longer retirements. Self annuitizing requires lower spending, and stocks could support higher spending with upside growth, but it does add risk as well. As for bonds, ultimately, the question is this: why hold any bonds in the part of the retirement portfolio designed to meet spending obligations? The income annuity invests in bonds and provides payments precisely matched to the length of retirement, while stocks provide opportunities for greater investment growth above bonds. Bonds alone hold no advantage.

The income annuity provides a license to spend more from the start of retirement by being able to pool risk. Supported spending from an income annuity is higher because it is based on reaching life expectancy, and should the retiree live beyond life expectancy, the higher income continues to be sustained because of the subsidies arriving from those who died early. The expectation that subsidies will arrive as needed allows spending to increase for everyone from the very start of retirement. Exhibit 8.1 highlights how mortality credits represent a third source of spending with an income annuity beyond the spenddown of principal and the interest generated by that principal.

Regarding sequence risk, for those who self-annuitize, there are two options for deciding how to spend from investments. One is to spend at the same rate as the annuity with the hope of either dying before running out of money, or the hope that the investments earn strong enough returns to sustain the higher spending rate indefinitely. This approach requires acceptance of the possibility that the standard of living may need to be cut substantially later in retirement should the hopes for sustained investment growth not pan out. The alternative is to spend less early on and, should good market returns materialize, increase spending later. The problem with intending to increase spending over time is that it is the reverse of what most people generally wish to do, which is to spend more early in retirement and cut back as life slows down at more advanced ages.

The four financial goals for retirement are lifestyle, longevity, liquidity, and legacy. We have just discussed how an income annuity potentially enhances lifestyle from the starting point of retirement, especially for more conservative individuals who spend less because they are more worried about outliving their assets. Additionally, longevity is the fundamental reason to consider an annuity. But what about liquidity and legacy?

Exhibit 8.1

Sources of Income Annuity Payouts

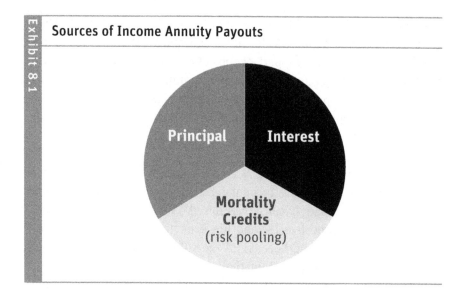

Income annuities do not provide liquidity or legacy without adding provisions which reduce the value of the mortality credits. For those less willing to subsidize the payments to others in the event of an early death, there is less right to earn the subsidies from others in the event of a long life.

But there is more to the story about liquidity and legacy, and it is related to how an income annuity fits into an overall plan. Often the discussion around income annuities frames the matter incorrectly, as if it is an all-or-nothing decision. Partial annuitization lets us think about how we allocate assets toward meeting different goals.

An important point to understand about assets in a liquid financial portfolio is that one's degree of control over the assets may be overstated. There is a stream of lifestyle spending goals which must be financed in order to have a successful retirement. Those spending goals represent a liability which must be financed by assets somewhere on the retirement balance sheet. The assets earmarked for that purpose do not provide true liquidity, as discussed in Chapter 1.

For example, consider a couple who believes that the 4 percent rule serves as an appropriate guide for their retirement spending. They seek to spend

$40,000 per year with inflation adjustments, and they have $1 million invested in stocks or bonds through their brokerage account. Does this couple have any liquidity? Technically, we could say yes, since they do have $1 million of liquid financial assets. But in a meaningful sense, this couple does not have liquidity. They are not free to use that $1 million for other purposes. The full amount must be tied up in order to support their spending objectives. Spending it for other purposes jeopardizes their ability to continue meeting their retirement spending goal later in retirement.

Certain assets on the balance sheet must be earmarked to fund liabilities and this has implications for how those assets should be managed. Many real-world retirees end up earmarking more assets than necessary to support income, and therefore spend less than possible because there is no guarantee component with investments, and they worry about outliving their assets. It is necessary to consider whether an income annuity provides an explicit way to earmark the assets needed for income in such a way that it does free up other assets to provide meaningful liquidity.

For a partial annuitization strategy, Iowa-based financial planner Curtis Cloke refers to the nonannuitized assets as "unfettered assets," as they are no longer tied down to cover the spending needs met by the income annuity. This creates more flexibility for the unfettered assets to support a liquid reserve to cover unexpected expenses or other surprises to the financial plan, or to otherwise support legacy goals. Allocating other assets in a way that accounts for a more secure spending floor can allow a spending goal to be met with fewer assets than a pure systematic withdrawal strategy based only on volatile investments. With each retirement income plan, it is important to investigate how to support spending goals most efficiently.

◉ Income Annuities and Legacy

With this extremely simplified example completed, we now return to our baseline market assumptions to add realism, though we will maintain fixed returns for a bit longer. The status of legacy will be clearer with another simple example comparing an investments-only retirement strategy with a partial annuitization strategy. Consider a sixty-five-year-old female who is ready to retire.

We return to the assumptions about investments and annuities from Chapters 3 and 4. Inflation is 2 percent and bonds provide an additional 1 percent real return. These values are fixed. Stocks support an arithmetic average 6 percent risk premium above bonds with a 20 percent volatility. A portfolio combining stocks and bonds will experience a weighted average return based on those components. For a 50/50 annually rebalanced asset allocation, for instance, the portfolio nominal arithmetic return is 6 percent, the real return is 4 percent, and the volatility is 10 percent. The compounded real return for this portfolio is 3.5 percent. For annuities, with the 3 percent bond yield, a life-only income annuity for this sixty-five-year-old female offers a 5.78 percent payout rate. In this section, we base the analysis assuming the portfolio earns the average compounded return, which represents a median outcome for a broader analysis that would include simulated volatile returns and sequence risk.

For this analysis, we will simplify fixed-income investments to assume a flat and unchanging yield curve. This eliminates interest rate risk from the analysis, as there is no possibility for fluctuating interest rates to create capital gains or losses for the underlying bond portfolio. In reality, if interest rates rise, the value of a fixed-income portfolio declines, but the present-value cost of funding a future spending objective also decreases. If the duration of the bond portfolio matches the duration of the spending liability, then interest rate fluctuations have offsetting effects on the asset and liability sides of the balance sheet and interest rate risk is hedged.

Alternatively, we could think of our retiree as holding individual bonds to maturity, which means that any capital gains or losses from interest rate fluctuations would not be realized as the bonds reach maturity and provide their face value as a source of retirement spending for that year. This simplification about fixed-income does not meaningfully impact the decision between stocks and income annuities; it simply lets us focus more directly on the equity risk premium and risk pooling without also having to worry about fluctuating interest rates. Bonds may be riskier for retired households than implied by our analysis, but this is not our focus.

With a nest egg of $1 million, she budgets for $47,873 of spending from her portfolio—with a planned 2 percent annual spending increase to cover inflation—for the rest of her life. This represents a 4.78 percent withdrawal rate from the retirement date portfolio balance. This spending amount is chosen as the value that will deplete the portfolio precisely after thirty-five years with the 3.5 percent compounded real return assumption. In this case, she does account for longevity risk by planning for a lengthy retirement to age 100 (for which she still has an 11 percent chance to outlive). But the market assumptions for this example are favorable to investments. The return corresponds to the median outcome for investments, and with her spending goal, she could expect to deplete her portfolio 50 percent of the time before the thirty-five-year planning horizon.

We know that her investment wealth will last for precisely thirty-five years in the investments-only case with a 50 percent stock allocation. Legacy is $0 at age 100 and she cannot support spending beyond that age. But what happens to her remaining investments if she allocates part of her portfolio to an income annuity? The answer will depend on how she adjusts the asset allocation for her remaining investments in response to the carve-out for the annuity premium. I will consider three asset allocation options for the remaining investments and base the accompanying example on a plan to allocate 30 percent of assets to an income annuity at the start of retirement.

First, the more conservative response to partial annuitization is to not change the asset allocation for her remaining investment portfolio. She maintains the same 50/50 asset allocation as in the investments-only case, but her overall stock holdings have been reduced since the stocks are 50 percent of the 70 percent that remains after annuitization. Stocks are now 35 percent of the overall asset base. As will be discussed, this is not the recommended approach for managing asset allocation when using any type of annuity with lifetime income.

The second option will provide the most aggressive overall adjustment. In this case, the fixed asset allocation for investments is permanently adjusted to treat the annuity premium as a bond and to hold the same amount of stocks both before and after annuitization. The stock allocation is adjusted upward so that stocks remain as 50 percent of the original wealth holdings before annuitization. With 30 percent of assets annuitized, the stock allocation for the remaining portfolio increases to be 50 percent divided by the 70 percent that remains, or 71 percent of the remaining investments. Treating the income annuity as part of the fixed-income investment, she shifts $300K into the income annuity from her bond holdings while preserving the same amount ($500K) of stocks as before. With the remaining $700K in the financial portfolio, the new asset allocation is 71 percent stocks.

The third approach is to adjust asset allocation over time so that the stock allocation remains at 50 percent of the combination of the remaining portfolio balance plus the present value of remaining annuity payments. This will be the most complex method to use in practice since it requires ongoing adjustments and updating calculations for the annuity present value. In this case, the present value of annuity payments is calculated using the 3 percent bond interest rate and the assumption that the retiree lives to her planning age of 100. This assumption about living until 100 to match the planning age increases the annuity present value relative to the premium paid. Annuity pricing is based on survival probabilities that do not assume such a long lifespan. With a 3 percent discount factor, the present value of the thirty-five annuity payments is $384K, which is $84K more than the $300K annuity premium.

The financial plan is not evaluated with objective mortality. The retiree seeks additional conservatism for the financial plan by choosing a planning age she is less likely to outlive, and this increases the perceived value of the annuity with respect to the role it will play in her financial plan. The annuity is not objectively worth $384K, but it holds this value given her conservative planning age. This higher annuity valuation does increase the initial stock allocation for the strategy, but over time the present value of remaining annuity payments will decline faster than the remaining portfolio assets, leading the stock allocation to decline as time passes. Overall, this approach is more conservative than the second one, which maintains a high stock allocation despite the decline in the present value of remaining annuity payments over time. Exhibit 8.2 illustrates these three stock glidepath assumptions.

With 30 percent of assets totaling $300K used to purchase an income annuity paying at 5.78 percent, annual annuity payments total $17,430. In the first year of retirement, this leaves $30,533 to be withdrawn from the remaining $700K in the portfolio. The initial withdrawal rate from the investment portfolio is reduced from 4.78 percent to 4.36 percent. The reduced withdrawal rate helps to reduce the initial exposure to sequence-of-returns risk as a market downturn is less likely to escalate an increase

Exhibit 8.2

Stock Allocation Glidepaths for the Three Responses to Partial Annuitization

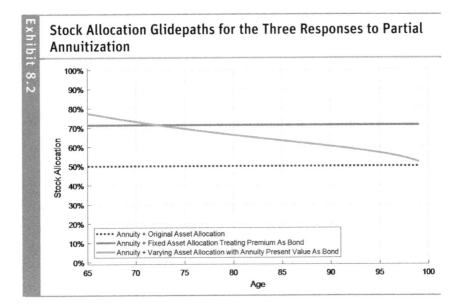

in the withdrawal percentage needed to meet ongoing expenses from what remains. However, the entire subsequent inflation adjustments for the spending goal will need to come from the remaining investments as the annuity payment is fixed. This creates more pressure for the portfolio over time. This is an interesting tradeoff pitting lower initial spending against greater subsequent spending growth that we can start to evaluate with the next exhibit. We will also discuss this point further when we consider whether to incorporate inflation protection into the annuity.

Exhibit 8.3 illustrates the amount of investment assets that remain over time for the different retirement strategies. As noted, with the investments-only strategy, the spending goal was specifically designed to deplete the investment portfolio precisely at age 100. Will partial annuitization cause portfolio depletion sooner or will it extend the life of the portfolio?

The exhibit reveals that the answer depends on how the asset allocation is adjusted in response to shifting some portfolio assets to the annuity. If the stock allocation remains at 50 percent of what is left, then the overall stock allocation has been reduced because the annuity is a bond-like asset. This loss of investment growth potential leads the portfolio to deplete two years prior to the planning age. A portion of spending is still available with the income annuity. But with the growth of the spending goal for inflation, the annuity income is far from adequate at this point in the retirement plan.

The results are much more favorable if the annuity is treated like a bond and the stock allocation for the remaining investments is increased to reflect this. With the more aggressive fixed stock allocation, $425K remains at the planning age, and with the variable asset allocation that accounts for the shrinking present value of remaining annuity payments, $362K still remains at the planning age. In these cases, the retiree is able to fund her spending goal equally well and partial annuitization supports a great subsequent legacy. In the long-term, these latter two cases are more efficient than an investments-only approach.

Exhibit 8.3 tracks the amount of liquid financial assets remaining after also meeting the spending goal. In early retirement, liquid financial assets will naturally be less with partial annuitization. The value of financial assets falls by 30 percent with this partial annuitization. With a lower required distribution rate, financial assets grow and eventually catch-up to investments-only by the mid to late 80s. As this is just below life expectancy, this places the odds squarely in favor of having more liquid financial assets at death with partial annuitization. Short-term sacrifice supports long-term gain. Because the income annuity provides a bigger initial payout, there is less pressure on the portfolio in the early retirement years. This allows liquid financial assets to grow more quickly over time.

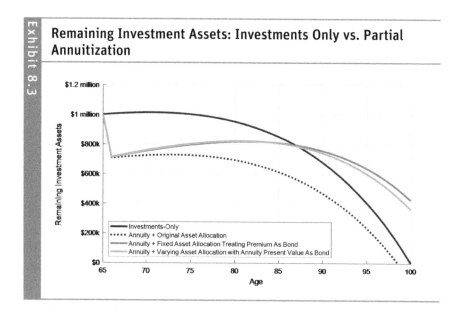

Exhibit 8.3

Remaining Investment Assets: Investments Only vs. Partial Annuitization

The portfolio withdrawal rate stays less with partial annuitization than the investments-only case for three reasons. First, the payout rate from the income annuity is higher than the sustainable spending rate from the investment portfolio. Even though the annuitized assets do not benefit from a risk premium, they do benefit from being calibrated to a shorter planning horizon through risk pooling.

Second, as retirement continues, the income annuity supports more of the income goal with mortality credits, while the bond component of the investment portfolio continues to create a drag on the sustainable amount of spending. Over time, more of the cumulative retirement spending has been funded by the mortality credits from the income annuity, which relieves pressure on the amount of withdrawals needed from the remaining financial assets.

Third, the partial annuitization approach also supports greater growth for remaining assets through the higher stock allocation, which is justified at the initial retirement date by considering the allocation to the income annuity as part of the fixed-income portfolio. The greater risk capacity afforded through partial annuitization allows remaining assets to be invested more aggressively for the subset of the retirement balance sheet representing the financial portfolio.

When retirement is short, partial annuitization leads to a smaller legacy, though the remaining legacy from investment assets is still reasonably large. For longer retirements, partial annuitization offers sound spending support while also fortifying a larger legacy. By requiring less assets to meet spending, risk capacity increases and the withdrawal rate from remaining assets decreases. Nonannuity assets can grow with less sequence risk, creating better long-term opportunities for legacy.

If income annuities include provisions for cash or installment refunds, an early death may not leave beneficiaries in any worse shape than a plan excluding income annuities. This would lose some of the kick from mortality credits, so it would effectively trade more legacy wealth in early retirement for less in later retirement. However, it is an option for retirees not fully convinced by the life-only strategy.

◉ Income Annuities and True Liquidity

As discussed, there are three general financial goals for retirement planning related to the four Ls: funding retirement spending (longevity and lifestyle), providing a legacy to the next generation, and supporting liquidity to cover contingencies. We have considered the first two, and it is worth adding a few comments about liquidity. When we compare the roles of risk pooling (income annuities) and risk premium (stocks) in a retirement income plan, the idea is that annuities do not necessarily provide a direct source of liquidity, but that risk pooling can help to support other goals more efficiently and leave more remaining investment assets available to provide true liquidity for the financial plan.

The *risk premium* strategy will use an investment portfolio to meet the financial goals. The *risk pooling* strategy is an integrated strategy: an income annuity (risk pooling) is used to meet spending goals, life insurance may contribute to legacy goals, and an investment portfolio is otherwise used to support liquidity and other goals that are more discretionary in nature.

Maintaining liquidity is an important tool for managing unanticipated spending shocks in retirement. But the nature of liquidity in a retirement income plan must be carefully considered. An investment portfolio is a liquid asset, but some of its liquidity may be only an illusion. Assets must be matched to liabilities. Some, or even all, of the investment portfolio may be earmarked to meet future lifestyle spending goals. In financial advisor Curtis Cloke's language, the portfolio is held hostage to income needs. A retiree is free to reallocate her assets in any way she wishes, but the assets are not truly liquid because they must be preserved to meet the spending goal. While a retiree could decide to use these assets for another purpose, doing so would jeopardize the ability to fund future spending.

This is different from true liquidity, in which assets could be spent in any desired way because they are not earmarked to cover other liabilities. True liquidity emerges when there are excess assets remaining after specifically accounting for ongoing spending goals. This distinction is important because there could be cases when tying up part of one's assets in something illiquid, such as an income annuity, may allow for the spending goal to be covered more cheaply (i.e. with less assets) than could be done when all assets are positioned in an investment portfolio.

In simple terms, an income annuity that pools longevity risk may allow lifetime spending to be met at a cost of twenty years of the spending objective, while self-funding for longevity may require setting aside enough from an investment portfolio to cover thirty to forty years of expenses. Because risk pooling allows for less to be set aside to cover the spending goal, there is now greater true liquidity and therefore more to cover other unexpected contingencies, such as long-term care or health care shocks, without jeopardizing core-spending needs.

In order to calculate the true liquidity for an investment portfolio that is also supporting a spending goal, we must make assumptions about how much of the portfolio shall be earmarked for the spending goal. We discussed this in Chapter 3 in terms of how asset allocation combined with capital market assumptions, the retirement time horizon, and the desired probability for plan success all work together to determine a sustainable spending rate for the retiree. The asset base to support a spending goal is the spending goal divided by this estimated safe withdrawal rate. If the current portfolio value is larger than this threshold, then the excess reflects the true liquidity for the financial plan. True liquidity can be negative (the spending goal has a shortfall at the accepted level of risk) if current assets are less than what is needed to create comfort that the retirement spending goal will be met.

$$True\ Liquidity = Current\ Portfolio\ Value - \frac{Spending\ Goal}{``Safe"\ Withdrawal\ Rate}$$

If a retiree chooses to fully cover a spending goal through the partial annuitization of her portfolio, then remaining assets in the portfolio are not earmarked to cover spending. With this integrated strategy, risk pooling is used to earmark assets for spending, and the risk premium is used for liquidity. True liquidity will be larger whenever the payout rate for the annuity is greater than the determined "safe" withdrawal rate from investments as based on the retiree's risk aversion.

● Allocation to an Annuity

The earlier example demonstrated the impact of allocating 30 percent of the investment assets to an income annuity. This amount was picked arbitrarily. What is the right amount? I am sometimes asked about how much to put into an annuity as though it was another asset class in an asset allocation problem: how much to stocks, to bonds, and to annuities? The better way to approach this is to ask how much annuity income is needed to meet the longevity spending goals.

The Retirement Income Optimization Map™ (RIO Map™) in Exhibit 8.4 provides a proper summary of how to approach the retirement income problem. This exhibit draws on attributes from the safety-first approach to consider the entire retirement balance sheet and to match assets and liabilities. At the same time, this approach is not overly regimented and includes both probability-based and safety-first plans, as the relative sizes of the reliable income and diversified portfolio boxes can be adjusted to create a plan that meets the psychological needs of the individual implementing it. It works by positioning the four Ls as the financial goals on the left and translating them into the liabilities and expenses associated with those goals on the right.

Retirement assets are matched to those goals after positioning assets in three general categories: reliable income resources, the diversified portfolio, and reserve assets. Reliable income includes protections to help manage retirement risks. Examples include Social Security and pension benefits, individual bonds, and different types of annuities providing lifetime income protections. The diversified portfolio is the traditional investment portfolio and can also include life insurance for matching to a legacy goal or for coordinating with investments to cover spending. Reserves are remaining assets that have not been earmarked to cover other goals and are available to help support retirement contingencies.

With this framework, the amount of portfolio assets to earmark as an annuity premium is based on how much is needed to support longevity goals after accounting for the other reliable income resources available to the household. For example, suppose an individual reaches retirement with $1 million in an IRA and Social Security benefits worth $30,000. This retiree seeks to spend $70,000 per year, of which $45,000 is deemed as essential expenses. After Social Security, there is a $15,000 gap for reliable income. The sixty-five-year-old female facing a 5.78 percent payout rate on a life-only income annuity with level payments could purchase an annuity with $259,516 and precisely close the gap. This represents 25.9 percent of portfolio assets, and it would serve as the starting point for analyzing the

Exhibit 8.4

Retirement Income Optimization Map™ (RIO Map™)

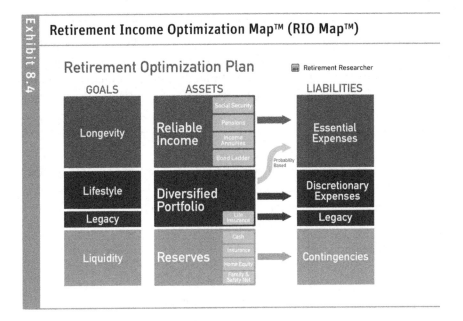

Retirement Optimization Plan · Retirement Researcher

GOALS	ASSETS	LIABILITIES
Longevity	Reliable Income (Social Security, Pensions, Income Annuities, Bond Ladder)	Essential Expenses
Lifestyle	Diversified Portfolio	Discretionary Expenses
Legacy	(Life Insurance)	Legacy
Liquidity	Reserves (Cash, Insurance, Home Equity, Family & Safety Net)	Contingencies

annuity allocation. This would be the portion of assets to earmark to the annuity and the retiree must evaluate whether this is a reasonable portion of the overall asset base.

● Partial Annuitization and Asset Allocation for Remaining Investments

In the earlier example, we could observe the importance of treating annuity premiums as a fixed-income asset so that overall stock holdings do not decrease with a partial annuitization strategy. Treating the matter in this way is justified. We now elaborate on why it is justified to treat the annuity as a bond and to become more aggressive with the remaining assets in the investment portfolio so that total stock holdings are not changed.

For someone who worries and loses sleep about outliving his or her portfolio, does not have much additional income from outside the portfolio, mostly faces fixed expenses without much room to make cuts, and does not have much in the way of backup reserves in the absence of annuitization, it may be necessary to spend and invest very conservatively in order to achieve a high probability of plan success. This will imply using a lower stock allocation and a lower spending rate.

However, for someone who has less fear about outliving his or her portfolio, has a number of additional income sources from outside the portfolio, has the flexibility to cut portfolio spending without adversely impacting the living standard, and has sufficient additional reserves, a higher spending rate and more aggressive asset allocation could be quite satisfactory and optimal. By repositioning a portion of assets into an income annuity, a number of these latter characteristics can be better achieved.

A good starting point for this discussion is to review the Retirement CARE Analysis™ introduced in my book *How Much Can I Spend in Retirement?* It is a framework I developed to outline the factors a retiree should consider when choosing an initial spending rate and asset allocation. This framework provides the details for how to decide on the aggressiveness of both spending and asset allocation within a retirement income plan. This framework is based on Capacities, Aspirations, Realities, and Emotions. Exhibit 8.5 provides the factors to keep in mind.

For our discussion about how to adjust asset allocation when using a partial annuitization strategy, the decision to use an annuity will have already been based on a number of these factors: lifestyle and legacy goals, capital market expectations, longevity risk aversion, financial tool aversion, susceptibility to behavioral mistakes, financial plan complexity, and the financial savvy of all household members. With the lifestyle and longevity distinction of the Four Ls financial goals, the issue of spending flexibility has also been addressed, as the annuity is matched to goals for which there is less flexibility.

The remaining factors from the Retirement CARE Analysis that still can apply to asset allocation include three of the capacity factors (reliable income, funded ratio, and availability of reserves) and the emotional comfort factor of traditional risk aversion.

This discussion implies that a retiree could become even more aggressive with an annuity in place, increasing their overall stock holdings. That is certainly a possibility, but I have not pushed the analysis quite so far. The partial annuity strategies considered were instead an effort to keep the overall exposure to market risk the same before and after the annuity purchase by treating the annuity as an alternative to a portion of the bond holdings.

Exhibit 8.5

The Retirement CARE Analysis™

CAPACITIES (Resiliencies)

Reliable Income
What proportion of your spending goals are covered through reliable income sources from outside the investment portfolio that will not be diminished by market downturns?

Spending Flexibility
Is it possible to reduce portfolio distributions by making simple lifestyle adjustments without significantly harming your standard of living?

Funded Ratio
Are there sufficient assets to meet retirement goals without taking market risk? Is there excess discretionary wealth, or are you underfunded with respect to goals?

Availability of Reserves and Exposures to Spending Shocks
How much exposure is there to large and uncertain expenses? What insurance policies or other reserves are available to manage these shocks? Are there reserve assets?

ASPIRATIONS (Goals)

Lifestyle
What is the retirement budget? How does it change over time? How closely connected is it to consumer price inflation?

Legacy
What are the legacy goals? How important is legacy, relative to other goals?

RETURNS (Assumptions)

Capital market expectations
What are reasonable market return assumptions for different asset classes and inflation to guide simulation of the retirement income plan? How are returns impacted by investor behavior, fees, taxes, and investment vehicle choices?

EMOTIONAL COMFORT (Constraints)

Traditional risk aversion
How much short-term portfolio volatility can you stomach before it affects your sleep and leads you to panic and change course if markets are down?

Longevity risk aversion
How fearful are you about outliving your investment portfolio? Greater concern means more longevity risk aversion, implying that one should choose a higher planning age.

Financial tool aversion
Are you willing to consider different types of retirement tools, such as annuities and reverse mortgages, or are some tools simply nonstarters for you?

Susceptibility to behavioral mistakes
When it comes to investing and long-term planning for complex situations, how prone are you to making a variety of behavioral mistakes? Will you be able to stick to your financial plan?

Financial plan complexity
What is the acceptable degree of complexity and involvement needed to manage your finances? Do you enjoy the planning process, or would you prefer to outsource management to others? Would you prefer more simple set-it-and-forget-it types of solutions?

Financial savvy of all household members
How is financial planning knowledge and savvy distributed among household members? What is the degree of vulnerability of others in the household if the more financially savvy member experiences cognitive decline or an unexpected death?

For those with longevity risk aversion, which helped prompt annuity use in the first place, the three capacity factors have all been strengthened in terms of being able to implement a more aggressive asset allocation for the remaining investment portfolio.

First, reliable income has increased through the annuity. More of the spending goal is now covered by reliable income assets that are not exposed to downside market risk. I use the term GRIP, or Guaranteed Retirement Income Percentage, to describe this concept. When the GRIP increases, more of the total spending budget is covered by resources with lifetime protections. This reduces the harm of investment portfolio depletion because more retirement spending is still available, and the longevity goals have been more fully covered. With less exposure to downside market risk, the retiree has greater risk capacity and can rest more easily with a higher stock allocation for what remains. In other words, adding protected lifetime income can strengthen one's GRIP on retirement.

I was part of a research effort with Michael Finke and Duncan Williams to explore these issues in a March 2012 article in the *Journal of Financial Planning* titled "Spending Flexibility and Safe Withdrawal Rates." We investigated withdrawal rates and asset allocation after adding other income sources from outside the investment portfolio. Also, instead of focusing on the traditional objective of worrying only about using a low failure rate, we sought a better balance between the competing trade-offs for wanting to spend and enjoy more while one is still alive and healthy against not wanting to deplete the investment portfolio and having to rely only on nonportfolio income sources in later retirement.

We completed this analysis using more formal economic models of utility maximization in which the retiree decided to maximize the expected lifetime satisfaction to be received from across the distribution of outcomes. As for what is most relevant here, we found that a risk tolerant retiree with $1 million of portfolio assets would be willing to increase the stock allocation by 10 to 30 percent when reliable income is increased from $20,000 to $60,000.

The second capacity factor is the funded ratio. The funded ratio is a tool that quantifies the shape of the RIO Map shown in Exhibit 8.4. It quantifies the size of the various asset and liability boxes. The idea of calculating an individual's funded ratio is to treat personal retirement planning in the same manner as a corporate pension fund. On a lifetime basis, are the assets large enough to meet the liabilities? A funded ratio of one means that a retiree has just enough assets to meet liabilities, while overfunded and underfunded individuals have more or less than this, respectively. We can also make those comparisons in terms of the subcategories on the RIO Map, looking at how well the different liabilities associated with the four Ls have been funded.

Assets are the resources available to fund liabilities, while liabilities are the planned expenditures to be made over the lifetime. Streams of lifetime income and expenses are each calculated as present values.

For future income and spending needs, it may be easiest to keep track of these cash flows in inflation-adjusted terms, as this provides a translation for the value of future amounts in terms of what can be understood today. To express matters in inflation-adjusted terms, future income and spending needs, as well as the discount rate used in the calculations, are all adjusted downward to account for inflation. It is important to be consistent about expressing all terms either with their real or nominal values. The natural discount rate is the bond yield, which we have treated as 1 percent in real terms and 3 percent in nominal terms.

Assets can be divided among three general categories: financial capital, human capital and social capital. The present discounted value of assets includes the current value of the financial portfolio and other resources currently owned (such as the value of a home) which could potentially be sold to fund future spending needs. It also includes the present value of other available income sources over the lifetime, such as future employment income, Social Security benefits, pensions, and annuities. Meanwhile, liabilities include current debts, such as a mortgage or loan balance, and the discounted present value of an individual's expenditures over the remaining lifetime. The funded ratio is then calculated as the present value of assets divided by the present value of liabilities.

An implication of the funded ratio is that optimal asset allocation varies with the funded status. Mathematically, the optimal allocation to volatile assets like stocks follows a U-shaped curve with a minimum equity allocation when the funded ratio is one, and allocations becoming more aggressive when moving further away from one in either the up or down direction. A few additional points about this are in order, however.

First, when the funded ratio is less than one, the mathematical optimization suggesting a higher stock allocation should be accepted with caution. While attempts to make a Hail Mary pass to salvage a financial plan may maximize the probability for a plan's success, matters could also just as easily backfire leaving the funded ratio in an even more dire condition.

Meanwhile, in fortunate situations where the funded ratio exceeds one, the implication is to think in terms of portfolio insurance in which investment risk increases as the funded status increases but decreases with a decreasing funded ratio to avoid it having fall below one. Regarding this point, financial author William Bernstein asks the question, why continue to play the game if you have already won? The danger is that the funded ratio falls below one, and the individual is subsequently unable to restore the funded status, which means that the individual had, and subsequently lost, the ability to meet the lifetime financial goals.

This returns us to the point about the impact of partial annuitization for a retiree experiencing longevity risk aversion and planning for a retirement lasting beyond life expectancy. With this subjective view toward longevity, the annuity asset is worth more than the premium, and it increases the funded ratio for the plan. This helps to reduce the risk that a market drop shifts the plan from overfunded to underfunded. The remaining portfolio is available for more discretionary uses, and the retirement is more secure, justifying a higher stock allocation for the portfolio piece of the asset base.

The third factor is the availability of reserves. What other resources are available that have not been earmarked to manage spending and can be used to cover contingencies? Having more reserves available means less reliance on the assets covering other goals to outperform and to create reserves through market gains. For this point, we have already discussed how by helping to meet spending goals with less assets, the income annuity creates additional reserves that provide true liquidity. With this added flexibility, the retiree can feel more comfortable with the aggressive asset allocation because they are less exposed to the possibility of having to sell assets at a loss to cover contingencies, and then not have enough left to cover their other spending needs in subsequent years.

Finally, traditional risk aversion is the countervailing force, and this is the factor that may receive the most attention. Though the investment portfolio is now a smaller portion of the overall asset base, the retiree must still be comfortable with the greater short-term portfolio volatility that a more aggressive asset allocation will imply. Conceptually this is justified, as we have discussed. But the retiree must accept and understand these points to avoid vulnerability to panicking and not following the strategy during market downturns.

We must clarify the meaning of risk from the perspective of retirement and personal finance. Risk is not only related to short-term market volatility, though the ability of a risk-averse investor to stomach portfolio volatility is an important constraint for asset allocation decisions. Rather, the fundamental nature of risk for retirees is the threat that events take place (unexpectedly long life, poor market returns, spending shocks) that trigger a permanently lowered standard of living in subsequent years. Retirees must decide how much risk to their lifestyle they are willing to accept, and this is a different decision than how much short-term volatility is found with their investments.

Ultimately, this is an important factor that will reduce the benefit of annuitization if the retiree cannot make the distinction about how the annuity is still an asset even though it does not appear on the portfolio statement. To be effective, retirees should view the annuity as part of their bond holdings and adjust their portfolio accordingly. If they cannot overcome the psychological hurdle to accept this rationale, then the effectiveness of partial annuity strategies will be weakened.

◉ Inflation Risk Management and Income Annuities

Another common question relates to inflation protection and whether it should be incorporated into the annuity. We can distinguish between whether the retiree needs the annuity to provide inflation protection and whether the retiree wants the annuity to provide inflation protection. With a lower payout rate, an income annuity providing income growth and inflation protection will require a larger premium to build up the same initial spending power. Alternatively, the same premium amount will buy less initial income when this income grows over time. This concept is illustrated in Exhibits 8.6 and 8.7, using the life-only annuity payout rates calculated in Chapter 4 for a sixty-five-year-old female.

The payout rates are 5.78 percent for a life-only income annuity providing a level amount of spending and 4.56 percent for lifetime income that grows annually by 2 percent. With a $1 million premium, annual spending is $57,800 for the level flavor, which starts 27 percent higher than the initial $45,600 for the cost-of-living adjusted flavor. With the 2 percent spending growth, spending from the COLA flavor surpasses the level flavor with the thirteenth payment received at age seventy-seven. With a 3 percent discount rate, cumulative lifetime spending received from the COLA flavor is larger at ages ninety-two and beyond. Obtaining inflation protection means trading less spending early on for more spending later.

Exhibit 8.6

Comparing Female Age Sixty-Five, Life-Only Income Annuities with $1 Million Premium (Nominal Dollars)
Level Amount (5.78 Percent Payout) vs. 2 Percent COLA (4.56 Percent Payout)

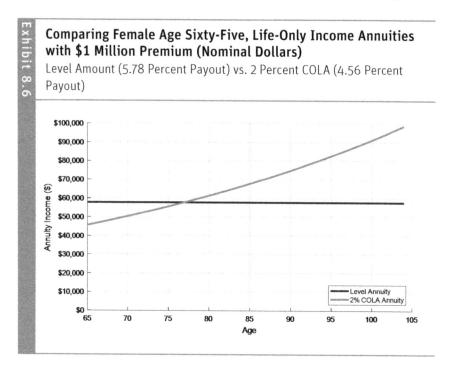

To be clear about the impact of inflation on the purchasing power of spending, Exhibit 8.7 shows the same dollar amounts as provided by the income annuity but adjusts them for their real purchasing power. With assumed inflation of 2 percent, the annuity with a COLA allows the purchasing power keep up with economy-wide price growth. Meanwhile, though the purchasing power of the level version starts off at a higher level, its lack of growth leads it to lose pace over time. Its real purchasing power will drop in half at age 100.

Exhibit 8.7

Comparing Female Age Sixty-Five, Life-Only Income Annuities with $1 Million Premium (Real Dollars)

Level Amount (5.78 Percent Payout) vs. 2 Percent COLA (4.56 Percent Payout)

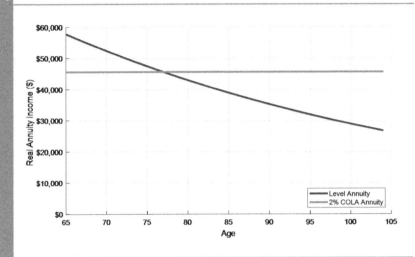

With these considerations in mind, an important question remains about how to best weigh the choice between income annuities with level payments and income annuities which provide a cost-of-living adjustment. To consider this further, we return to the earlier example about partial annuitization and the impact on legacy. The retiree has $1 million and a spending goal of $47,873 that subsequently grows with inflation. With an investments-only strategy and a 50/50 asset allocation, this spending goal was chosen alongside the capital market expectations so that the investment portfolio depletes precisely at age 100. In addition to this investments-only strategy, we consider two partial annuitization strategies that involve a decision to use an annuity to support 30 percent of the initial spending goal. Initial annuity income of $14,362 is sought, and the rest of the spending goal will then be distributed from the remaining investment assets.

With these partial annuitization strategies, we do use the more aggressive way to adjust asset allocation for the remaining investments, which is to treat the annuity premium as a fixed-income asset and permanently adjust the asset allocation for the remaining investments so that stocks still represent 50 percent of this wealth. For this comparison, the income annuity with level payments requires annuitizing 24.9 percent of the asset base so that the annuity covers 30 percent of the initial spending goal. It is a lower percentage because the payout rate is higher than the necessary withdrawal rate from the full initial wealth. Meanwhile, with its lower initial payout rate, the income annuity with the COLA requires annuitizing 31.5 percent of assets to initially cover 30 percent of spending. The tradeoff is that with level annuity spending, the remaining investment portfolio must also cover the subsequent inflation adjustments that the level annuity does not provide. This leads to a larger distribution amount over time. As well, for the annuity with level payments, the asset allocation for the remaining investments is 66.5 percent. Because more assets are annuitized, the stock allocation for remaining investments is 73 percent in the case of the annuity with a COLA. Exhibit 8.8 illustrates this differing distribution need as the level annuity will call for faster growth in the distribution from remaining investments in order to also cover the inflation adjustment for the annuity portion.

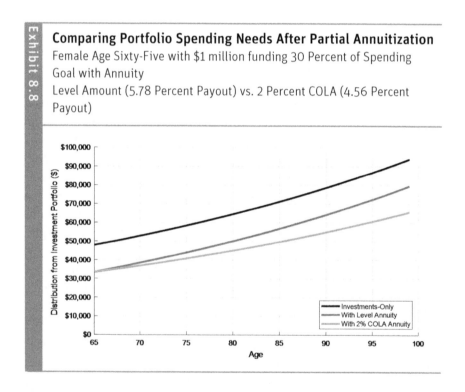

Exhibit 8.8

Comparing Portfolio Spending Needs After Partial Annuitization
Female Age Sixty-Five with $1 million funding 30 Percent of Spending Goal with Annuity
Level Amount (5.78 Percent Payout) vs. 2 Percent COLA (4.56 Percent Payout)

Exhibit 8.9 plots the evolution for the remaining investment assets with these three strategies. As before, we see that the annuity premium payment does initially reduce the amount of remaining investments. For the COLA flavor, the drop is a bit larger to meet the initial goal with the lower payout rate. Over time, the advantage moves in favor of the partial annuity strategies as they support a higher stock allocation and a lower distribution need from the remaining investment assets. The lower withdrawal rate from investments can help assets to grow and to manage sequence risk, such that the higher spending need later in retirement can be more effectively managed. The level annuity case supports more investment wealth than investments-only by age eighty-seven, and the COLA annuity supports more investment wealth by age ninety. After age ninety-four, the COLA strategy supports the most investment wealth. At age 100, the investments-only strategy has depleted the portfolio, while $346K remains with the level annuity strategy and $451K remains with the COLA annuity strategy.

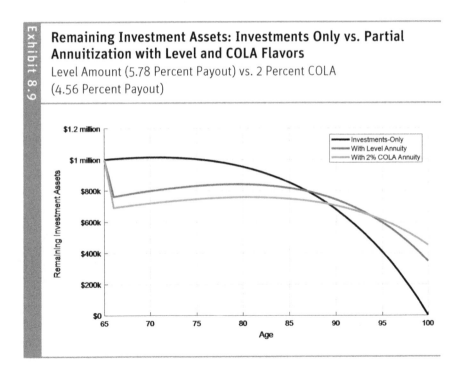

Exhibit 8.9

Remaining Investment Assets: Investments Only vs. Partial Annuitization with Level and COLA Flavors

Level Amount (5.78 Percent Payout) vs. 2 Percent COLA (4.56 Percent Payout)

In comparing the investments-only strategy with the level annuity strategy, these results show that the retiree does not need the annuity to provide inflation protection. The level annuity approach has better positioned the investment portfolio so that it can more easily support the inflation adjustments that the annuity misses in subsequent years. Meanwhile, the decision about whether the retiree will want inflation protection for the annuity involves comparing the results for the level annuity case with the 2 percent COLA case. This is a tougher decision. The income annuity with a COLA provides more mortality credits because it backloads payments to later in life when survival probabilities are less. Eventually, it will provide a better outcome. But in this example, it requires waiting until age ninety-four before this happens. This is well beyond life expectancy and it is a personal decision as there is no correct answer. It is more understandable if a retiree opts against a strategy that does not provide a better outcome until she is in her midnineties.

A final important matter must be addressed regarding the fact that this discussion has been based on a simplified model in which future inflation is fixed and known. There was no possibility for unexpectedly high inflation. The possibility of high inflation would make the inflation-adjusted annuity a more attractive choice. In that regard, we can also consider what real world pricing implies for the cost of inflation protection in the annuity.

To better understand this point, it is not necessary to introduce an entirely new model for the capital market expectations that integrates randomized inflation. Instead, we can just look to the situation with current real-world annuity pricing.

In May 2019, the market for CPI-adjusted income annuities is not well developed. ImmediateAnnuities.com only lists one company as offering this type of annuity. The payout rate for a true CPI-adjusted income annuity for a sixty-five-year-old female is 4.28 percent. Meanwhile, the top two payout rates for an income annuity with a 3 percent annual cost-of-living adjustments are 4.3 and 4.4 percent. Lifetime inflation would have to exceed an annualized amount of a bit less than 3 percent for the CPI-adjusted annuity to provide more real income. This is higher than the 2 percent inflation that markets anticipate over the next thirty years as determined by the differences between traditional treasuries and TIPS. Two reasons for this higher break-even inflation rate within the CPI-adjusted annuity include the difficulty of hedging lifetime inflation risk with TIPS that only have maturities for up to thirty years and the lack of competition in this specific market.

Nevertheless, it is possible that inflation could exceed the break-even level. The retiree must decide whether it is worth paying the additional cost to obtain contractually protected lifetime inflation-adjusted income beyond what Social Security provides, or whether to instead use a lower initial premium to obtain level income from the annuity. The retiree can then try to manage the inflation risk through the investment portfolio and through the synergies of reducing sequence risk by being able to use a lower distribution rate from the remaining investments. My research suggests that the latter approach is generally worthwhile, and it is not just because the portfolio is assumed to grow faster than inflation.

It is important to understand that while the probability-based mind-set leads to a conclusion that stocks will grow faster than inflation, this relationship is far from perfect and there can be significant periods of time where this does not happen. The benefit of the annuity with level payments is also that it allows for the distribution rate from remaining investments to be lower as well. Less premium is needed to meet a targeted initial spending amount, which leaves more in the investment portfolio, which then allows for a lower withdrawal rate to cover the rest of the spending goal from the remaining investments. This reduces the exposure to sequence-of-returns risk, making it more likely that the portfolio will be better positioned to support the later stress of funding the inflation adjustments for all the spending, including what the annuity does not provide. Level annuity purchases could also be laddered over time to support inflation adjustments. Nonetheless, for someone sufficiently concerned about inflation risk, the value of inflation-protection is greater, and it is not a bad decision to use the inflation-adjusted annuity.

One additional important point about this discussion is that it has presupposed that retirees desire their overall spending to consistently keep pace with inflation. The reality, which I addressed in greater detail in my book *How Much Can I Spend in Retirement?*, is that the inflation-adjusted spending for many retirees can be expected to decline with age. Other income sources, such as Social Security, will adjust their benefits with inflation. And as partial annuitization means that only a fraction of overall income is provided by the annuity, it may be the case that an income annuity with level payments will match the spending needs of real retirees more precisely. In other words, having those inflation adjustments may not even be necessary for many retirees. In cases where retirees do find that their income is falling short of their spending on account of inflation, it is always possible to ladder in purchases of additional annuities over time to support growth for reliable income.

In this regard, retirees may wish to consider whether using a level income annuity might be more advantageous to their situation to obtain more income early on for the same premium (or, the same amount of initial income could be purchased for a smaller premium). As well, as more initial income could mean devoting less to the annuity, remaining financial assets could be focused toward growth which may outpace inflation. This could allow additional annuity purchases to be made over time to provide additional income. The decision to annuitize more income can then be revisited later in retirement once it is clear how spending needs are evolving.

A CPI-adjusted income annuity is the closest thing to a risk free asset in retirement. Any other approach to seeking investment growth which outpaces inflation will require accepting some degree of risk. Investment growth does not always outpace inflation in the relatively short time horizons which may matter to retirees. Nonetheless, with the lower distribution rate needed, investments will have a better fighting chance to accomplish this.

When to Purchase and When to Start Income

This discussion has been about immediate annuities. Deferred income annuities were also introduced in Chapter 4. In this section we will consider issues related to when to annuitize assets and when to begin income payments. We look at longevity insurance for an individual retiring at sixty-five. Would it make more sense to purchase an immediate annuity at sixty-five, purchase a longevity insurance deferred income annuity at age sixty-five, which begins income at age eighty-five, or wait until age eighty-five and then purchase an immediate annuity at that time? We will dig deeper into the tradeoffs involved with these decisions.

Participating Income Annuities with Dividends

For another angle on inflation protection, a recent innovation for income annuities is the creation of participating income annuities that may help to provide protection against unexpected inflation. A participating income annuity will offer a lower guaranteed payout rate than a traditional income annuity, but payments enjoy the opportunity to grow through the receipt of dividends from the general account. This process works in the same general way as participating whole life insurance.

As a reminder, dividends are a return of surplus to policy owners of the insurance company after accounting for investment returns, company expenses, and the mortality experience of policy owners. Higher than anticipated returns on the general account funds, then, is one of several factors that could lead to higher dividend payments. Payments will grow over time if interest rates rise and new bonds are purchased offering higher yields. An important explanation for rising interest rates is an uptick in inflation. The owner is not locking into the bond yield curve at the time of purchase as with traditional income annuities. A changing interest rate environment will impact subsequent dividend payments.

Participating income annuities can also provide a way to help manage sequence risk, as dividends can be received as cash to spend when markets are down, and reinvested for increased protected income when markets perform well. Participation in the general account through the ability to receive dividends can lay a foundation for retirees to earn higher income payments over time in a manner that may be able to better keep pace with inflation. This provides an alternative way to seek inflation protection outside of using a COLA or CPI adjustment for income annuity payments.

As well, though we do not provide simulations, another possibility relates to actions taken in the final preretirement accumulation years. For someone aged fifty-five who is seeking to retire at sixty-five, would it make more sense to purchase a deferred annuity at fifty-five or to wait until sixty-five to purchase an immediate annuity? We will also consider how laddering annuity purchases over time can provide another way to manage these tradeoffs and provide better diversification opportunities.

There are risks related both to annuitizing assets sooner and later. First, for risks related to annuitizing sooner instead of waiting, it is important to consider how an income annuity is generally an irreversible decision.

By annuitizing today, an individual loses flexibility for the decision and the option value of waiting. There is value from maintaining the option to annuitize without following through, as it keeps the option open. Benefits from waiting include that the retiree could die early, making the annuity decision unnecessary. A health shock or other spending shock requiring liquidity could also take place, and annuitized assets are no longer available to provide liquidity.

However, as discussed, partial annuitization may increase the true liquidity of the plan. As well, interest rates could increase in the future, which would help support a higher subsequent payout rate from annuities. Payout rates on income annuities also otherwise increase with age as remaining longevity shortens. If the assets waiting in reserve to be annuitized do not experience too large of capital losses with the rising interest rates, it is possible that a greater amount of annuitized income could be generated in this way. Less likely, but still a possibility, is that mortality rates could systematically increase in unexpected ways that would allow for higher payout rates in the future.

There are also risks associated with waiting to purchase an annuity. Unexpected mortality improvements or declining interest rates would both make annuitization more expensive in the future. If people live even longer than actuaries are currently projecting, future payout rates will be further reduced and those who purchased before this realization will be better off. Insurance companies can better manage this systematic mortality risk by also selling life insurance. Unexpected mortality improvements mean the annuities will have to pay more but life insurance claims will decrease, and vice versa. Also, by waiting, one does miss out on receiving mortality credits at younger ages. These lost mortality credits may be relatively small until reaching the age range where mortality rates start to increase in earnest. As well, if the assets are kept invested in the markets, market volatility could lead to portfolio losses so that fewer assets are available to annuitize in the future.

Laddering income annuity purchases over time does provide a practical way to balance these tradeoffs. Laddering creates option value as not all annuitization takes place at once. This also reduces the risk of exposure to current interest rates and does provide an opportunity to diversify annuity purchases between different companies, reducing the impacts of a company failure and helping to keep annuity purchase amounts under state guarantee limits.

On the matter of the low interest rate environment, this is sometimes used as a reason to avoid annuitizing at the present and forever locking in the current bond yield curve. This idea is worth a discussion, as it is not correct. The case for an income annuity becomes stronger in a low interest rate environment for someone who is already retired and spending from assets.

With low rates, the mortality credit component of the annuity payout becomes even more important, making annuities even more attractive relative to bonds. The bond interest component for spending is reduced for both tools as interest rates decrease, but annuities are hurt less by lowering interest rates, since the mortality credit component for spending is not impacted by interest rates.

Exhibit 8.10 illustrates this by showing the costs for an income annuity and a bond ladder through age 100 for flat yield curves at different interest rates. The exhibit shows the cost of purchasing a dollar of lifetime income, which is just one divided by the annuity payout rate, or the sustainable spending rate from the bond ladder. We can observe how lower interest rates do increase the cost of funding an income stream with an annuity. But the point is that the cost of funding a bond ladder grows faster than the cost of an annuity with lower interest rates. At the 3 percent interest rate we have been using, the life-only income annuity payout for a sixty-five-year-old female is 5.78 percent. The cost of funding one dollar of lifetime income is 1 / 0.0578, or $17.30. As for the bond ladder cost, the present value of thirty-five annual dollar payments to age 100 with a 3 percent interest rate is $22.14. The bond ladder cost is 28 percent higher than the annuity cost. If interest rates are higher, the gap in costs narrows. For instance, at 5 percent interest rates, the annuity cost for one dollar of lifetime income is $14.10, compared to $17.19 needed to purchase a bond ladder through age 100. At this interest rate, the bond ladder cost is 21.9 percent higher. Though the absolute cost for any strategy increases with lower interest rates, the bond ladder cost grows faster than the annuity as the mortality credits become a relatively more important source of spending power.

Exhibit 8.10

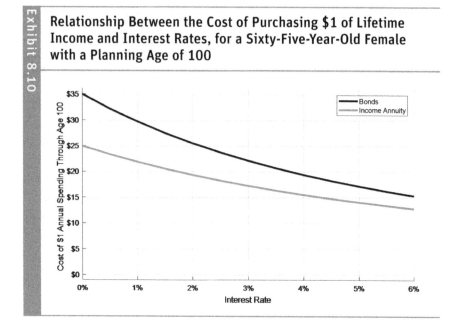

Relationship Between the Cost of Purchasing $1 of Lifetime Income and Interest Rates, for a Sixty-Five-Year-Old Female with a Planning Age of 100

As well, if we consider changing interest rates and their associated risk, increasing interest rates would mean capital losses for the bonds. One could not simply sell bonds for their earlier value to take advantage of the higher annuity rates. While waiting for rates to rise, if that happens, the retiree will be spending their principal when spending exceeds interest and dividends. The likelihood of needing to dip into the principal increases.

Even if rates do rise, retirees may not be able to purchase more income as they are multiplying a higher rate by a smaller pool of assets at this stage. If interest rates do not rise, bonds do not have capital losses, but the annuity payout rates do not increase. Waiting entails risk. For retirees investing conservatively like the insurance company, it is likely that one burns through assets fast enough to not benefit from any possible future increased annuity payout rate. Retirees also give up some mortality credits by waiting.

This brings us to the relationship between annuity payout rates and age. We return to the 3 percent interest rate assumption used throughout the book. Exhibit 8.11 shows simulated payout rates with immediate annuities for females with purchase ages ranging from sixty-five to eighty-five, and for deferred income annuities purchased at sixty-five with income start ages ranging from sixty-six to eighty-five. These relationships are not linear. Payout rates rise more quickly as purchase age increases due to higher mortality rates at advanced ages. The effect is particularly pronounced as the deferred income annuity becomes longevity insurance with the more advanced income start ages. As described in Chapter 4, the immediate annuity at age sixty-five has a payout rate of 5.78 percent. The payout rate on the immediate annuity purchased at age eighty-five is 12.34 percent, and the payout rate for longevity insurance purchased at sixty-five with an income start age of eighty-five is 30.82 percent.

The difference between the 12.34 and 30.82 percent payout rates is determined by both the opportunity for annuity premiums to grow for twenty years inside the annuity and by the probability that a sixty-five-year-old female lives to receive the first payment at age eighty-five. Intuitively, higher ages support higher payout rates because the remaining life expectancy is less, so the annuity provider expects to make fewer payments. In this regard, nothing is gained by waiting to annuitize assets or to begin income. For immediate annuities, mortality credits at the younger ages are lost as one ages.

Longevity insurance provides the opportunity to more highly leverage the mortality credits by committing at a younger age and then skipping payments for which there is still a high probability to be alive to receive. This is an important part of the explanation for the higher payout rate relative to just waiting to a more advanced age to annuitize assets. In this example, the probability of surviving from sixty-five to eighty-five is 72.3 percent. The other aspect is the growth of the annuity premium at 3 percent for twenty years, which leads to a discount factor of 55.4 percent for the assets needed at age sixty-five to start income which begins at age eighty-five. The longevity insurance payout rate of 30.82 percent can be converted to the payout rate for an immediate annuity at age eighty-five by multiplying these factors: 30.82 x 0.723 x 0.554 = 12.34 percent.

Exhibit 8.12 repeats this analysis to show how the cost of one dollar of lifetime income relates to the age it is purchased. The cost decreases with age because every year someone lives before purchasing an income annuity is another year income does not have to be paid. However, the cost does not reduce by one dollar per year. Life expectancy does not reduce on a one-to-one basis as people continue to live. That difference is

Exhibit 8.11

Relationship Between Purchase Age and Annuity Payout Rates for a Female

Immediate Annuities (SPIA) and Deferred Income Annuities (DIA) at a 3 Percent Interest Rate

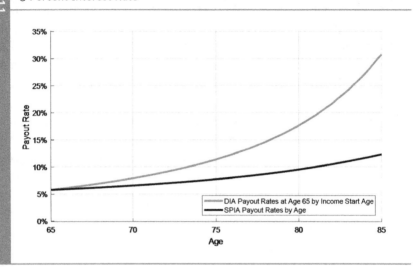

Exhibit 8.12

Relationship Between the Cost of Purchasing $1 of Lifetime Income and Purchase Age for a Female

Immediate Annuities (SPIA) and Deferred Income Annuities (DIA) at a 3 Percent Interest Rate

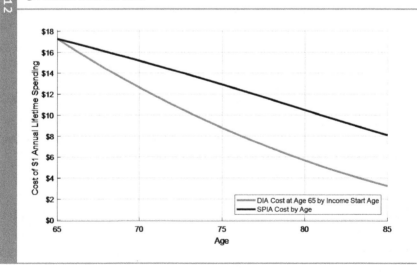

the mortality credit lost by waiting to annuitize. With the deferred income annuity, the costs plummet more quickly with the delayed start date, making it possible to hedge the tail risk for longevity at a lower cost.

To provide more clarity for this discussion, consider an example which uses partial annuitization in three ways for a sixty-five-year-old female based on the same spending, market, and annuity pricing assumptions as in the earlier examples. Her spending goal is to start retirement with $47,873 of spending and to adjust this for inflation in subsequent years. In addition to an investments-only strategy, she could immediately annuitize 30 percent of her spending goal with a life-only and level income annuity offering a 5.78 percent payout rate. This requires 24.9 percent of her assets, and she permanently adjusts her stock allocation from 50 percent to 66.6 percent to treat the annuity premium as a bond.

The second option is to purchase longevity insurance as a level and life-only annuity that covers 100 percent of her spending goal at age eighty-five but will lag by inflation in subsequent years. This option will require 23.1 percent of her assets and she adjusts her stock allocation to 65 percent.

The third option is to wait until age eighty-five and to then purchase a level life-only immediate annuity at that time to cover 100 percent of her age eighty-five spending goal. This requires a premium of $576,473 from her remaining $851,614 at age eighty-five. Because she is doing this late in life it may be more difficult to treat this annuity premium as a bond, as it would require using 100 percent stocks for the remaining portfolio at an advanced age. To be more realistic with this third option, I assume she keeps the 50 percent stock allocation for her remaining assets after this partial annuitization.

Exhibit 8.13 compares the outcomes for these three different approaches to the timing of partial annuitization and how they compare to each other as well as an investments-only strategy. At age 100, the longevity insurance strategy has come out ahead with the largest remaining legacy value for assets. However, the road to get there was rough, as the legacy value of assets was dramatically less at various earlier points in retirement. Remaining assets were the lowest at age eighty-five, as it was necessary to spend down the remaining investment assets more aggressively using a higher withdrawal rate after paying for an annuity which does not begin income until later. This concept is similar to viewing the decision to delay Social Security benefits, though it is more extreme in this case even though about the same amount of assets were annuitized as with the immediate annuity case.

With volatile markets, this strategy would also increase exposure to sequence risk by requiring a higher distribution rate from remaining investment assets, and it is important to build a bridge to help avoid this exposure, such as the strategy to combine a twenty-year bond ladder with a deferred income annuity beginning payments in year twenty-one.

Longevity insurance also requires overcoming another behavioral hurdle, which is the concern one may have with paying a premium to a company and then hoping the company is still in business in the distant future when payments finally begin. In the end, it is understandable if the wealth glidepath for this longevity insurance strategy is not appetizing.

Coming in second at age 100 is the strategy to wait until age eighty-five and then purchase an immediate annuity. This strategy benefits from the growth rate on investments at 3.5 percent being larger than the growth rate inside the annuity of 3 percent. But the ultimate outcomes are similar to the longevity insurance case, which reflects the actuarial nature of the decision. Mathematically the decision for when to annuitize does not matter as much in the end. There are various tradeoffs along the way, and it is important that individuals make a decision that is right for them.

Finally, the strategy to immediately annuitize a portion of assets provides the third largest legacy at the end, but it also offered the highest legacy for the period between ages eighty-seven and ninety-seven. Using an immediate annuity at the start of retirement is quite competitive with the other two strategies that defer in some way. It is a reasonable baseline for us to use, and there is no single correct answer for choosing among these options. The decision must be based on the tradeoffs we have discussed and the comfort one has with the different strategies. The ultimate point from this discussion is that any form of risk pooling can help manage longevity risk more effectively than reliance on an investments-only strategy.

The previous example helped us to delve a bit deeper into the issue of what age to purchase an immediate annuity. Though purchasing at the start of retirement is a very reasonable baseline, as I suggested, it is not

Exhibit 8.13

Remaining Investment Assets: Investments Only vs. Partial Annuitization with Various Timings for Payments

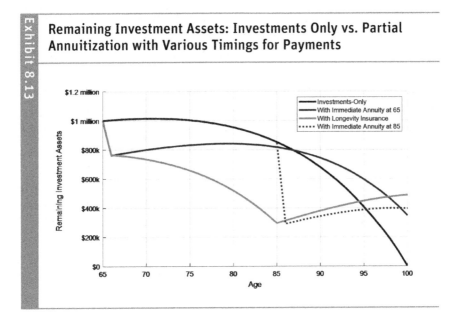

necessary to purchase the annuity right away. There is value in waiting, and the case for annuitization does become stronger with age.

York University professor Moshe Milevsky developed and trademarked a measure he calls the Implied Longevity Yield (ILY) to better understand the implications of delaying an annuity purchase. Assuming interest rates and mortality rates do not change, his measure identifies the rate of return that would be required on an investment portfolio to match payments from an annuity and then leave enough to purchase an annuity providing the same income at a later age. It shows the return hurdle that investments need to meet to justify procrastinating on the decision to buy an annuity. We can consider an example of this using the income annuity payout rates illustrated in Exhibit 8.12.

Exhibit 8.14 provides an example for a female seeking $1,000 of annual lifetime income provided at the start of each year who is deciding whether to purchase an income annuity today or to wait five years and then purchase an income annuity. For example, a sixty-five-year-old would need pay $17,291 today for this lifetime income through a life-only immediate annuity with a 5.78 percent payout rate. Alternatively, if she has this amount of assets today, she could take $1,000 annual distributions from her investments with the intention to purchase an income annuity at age seventy. At seventy, the annuity payout rate is 6.58 percent, and it takes

$15,197 to fund the subsequent lifetime payments. The implied longevity yield is the internal rate of return needed on her assets at age sixty-five to fund the five years of distributions and still have enough left to purchase the annuity at age seventy. In this case, it is 3.75 percent. Assuming no changes in interest rates or surprises to mortality rates, so that today's payout rates can be applied in the future, she would need to earn at least 3.75 percent annually on her investments to justify delaying the purchase of an income annuity to age seventy.

To match risk levels for the annuity, we should think of the investment portfolio as being primarily bonds, which we are assuming will provide a 3 percent return. It falls short of the implied longevity yield. This is a justification for purchasing the annuity today at age sixty-five.

Nonetheless, what we also observe in Exhibit 8.14 is that the implied longevity yield increases with age. By age eighty-five, the implied longevity yield is 9.25 percent, which is greater than the arithmetic average return assumed for the stock market. These increases result from the acceleration of payout rate increases with age, as mortality rates increase and the remaining life expectancy shortens. This is the source of the common notion that it is best to wait until more advanced ages to purchase an annuity, as mortality credits increase with age. To be clear, mortality credits do not increase by waiting. Mortality credits for the younger ages are lost by waiting to purchase the annuity. But with advancing age, the higher mortality rates serve to amortize the mortality credits over a shorter period which makes it appear that mortality credits increase. The mortality effects start to dominate the interest rate effects on annuity pricing. It becomes increasingly difficult for investments to beat the return hurdle needed to keep pace with an annuity.

Though the rising ILYs with age are often treated as a justification to delay buying an annuity, the ILY at age sixty-five is already sufficiently high to consider the annuity at that age. It exceeds the return that can safely be obtained from bonds, and accepting risk is required for investments to beat the ILY from delaying the purchase. The case for annuitizing at sixty-five is already strong, it just becomes even stronger at more advanced ages. Again, there is no single correct answer about the best age to purchase an income annuity, as it depends on the comfort each individual has when assessing the various tradeoffs. But this analysis certainly allows for the conclusion that it is justified to purchase the annuity sooner rather than later.

Exhibit 8.14

Implied Longevity Yield: Waiting Five Years to Purchase an Income Annuity for $1,000 of Annual Lifetime Income

Female with Simulated Immediate Annuity Payout Rates at 3 Percent Interest Rate

Current Age	$1,000 of Lifetime Income with SPIA today	$1,000 of Lifetime Incomewith SPIA in 5 Years	Implied Longevity Yield
65	$17,291	$15,197	3.75%
70	$15,197	$12,920	4.09%
75	$12,920	$10,493	4.68%
80	$10,493	$8,105	6.08%
85	$8,105	$6,045	9.25%

● Risk Pooling vs. Risk Premium: A Monte Carlo Investigation

Thus far in this chapter we have been considering the impact of longevity risk by using a planning age of 100. For a sixty-five-year-old female and assuming the Society of Actuaries (SOA) 2012 Individual Annuity Mortality tables with built-in projections for mortality improvements through 2019 is the appropriate data to reflect her situation, she has an 11 percent chance to outlive this age. But she accepts this risk because the tradeoff would be spending even less to further stretch out the asset base for investment-only strategies. She plans for thirty-five years of retirement spending with an assumption she will pass away on her 100th birthday.

Market and sequence risks have not directly appeared yet in this chapter since markets are assumed to provide their median fixed rates of return. In this section, we reintroduce market risk for stocks in order to make a more complete comparison between risk pooling and the risk premium. We maintain the simplified approach for bonds in which retirees and the insurance company have access to a flat and unchanging yield curve at 3 percent. But now, stocks provide a risk premium of 6 percent above bonds with a 20 percent volatility. We consider funding retirement spending with bonds, with an income annuity, or with a diversified investment portfolio.

With a one percent real interest rate and two percent inflation, a retiree with $1 million could build a bond ladder providing annual inflation-adjusted income starting at $33,667. With this spending level, her asset base depletes at age 100.

Alternatively, an income annuity allows risk pooling to become an additional source of spending power for her retirement income plan. As described in Chapter 4 for these assumptions, the payout rate for the income annuity providing inflation adjustments is 4.56 percent for a sixty-five-year-old female. A $1 million premium could support $45,600 of annual inflation-adjusted income for her entire lifetime.

Exhibit 8.15 illustrates the spending sources for these two retirement income tools. The bond ladder supports spending through the spenddown of principal and the interest earned on remaining principal. With the same assumptions for interest rates, the income annuity also provides these sources of spending plus risk pooling through mortality credits. The mortality credits are the subsidies to the long-lived, but they are amortized to the present to allow a higher spending level throughout retirement. Retirees can feel more comfortable spending at a higher level because protections are in place to support retirement spending in the event of an extremely long lifetime. Risk pooling allows for 35 percent more inflation-adjusted spending over her lifetime when her planning age for investments-only strategies is 100. Risk pooling provides a unique additional source of spending power beyond what bonds can provide. For those demonstrating longevity risk aversion (and who therefore use a planning age somewhere beyond their statistical life expectancy), higher income is supported no matter how long one actually lives.

The question then becomes whether the risk premium from the stock market will provide sufficiently higher returns for a diversified investment portfolio to sustain the same spending level that is contractually protected by the annuity. For this comparison, stocks receive the benefit of the doubt that historical risk premiums will persist. As explained in Chapter 3, the premium used here is 6 percent in arithmetic terms with a 20 percent volatility. Stock returns are modeled using a lognormal distribution based on a 9 percent arithmetic average and a 20 percent standard deviation.

Exhibit 8.15

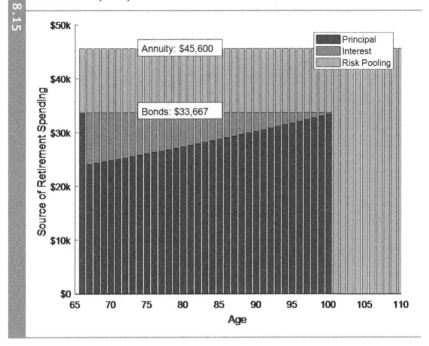

Sources of Inflation-Adjusted Spending for a Bond Ladder and an Income Annuity
Purchased by Sixty-Five-Year-Old Female with $1 Million

Exhibit 8.16 shows the probability of success for meeting this spending goal for different asset allocations using 10,000 Monte Carlo simulations. The retiree only cares about the curve for the planning age of 100, but others are included to tell a more complete story. Starting with 0 percent stocks, or an all-bond portfolio, bonds can successfully match annuity spending for a twenty-year planning horizon to age eighty-five, but the bond portfolio will deplete before age ninety and success falls to zero. By ninety, the annuity has reached beyond what bonds could accomplish on their own. The exhibit also makes clear that for someone to consider the risk premium as a retirement solution, it is important not to be timid with the stock allocation. Without risk pooling, only the portion of assets exposed to the risk premium can create the opportunity for returns exceeding bonds. With a planning age of 100, the best opportunity for matching the annuity is with 100 percent stocks, but the probability of success is only 66 percent. In 34 percent of cases, an all-stock portfolio will deplete before the planning age when trying to match the spending protected by the annuity.

Exhibit 8.16

Probability of Success for a Sixty-Five-Year-Old Female Seeking to Match Protected Income Annuity Spending through Portfolio Distributions

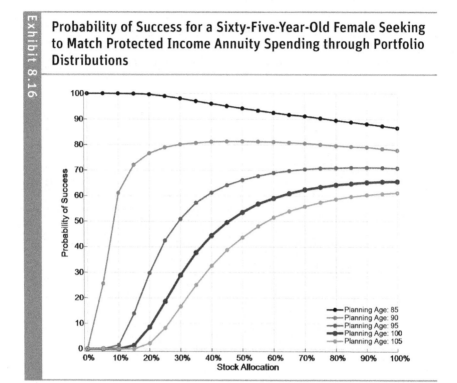

The introduction of stock market risk requires two additional elements for the decision-making of our risk averse retiree. What failure probability does she comfortably and willingly accept that her portfolio will not be able to support spending through the planning age? As well, how high of stock allocation is she willing to accept, in terms of her ability to stomach the daily volatility experienced by her investment portfolio? With volatile investments and a fixed spending goal, some probability for portfolio depletion must be accepted by anyone seeking upside growth potential through the equity risk premium. Though success is highest with 100 percent stocks, it is still not particularly high, and the retiree may not feel comfortable with that much exposure to market volatility. If the retiree considers 50 percent stocks, the success rate is 54 percent.

In almost half of the simulations with a balanced portfolio, investments are not able to keep pace with the spending that is protected by the annuity. As well, this assumes the historical risk premium, and these estimated success rates would be even less for those concerned that the outperformance of the stock market will be less in the future.

For the retirement income showdown between risk pooling and risk premium, we have seen that risk pooling provides stronger support for meeting a retirement spending goal than may be commonly assumed. Though not impossible, it is difficult for the risk premium from the stock market to provide enough excess returns to match what an income annuity is able to contractually protect through risk pooling.

This example did use a specific set of assumptions and it is worth providing comment on how varying the assumptions could impact the outcomes. First, regarding the choice of a sixty-five-year-old female, retirees could of course have different ages or genders, and we could consider the case for a couple. This assumption is fundamentally about the length of the planning horizon. If the planning horizon is longer (because younger or a couple), spending must be reduced for either strategy. A joint and survivor income annuity may be used. Income annuities will pay less, but portfolio distributions must also be reduced to account for the longer planning horizon. Likewise, the planning age could be higher (greater longevity risk aversion) or lower (less longevity risk aversion). A retiree with less longevity risk aversion could plan for a shorter time horizon, which would allow for relatively more spending from investments with greater accepted risk. Risk pooling becomes increasingly favorable as longevity risk aversion increases.

As well, this example assumes that the retiree seeks inflation-adjusted spending. Switching to a level spending goal shifts the focus to nominal interest rates, which increases initial spending for both strategies. By using a higher interest rate (3 percent nominal instead of 1 percent real, in this case), the gap between the annuity and the bond ladder would narrow from 35 percent to 28 percent.

Finally, instead of using a life-only income annuity, provisions could be added to refund a portion of the premium in the event of early death, which reduces the payout rate. Such annuity provisions will work to improve the chance that investments can keep pace as the income payout rate of the annuity is reduced.

Ultimately, the key message is that risk premiums do not obviously outperform risk pooling to meet retirement spending goals as well as providing support for contingencies and legacy.

For risk averse retirees, risk pooling funds retirement spending goals more cheaply and with contractual protections, which in turn allows for greater true liquidity for nonannuitized investment assets. The main advantage for the investments-only risk premium strategy is that it allows for a larger legacy should the retiree die early, but at the cost of not having a contractual guarantee for income, and having less true liquidity, as more must be set aside to provide sufficient confidence that the spending goal can be funded. In the event of a long retirement, the legacy advantage of the risk premium strategy gradually declines as partial annuitization can ultimately support a larger legacy in the long-term. These tradeoffs suggest that greater care should be taken to consider how risk aversion and desires for legacy impact the relative advantages of risk pooling and the risk premium as strategies to fund retirement spending goals. It is not obvious that an investments-only retirement income strategy will outperform a partial annuity strategy when seeking to meet various retirement goals and managing retirement risk.

Further Reading

Branning, Jason K., and M. Ray Grubbs. 2010. "Using a Hierarchy of Funds to Reach Client Goals." *Journal of Financial Planning* 23, 12 (December): 31–33.

Cloke, Curtis V. 2011. "Breaking the Income Annuity Liquidity Myth." LifeHealthPRO (March 25).

Finke, Michael, Wade D. Pfau, and Duncan Williams. 2012. "Spending Flexibility and Safe Withdrawal Rates." *Journal of Financial Planning* 25 (3): 44–51.

Frank, Sr., Larry R., John B. Mitchell, and David M. Blanchett. 2012. "An Age-Based, Three-Dimensional Distribution Model Incorporating Sequence and Longevity Risks." *Journal of Financial Planning* 25, 3 (March): 52–60.

Milevsky, Moshe A. 2005. "The Implied Longevity Yield: A Note on Developing an Index for Life Annuities." *The Journal of Risk and Insurance* 72, 2 (June): 302–320.

Milevsky, Moshe A., and Huaxiong Huang. 2011. "Spending Retirement on Planet Vulcan: The Impact of Longevity Risk Aversion on Optimal Withdrawal Rates." *Financial Analysts Journal* 67, 2 (March/April): 45–58.

Pfau, Wade D. 2017. "Retirement Income Showdown: Risk Pooling Versus Risk Premium." *Journal of Financial Planning* 30 (February): 40–51.

Pittman, Sam, and Rod Greenshields. 2012. "Adaptive Investing: A Responsive Approach to Managing Retirement Assets." Retirement Management Journal 2, 3 (Fall): 45–54.

CHAPTER 9

Product Allocation for Retirement

We have now provided context for how a retirement income strategy should extend beyond traditional wealth management to better manage the changing risks of retirement. We have covered important topics to help inform decisions about sustainable spending rates from investments and insurance.

The process of building a retirement income strategy involves determining how to best combine retirement income tools to optimize the balance between meeting your retirement goals and protecting those goals from the unique risks of retirement. Retirement risks come in many forms, including unknown planning horizons, market volatility, inflation, and other spending shocks. Each of these risks must be managed by combining different tools and tactics, each with different relative strengths and weaknesses. No single tool can cover every risk. We require a framework that incorporates capacities, aspirations, realities, and emotional comfort. Then we can combine tools to determine how to best develop an overall plan.

In doing this, it becomes hard to counter the notion that risk pooling and insurance can play an important and valuable role. We have introduced various types of annuities, and in this chapter, we consider further about advantages and disadvantages for each and how to think about choosing between them.

As a simple starting point, income annuities, when treated as bonds, will frequently be the most efficient way to incorporate lifetime income into planning. However, there can be exceptions. Deferred variable annuities and fixed index annuities play a role for those attracted to the upside and liquidity features they offer compared to income annuities. There are also cases where these types of annuities may provide greater efficiency in terms of higher protected income levels or a better overall asset allocation for retirees struggling with the concept that income annuities should replace bonds. Deferred annuities also offer greater flexibilities for the income start date and the opportunity to exchange into a better annuity in the future, as there is less lock-in when the contract has not already been annuitized. FIAs also provide principal loss protection.

This chapter is about product allocation. Exhibit 9.1 illustrates the idea. Retirement spending goals can be met through distributions from the investment portfolio, through annuitized income annuities, and through lifetime distributions from deferred annuities. Product allocation is about how to combine them into an overall plan.

● The Efficient Frontier for Retirement Income

In 2003, Peng Chen and Moshe Milevsky published an article in the *Journal of Financial Planning* that developed the concept of an efficient

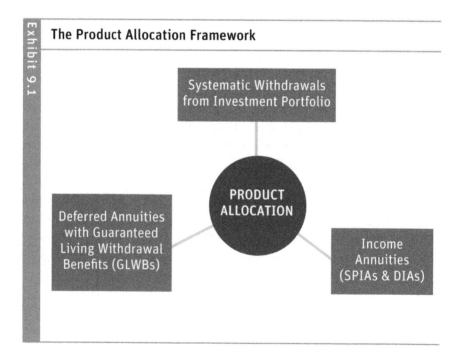

Exhibit 9.1

The Product Allocation Framework

Systematic Withdrawals from Investment Portfolio

PRODUCT ALLOCATION

Deferred Annuities with Guaranteed Living Withdrawal Benefits (GLWBs)

Income Annuities (SPIAs & DIAs)

frontier for retirement income. They extended the efficient frontier from modern portfolio theory (described in Chapter 3) beyond its single-period focus into a concept that works for lifetime financial planning. The efficient frontier is about the tradeoffs between risk and return and finding asset allocations that cannot provide greater advantage for one without creating loss for the other. Rather than looking at single-period portfolio returns and volatility, Chen and Milevsky focused on the trade-off between satisfying spending goals for life and preserving financial assets for legacy and liquidity. Product allocation considers how different combinations of stocks, bonds, and annuities with income provisions perform in meeting these objectives. Efficient allocations will do a better job at meeting both lifetime objectives by supporting spending even in bad market environments while preserving the legacy value of assets.

In a February 2013 *Journal of Financial Planning article,* "A Broader Framework for Determining an Efficient Frontier for Retirement Income," I developed my own take on their product allocation research. Among the assets I considered in the article were stock funds, bond funds, income annuities, and a simple variable annuity with a GLWB. I focused on how to best meet two competing financial objectives for retirement: satisfying spending goals for life and preserving financial assets. What I found with my simulations is that the efficient frontier for retirement income generally consists of combinations of stocks and income annuities. Bond funds do not make it to the frontier, and they do not serve a useful role for meeting spending goals in the optimal retirement income portfolio. Though they may not be as efficient as income annuities, competitively priced deferred annuities with lifetime income provisions will beat bonds because of the mortality credits they provide to help support spending in the event of a long retirement. They can provide a better outcome for those who are otherwise not comfortable with using a life-only income annuity along with a very aggressive asset allocation for the remainder of the portfolio.

Exhibit 9.2 provides a stylized representation of the efficient frontier from that research. Meeting more spending and preserving more assets means moving in the upper-right hand direction, and the shark-fin shape of the efficient frontier shows how combinations of stocks and income annuities beat combinations of stocks and bonds.

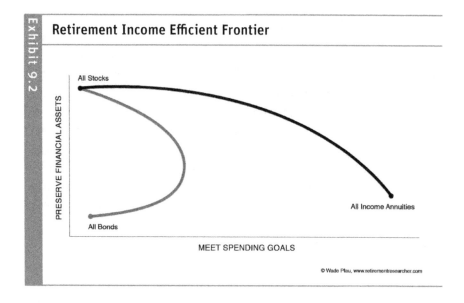

Exhibit 9.2

Retirement Income Efficient Frontier

All Stocks

PRESERVE FINANCIAL ASSETS

All Bonds

All Income Annuities

MEET SPENDING GOALS

© Wade Pfau, www.retirementresearcher.com

Mixing in other deferred annuities may not lead to product allocations that are right on the efficient frontier, but they can be close. In cases that variable or index annuities offer payout rates that are comparable to income annuities, this can help greatly in moving the annuities toward the efficient frontier. Similar levels of income are protected on the downside through the guarantee provisions, while the upside exposure can create more opportunity to support legacy relative to a cash refund provision on the income annuity that implies a 0 percent rate of return on the underlying assets. When not on the frontier, deferred annuities can also provide a more satisfying outcome for retirees that seek to maintain control over their assets and to avoid any regret about the irreversible nature of the annuitization decision.

For those who do not accept the aggressive asset allocation for remaining investments when using the annuity, deferred variable annuities have another possibility to shine. Perhaps the put option style guarantee on the variable annuity allows the retiree to feel more comfortable increasing their stock allocation in the variable annuity relative to an unprotected portfolio. A higher stock allocation in the variable annuity provides greater upside potential for growing income and assets, which can make it hard for the unprotected portfolio with a lower stock allocation to keep pace. Greater exposure to the equity premium inside the variable annuity in these cases can potentially provide additional returns that more than offset the annuity fees. This can support greater legacy after meeting the same spending goal. Meanwhile, in poor market environments, the income protection will continue to cover a portion of spending after the contract value or investment portfolio depletes.

○ Upside Exposure, Downside Protection, and Liquidity Provisions

A key criterion for choosing among annuities with the objective of supporting retirement income is to understand the amount of contractually guaranteed income offered through annuitization or through taking lifetime distributions with an optional living benefit rider attached to the contract. Writing in his book *The Annuity Stanifesto* Stan Haithcock argues that focusing on the minimum guaranteed income is the only worthwhile matter for those using the annuity tool as a source of spending. Liquidity and upside potential are not relevant for the decision-making, he argues, because it is too easy to be blinded by upside potential without fully understanding whether it is likely to ever be realized. It is hard to assess the true upside potential with so many moving parts in deferred annuity contracts. His slogan is to, "Own an annuity for what it *will do*, not what it *might do*."

Nonetheless, an important selling point of deferred annuities is that they provide more than just a minimum guarantee withdrawal benefit. There is also a tradeoff in that higher fees on deferred annuities can support better downside protections with less upside exposure, and a focus only on guarantees would lead one to only one factor in the decision without considering the tradeoffs.

The difference in worst-case guaranteed income levels from different annuities reflects the effective cost one must accept for other features of the annuity such as liquidity provisions, upside growth potential, and additional death benefits. If growth potential is achieved for deferred annuities, then step-ups may be realized, and lifetime income could be higher than the minimum guaranteed level.

In theory, simple income annuities should offer the highest payout rates. Their simple design lacks any special features like liquidity and upside potential. More generally, fixed annuities should have higher payout rates than variable annuities because they do not have to support guarantees even in the event of capital losses for the contract value. We also covered how fixed index annuities can provide competitive payout rates to income annuities on their optional guaranteed lifetime withdrawal benefits on account of the insurance company being able to assume some lapsation for income guarantee owners. Not everyone paying for the income rider will take advantage of their guaranteed lifetime distributions to the full potential and therefore will be less likely to deplete the contract value and make the insurance company responsible for continued payments. For those seeking a deferral period, this could especially be true, and it is worth comparing the payout rate on deferred income annuities against the guaranteed income payments offered through guaranteed living withdrawal benefit riders on fixed index annuities. The latter could be higher. Nonetheless, for annuities purchased at advanced ages, simple income annuities will often have the edge in terms of providing a higher payout because there will be less time for FIA owners to lapse.

Payouts for variable annuities will typically be less as their age-based brackets are based on annuitization rates for younger ages. There can occasionally be exceptions in which variable annuities can offer comparable guarantees. I am aware of one commercial variable annuity that requires the use of a bond fund for the subaccount and provides competitive payouts to other types of annuities for a broad range of ages. Couples should also check variable annuities more closely as the reduction in guaranteed benefits for couples in a variable annuity can be less than the reductions in fixed annuities.

Indeed, the type of annuity offering the most guaranteed income can vary depending on household characteristics, the length of deferral, and as product offerings and pricing change over time. It is worth shopping around between different types of annuities to make sure that one is finding the best opportunities at any given moment.

We can move beyond minimum guaranteed income provided by the annuity. Annuities with competitive guaranteed payouts alongside other benefits for upside and liquidity have an edge. The next part of deciding about an annuity is to choose whether it is worth accepting a lower guaranteed payout in order to have access to other benefits from the annuity.

As mentioned, accepting a lower guaranteed income from one annuity is a way to understand its costs in terms of receiving the other benefits provided. This does become a harder decision because it can be quite difficult to assess the true upside potential of a deferred annuity when there are so many moving parts inside the contract. Companies focus on a particular angle to market their variable annuities, and this can add complexity that becomes harder to analyze and compare. Upside exposures and step-ups can also depend on whether aggressive asset allocations are allowed within the annuity.

In separate research, I compared the potential for step-up opportunities from a stylized variable annuity and found that they do depend on asset allocation. In terms of median outcomes, step-ups were not provided with an all bond allocation. For 50 percent stocks in the variable annuity, I found that step-ups supported 11 percent more income after a ten-year deferral period, and then another 13 percent income growth over a subsequent thirty-year distribution phase. Meanwhile, if 100 stocks were allowed, step-ups allowed 48 percent more guaranteed income after ten years, and another 70 percent increase in income over a subsequent thirty-year distribution period. Upside potential is real, and it does depend on asset allocation. As well, upside potential may be greater for contracts with weaker guarantees and lower expenses. There are tradeoffs to be considered.

As mentioned, in my research, I have made attempts to simulate the upside potential for different types of representative annuities. Gradually, there are starting to be more commercial services that seek to provide tools to compare different annuities in terms of their guaranteed benefits and potential for upside. Cannex, for instance, now has Monte Carlo simulation tools to estimate average income provided by different commercial annuities after accounting for upside potential within the contracts. These tools can be helpful to make decisions.

Competitive variable annuities provide the most upside potential, especially with lower costs, higher quality investment choices, investment freedom to choose an aggressive asset allocation, and the ability to stack rollups on step-ups. FIAs will fall in between variable annuities and income annuities regarding upside potential. They provide some upside potential, but it is more limited, and there may be little potential to provide step-ups after lifetime withdrawals have begun. Income annuities do not provide upside potential. Generally, accepting less upside potential allows for the possibility of more robust downside protections, but there can be exceptions. In comparing about this tradeoff, retirees should also consider about the tax treatment and credit risk for different types of annuities.

◉ Tax Treatment

Taxation on annuities can get complex, especially when it comes to issues related to their death benefits or when using them in trusts. Our discussion will not consider these cases, but it is worth having a basic understanding about how the taxes for annuities work when they are being used by households as a source of ongoing spending during the owner's lifetime. This discussion will remain basic and should not be interpreted as specific tax advice. A tax professional should always be consulted for specific tax questions, but it is nonetheless possible to provide a basic understanding of the tax issues at work. A great resource for more in-depth treatment of annuity tax issues is John Olsen and Michael Kitces' book *The Advisor's Guide to Annuities*.

When it comes to basic tax treatment for annuities, we distinguish between annuities held in nonqualified or taxable accounts, and annuities held in qualified retirement plans such as IRAs and 401(k)s. As well, we must distinguish between annuities that have been annuitized into a stream of payments and annuities that remain in the deferral stage, which includes nonlifetime distributions from annuities and lifetime distributions from annuities obtained through an optional lifetime withdrawal benefit rider. Income annuities, including single-premium immediate annuities and deferred income annuities, are already annuitized and provide the ability to lock in income.

Deferred annuities such as variable and index annuities provide more flexibility because they are not annuitized, and they offer upside potential, the ability to annuitize within the contract, and the option to add a lifetime income rider that will support guaranteed lifetime distributions without annuitization. Deferred annuities are purchased for growth with an option to guarantee income later by annuitizing or with an income rider. We consider these cases in greater detail.

Annuitized Contracts in Taxable Accounts

In taxable accounts, the basic idea for annuities is that distributions representing return of premium are not taxed, but distributions representing any interest or gains through market growth or mortality credits are taxed. Taxation occurs at the point of distribution rather than when interest is earned, which allows for continued tax deferral for the underlying annuity assets until distributions are made.

For income annuities and other annuitized contracts that were purchased in a taxable account, the basic idea is that two of the three sources of annuity payments (interest and mortality credits) are taxed as income, and the third source (return of premium) is received tax-free. To determine how much of the annuity payment is classified as the return of the initial premium, the IRS provides details for how long an annuitant should expect to receive payments from the annuity. The portion of each annuity payment considered to be a return of principal is the amount of the premium payment divided by the total annuity income to be received during the expected lifetime. This is the exclusion ratio. It is the portion of annuity payments excluded from taxable income.

Once the full amount of premium has been returned as income at the life expectancy, subsequent annuity income then becomes fully taxable for the remainder of one's lifetime. This process helps to defer some taxes to the latter part of retirement after surpassing the IRS measure of life expectancy. This concept also applies to deferred income annuities, as annuitized assets grow tax deferred within the contract and then the exclusion ratio is applied once payments begin.

For example, consider our sixty-five-year-old female with an income annuity that begins payments immediately and is life-only. The payout rate is 5.78 percent. For a premium of $100,000, the annuity pays $5,780 per year. As a simple example, suppose the IRS documentation requires using a life expectancy of 18.2 years. This is a shorter life expectancy than what the average annuity owner will experience. The total income received over the life expectancy is 5,780 x 18.2 = $105,196. The portion treated as the return of premium is the $100,000 premium divided by the total $105,196 income, or 95.1 percent. This portion is excluded from taxable income.

The inclusion ratio represents the remainder of the income that is treated as gains through interest and mortality credits. It is 4.9 percent of the payment. This is $283 per year, and it is the taxable income for the first eighteen years of the contract. After that point, the full $5,780 becomes taxable income as it fully reflects gains to the recipient beyond the premium paid, at least with respect to the mortality tables used by the IRS. Most services providing annuity quotations will provide either the inclusion ratio or the actual amount of annuity payments that are taxable when the premium will be drawn from a taxable account.

This nature of taxation for annuitized annuity contracts can be beneficial when combined with other strategies, such as Roth conversions, that lead to generating more taxable income in early retirement in order to reduce the amount of other taxable income later in retirement when the annuity income switches to become fully taxable. These actions will help keep the marginal tax rate lower early on because less annuity income is taxable, and lower in the future when higher taxes on the income annuity are offset by having other taxable income sources already reduced.

Annuitized Contracts in Qualified Retirement Plans

For annuities that have been annuitized inside of retirement plans, distributions are taxed at ordinary income tax rates as they are received. This is straightforward. The aspect that can get trickier relates to determining RMDs for the annuity assets.

For annuitized contracts, the RMD calculation does not include any annuity premium or present value of payments. The annuity income is accepted as covering the RMDs for the annuitized assets. At younger ages, annuity income might be larger than the RMD that would have been required for those assets, but the annuity income could be less than the RMD at later ages. These differences are assumed to balance out over time, though, since the annuity is treated as an accepted way to spend down the assets over retirement.

To be clear, in the early years, when the annuity income is larger than the RMD would have been on the annuitized assets, the retiree does not get to use the annuity income to cover the RMDs on other assets remaining in the qualified plan. This could be viewed as a disadvantage with a partial annuity strategy, as the retiree pays taxes on the annuity distributions and the annuity distributions cannot be counted against any other RMDs due on remaining assets.

Though the tax treatment is relatively simple for an immediate annuity in a qualified plan, there are problems with using a deferred income annuity in a qualified plan when income is to begin past the age 70.5 RMD starting point. This creates a technical violation for RMD rules as annuity income covers the RMDs for the annuitized assets, but there is no annuity income when that income was deferred. In July 2014, the Treasury Department created new regulations for QLACs to help rectify this problem. Qualifying contracts for annuitized premiums up to $130,000 or 25 percent of the combined balances held in qualified plans, whichever is smaller, can now delay annuity income to age eighty-five without violating the RMD rules.

Not many 401(k) plans or other qualified retirement plans that are set up by employers offer the ability to purchase annuities. This may become more common in the future. For those who do have this option, it is worth exploring whether the annuities inside the employer plan may provide a better opportunity than annuities outside the plan. Women can particularly benefit from the unisex pricing that is required for annuities held inside employer retirement plans. If good annuity choices are not available in the 401(k), then the common process after retiring would be to rollover the 401(k) assets into an IRA and then purchase the annuity inside of the IRA. When these steps are correctly followed, no taxable events have transpired until distributions are received.

Deferred Annuities in Taxable Accounts

Deferred annuities provide a way to obtain tax deferral for assets that would otherwise experience ongoing taxation in a taxable account. This tax deferral is subject to the usual limitations the government provides, which are that all subsequent gains, even long-term capital gains, are taxed at ordinary income tax rates. A 10 percent penalty also applies for distributions taken prior to age 59.5, if certain conditions are not met to allow an exemption for the penalty.

The tax penalty was created to deter using the annuity for reasons other than as part of a retirement plan. There are exceptions to paying the penalty for distributions taken before age 59.5. These include events such as death of the owner, the taxpayer becomes disabled, or for payments from an immediate annuity (but not a deferred income annuity). An exception also exists for those taking substantially equal periodic payments over the lifetime.

Tax deferral can be a powerful benefit for annuities in taxable accounts. Assets held in taxable accounts face ongoing taxes on interest, dividends, and realized capital gains, which can eat into the compounding growth potential for the assets. A tax drag is created relative to being able to defer those taxes until later. As discussed in earlier chapters, this tax deferral has motivated the use of annuities as accumulation vehicles with a de-emphasis on their original purpose of provided periodic distributions on fixed dates. If annuities are used for less tax-efficient asset classes that mostly generate ordinary income rather than long-term capital gains, then this tax deferral could provide net positive value for the owner.

When distributions are taken from a deferred annuity, the tax treatment is different than the exclusion ratio used for annuitized contracts. Both types of annuities will provide the return of premium tax-free, but rather than having premium returned as an ongoing part of the distributions, a deferred annuity is taxed on a last-in-first-out (LIFO) basis. Any distributions from the deferred annuity, either as guaranteed distributions through a living benefit rider or unguaranteed distributions, are treated first as gains from the contract. The original principal is received only when there are no remaining gains to be taken. When a deferral period has been used, this pushes larger taxable income distributions toward the early part of the contract distribution period, rather than later like with the exclusion ratio for annuitized contracts. On a case by case basis, there could be value in diversifying between annuitized and deferred contracts in order to smooth the levels of taxable income over time.

One other point that is relevant for deferred annuities is that the IRS allows for 1035 exchanges. These rules prevent a taxable event from being created when exchanging a life insurance policy into an annuity, or for exchanging from one annuity contract to another. This can provide a way to switch to an annuity offering more attractive guaranteed income payments or other features.

For example, perhaps one has used a variable annuity with an income rider that has experienced strong growth for investments, and the contract value is worth about the same amount as the benefit base. Rather than turning on the guaranteed income for this contract, it may be possible to exchange into a fixed annuity contract with better annuitization rates, or even a fixed index annuity (or another type of variable annuity) with more attractive withdrawal benefits. This can be accomplished without creating a taxable event. This feature of the tax code only applies to deferred annuities since annuitized contracts are not liquid and cannot be exchanged in such a way.

Deferred Annuities in Qualified Retirement Plans

With deferred annuities in qualified plans, distributions from the annuity are treated as taxable income when they are received. This is the same as for annuitized contracts. It is important to emphasize that since retirement plans already provide tax deferral, this is not a distinct advantage of holding an annuity inside a qualified plan. There must be some other benefit from the annuity, such as the desire to receive protected lifetime income, to justify its placement this way. For lifetime income, a reason why the annuity may be more attractive inside a retirement plan, despite already having the benefit of tax deferral, is that taxable investment holdings may have large embedded capital gains that would trigger a large tax bill if sold to pay the annuity premium. There is no 1035 exchange for moving assets from a taxable investment portfolio to an annuity.

For deferred annuities, the contract value of the annuity remains liquid, and RMDs are calculated on it. Unlike with annuitized contracts, deferred annuities allow their distributions to be aggregated into the overall RMD calculations. This can be a benefit at younger ages, when the distribution from the annuity may exceed the RMD on the underlying contract value, so that part of the annuity income can also be counted against the RMDs for nonannuity assets. In cases that the contract value declines over time, this benefit could even increase further as the annuity income may be much larger than the RMD on the smaller remaining contract value. This can help to lower the need to take distributions from the remainder of the IRA to cover RMDs, which could prove useful in helping to manage sequence-of-returns risk.

However, there are complications related to this point because the RMDs on a deferred annuity contract may not only be applied to the contract value. RMDs may also be due on the present value of any living or death benefits with the contract. Two simplifications provided about this are that the actuarial value of these benefits can be ignored if they are worth less than 20 percent of the contract value, and a standard return of premium death benefit can be ignored for these calculations. These requirements can complicate taxes because it is necessary to obtain estimates for the actuarial present value of the annuity benefits in order to determine the total RMDs for the annuity.

This taxation matter also speaks to the value of not placing all retirement plan assets into a deferred annuity. One potential calamity could relate to an optional death benefit rider that only paid a death benefit if the contract value exceeds zero. If the contract value is close to zero, one might wish to stop taking distributions, but the RMD required on that death benefit could exceed the remaining contract value and require a complete liquidation of the annuity if there were no other assets that could be used to cover the RMD. Having other IRA assets can be an important way to manage tax surprises related to this complex aspect of calculating RMDs for deferred annuities.

⊙ Credit Risk for Annuities

Aside from general views that annuity fees are too high and that the stock market can easily outperform anything that an annuity is able to offer, the primary objection to annuities is that insurance companies may fail to support their contractual payment obligations. This matter is worth addressing. While the risk that guarantees cannot be fulfilled is not zero, I think the concern tends to be overstated and there are steps retirees can take to mitigate these risks. There are also differences to consider between annuitized contracts and guaranteed lifetime withdrawal benefits for deferred annuities.

First, this concern about insurer viability is often stated as if conditions within financial markets are so bad that the 4 percent rule of thumb fails to work, then surely insurance companies will be bankrupt in the ensuing financial calamity. But sequence-of-returns risk means that a particular cohort of retirees may find that the 4 percent rule is unsustainable without

Charitable Gift Annuities

For those with charitable inclinations, a charitable gift annuity is another alternative. With charitable gift annuities, a charitable organization receives the premium. In turn, the charity provides a protected lifetime income. Charitable gift annuities will offer lower payout rates than competitive commercial annuities (i.e. their money's worth measures will be lower) to better ensure that the average participant leaves something for the charity.

The American Council of Gift Annuities provides a table of suggested maximum annuity rates that charities should offer with the goal of trying to preserve half of the gift as a charitable contribution after making the required lifetime payments to the donor through life expectancy. These tables are provided both for immediate and deferred payments, as well as for single and joint lives. Charitable gift annuities provide the opportunity to receive a charitable tax deduction for a portion of the premium in the year that the premium is paid, which reflects an estimate of the amount that will eventually be available for the charity after lifetime payments are provided. The premium can also be paid with appreciated stock, but long-term capital gains tax may then have to be paid on income received through the annuity.
One planning idea related to this potentially large tax deduction is that it could provide a further opportunity to do a Roth conversion and generate offsetting taxable income in the same tax year.

Some charities may keep the premium on their books. Charities could try to manage the risk of providing protected lifetime income on their own. But charities do not necessarily have the toolset to properly manage longevity and investment risk. A more sensible approach would be for the charity to offload these risks to an insurance company that is better able to manage the longevity and market risks related to managing a pool of income annuity payouts. In this case, the charity would provide an annuity on your behalf with the required amount of your premium, and then would be able to book the rest of the amount as a charitable contribution, assuming their offer is less competitive than a commercial annuity.

A final related point is that the protected lifetime income is dependent on the financial health of the charity. If the charity fails and does not have the capacity to make the promised payments, there is no recourse for the donor.

an overall economic catastrophe. Financial markets may recover, but the portfolios for those taking distributions will not get to enjoy the full recovery on account of the increasing distribution demands from what is left in the portfolio. As well, the 4 percent rule assumes an aggressive stock allocation, while the general accounts of insurance companies hold little stocks. Insurance companies mostly hold fixed-income assets to maturity and are highly regulated to maintain appropriate backup reserves. Stock market volatility will have little impact on their abilities to pay claims.

Financial calamity for insurance companies would instead have to be triggered either by a widespread default on their bond holdings, by efforts to invest more aggressively in riskier assets that circumvent regulations, or by facing unanticipatedly large claims that exceed what their assets can support. These outcomes are possible.

The first, though, would imply an economic catastrophe in which not receiving annuity payments may be the last of one's concerns. The second would require regulators falling asleep at their jobs. As for the third, a concern may be, what happens if cancer is cured and everyone starts living longer than the insurance company expected? In this case, insurance companies would see reduced death benefit claims on their life insurance business that would help to offset the increasing claims on their annuity business. They may not be able to fully manage this longevity surprise, but neither is a household investor. Arguably an insurance company is better suited to handle this systematic longevity risk.

Another avenue for the protection of income annuity owners and owners of other fixed annuities are the state insurance guarantee associations that guarantee annuity premiums up to certain levels defined for each state. While these insurance funds do not have sufficient assets to support a systematic collapse of multiple insurance companies, they are positioned to stand behind guarantees on the rare occasion that an individual insurance company falters.

The National Organization of Life and Health Insurance Guarantee Association maintains a website (www.nolhga.com) that provides details about the specific guarantees offered in each state. They often range from between $100,000 and $300,000 of premium. A common strategy for those seeking annuity amounts that exceed state guarantee limits is to diversify across insurance companies and to not exceed the premium limit with any one company. Nonetheless, relying on the state guarantee association is not an alternative to choosing a well-managed company.

Another important point about state guarantee associations is that they do not apply to optional income riders. The state guarantee associations are for fixed annuities and provide protection for annuitized contracts and for the contract value of deferred contracts. Variable annuities are not covered, but the investment subaccounts are separately managed and are protected from company failure in the same manner as mutual funds or ETFs are not exposed to risks for the custodian of the assets. But the income riders are not protected. With deferred annuities, the contract value could be recovered, but there is no recourse to obtain guaranteed income through the benefit rider if the insurer fails. This is a key consideration for considering how income annuities provide an additional layer of protection over optional riders on deferred annuities.

As such, credit ratings are also extremely important to consider when choosing from among insurance companies offering income annuities. It is not a good idea to blindly go with whichever company is offering the highest monthly payout on a given premium, as that may be a lower-rated company that could potentially run into trouble with meeting payments in the future.

Several credit ratings agencies provide ratings on insurance companies, with AM Best probably being the most well-known on the insurance side. Others include Fitch, Standard and Poor's, and Moody's. They assess insurance companies based on the riskiness of their investment holdings and whether the company can be expected to successfully pay its liabilities (annuity payments and other insurance claims) in a timely matter. Consider sticking with larger insurance companies with long histories of paying claims that also rank among the highest levels offered by the rating agencies.

Exhibit 9.3 provides the rating scales for several well-known companies. These can be confusing to keep straight. Another measure one may come across is the Comdex ranking, which aggregates the ratings of various ratings agencies in order to provide an overall score between one and 100.

Exhibit 9.3

Credit Rating Scales for Insurance Companies

AM Best		S&P		Moody's	
Category	**Description**	**Category**	**Description**	**Category**	**Description**
A++	Superior	AAA	Extremely Strong	Aaa	Exceptional
A+	Superior				
A	Excellent	AA+	Very Strong	Aa1	Excellent
A-	Excellent	AA	Very Strong	Aa2	Excellent
		AA-	Very Strong	Aa3	Excellent
B++	Good	A+	Strong	A1	Good
B+	Good	A	Strong	A2	Good
		A-	Strong	A3	Good
B	Fair	BBB+	Good	Baa1	Adequate
B-	Fair	BBB	Good	Baa2	Adequate
		BBB-	Good	Baa3	Adequate
C++	Marginal	BB	Marginal		
C+	Marginal				
C	Weak	B	Weak		
C-	Weak				
		CCC	Very Weak	Ba1	Questionable

Ratings agencies provide credit ratings for insurance companies based on assessments for the reliability that the insurance company will be able to make good on its promised payments. These ratings can be used as a tool to help assess the quality of an insurance company. A lower rated company may offer a higher level of protected income, but the contract owner would need to accept greater risk about whether the insurance company can make good on its promises.

Annuity company failures are rare. The annuity industry on a whole maintains a strong motivation to maintain consumer confidence in the ability for insurers to provide the promised lifetime payments. In this regard, it is highly likely that a large insurer will step in and support promised payments for any small insurer that fails. Joe Tomlinson reviewed the history of annuity provider failures in a 2012 Advisor Perspectives column, and he found only a few cases where annuity owners ended up with less than they had been promised after accounting for rescues by large insurers or state guarantees. In 1983, Baldwin-United, a piano company that decided to enter the insurance business, declared bankruptcy, and was taken over by MetLife, but policyowners eventually faced a court-

Fee-Only Advisors and Annuities

Historically, annuities have mostly been sold through financial advisors who serve as intermediaries and receive a commission on the sale, rather than being sold directly by the insurance company to the consumer. Having insurance companies compensate the advisor through a commission has created problems for financial advisors who only accept fees from their clients rather than commissions for selling financial products.

In recent years, the fee-only model for financial advice has grown in popularity. It is often designed to charge a percentage of assets under management or charge hourly fees or fixed fees for providing planning services. Fee-only advisors have effectively won the public debate about this type of compensation model being more aligned with serving consumer interests. Commissions were argued to create a conflict of interest, as a commission-based advisor need only to sell suitable financial products that are not necessarily putting the consumer's needs first.

While fee-only advisors can be aligned with client interests during the accumulation phase by seeking to accumulate more assets and grow the investment portfolio, the fee-only model does not necessarily align with managing retirement risks during the distribution phase that focuses on lifetime income rather than portfolio growth. Fee-only financial advisors have been particularly slow to adopt the use of annuities. Caution about annuities relates to their complexity and the confusion this complexity can create among consumers, their built-in fees and surrender charges for early distributions, and their commission-based compensation model. This has left their clients more exposed to market volatility and longevity risk when seeking to build retirement income plans.

Insurance companies are now creating annuities that can fit into the toolbox of fee-only financial advisors in a much more effective manner. It is now increasingly possible to treat the annuity assets in the same manner as other investment options are treated on the platforms used by fee-only advisors to consolidate and manage client assets. For deferred variable and index annuities, the contract value is known, and income annuities can be managed by accounting for the present value of their remaining payments. This makes it possible for advisors to charge their fees on the assets held inside the annuity in the same way as for other investment assets.

For fee-only annuities, internal costs can be reduced because advisors can charge their fees from outside the annuity. The insurance company no longer needs to charge more from within the annuity in order to collect fees to compensate the advisor. This can result in lower mortality and expense charges on the annuity, and surrender charges can be reduced or even eliminated. For variable annuities, lower internal expenses can allow for more step-up opportunities and upside potential. A fee-only index annuity can provide more to the options budget, since advisor fees do not have to be supported internally. This can allow for better parameters to provide the owner with more participation in the market upside. Allowing fee-only advisors to also incorporate annuities in their planning should help to increase their exposure to the public in the coming years.

ordered reduction in benefits. The Executive Life Insurance Company of New York failed in 1991, and while it continued to pay benefits until 2012, the company was liquidated at that time and owners with contracts in excess of the state limits then faced losses. Past performance is not a predictor of future performance, and so it is understandable to have concerns about the credit risk for annuity providers. But it is important to recognize that this concern can be overstated.

◉ Final Thoughts and Best Practices

As we near the end, we can review some key concepts and highlights from the book. First, we consider characteristics that could make annuity use more advantageous for the financial plan. The first is how the retiree feels about using an aggressive stock allocation. The risk premium has a better shot at competing with the extra spending supported through annuity risk pooling. Bonds alone do not have an opportunity to compete with risk pooling, making the case for annuities stronger for conservative or risk averse retirees who are less comfortable holding stocks.

Another area in which some retirees may be conservative relates to longevity risk aversion. Those who are more greatly concerned with outliving their assets are better positioned to benefit from annuities because their alternative is to spend even less from an investment portfolio in the hope of sustaining it for a longer retirement horizon. Longevity risk aversion reflects subjective views about life expectancy, but some individuals may also objectively expect to live longer than the average member of the risk pool, which also increases the value of an annuity. The spread between the spending supported through an annuity and the spending supported from investments grows with the length of the planning horizon and longevity risk aversion. Though difficult to prove, there is a possibility that annuities help people to live longer than otherwise because of the reduced stress from dealing with their investments and market volatility.

With annuitization, it is no longer necessary to manage investments, freeing up a lot of time and stress, and the worry about market volatility and its impact on outliving wealth is minimized. Retirees no longer need to worry about "safe" withdrawal rates and trying to figure out just how much they can spend sustainably. Income protections, especially, benefit those who are more prone to making behavioral mistakes with their investment portfolio, who experience less self-control and may be tempted to overspend from their investment portfolio, and those who are intimidated by investments. This can especially apply to households with one member who is financially savvier than the others. Remaining household members become more vulnerable if something happens to the person who had been handling the family finances. Setting up a strategy with protected income can be a way to subsequently protect members of the household in this situation.

Retirees without children may have a stronger reason to consider annuities as they are less able to create risk sharing within the family. On occasion, children may offer to care for parents if assets deplete, with the understanding that an inheritance will be provided from what is otherwise left. However, this scenario creates the possibility of a reverse legacy. Children may have to care for parents, and parents may not want to put their children in that situation anyway. Nonetheless, if there are no children, then this idea of a reverse legacy as a way to opt out of using an annuity is not even an option.

Those who are pessimistic about financial markets can also become paralyzed regarding spending from investments in retirement. The annuity can provide a license to spend and enjoy because risk pooling will help to support late-life spending.

Related to behavioral and cognitive issues, income protections contribute the most when the purchaser maintains an openness and willingness to treat the annuity as part of the bond allocation and use a higher stock allocation with remaining investment assets. The idea is to draw from bonds to purchase the annuity. Likewise, fixed index annuities that are linked to stock indices will also be more effective for those who treat them as bond alternatives rather than stock alternatives. Variable annuities gain an edge for those who are willing to use a more aggressive asset allocation inside the variable annuity because they are comfortable with the downside risk protections for the annuity provided by the income guarantee provisions.

Annuities create more benefit when one would otherwise be invested in bonds, or when one is willing to view the annuity as a bond and invest more aggressively with the rest. Where annuity benefits are relatively weaker is for those who are more comfortable with an aggressive asset allocation but who have trouble with the big picture thinking on assets and allocate partly from stocks into the annuity rather than just from bonds.

Annuities can also provide greater value to those with less reliable income resources. Annuities can augment Social Security and other company pensions to create a secure base of spending resources not exposed to stock market volatility. Those with enough assets may find that earmarking a portion to strengthen reliable income will increase risk capacity and improve long-term outcomes.

If the payout rate on the annuity is higher than the withdrawal rate from investments to meet a goal, then a partial annuity strategy will allow for an even lower withdrawal rate from what is left in the investments. This increases the success rate for the partial annuity strategy, and it increases the retirement GRIP (guaranteed retirement income percentage), which reduces the magnitude of shortfalls if investments do deplete because a greater portion of spending is available from outside the investments. With less earmarked to cover spending, true liquidity increases, sequence risk decreases, and the potential for greater legacy in the long-term grows. As well, for those with less flexibility for spending, the annuity can help to avoid the need to reduce portfolio distributions in response to poor market performance.

As for specific advice, it is important to take your time with the decision about an annuity. Annuities are complex and this is a big decision that can affect lifelong financial security. It is important to also discuss the decision with family members to coordinate both with the spouse and with any potential heirs. Work with someone who is familiar with the vast array of available annuities and understands which work better for different purposes, ages, and deferral periods. Only add optional living or death benefits if you plan to use them. Do not make these decisions quickly or take them lightly.

When comparing annuities for lifetime income, it is essential to focus on the dollar amount of guaranteed withdrawals. The dollar amount is what matters, and it is a complicated function of the interactions between rollups, withdrawal rates, and the length of the deferral period. This also helps to avoid thinking about the annuity strictly as an investment. The purpose is to protect lifetime income, so it is important to focus directly on what that lifetime income will be.

Try to view annuities and whole life insurance as a replacement for bond holdings in the investment portfolio. For retirees who view these actuarial bonds as a replacement for other fixed-income assets, the partial insurance strategies can increase success rates, raise the proportion of lifetime spending goals that can be covered, and improve legacy, relative to an investments-only strategy. Partial annuity strategies also provide more reliable income throughout retirement to help support spending goals even in the event of bad market scenarios and portfolio depletion.

Partial annuity strategies mean not putting everything into the annuity, and it is okay to diversify purchases between different companies and even different types of annuities.

For other ideas about best practices, please see the call-out box on what the National Association of Insurance Commissioners (NAIC) suggests for consideration when determining if an annuity is a suitable tool for the financial plan.

Finally, it is important to understand how insurance products work for retirement income. It can be complicated. I conclude with a list of questions for which it is important to understand the answers for an annuity product.

First, Exhibit 9.4 covers income annuities. This list is relatively short. Exhibit 9.5 then covers questions for variable annuities, and Exhibit 9.6 is for fixed index annuities. Some questions overlap, but others are quite different or are not relevant for all types of annuities. These lists are provided without further comment.

For deferred annuities, make sure you understand how the annuity works with respect to its various features. This will help to assess the potential upside and liquidity to be compared with an income annuity.

Retirees may wonder about which type of annuity to use, and this depends on personal preferences. The variable annuity maintains a contract value that can rise and fall with the markets, creating more upside potential and downside risk than other annuities. The fixed index annuity offers upside potential and liquidity, but generally less upside potential than a variable annuity and less minimum guaranteed income than an income annuity. Income annuities do not have liquidity, but they are the most efficient way

NAIC Suitability Requirements

The National Association of Insurance Commissioners (NAIC) is a consortium of state insurance regulators that includes an advisory board which creates a set of best practice model regulations that states can consider and adopt to regulate insurance within their borders. States are not required to adopt the model regulations, but most do, at least in a modified form. It is worth considering their approach to annuity suitability, as it can speak to issues relevant for consumers thinking about an annuity purchase. Insurance commissioners want to know that agents are properly trained about the annuities and that the annuity is suitable for their clients. The twelve factors that they have outlined for determining the suitability of any annuity recommendation include:

1. Age: The age of the annuity owner and annuitant are both important considerations, with the important point being that older individuals may experience cognitive decline or diminished capacity and be less able to understand the annuity terms. Another concern is that the surrender charges for the annuity extend beyond the owner's remaining lifetime.
2. Annual income: Annual income is particularly important for annuities with flexible premiums in order to make sure that the owner will have the resources to support future contributions. Single premium annuities will also benefit from information about income in order to get a better sense of the type of spending level support that will be needed.
3. Financial situation and needs, including the financial resources used for funding of the annuity: It is important to always focus on the big picture of retirement assets and liabilities and to think about the change in the composition of these assets when using a portion of them to purchase the annuity.
4. Financial experience: As the complexity of the annuity grows, more financial experience is important to better clarify that the owner can understand the terms of the annuity. With a variable annuity, the owner must also be able to manage the asset allocation decisions for the subaccounts.
5. Financial objectives: It is important to be clear about how the annuity will work to meet a specific financial objective for the household.
6. Intended use of the annuity: Related to the financial objective, it is important to clearly understand how the annuity will be used to meet a specific objective in the financial plan. Most often with retirement, the use will be to generate longevity-protected spending power, but other uses could include accumulating assets with

downside protection, obtaining tax deferral for assets, protecting assets from creditors, or meeting a legacy goal.

7. Financial time horizon: It is important to recognize that annuities are meant to serve as long-term tools, so the retiree time horizon must be considered.

8. Existing assets, including investment and life insurance holdings: The annuity will serve as a tool within a broader overall plan and understanding how it fits into a plan means knowing about the other resources available.

9. Liquidity needs: A key issue to consider is that there must be enough remaining liquidity after the annuity purchase to avoid experiencing surrender charges because the annuity assets are needed for unanticipated expenses.

10. Liquid net worth: The liquid net worth is important to consider with respect to ensuring that enough liquidity will remain after the annuity purchase for unexpected needs.

11. Risk tolerance: Risk tolerance can be an important factor in relation to the discussion about funding retirement spending through bonds, a diversified portfolio, or an annuity. A lower risk tolerance means less exposure to the risk premium to fund retirement, which will make the case stronger for using risk pooling through an annuity to support more spending than bonds.

12. Tax status: It is important to understand how the annuity is taxed and whether its taxation will help improve the tax characteristics of the overall financial plan.

Exhibit 9.4

Questions to Ask About an Income Annuity

Income guaranteed amount	What is the minimum guaranteed amount of lifetime income?
Guaranteed withdrawal rates	What is the guaranteed payout rate? How does it vary by age and length of deferral period?
Other withdrawal features	Does the contract provide liquidity to take nonguaranteed withdrawals? (Answering yes is uncommon)
Death benefit	What are the death benefit provisions, such as cash refund, installment refund, or period certain payments?
Insurance company credit rating	What credit ratings has the insurance company earned from the major credit rating agencies?

Exhibit 9.5

Questions to Ask About a Variable Annuity

Deferral Period

Rollup rate	Is the rollup rate simple or compounded?
Other rollup features	How long will the rollup rate be applied?
Step-up frequency	How frequently are step-up opportunities provided?
Stacking	Do step-ups stack on top of rollups?
Vesting frequency	How frequently are step-ups and rollups vested into the benefit base?

Distribution Period

Income guaranteed amount	What is the minimum guaranteed amount of lifetime income as determined by the interaction of rollup rates and withdrawal rates after an assumed deferral period?
Guaranteed withdrawal rates	What are the guaranteed withdrawal rates? Do they depend on the age at first guaranteed withdrawal? Or do they depend on age at contract issue and length of deferral period?
Adjustment for couples	Are withdrawal rates or fees adjusted for couples relative to singles?
Other withdrawal features	Does the contract provide liquidity to take nonguaranteed withdrawals?
Impact of nonlifetime withdrawals	How does the amount of guaranteed lifetime income adjust to nonguaranteed withdrawals (including excess withdrawals beyond the guaranteed amount)?
Death benefit	What are the death benefit provisions?

Risk Management Approach

Maximum allocation to risky assets	What is the maximum allowed allocation for risky assets?
Range of investment offerings	What are the fund choices for the sub-account investments?
Other restraints on investment allocation	Are there any other requirements about using volatility-controlled funds or holding cash positions?
Variable annuity and subaccount fees	What are the ongoing mortality and expense charges? What fees are applied to the investment options in the sub-account? Are these fees applied to the contract value, the benefit base, or some other metric for the annuity?
Additional fees for guarantee	What are the ongoing fees for optional guaranteed living and death benefits? Are these fees applied to the contract value, the benefit base, or some other metric for the annuity?
Fee adjustments	How much flexibility does the insurance company maintain to adjust fees? What are the maximums?
Surrender charges	What surrender charge schedule is applied to excess distributions in the early years of the contract?
Insurance company credit rating	What credit ratings has the insurance company earned from the major credit rating agencies?

Exhibit 9.6

Questions to Ask About a Fixed Index Annuity

	Deferral Period
Linked index	What financial market index is used for crediting interest?
Downside protection	Is principal protection provided? What is the worst-case interest to be credited? What is the guaranteed minimum surrender value?
Crediting method	What crediting method is used to determine upside participation?
Rollup rate	Is there a rollup rate? Is it simple or compounded?
Other rollup features	How long will the rollup rate be applied?
Step-up frequency	How frequently are step-up opportunities provided?
Possibility for step-ups	Given the crediting method, how likely are step-up opportunities?
Stacking	Do step-ups stack on top of rollups?
Vesting frequency	How frequently are step-ups and rollups vested into the benefit base?

	Distribution Period
Income guaranteed amount	What is the minimum guaranteed amount of lifetime income as determined by the interaction of rollup rates and withdrawal rates after an assumed deferral period?
Guaranteed withdrawal rates	What are the guaranteed withdrawal rates? Do they depend on the age at first guaranteed withdrawal? Or do they depend on age at contract issue and length of deferral period?
Adjustment for couples	Are withdrawal rates or fees adjusted for couples relative to singles?
Other withdrawal features	Does the contract provide liquidity to take nonguaranteed withdrawals?
Impact of nonlifetime withdrawals	How does the amount of guaranteed lifetime income adjust to nonguaranteed withdrawals (including excess withdrawals beyond the guaranteed amount)?
Death benefit	What are the death benefit provisions?

	Risk Management Approach
Changes to crediting method	How much flexibility does the insurance company maintain to adjust parameters with the crediting method at each new term?
History of crediting method	Has the insurance company demonstrated the ability to not adjust crediting method parameters in an adverse direction at least during the surrender period?
Additional fees for guarantee rider	What are the ongoing fees for option guaranteed living and death benefits? Are these fees applied to the contract value, the benefit base, or some other metric for the annuity?
Fee adjustments	How much flexibility does the insurance company maintain to adjust rider fees? What are the maximums?
Surrender charges	What surrender charge schedule is applied to excess distributions in the early years of the contract?
Insurance company credit rating	What credit ratings has the insurance company earned from the major credit rating agencies?

to secure a stream of protected lifetime income with the least amount of assets. The analysis makes clear that including risk pooling as a retirement income tool can help to lay a foundation for improved retirement outcomes no matter which approach is chosen.

In conclusion, we must step away from the notion that either investments or insurance alone will best serve retirees. More emphasis is needed on different forms of insurance products and how they may behave as part of an integrated retirement income plan. I hope this text has helped to expand knowledge about the topic. Thank you for reading, and please check my website www.retirementresearcher.com to stay up-to-date with the latest developments in the evolving field of retirement income planning.

Further Reading

Chen, Peng, and Moshe A. Milevsky. 2003. "Merging Asset Allocation and Longevity Insurance: An Optimal Perspective on Payout Annuities." *Journal of Financial Planning*. 16 (6): 64–72.

Haithcock, Stan G. 2014. *The Annuity Stanifesto*. Ponte Vedra Beach, FL: AnnuityMan Publishing. [https://amzn.to/2N5mL7I]

Milevsky, Moshe A., and Alexandra C. Macqueen. 2015. *Pensionize Your Next Egg: How to Use Product Allocation to Create a Guaranteed Income for Life (2nd Edition)*. Hoboken, NJ: Wiley. [https://amzn.to/2XqpRqO]

Olsen, John L., and Michael E. Kitces. 2014. *The Advisor's Guide to Annuities, 4th Edition*. Cincinnati: The National Underwriter Company. [https://amzn.to/2IPFChG]

Pfau, Wade D. 2013. "A Broader Framework for Determining an Efficient Frontier for Retirement Income." *Journal of Financial Planning*. 26 (2): 44–51.

Tomlinson, Joe. 2012. "How Safe are Annuities?" *Advisor Perspectives* (August 14).

Further Resources

Other Books in the Retirement Researcher's Guide Series

How Much Can I Spend in Retirement?
Available from Amazon:
http://amzn.to/2xLgXGC

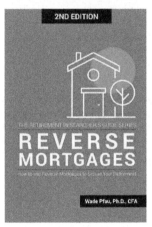

Reverse Mortgages (2nd Ed.)
Available from Amazon:
http://amzn.to/2GgCt7v

The American College of Financial Services—RICP® Designation

The American College of Financial Services pioneered the Retirement Income Certified Professional® (RICP®) designation in late 2012. It is a three-course sequence providing comprehensive coverage for the different schools of thought and philosophies about retirement income planning. I became the RICP® curriculum director in early 2019 and am now responsible for incorporating the latest innovations in the field and keeping the curriculum up to date. For those seeking to further study about retirement income planning, the RICP® designation provides a great opportunity (https://www.theamericancollege.edu/designations-degrees/RICP).

GLOSSARY OF ACRONYMS

- AGI: Adjusted Gross Income
- CD: Certificate of Deposit
- CFA: Chartered Financial Analyst
- CFP: Certified Financial Planner
- DIA: Deferred Income Annuities
- FIA: Fixed Index Annuities
- FPA: Financial Planning Association
- GLWB: Guaranteed Living Withdrawal Benefit
- IRA: Individual Retirement Account
- IRS: Internal Revenue Service
- MPT: Modern Portfolio Theory
- MRT: Modern Retirement Theory
- QLAC: Qualified Longevity Annuity Contract
- RIA: Registered Investment Advisor
- RICP®: Retirement Income Certified Professional
- RMD: Required Minimum Distribution
- SPIA: Single Premium Immediate Annuities
- STRIPS: Separate Trading of Registered Interest and Principal of Securities
- TIPS: Treasury Inflation-Protected Securities
- VA: Variable Annuities

INDEX

illiquid, 10, 43, 122, 251, 288

immediateannuities.com, 128, 136-138, 163, 302

implied longevity yield, 313-315

index fund, 52-54, 73-74, 153

installment refund, 105, 108, 237, 287, 345

integrated strategy, 8, 243, 288-289

internal rate of return, 31, 87, 121-126, 254, 314

irreversible, 142, 305, 324

lapse, 205, 218, 258-261, 326, 336

last-in-first-out, 270, 332

Markowitz, Harry, 58, 62, 79

Marrion, Jack, 195

Milevsky, Moshe, 92, 133, 141, 164, 178, 205, 313, 322-323

Modern Portfolio Theory, 13, 21, 28, 58-60, 323

modified endowment contract, 270-271

nonqualified, 108, 328

Olsen, John, 195, 328

policy loan, 245, 251, 256, 265, 267

probability of success, 63, 69, 86, 96, 210, 241, 271, 276, 317-318

probability-based approach, 1, 7, 15, 19-21, 25, 51, 63, 65-66, 92, 290, 303

product allocation, 27, 274, 321-324

put option, 172, 324

qualified longevity annuity contract, 104, 331

qualified plan, 232, 272, 330-333

regulation, 104, 331, 336, 344

reliable income, 116, 144, 271, 290, 292-294, 304, 342-343

required minimum distribution, 168, 175, 207, 268

retirement balance sheet, 9-10, 23, 94, 140, 142, 240, 280, 287, 290

Retirement CARE Analysis, 292-293

reverse engineer, 86, 88, 96-99, 127-128, 185

risk capacity, 4, 12-13, 89, 147, 178-179, 274, 287, 294, 342

rollover, 229, 238, 331

safe withdrawal rate, 24, 49, 289, 294, 340

safety-first approach, 1, 22, 63, 290

ABOUT THE AUTHOR

Wade D. Pfau, PhD, CFA, RICP is a professor of retirement income and the director of the Retirement Income Certified Professional® (RICP®) designation program at the American College of Financial Services in King of Prussia, Pennsylvania. He is a codirector of the college's New York Life Center for Retirement Income. He also serves as a principal and the director of retirement research for McLean Asset Management and chief planning scientist at inStream Solutions.

He hosts the Retirement Researcher website as an educational resource for individuals and financial advisors on topics related to retirement income planning. He holds a doctorate in economics from Princeton University and publishes frequently in a wide variety of academic and practitioner research journals. His research has been discussed in outlets including the print editions of the *Economist, New York Times, Wall Street Journal, Time, Kiplinger's, and Money* magazine.

Wade is a past selectee for the InvestmentNews Power 20 in 2013 and 40 Under 40 in 2014, the *Investment Advisor* 35 list for 2015 and 25 list for 2014, and *Financial Planning* magazine's Influencer Awards. In 2016, he was chosen as one of the Icons and Innovators by *InvestmentNews*. He is a two-time winner of the *Journal of Financial Planning* Montgomery-Warschauer Editor's Award, a two-time winner of the Academic Thought Leadership Award from the Retirement Income Industry Association, and a Best Paper Award winner in the Retirement category from the Academy of Financial Services. Wade served for four years as a coeditor of the *Journal of Personal Finance.*

Wade is a contributor to *Forbes,* an Expert Panelist for the *Wall Street Journal,* and a columnist for *Advisor Perspectives.* He has spoken at the national conferences of organizations such as the CFA Institute, Financial Planning Association, National Association of Personal Financial Advisors, and Academy of Financial Services.

He is also author of two other books, *Reverse Mortgages: How to Use Reverse Mortgages to Secure Your Retirement* and *How Much Can I Spend in Retirement: A Guide to Investment-Based Retirement Income Strategies.*

Made in the USA
Middletown, DE
28 November 2019

79165088R00205